T0246285

Praise for Louis Ferrante

"A detailed work that covers major events in American mafia history . . . highly entertaining."

—*Wall Street Journal*

"He may be a loss to the criminal fraternity, [but] he is most certainly an asset to the literary world."

—Aspects of History

"A fascinating inside look at the history of the mafia . . . Ferrante's familiarity with mafia customs gives flesh and immediacy to what could otherwise be a rote historical tome, but he doesn't draw his authority from affiliation alone: this is a well-researched history in its own right. True crime fans will be captivated."

—*Publishers Weekly*

"It's very rare when someone from Lou's world has the heart of a writer . . . his talent for storytelling shines through."

—Nicholas Pileggi, author of *Wiseguy* and *Casino*

"You could fill a whole library with books about the mob and the history of the mafia. [*Rise of Empire*] stands out thanks to the background of its author, Louis Ferrante."

—NPR

"Drawing on his experience as an ex-mobster, Ferrante peppers his stories with enlightening morsels about the conditions that facilitated the rise and impunity of organised criminals."

—*Kirkus Reviews*

"Being inside Ferrante's mind is an amazing experience."

—Joel Stein, *TIME*

BORGATA

CLASH OF TITANS: A HISTORY OF AMERICAN MAFIA

VOLUME 2 OF THE BORGATA TRILOGY

LOUIS FERRANTE

PEGASUS BOOKS
NEW YORK LONDON

BORGATA: CLASH OF TITANS

Pegasus Books, Ltd.
148 West 37th Street, 13th Floor
New York, NY 10018

First Pegasus Books cloth edition January 2025

ISBN: 978-1-63936-748-1

10 9 8 7 6 5 4 3 2 1

Printed in the United States of America
Distributed by Simon & Schuster
www.pegasusbooks.com

For Gabriella

CONTENTS

Introduction

In the first volume of the *Borgata* trilogy, *Rise of Empire*, we deciphered the American mafia's earliest origins in Sicily and traced its relatively uninterrupted hundred-year run in which the secret society moved across the ocean and sunk its roots deep into the American soil, taking center stage as the nation's premier underworld power, with an astonishingly long reach into the overworld in the way of law enforcement, politics and industry. But can the American mafia truly be referred to as an empire, a label attributed to it by *Time* and *Life* magazines, and a theme we will continue to assert over the course of the *Borgata* trilogy? The use of deadly force to acquire wealth and expand territorially is common to all empires, from Egypt and Babylon, Rome and Carthage, to France, Spain and Great Britain. These criteria – deadly force, acquisition of wealth and territorial expansion – have certainly allowed us to imagine the American mafia as an empire, but can mafia dons be considered emperors?

In *The City of God*, St Augustine relates a story from a lost portion of Cicero's *De Republica* in which a pirate, who was taken captive by Alexander the Great, was asked by Alexander, 'What is your idea, in infesting the sea?' The pirate adamantly replied, 'The same as yours, in infesting the earth! But because I do it with a tiny craft, I'm called a pirate: because you have a mighty navy, you're called an emperor.'

According to this pirate, as well as Cicero and St Augustine who both concurred with his logic, a crime is a crime, the difference being the size and scope of the endeavor. As Voltaire said, 'History is nothing more than a tableau of crimes,' and our mafia history certainly fits Voltaire's bill just as our subject matter meets the broad definition of empire, and although a mafia don does not command a navy, he does command an army of sworn assassins.

Like all empires that experience a period of marvelous growth while being tested on numerous fronts in a way that threatens their survival, in this second volume of our trilogy, *Clash of Titans*, the American mafia will encounter severe threats from within and without, all involving deadly human conflict between some of the most powerful men in America.

Although mobsters appear to have very little in common with the badass cowboys we have come to know through spaghetti westerns, most of the classic western movies revolve around outlaws, vengeance and murder – very much like La Cosa Nostra – and there is often a riveting scene in which two men face off against one another in a showdown. In the classic movie, *The Western Code*, rancher Nick Grindell says to a rival, 'This town ain't big enough for both of us.' In another classic western film, *The Virginian*, cowboy Trampas says to a rival, 'This world isn't big enough for both of us.' Whether a small town or a big world – or underworld – history is replete with arch-rivals who feel the same as Trampas and Grindell – that someone has to go! Whether we like it or not, conflict is part of the human condition and contests are usually governed by natural selection: the strong survive. But strength does not always mean physical strength, which is never enough to carry the day in the savage but calculating arena of human affairs. Oftentimes, one person achieves victory over another by perfecting what the political theorist, Niccolò Machiavelli, referred to as *virtù*. Modern translators have different interpretations of Machiavelli's use of the word, which has nothing to do with our contemporary definition of virtue, meaning moral integrity. The word is derived from the Latin *vir*, meaning man, and very much like the original meaning of *omertà*, *virtù* meant being a man in all things. Machiavelli believed that a leader must be possessed of *virtù*, meaning a peculiar strength of mind that can outmaneuver opponents through intrigue and guide his own destiny. Since Machiavelli's philosophical advice has been studied and perfectly executed by American godfathers such as Carlo Gambino and Joe Bonanno – who, among others, will square off in the pages of this book – and Machiavelli's inspiration to write his most prominent work, *De Principatibus*, or *The Prince*, followed his torture and unlawful imprisonment at the hands of the powerful Medici family, who have been accurately referred to as the 'Godfathers of the Renaissance', let us travel through time and begin our story with a brief drama from fifteenth-century Florence. This is where we will find not only the distant ethno-cultural ancestors of the mafiosos you will meet in the pages of this book, but a perfect clash of titans that will form the ideal introduction to this second volume of the *Borgata* trilogy.

In 1469, the same year Machiavelli was born, the patriarch of the Medici family and de facto godfather of Florence, Piero de' Medici, died. The family's banking fortune and far-flung enterprises passed into the hands of his twenty-year-old son, Lorenzo.

Two years after Lorenzo assumed power, Francesco della Rovere became Pope Sixtus IV and transformed the papacy in Rome into an Italian principality. An imposing man with no teeth and a flat nose, he was known to wade 'deep in crime and bloodshed'. The Pope used his power to dish out favors to his own mafia-like family, including unaccomplished nephews who were made cardinals, one of whom was believed to be his biological son, incestuously conceived by his sister. This alleged bastard, Cardinal Girolamo Riario, wanted to buy the small town of Imola, which had a price tag of 40,000 ducats. His uncle (or father), the Pope, tapped Lorenzo for the loan, but Lorenzo wanted the town for himself so he made endless excuses as to why he could not come up with the cash. When the Pope realized that Lorenzo was blowing him off, he asked to borrow the money from another mafia-like banking family, the Pazzis. The Pazzi family had long desired the Vatican account so they promptly advanced the loan for Imola, putting added pressure on the already competitive relationship between themselves and the Medici family, and setting the stage for a showdown.

While this drama was unfolding, the archbishopric of Pisa became vacant and the Pope appointed Francesco Salviati to the post, a move that was in breach of an agreement the Pope had with the Republic of Florence in which the republic, i.e. Lorenzo, had to consent to any ecclesiastical appointments in the region. Lorenzo hit back, denying Salviati access to Pisa by forbidding him passage through Tuscany. As Salviati sat on his hands in Rome, Lorenzo anticipated a papal plot coming down the pike and tried to head it off by forming a triple alliance with two other city-states, Milan and Venice. The Pope accurately discerned the alliance as a direct threat to himself and called on his own allies in the region, including King Ferrante of Naples and the Pazzi family, who, as mentioned above, wanted to displace the Medicis as the Vatican's premier bankers. Before long, a conspiracy was afoot to remove Lorenzo from power. The main conspirators were Francesco Salviati, the Archbishop of Nothing and Nowhere, who was stuck traipsing around Rome until the gatekeeper of Pisa, Lorenzo, allowed him entry; Francesco de' Pazzi, a spoiled, arrogant member of the Pazzi family, who managed their bank branch in Rome; and Cardinal Riario, who scooped up Imola with Pazzi money after Lorenzo denied him the loan. Behind these men stood the Pope, who 'was restrained by no scruple from rendering his spiritual power' in pursuit of 'temporary intrigues in which his ambition had involved him'.

The patriarch of the Pazzi family was Francesco de' Pazzi's uncle, Jacopo, a cheap, old gambler given to temper tantrums whenever his luck ran dry. But although the old man had some character flaws, often displayed in public, he was no dummy when it came to politics and, after being apprised of the plot developing in Rome, told his nephew Francesco that any stunt against the popular Lorenzo had little chance of success. But the younger Francesco did not let up on trying to convince his uncle that the plot would succeed and that they would reap untold riches once the Medicis were out of the way.

In an attempt to change the old man's mind, Francesco visited a salty old warhorse, Giovan Battista da Montesecco, who led a mercenary force that was regularly employed by the Pope. Montesecco was asked to participate in the plot but politely declined. When Francesco assured him that the plot had the Pope's blessing, Montesecco insisted that he hear this with his own ears. The conspirators quickly arranged for an audience with the Pope, who told Montesecco that he did indeed want Lorenzo removed, but he never openly said that he wanted him knocked off. It was a replay of England's Henry II calling for the death of Thomas Becket by way of sly language that Henry could – and did – later deny after Becket was murdered by the king's loyal knights. Montesecco left the Pope's presence, convinced that the murder of Lorenzo was condoned by His Holiness, albeit by means of crafty language.

When the Pazzi patriarch, Jacopo, learned that the hardened soldier, Montesecco, had joined the conspiracy which had the Pope's blessing, the old gambler was ready to wager the family fortune. The plotters decided that, in order to dethrone Lorenzo, they also had to whack Lorenzo's younger and only brother, Giuliano. After several unsuccessful attempts at luring the Medici brothers into a trap, it was at last decided that they would be stabbed while attending High Mass together inside of a cathedral in Florence. After hearing the hit would take place in a church, the faithful old mercenary, Montesecco, balked; he was indeed prepared to run a dagger through Lorenzo with the Pope's blessing, but was not about to 'add sacrilege to murder' by killing in a place where 'God would see him'. Believing God's vision to be quite limited to houses of worship, Montesecco withdrew from the plot. He was quickly replaced by men with fewer scruples – two priests. Enter Stefano da Bagnone and Antonio Maffei, 'who were familiar with the sacred place'. While two assassins killed Giuliano, the priests would murder Lorenzo.

The most sacred ritual of the Catholic Mass is when the priest elevates the host, transforming an edible wafer into the body of Christ. What coincides with the elevation of the wafer is the ringing of the altar bells. The hit team agreed that the sound of the bells would signal the cue for the priest-assassins to run their daggers through Lorenzo while Francesco de' Pazzi and his sidekick, Bernardo Baroncelli, a down-and-out opportunist who was indebted to Pazzi, stabbed Giuliano.

On Sunday morning, Giuliano, who had an injured leg, decided to skip Mass but was persuaded by the plotters to attend. With the Medicis and their would-be killers in attendance, the Mass was celebrated according to the ancient Latin tradition until the wafer went up – and the daggers came down. As Giuliano lowered his head, an expression of humility before the body of Christ, the lead executioner, Baroncelli, delivered a stunning blow into Giuliano's scalp, nearly splitting his skull in half. Giuliano collapsed to his knees as Pazzi drew his dagger and plunged it into Giuliano nineteen times.

One of the priest-assassins, Antonio Maffei, lunged at Lorenzo, but the attack on Giuliano must have cost him the element of surprise. Lorenzo leaned away from the blow, was nicked in the neck but drew his dagger and slashed at both priests who lost their nerve and fled. Lorenzo left the church and took refuge in the Medici palace, where he and his supporters planned their revenge.

Montesecco, the holy soldier who backed out of the plot, was still on the hook. He was brutally tortured until he gave up all the conspirators, including the Pope. He was then beheaded in a courtyard, a welcome blow that put an end to his misery. The two priests were also tortured; their testicles were hacked off while they were alive then both men were hung from nooses. Archbishop Francesco Salviati, who was denied entry into Pisa, was promised the more prominent archbishopric of Florence if the plot succeeded. He was at least given a splendid view of Florence when a rope was tightened around his neck and he was hurled from a high window of the Palazzo della Signoria, along with Francesco de' Pazzi who was stripped naked and beaten before being flung from a window. A witness to the slaughter said that Salviati, at the end of his rope, struggled along the wall and sank his teeth into Pazzi's naked flesh. They hung like slabs of salami and pepperoni in a *salumeria* until their heads were cut off and impaled on lances for everyone to see.

Jacopo de' Pazzi, the patriarch who had initially warned his nephew against the plot, escaped the city but was dragged back by angry villagers who were loyal to Lorenzo. He was stripped naked, tortured, had a rope tightened around his neck and was also flung from a window of the Palazzo della Signoria. After he was cut down and buried, the people of Florence dug up his body and dragged it through the streets before fixing his rotted head to the grandiose doors of the Pazzi palace, where it was used as a knocker.

Because Lorenzo, the much more powerful older brother, had survived the plot, he was able to destroy the Pazzi family. With the Pazzi name wiped out due to a bungled hit, let us leave behind these 'Godfathers of the Renaissance' for more contemporary godfathers as we skip through five centuries of Machiavellian plots, coups, assassinations and bloodshed to arrive at the start of the next stage of our history which is, in many ways, similar to this Florentine drama.

In January 1961, John Fitzgerald Kennedy was inaugurated as the thirty-fifth president of the United States. He and his younger brother, Robert Francis Kennedy, who John appointed as his attorney general, can easily be compared to Lorenzo and Giuliano de' Medici: both pairs of brothers were born into money and power, both received the finest educations, both were immersed in politics where they created many powerful enemies, both were religious and attended church together, and both would become targets of assassins. Kenny O'Donnell and Dave Powers, who were known to the press corps as the 'Irish mafia', were close friends and advisors to President Kennedy. In a bestselling memoir that recalls their experiences with the president, O'Donnell tells us that Powers was convinced that John, like Lorenzo, would be targeted for death inside of a church. 'Going to church with the President . . . made Dave a nervous wreck,' wrote O'Donnell. 'Dave was sure that if the President was to be killed, it would happen in a church, either by a shot from the choir loft or by a gunman walking past the President's pew in the procession of people going to the altar for communion. Instead of praying, Dave spent his time at mass eyeing the kneeling Catholics around him and glancing over his shoulder at the choir loft.'

Unlike the botched hit carried out by the Pazzi family, the cabal who plotted against the Kennedys, one of whom adorns the cover of this book, would not make the same mistake of using amateur assassins and killing the younger, weaker brother and allowing the stronger to survive and exact vengeance on the plotters.

In July 1962, Louisiana don Carlos Marcello invited friends and family to his Grand Isle fishing camp and vacation lodge in the Mississippi Delta. While Marcello was drinking a Scotch, a friend of his commented about the Supreme Court's recent decision to uphold Marcello's deportation order, instigated by US attorney general Robert Kennedy, who was also behind a spate of indictments and suffocating tax liens aimed at Marcello. In a fit of sudden anger, Marcello spat out his Scotch and shouted in his Cajun-Italian-American drawl, 'Don't worry, man, 'bout dat Bobby. We goin' to take care a dat sonofabitch!' Someone asked Marcello if he meant that Bobby would be whacked. 'What good dat do?' answered Marcello. 'You hit dat man and his brother calls out the National Guard. No, you gotta hit de top man.'

When Marcello shouted those ominous words in a whiff of fiery Scotch, President Kennedy had just over a year to live.

Part One

Politics and Power

Chapter 1

Father and Sons

Joseph Patrick Kennedy was born in Boston, Massachusetts, on 6 September 1888. As a young man, he made a fortune as a stocks and commodities trader, perfecting what we would refer to today as 'pump and dump' schemes in which stock prices are artificially inflated then sold off at their height. Kennedy also sold short before the stock market crash of 1929 and always exhibited, according to one biographer, 'an almost uncanny knack for being in the right stock, short or long, at precisely the right time', leaving many to suspect insider trading. Another Kennedy biographer wrote, 'better than any Mafia chieftain, Joe covered his tracks', and he was able to avoid brushes with the law and maintain a cleaner image than many of his underworld associates.

During Prohibition, Joe acquired liquor from overseas distilleries and needed the mob's help in distributing it across the United States. Frank Costello said that he and Joe were 'partners' in the liquor business before and after Prohibition. Columnist John Miller, who was close friends with Frank Costello, said, 'The way [Costello] talked about [Joe Kennedy Sr], you had the sense that they were close during Prohibition . . . Frank said that he helped Kennedy become wealthy.' Testimony has also come from Joe's side, beginning with author Gore Vidal, who was related to the Kennedy family through marriage. Vidal wrote in his memoirs, 'the father belonged in jail, along with his close friend Frank Costello. In fact, once a week . . . the boss of the mob and the president's father had dinner together in the Central Park South Kennedy apartment . . . Of course, Joe made no secret of his underworld connections, unavoidable for a man who had cornered the Scotch whiskey market.'

Harold E. Clancy, a Bostonian who was employed by Joe Kennedy, not only confirmed that Joe worked with Costello during Prohibition, but also said that Costello tried to get Joe to invest in his large and profitable slot machine business, an offer Joe declined.

Meyer Lansky and Owney 'The Killer' Madden also claimed to

have worked with Joe Kennedy in the world of bootlegging. Madden's longtime attorney, Q. Byrum Hurst, who also served in the Arkansas state senate while Hot Springs was a mob sanctuary, said, 'Owney and Joe Kennedy were partners in the bootleg business for a number of years. I discussed the Kennedy partnership with him many times . . . Owney controlled all the nightclubs in New York then . . . and Joe wanted the outlets for his liquor.'

Don Joe Bonanno once told his son, Salvatore 'Bill' Bonanno, 'Kennedy was no different from the rest of us, except his whiskey went mainly to society people.' The Bonannos, father and son, especially disliked Kennedy after hearing that one of his boats, 'heavy with her cargo of bootleg whiskey and illegal aliens', was spotted by the Coast Guard, and, in an effort to lighten the load and pick up speed, dumped the aliens overboard instead of the liquor, which was worth more. Bonanno's assertion was backed by FBI deputy associate director Cartha 'Deke' DeLoach, who said that Joe Kennedy 'had associates in organized crime . . . he had considerable experience in the bygone era of smuggling, and that's how he made his fortune, according to [FBI director] Hoover'.

Pulitzer Prize-winning author Seymour Hersh wrote a book about the darker side of the Kennedys. 'In scores of interviews for this book over four years,' wrote Hersh, 'former high-level government officials of the 1950s and 1960s, including Justice Department prosecutors, CIA operatives, and FBI agents, insisted that they knew that Joe Kennedy had been a prominent bootlegger during Prohibition.' One man Hersh interviewed was Abraham Marovitz, a Chicago attorney who represented top mobsters and would one day be appointed to the federal bench by President John Kennedy. Marovitz said of the old man, 'Kennedy was bootlegging . . . he had mob connections. Kennedy couldn't have operated the way he did without mob approval. They'd have knocked him off, too.'

Around the same time that the mob had met in Atlantic City to discuss what the future might look like for them after Prohibition was repealed, Joe Sr jetted off to London to secure contracts making him the exclusive American distributor of Gordon's gin and two premium Scotch whiskies. Back in the United States, Joe established Somerset Importers Ltd, which he sold to Abner 'Longie' Zwillman in July 1946. Joe Kennedy's defenders, who have attacked the many personal testimonies linking him to bootlegging as a pack of lies, have more trouble explaining away business records which show that Zwillman, who was partners with Frank Costello (before Zwillman was murdered by Vito Genovese), somehow ended up with Kennedy's liquor company. Historians have speculated as to Kennedy's timing and reason for selling the company to Zwillman, one saying that, with a son entering Congress, Joe no longer wanted the image of a liquor baron, as if, once the company was sold, no one would utter another word of it. With all of the local and regional representatives for Somerset being

Joe Kennedy Sr

mob-connected, Frank Costello, who was already part owner of Alliance Distributors which distributed House of Lords and King's Ransom whiskies, must have thought it high time to squeeze Kennedy into a sale. If Costello ordered the sales reps to suddenly become lazy, Joe would have gone under overnight. At the time Joe sold his company, Costello was also in complete control of New York's corrupt political machine, Tammany Hall, and since Joe wanted his son to enter politics and carry New York in a general election, it was smart to make Costello happy.

Before Joe pushed his children into politics, three of whom we will be meeting shortly, he had ambitions himself of becoming president of the United States. To this end, he aligned himself with the brilliant but sly Franklin Roosevelt who, as we may recall from volume one of the *Borgata* trilogy, double-crossed Charles 'Lucky' Luciano, Meyer Lansky and Frank Costello at the 1932 Democratic convention. Unlike the mobsters who backed Roosevelt but got nothing out of it, Joe Kennedy's support for Roosevelt was repaid when he was offered the chair of the United States Securities and Exchange Commission (SEC), which was like appointing Lucky Luciano head of the anti-mafia squad. Upon being offered the appointment by Roosevelt, Kennedy told the president, 'I had been involved in Wall Street, and, over a business career of twenty-five years, had done plenty of things that people could find fault with.' The president was unmoved by Kennedy's candid admission and is reported to have said, 'It takes a thief to catch a thief.' On 2 July 1934, Kennedy was sworn in as the head of the SEC.

By March 1938, following his term at the SEC and after a brief stint as chairman of the Maritime Commission – another odd job for a former high seas smuggler – Roosevelt appointed Kennedy as ambassador to the Court of St James's in London. The post was one of, if not *the* most prestigious ambassadorships in the world. In the past, five US ambassadors to the Court of St James's had gone on to become US presidents, which was Kennedy's overriding ambition. Many Americans publicly and privately criticized the appointment, including Roosevelt's secretary of the interior, Harold Ickes, who wrote in his diary, 'At a time when we should be sending the best that we have to Great Britain [which was preparing for war with Nazi Germany], we have not done so. We have sent a rich man, untrained in diplomacy, unlearned in history and politics, who is a great publicity seeker and who is apparently ambitious to be the first Catholic President of the United States.'

The Brits, who graciously welcomed Kennedy, were quickly appalled by him. Sir Robert Vansittart, undersecretary at the Foreign Office, called Kennedy 'a very foul specimen of double-crosser', which was an opinion shared by the Chicago mob's brilliant consigliere, Murray 'The Camel' Humphreys, who had illegal business dealings with Kennedy, and called him a 'four-flusher and a double-crosser'.

Kennedy was also a war profiteer, using his clout as ambassador to secure precious cargo space on transatlantic voyages. 'Using his name and the prestige of the embassy . . . I was able to get shipping space for up to, I think, around 200,000 cases of whiskey,' said an employee of Kennedy, 'at a time when shipping space was very scarce.' As ambassador, Kennedy also used his insider information about world events to trade stocks on Wall Street.

Any hopes Kennedy had of becoming president were dashed in November 1940 at a time when Great Britain stood alone against Nazi Germany, whose war machine had recently overrun much of Europe. According to Assistant Secretary of State Breckinridge Long, Kennedy had been pushing for 'an economic collaboration' with the Axis powers and did 'not believe in the continuing of democracy' in the United States, an odd viewpoint for a presidential hopeful in the world's leading democracy. Although Long's concerns about Kennedy's pessimism were kept confidential, Kennedy imprudently exposed his thoughts during a long interview at Boston's Ritz Carlton hotel. Three days after President Roosevelt was elected for an unprecedented third term in office, Louis Lyons of the *Boston Daily Globe*, accompanied by Charles Edmundson and Ralph Coghlan of the *St Louis Post-Dispatch*, visited Kennedy in his suite and spoke with him off the record as he munched on a slice of apple pie. 'Democracy is all done,' he told the reporters, meaning in both Britain and the United States, the latter of which he did not want to enter the war under any circumstances. Kennedy, moreover, insinuated that Prime Minister Winston Churchill was a drunk, the king was a stutterer, and the queen looked like a shlumpy housewife. The reporters from St Louis respected Kennedy's confidentiality but the reporter from Boston could not resist such a good scoop. When the article went to print, Kennedy was forced to explain himself or resign as ambassador; he did both, and his lifelong dream of becoming president was ruined. But the determined former bootlegger, maritime smuggler, stock swindler and mafia associate was not done; he simply transferred his ambitions of becoming president to the oldest of his nine children, Joseph Patrick Kennedy Jr.

Born in Massachusetts on 25 July 1915, eighteen-year-old Joe Kennedy Jr toured the European continent in 1933, while he was enrolled at the London School of Economics. In a letter to his father from Munich, Germany, he wrote that Adolf Hitler's ruthless Brownshirts were 'very nice and polite . . . and no one sees no sign of brutality'. He also noted that the Nazi Party's dislike of Jews was 'well-founded', and that Germany's sterilization law, designed to eradicate the procreation of *Untermenschen* (sub-humans), meaning anyone with real or perceived mental or physical flaws, was 'a great thing . . . it will do away with many of the disgusting specimens of men which inhabit this earth'. (Joe had a sister, Rosemary, with an intellectual disability since birth; she would have fallen victim to such a law and ultimately subjected to a 'mercy death'.) Perhaps we can excuse an ignorant and insensitive teenager who was still feeling his way through a confusing world, but it is much more difficult to dismiss his father's response. Joe Sr wrote back that he was 'very pleased and gratified' with his son's letter and that his 'conclusions are very sound'.

Joe worked hard to keep the United States out of the war with Germany but the country was dragged in after Germany's ally, Japan, attacked the US naval base at Pearl Harbor in Hawaii, on 7 December 1941. That night, Prime Minister Winston Churchill 'went to bed and slept the sleep of the saved', knowing Britain finally had a powerful ally in the fight, while Kennedy worried about losing his fortune as well as his sons, two of whom were of fighting age.

In 1941, Joe Jr had become a cadet in the Naval Aviation Reserve. He took flight training in 1942 and was stationed with a patrol squadron in England in 1943. On 12 August 1944, the 29-year-old navy lieutenant had twenty-five combat missions under his belt, which earned him enough points to return home, when he heroically volunteered for an incredibly dangerous mission. Not long after he took off in his bomber, the explosives in his aircraft accidentally detonated in the skies over Suffolk. Following that tragedy, a silently inconsolable Joe Kennedy Sr shifted his political aspirations to his next oldest son, John Fitzgerald Kennedy, who was also fighting in the war.

John Fitzgerald Kennedy was born on 29 May 1917. Like his older brother, he also joined the navy but instead of becoming a bomber pilot in the European theatre, he commanded a torpedo patrol boat in the Pacific. On Sunday, 2 August 1943, as Lieutenant Kennedy and his twelve-man crew patrolled the dark waters of Blackett Strait in the Solomon Islands, cruising in their relatively small PT boat, they were rammed by a Japanese destroyer, its steel bow slicing the mahogany wood-plank hull in half. One young sailor was crushed to death in the impact while another was lost and presumed to have met the same

fate. Kennedy and the other survivors clung to life in a sea of burning gasoline. In an act of awe-inspiring heroism, Kennedy swam around the fiery sea, infested with Japanese ships and sharks, while calling out for his crew. He rounded up ten survivors and was so cool and courageous throughout the ordeal that, when one 'exhausted and dispirited' sailor told him, 'I can't go any further,' Kennedy snapped back,

John F Kennedy on his Naval patrol boat

'For a guy from Boston, you're certainly putting up a great exhibition out here.' Kennedy's goal was not to insult but motivate him to push on; he saved him and others who were injured, several of whom would have certainly gone under if he had not dragged them to floating pieces of hull. The survivors eventually made it to a deserted island approximately three and a half miles away, with Kennedy literally towing one injured man as he swam. Since they had no provisions, Kennedy swam to other islands searching for food and help, both of which he and his crew received when they encountered friendly natives and were rescued by a plucky Australian on 7 August. 'Bearded, gaunt, unwashed, half-starved, half-naked, blotched with festering coral wounds, cast away on a miserable patch of jungle surrounded by sharks,' Kennedy was asked by the lieutenant on His Majesty's service, 'Come and have some tea.'

During the five-day ordeal, in which Kennedy displayed the utmost grit, he had indelibly etched his name into the nation's annals of outstanding heroism while providing his father with a record of valor he could market back home and fulfill his dream of getting a Kennedy into the White House.

After coming home from the war, John Kennedy (who I will refer to as Jack) said that his father wanted him in politics. 'It was like being drafted,' Jack later told a reporter. 'My father wanted his eldest son in politics. "Wanted" isn't the right word. He *demanded* it.' Joe Sr confirmed Jack's story when he said, 'I got Jack into politics; I was the one. I told him Joe was dead and that it was therefore his responsibility to run for Congress. He didn't want to. He felt he didn't have the ability and he still feels that way. But I told him he had to.' And so Jack ran for Congress in Massachusetts and was elected in 1947, remaining there until 1953, at which point he was elected to the US Senate, placing him one step away from the Oval Office. But getting into the White House would depend on the help of yet another Kennedy son, the third eldest boy, Robert, who, in his ongoing effort to garner national fame for him and his older brother, would take on the mafia as well as the International Brotherhood of Teamsters, a nationwide labor union that was thoroughly infiltrated by the mob.

Chapter 2

The Runt of the Litter

On 20 November 1925, Robert Francis Kennedy was born into the large, wealthy Kennedy clan, who believed that winning was everything. 'We don't want any losers around here,' said his father, Joe. 'In this family we want winners . . . Don't come in second or third – that doesn't count – but win.' Jewel Reed, wife of James Reed who served with Jack, later said that Joe 'wanted them to be number one . . . I remembered how intensely he had focused on their winning.' To win, even by cheating, if not openly promoted, was permitted, as long as you did not get caught; Joe Kennedy Jr cheated in a sailboat race and youngest brother, Ted, would be expelled from Harvard for cheating.

Joe Sr also believed that sibling rivalries strengthened character and encouraged his children to compete among themselves. Jack once said, 'We soon learned that competition in the family was a kind of dry run for the world outside.' Robert (who we will refer to as Bobby) was, according to a close family friend, 'the runt of a pretty competitive family'. His mother, Rose, was concerned about his lack of masculinity. 'He was the smallest and thinnest,' she said, 'and we feared he might grow up puny and girlish.' According to his sister, Eunice, Bobby was also 'very sensitive' and 'got hurt easily'. Sensitive children can be given to tears, but crying was forbidden in the Kennedy household. 'We don't want any crying in this house,' said Bobby's father, stifling emotions that can, when suppressed at length, spoil someone's character.

When the Second World War broke out, Bobby dreamed of being a war hero like his two older brothers, but he unfortunately spent six months in the Caribbean where the greatest danger he had faced was 'a fistfight with a Puerto Rican', which he lost, and the slim chance of being hit on the head by a falling coconut. His failure to see action left a chip on his shoulder and he became agitated whenever someone asked what he had done during the war.

Following the war, Bobby picked up with his education at Harvard, where he earned a Bachelor of Arts degree in 1948, even though he candidly admitted, 'I didn't go to class very much. I used to talk and argue a lot, mostly about sports and politics.' One professor, who remembered Jack as a hard worker, said that Bobby 'didn't pay much attention to academic work'. Another professor said that Bobby 'liked to play around rather than work'. Not surprisingly, Bobby later commented, 'I just didn't know anything when I got out of college' – which explains why he was turned down by Harvard Law, a devastating rejection that was especially humiliating in the competitive Kennedy clan. Bobby was accepted at the University of Virginia Law School and, after graduating in 1951, he went to work as an attorney for the Justice Department in Brooklyn's Criminal Division, where he got his first glimpse of mobsters.

Late the following year, Joe Kennedy Sr asked Senator Joseph McCarthy of Wisconsin to appoint Bobby as an assistant counsel to his Permanent Subcommittee on Investigations into American communists. Bobby eagerly joined the now infamous senator's notorious hunt for Reds and enjoyed it so much that Joe Sr once mused, 'had [Bobby] lived in Germany, he could have joined the Gestapo and been sincere about it'. However, Bobby resigned in July 1953 after becoming embroiled in a feud with chief counsel Roy Cohn. After briefly working for the Hoover Commission, which Bobby found to be a 'dull' experience, he landed a job as chief counsel to the Senate committee that was investigating the illegal procurement of military uniforms, which was led by Senator John McClellan from Arkansas. While Bobby was involved in this investigation, journalist Clark Mollenhoff, a Pulitzer Prize-winning reporter for the *Des Moines Register* and *Minneapolis Star Tribune*, convinced Bobby to expand the committee's reach and look into widespread corruption inside the mob-infested Teamsters Union. Bobby's interest was piqued. The young man who missed the war spotted a chance at achieving a different kind of glory.

In 1903, the International Brotherhood of Teamsters began as a union of truck drivers who delivered necessities like milk, bread, ice and coal. By the middle of the century, the Teamsters were the wealthiest union in the country with over a million dues-paying members nationwide, and were heavily infiltrated by various mafia families across the country who controlled the cities where union locals were headquartered.

In the summer of 1954, President Dwight D. Eisenhower saw the need for more and better roads crisscrossing the United States and formed a five-man committee that recommended a national highway system. One member of the committee was Teamster president Dave Beck, whose interstate truckers would benefit immensely from the new federal funding that poured into the construction of highways. In 1956, Beck broke with most labor unions and endorsed Eisenhower's re-election campaign on behalf of the Teamsters. Until then, the Teamsters, who made generous campaign contributions to both political parties, had sufficient clout to keep any federal investigations into their mode of operations short and fruitless. When one previous investigation was halted, a surprised congressman pointed to the ceiling of the hearing room and said to the press, 'The pressure comes from away up there, and I just can't talk about it any more specifically than that.' The congressman was referring to the executive branch.

Since politicians rely on votes and do not like to tangle with the labor force, Joe Kennedy warned Bobby that a congressional attack on the Teamsters was 'political suicide' and would ruin Jack's chance of becoming president. A family friend, LeMoyne 'Lem' Billings, enlarged the scope of Papa Kennedy's concerns beyond politics when he said, 'The old man saw this as dangerous, not the sort of thing, or the sort of people to mess around with.' But Bobby would not back down, even getting into a 'furious argument' with his father. Bobby felt, since the Teamsters had endorsed a Republican in the 1956 presidential election, and Jack would be running for president as a Democrat in the 1960 election, that smearing the Teamsters and exposing them as a hornets' nest of mob activity would turn the union's support for any Republican nominee into a negative endorsement. Bobby had also watched Senator Estes Kefauver rise to national prominence as a televised crime crusader during the Kefauver hearings; Clark Mollenhoff pointed out that Kefauver, who 'edged out' Jack for the 1956 vice presidential nomination, 'did his investigations five years ago and it got him enough clout to beat your brother's butt'. Knowing Mollenhoff was right, Bobby asked Jack to help him fight the corruption inside the Teamsters and earn for himself a national name. Jack, who felt 'that one Kennedy connected with the committee was enough', was dissuaded from participating by a number of colleagues including Senate majority leader Lyndon Johnson, who referred to Bobby as a 'grand-standing little runt'. But, on account of Bobby's incessant prodding, Jack eventually agreed to work alongside his brother while Papa Joe gave in when at last convinced that the publicity would make Jack 'known to everybody in the country'.

To prepare for the hearings, Bobby crisscrossed America interviewing victims of Teamster violence and intimidation, while also investigating rigged leadership elections and the misuse of union funds. It was soon apparent to Bobby that union locals were 'completely dominated by racketeers and hoodlums', and the endemic corruption reached as high as Teamster president Dave Beck.

Dave Beck, who had become president of the Teamsters in 1952, was born in California and grew up in Seattle, Washington. At age sixteen, he quit school to work and help provide for his poor family, eventually becoming a truck driver and then a union organizer. As president of the Teamsters, Beck moved the union's primary headquarters from Indianapolis, Indiana, to Washington DC, so that the Teamster hierarchy could be closer to the high-powered lobbyists and politicians who make national policy decisions and pass labor laws. Using five million dollars of union funds, Beck constructed a five-story glass and marble building known as the Marble Palace, located across the street from the US Capitol. Beck's opulent office was on the third floor with a view of the Capitol dome. But it was not the steep price tag for the Marble Palace that Bobby had a problem with, it was Beck's misuse of union funds when it came to his and his son's personal homes in Seattle, Washington. Bobby dragged Beck before the committee, where Bobby produced evidence that Beck had used hundreds of thousands of dollars in union funds to build and renovate his spacious Seattle residence on Lake Shore Drive, which had an artificial waterfall in the backyard and a movie theatre in the basement. Beck had also used union funds to cover personal expenses and had built his son a house. After Beck was disgraced in public and exposed as a criminal, he repaid the stolen money and was ultimately convicted of larceny and tax evasion. Thanks to Bobby, Beck's downfall was inevitable and paved the way for a new union president whose name would become synonymous with the Teamsters: Jimmy Hoffa.

Chapter 3

The Brother Act Versus the Brotherhood

James Riddle Hoffa was born in the small coal-mining town of Brazil, Indiana, on 14 February 1913. He was the third of four children born to John Cleveland Hoffa, of Dutch descent, and Viola Riddle Hoffa, of Irish descent. John operated a drilling machine for a coal-mining company and died in October 1920 at the age of thirty-eight. The cause of death was a stroke but, given his young age, it is easy to imagine his death being connected to the unhealthy working conditions, which is what Jimmy Hoffa believed throughout his life.

In 1922, Viola, the widowed mother of four who has been described as a 'staunch Baptist mean motherfucker', took her family to Clinton, Indiana, in search of work, ultimately landing in Detroit, Michigan, where she sometimes worked three jobs and was known to never accept a handout. Her best job, if we can call it that, was polishing radiator caps at an automotive plant. Jimmy Hoffa later said, 'She worked damned hard and always looked tired.'

At fourteen, Jimmy Hoffa quit school to bag groceries then worked as a stock boy for a general store before landing a job on the loading docks of the Kroger Grocery and Baking Company. Hoffa and his co-workers received thirty-two cents an hour but were only paid when they were actually unloading produce from a boxcar; if that took four hours of a twelve-hour shift, the other eight hours were lost without pay. Between lost hours of unpaid labor and a mean manager who made the irascible Captain Bligh of the HMS *Bounty* look like the cheerful Captain Stubing of the Love Boat, the gutsy seventeen-year-old Hoffa, along with some older co-workers, planned a strike. To maximize their chance of dragging Kroger to the negotiating table, Hoffa and his crew strategically waited for a load of perishable Florida strawberries to arrive at the loading dock when they suddenly walked off the job.

Five men, including Hoffa, spoke on behalf of over a hundred angry workers. In the first step toward his enduring legacy, Hoffa, who proved to be a skilled negotiator, got management to cave in to a number of demands, the first being their right to strike which was, at the time, unlawful in Michigan. The 'Strawberry Boys', as they came to be known, also negotiated a pay raise, a guarantee of six hours' paid wages on a twelve-hour shift, an insurance plan, lunch breaks and smoke breaks.

About a year after his first strike, Hoffa was offered a job as an organizer for Detroit's Joint Council 43, an affiliate of the International Brotherhood of Teamsters. Hoffa was a relentless union organizer, recruiting new truck drivers at every turn. One truck driver was sleeping in his cab at a rest stop when Hoffa swung open his door. 'This little guy looked up at me, grinning,' the truck driver later said. 'I thought he was a bum looking for a ride. But he said, "My name is Hoffa. Can I talk with you about the Teamsters?" I said, "No, you can't. Now get out of here and let me sleep." He said, "Just five minutes; that's all I ask . . ." He really bore in on me. I told him I was scared I'd get fired if I joined a union . . . He had an answer for everything and he never let up. If I hadn't signed that membership card we'd still be there.'

Half-asleep truck drivers at rest stops could be considered easy pickings compared to the other ways Hoffa recruited and organized members. Speaking about his rise in the 1930s, Hoffa said, 'Every time you went near a place to organize you'd get picked up and sent to jail. The police beat you on the head with night-sticks. It was a mess. We fought on the streets. The employers hired every hoodlum strikebreaker in town . . . the police and the ex-cons lined up together against us.' Hoffa also said, 'We had a number of knockdown bloody battles. Six times I was beaten up and my scalp was laid open wide enough to require stitches . . . in one twenty-four-hour period I went to jail eighteen times while walking the picket line.' In time, Hoffa began to recruit 'professional hoodlums and gangsters' to combat the thugs hired by management. One associate said that it was not long before 'Jimmy dealt with the mob on a regular basis'.

By 1935, 22-year-old Hoffa became an agent for the 250-member Detroit Local 299, and by 1942, he helped organize the Michigan Conference of the International Brotherhood of Teamsters and was named its first chairman. After the Detroit mafia helped Hoffa rise to power in Michigan, the Chicago mob handed him the Midwest while introducing him to New York mobsters, whose help he needed to clinch the national election and replace the fallen Dave Beck.

Most of the Teamster locals in New York were under the tight grip of Giovanni Ignazio Dioguardi, aka 'Johnny Dio', a capo in Tommy 'Three-Finger Brown' Lucchese's borgata. As we may recall from volume one of this trilogy, Tommy Lucchese wrested control of the garment unions away from Lepke Buchalter. Since then, Lucchese had infiltrated most of the Teamster locals while peacefully taking over his own borgata from Gaetano 'Tom' Gagliano who, after many years in charge, bowed out on a high note, calling a Commission meeting where he asked the other bosses if he or anyone in his borgata had any outstanding debts or obligations to anyone. When they said they did not, Gagliano graciously stepped down and ceded the throne to Tommy Lucchese.

In the 1930s, Johnny Dio was a young hoodlum who worked for Lucchese, once getting into a shootout with other hoods and twice being indicted and acquitted of extortion. He was at last convicted by District Attorney Thomas Dewey, who referred to Dio as a 'young gorilla who began his career at the age of 15'. The description was apt: one victim testified that Dio's gang 'threatened to cut his ears off' if he did not give in to their demands. Dio served three years in Sing Sing then returned to assume his managerial role in Lucchese's gorilla squad. With the help of his brother, Tommy Dio, and their uncle, James 'Jimmy Doyle' Plumeri, Johnny Dio steamrolled over the Teamster unions with little patience for obstacles. Even investigative reporters were fair game. When columnist Victor Riesel wrote and talked about the crooked Teamsters in New York, he was told to back off. Riesel did not listen to this sound advice and was walking out of Lindy's restaurant in Manhattan when someone threw acid in his eyes. Mob informants said that Johnny Dio ordered the assault, then erased the scent back to himself by ordering the murder of Riesel's assailant.

Johnny Dio not only controlled the powerful Joint Council 16 and a half-dozen other locals, he also set up a number of paper locals, meaning they existed only on paper. Not unlike England's notoriously corrupt 'rotten boroughs', outlawed in 1832, paper locals were designed to steal elections. After the proper paperwork was drawn up, paper locals – referred to by the press as 'Dio Locals' – were assigned administrative officers but had no working members. Because the officers had voting power, they could sway an election and did just that when they helped Jimmy Hoffa secure the powerful New York delegation at the 1957 Teamsters convention held at the oceanfront Eden Roc Hotel in Miami, Florida. Thanks to the mob's help, the 44-year-old former strawberry striker with a criminal record 'as long as your arm' was elected as the new Teamster president.

In return for their support of Hoffa, the mafia expected everything from cushy jobs with big expense accounts, to easily approved loans from the Teamsters' multimillion-dollar pension fund. Although the fund was technically controlled by a board of trustees, Hoffa personally directed the investments, usually without a hint of advice from the board. (Over time, the fund dumped in excess of three hundred million dollars into construction loans for Las Vegas hotels and casinos, jointly owned by the New York and Chicago mobs who both had their talons deep into Hoffa. Although the loans were not approved according to proper standards, and Hoffa is reported to have taken a 10 percent vig for himself off the top, there is no question that they were profitable for the Teamsters, allowing Hoffa's defenders to argue on behalf of his unethical lending practices.)

If the Teamsters were, as Bobby wrote, 'The most powerful institution in this country – aside from the United States Government

Johnny Dio socks a photographer during a break at the Rackets Committee

itself,' then it was disconcerting for him to think that the mafia had almost complete control of its piggy bank. He placed a target on Hoffa's back and subpoenaed Teamster-connected mobsters to appear before the McClellan Committee, which the press dubbed the 'Rackets Committee', and which quickly 'evolved into the biggest Committee operation in the history of Washington'. Johnny Dio was especially entertaining when, during a cigarette break from the hearings, he socked a photographer.

Notwithstanding his violent nature, Dio was clever and fronted many of his unions with semi-legitimate Jews, creating more Jewish millionaires in America than New York University. With the help of his Jewish pals, he also wrested control of the kosher meat industry. Under questioning, Dio repeatedly invoked his Fifth Amendment right to remain silent, which frustrated Bobby as well as Senator Irving Ives of New York, who said, 'I would like to ask Mr. Dioguardi if there was anything he ever did from the time he was born until the present moment that would not incriminate him?' Dio conferred with his lawyer then took the Fifth on that, too. Of course, Dio refused to acknowledge that he had ever met Jimmy Hoffa, even though Dio's 'lurking presence' was often nearby when Hoffa negotiated trucking contracts. Bobby was sure that Dio's ominous glare was Hoffa's strongest negotiating tactic. The committee also produced wiretap evidence of Dio and Hoffa discussing business together. During the spring of 1953, the duo had discussed bringing New York's army of taxi drivers into the Teamsters Union. (At a later date, Hoffa tried to bring the 24,000-member New York City police force into the Teamsters.) Dio took the Fifth while Hoffa admitted, 'I recognize my voice, and I believe it is Dio's voice,' but denied any wrongdoing.

A longtime ally of Hoffa, Rolland McMaster, said that Hoffa 'knew that organized crime people could hurt him and his organization. So he got along with them . . . If you don't have some of those friends, you could get ate up, and you wouldn't know what happened to you.' Hoffa had plenty of 'those friends' and the Rackets Committee concluded that

Hoffa testifies before the Rackets Committee

Johnny Dio alone 'brought 40 men into the labor movement in positions of trust and responsibility – men who, among them, had been arrested a total of 178 times and convicted on 77 of these occasions for crimes ranging from theft . . . extortion, conspiracy, bookmaking, use of stench bombs, felonious assault, robbery . . . burglary, violation of the gun laws, being an accessory to murder, forgery, possession of stolen mail, and disorderly conduct'. No one had previously mistaken the tough

Teamsters for the Rotary Club but these revelations were shocking to the American public.

Among the many other witnesses Bobby called before the committee were Lucchese capo and union specialist Anthony 'Tony Ducks' Corallo, a nickname he was given for ducking convictions; Louisiana don Carlos Marcello; and Sam 'Momo' Giancana. Giancana, the Chicago mob's acting boss since 1957, has been portrayed in numerous books and documentaries as one of the biggest mafia bosses of all time, but he was never more than a front man for the official boss, Anthony 'Joe Batters' Accardo. Following the unwanted publicity from the Kefauver hearings, Accardo decided to recede into the shadows. Paul 'The Waiter' Ricca, who was one of Accardo's closest confidants, had groomed Giancana and recommended the relatively young forty-year-old for the role of acting boss, earning him a trip before the Rackets Committee which led to a memorable exchange between him and Bobby Kennedy. After Giancana laughed at one of

Sam Giancana, acting boss of the Chicago mob

Bobby's uncomfortable questions, Bobby shot back, 'I thought only little girls giggled, Mr. Giancana.' Bobby's taunting remark was meant to get under Giancana's skin and humiliate him on live television. Author Nancy Gager Clinch wrote a brilliant psychohistory of the Kennedy family in which she pointed out the male members' condescending attitude toward women. 'To be womanly,' wrote Clinch, 'was considered a deadly insult by Kennedy men, particularly Bobby.' Although Clinch makes no mention of Bobby's public jab at Giancana, or any references at all to the mafia, it is in this author's opinion that she unwittingly uncovered the root of Bobby's public insult – he was aiming for Giancana's jugular vein by calling him a girl, while hoping he would angrily respond and come out from behind the protection of the Fifth Amendment.

Bobby once admitted, 'It makes me boil inside to see people

come before the United States Senate and just lie and evade.' Clark Mollenhoff, the journalist who first suggested that Bobby go after the mob-infested Teamsters, agreed that Bobby 'sometimes lost his temper, and occasionally a little-boy impetuousness marred his performance'. Biographer Evan Thomas wrote of Bobby, 'Without quite realizing why, he seemed to be searching, with a kind of grim determination, for an outlet for his anger – for an enemy he could attack.' Anyone who watched the hearings could clearly see that Bobby got a cheap thrill out of degrading sworn killers, and was more intent on badgering witnesses than conducting a proper inquiry that could add value to a congressional investigation. The problem seems to have been embedded in Bobby's character. He took everything personally, and if someone lied, did not answer, or refuted his accusation, he was visibly annoyed and could not conceal his loathing. Even Bobby's own family understood this about him; Joe Kennedy once remarked, '[Bobby] hates the same way I do.' On another occasion, Joe told fashion designer Oleg Cassini, 'I'm like Bobby. I'm a hater.'

Another part of Bobby's problem was his strict ideas about good and evil. 'For him the world is divided into black and white hats,' said Bobby's wife, Ethel. 'Bobby can only distinguish good men and bad.' The witnesses before Bobby were deemed evil and therefore not entitled to equal justice under the law. And once Bobby had judged a person as evil, he did not need evidence to support his conclusion. Arthur Schlesinger, Harvard professor, family friend, advisor and Bobby's pre-eminent biographer, wrote that Bobby was 'driven by a conviction of righteousness, a fanaticism of virtue, a certitude about guilt that vaulted over gaps in evidence'.

The Teamster attorneys Bobby engaged with drew a similar conclusion, one calling Bobby 'a sadistic little monster', while another spoke about how far and wide he would cast his net: 'We had guilt by association, guilt by marriage, guilt by eating in the same chophouse, guilt by the general counsel's amazement, guilt by somebody else taking the Fifth Amendment, guilt by somebody else refusing to testify.'

Not surprisingly, Bobby was also hardwired to cultivate lasting personal vendettas. Rackets Committee investigator and future White House press secretary, Pierre Salinger, compared the rift between Hoffa and Bobby to a 'blood feud', which likely started when Hoffa seemed to get the better of Bobby in front of the nationally televised proceedings. 'Bobby wasn't too much on the law – had not practiced it very often . . .', said a justice department attorney. 'During his work as counsel for the [Rackets] committee, Hoffa made Kennedy look pretty bad. Bobby never forgave him for this.'

There was also a lot of jealousy between the two men: Hoffa was envious of Bobby's privileged upbringing, calling him 'a spoiled young millionaire that never had to go out and find a way to live by his own efforts'. Bobby was, in fact, a millionaire by the age of four when his father formed a trust fund for each of his children. By age twenty-one, he was handed a cool million and married Ethel Skakel, who also grew up swimming in a pool of money. In contrast, when Hoffa was age four, his father's lungs were already black from coal. Hoffa literally fought his way to the top, which seemed to create equal envy in Bobby who desperately wanted to be known for his own achievements, once complaining to Clark Mollenhoff – who actually wrote a flattering piece about Bobby – 'Why do you reporters have to bring politics, family and my money into it?'

Given that Hoffa and the mob were Bobby's primary targets, we cannot be surprised by how little they thought of him, but it is surprising to learn what Bobby's friends and colleagues in Washington thought of him. Lem Billings called him an 'unhappy, angry young man'. Kenny O'Donnell described him as 'not a simple man but many different simple men' and 'incredibly naive'. Journalist and Kennedy watcher Jim Bishop wrote that Bobby was an 'irritating little man' who treated people like 'serfs on some big Kennedy estate'. Senator Barry Goldwater called him a 'mean, little asshole'; former president Harry Truman called him 'a son of a bitch'; Senator Herbert Lehman called him a 'nasty little man'; Senator Lyndon B. Johnson called him a 'snot-nosed little son-of-a-bitch', a 'little fart' and a 'little shitass'. The latter three, being from Bobby's own political party, rendered the consensus bipartisan. They also thought that Bobby was ruthless, as did the mob.

If Bobby believed mobsters were ducking his subpoenas, he would have their wives served with subpoenas in order to bully their husbands into compliance. In most cases, this was pure harassment and abuse of power, although there was one episode in which an entire family was indeed deserving of subpoenas: the Gallos.

Chapter 4

A Paranoid Schizophrenic with Homicidal Tendencies

Umberto and Mary Gallo were immigrants from Naples, Italy, who settled in Brooklyn where they worked hard and opened a small diner named Jackie's Charcolette. They raised five children, three of whom were boys who all got involved with the mob and joined Joe Profaci's borgata.

The oldest boy, Lawrence 'Larry' Gallo, was born in November 1927. When he reached military age, he enlisted in the army but sought an early discharge by repeatedly throwing himself onto the floor and claiming dizzy spells. It worked; he was given a medical discharge and a monthly government check for the rest of his life which allowed him plenty of idle time to pursue the rackets. By adulthood, Larry had a long criminal record with thirteen arrests and four convictions, and once took the rap for his younger brother, serving a year in jail for a crime he did not commit.

Joseph Gregory Gallo, known as 'Crazy Joe' or 'Joey', was born on 7 April 1929. His rap sheet, with seventeen arrests and four convictions, dated back to age fifteen. As a young man, he briefly attended automotive trade school but was deemed 'defiant, uncooperative and in need of guidance'. He dropped out and joined the navy at age seventeen. Six months later, he was discharged and judged to be 'emotionally immature, egocentric, and demanding'. At twenty-one, after being arrested for breaking and entering, he appeared in court recognizably imbalanced. The magistrate sent him for an evaluation at Kings County Hospital, where doctors diagnosed him as 'insane', placing a clinical label on what his friends and

Joseph 'Crazy Joe' Gallo

family had known all along. The diagnosis unwittingly helped Crazy Joe's criminal career. 'I'm a paranoid schizophrenic,' he often told men he wished to frighten into submission, pretending he had no control over his actions. When one man did not heed the warning, Joey broke the guy's forearm over the end of a desk as if he were snapping a broomstick over his knee.

The third and youngest Gallo brother was Umberto, better known as Albert or 'Kid Blast', which made him sound like a notorious gunman who blasted people. The moniker was, quite to the contrary, given to him for 'blasting' a lot of girls as a teen, 'blast' being the local slang for getting lucky on a date. Blast was born on 6 June 1930 and, like his older brothers, he also had a long rap sheet.

The Gallo brothers grew up in a mafia-ridden section of Brooklyn known as Red Hook, which comprised a large part of the Brooklyn waterfront. Once the home of Dutch settlers, it became a magnet for southern Italian immigrants who sought work on the docks, and ultimately led to the mob's control of the waterfront, a phenomenon discussed at length in volume one. The local bars catered to longshoremen whose union was controlled by the heirs to Albert Anastasia. Anastasia's early departure from this world was expedited by the Gallo brothers who were assigned the hit by Profaci. Police believed that Larry Gallo's best friend, Joseph 'Joe Jelly' Gioielli, and Ralph Mafrici were the lead gunmen on the Anastasia hit, with Larry and Joey Gallo positioned as back-up shooters.*

Following the Anastasia hit, the Gallos were proposed for initiation into the Profaci borgata. When their names were circulated among the five families, allowing any made man an opportunity to object, no one raised any concerns over Larry though some protested Joey's initiation, concerned that he was an habitual drug user. Joey did indeed smoke marijuana and chew hashish, which was obviously frowned upon by older mobsters, but the real concern was highly addictive drugs like heroin, which Joey was rumored to use. To make sure his system was drug-free, Joey was kept in a hotel room for a few days

---

* Carmine Persico, who we will be meeting, later claimed to be on the hit, and Joey Gallo once referred to the hit team as the 'barbershop quintet', so it is possible that five men participated. However, some question Persico's presence and point out that no one else was alive when Persico began to tell people he was there. The quintet Joey referred to, moreover, consisted of Crazy Joe, Joe Jelly, Ralph Mafrici, Punchy Illiano and Sonny Camerone. (Joey did not include Larry.)

with a babysitter. After showing no signs of heroin withdrawal, he was cleared for membership. Even though Joey was not addicted to heroin, we must still wonder why a recreational drug user was admitted into the borgata by a square like Joe Profaci, who once commented to his fellow don, Joe Bonanno, 'These Americans are going to dirty us with their new ways.' The reason is because old-timers like Profaci needed young hoods like Joey to fight their battles and help them hold on to their power and assets. For the same reason, a superpower like the United States has drastically lowered its military recruitment standards to allow for members with medical issues, lower aptitude scores and criminal records. As history can attest, such dire adjustments are typically made when empires are beginning to crack, exactly where we find ourselves in this history as Joey is welcomed into Profaci's army for his willingness to kill, which canceled out the fact that he was certifiably crazy and enjoyed using recreational drugs, infractions that would have cost Joey his life at the hands of Profaci just a decade earlier.

Larry and Joey Gallo were suspected of planning or committing numerous murders while robbing, loansharking and extorting, but their mainstay was Teamster Local 266, whose members installed and repaired vending machines, pinball machines and jukeboxes, placing them in the crosshairs of Bobby Kennedy and earning them a formal invitation to appear before the Rackets Committee. Bobby believed that Local 266 was a front for a Gallo strong-arm operation to have every last bar and tavern in Red Hook, Brooklyn, display their vending machines.

For the trip to Washington, Crazy Joe exchanged his usual leather jacket and newsboy cap for a black suit and dark sunglasses. He told his brother Larry, 'They want to see a gangster? That's how I'm going – looking like one.' Joey also acted like one, and the press as well as the public ate him up like a powdered zeppole. After arriving in the Capitol, Bobby said, '[Crazy Joe] strode into my office, dressed like a Hollywood Grade B gangster, he felt the rug and said, "It would be nice for a crap game."' Joey then offered one of Bobby's secretaries a job in one of his floating casinos, telling her she 'could determine her own salary by taking as much as' she wanted from the pot. Joey later recalled his introduction to Bobby, saying that when he walked into his office, Bobby looked up and said, 'So you're Joe Gallo, the Juke Box King. You don't look tough. I'd like to fight you myself.'

Hoping that the privacy of his office would encourage the talkative Crazy Joe to open up about a few crimes, Bobby asked him about a murder he was suspected of committing in which the victim's face was blown to bits. Bobby said that Joey just giggled and shrugged. When another man entered Bobby's office, Joey played the role of Bobby's personal bodyguard and searched the man's pockets. 'No one is going to see Mr. Kennedy with a gun on him,' he said, sternly.

After all of Joey's behind-the-scenes antics, he sat before the committee and invoked his Fifth Amendment right to remain silent forty-eight times in his heavy Brooklyn accent. Older brother Larry was just as mute. The Gallos' victims had more to say. One man, who resisted the constant pressure to join their union, said, 'They split my skull open.' Another victim, who was beaten like an egg, said, 'My nose was completely out of shape, and it was formed like a horseshoe, like a U.' While pleading for his life, he said the brothers would only pause to comment that he was an 'excellent actor'.

Before leaving the Capitol and heading back to Brooklyn, Crazy Joe made a campaign promise to Bobby. Knowing Jack was running for president, he said, 'I'll line up my people for your brother in 1960.' Bobby replied, 'The biggest favor would be to announce for my brother's opponent.' Crazy Joe burst into a fit of laughter and, according to Bobby, 'went merrily on his way'.

Bobby called Joey 'one of the most extraordinary witnesses to appear before the Committee', but his relatively small union of vending machine repairmen was nothing compared to the vast domain of Teamster president Jimmy Hoffa, who remained Bobby's chief target throughout the hearings. Bobby all but proved that Hoffa was the gatekeeper who swung open the doors of the Marble Palace for mafiosos across the country, from low-level hoodlums like the Gallo brothers to heavy hitters like Louisiana don Carlos Marcello, Florida don Santo Trafficante, Chicago acting boss Sam Giancana, and the heads of New York's five families who all had a stake in the Teamsters which meant they also had control of the US economy. According to Pierre Salinger, 'A national strike by the union could strangle the nation's economy within hours.' Senator John McClellan was especially unnerved by all he had heard throughout the hearings, adding that 'such power constitutes a threat to the security and well-being of our country'.

In contrast to Senator McClellan, there were, however, plenty of senators on the Rackets Committee who were opposed to Bobby's fanatical pursuit of the Teamsters, which represented the largest bloc of American labor. Many senators believed that Bobby was simply advancing his family's political ambitions and the Teamsters were being singled out for supporting a Republican president. Case in point was Bobby's hands-off treatment of the president of the United Automobile Workers (UAW), Walter Reuther. The monolithic auto union, which was also infiltrated by the mob, was a powerful Democratic donor and supporter of Jack Kennedy for president. Whereas Hoffa was publicly pilloried for the slightest whiffs of corruption inside his union, Bobby was entirely unmoved when a UAW worker testified that, in order to keep his job, he was forced to contribute to a fraudulent fund that returned little, if anything, back to the workers. Instead of Bobby's usual cries of extortion, he told the UAW worker, 'If you did not like it, you should have worked someplace else.' In July 1957, *Newsweek* wrote that 'Robert Kennedy has ignored continual demands for an investigation of Reuther', while the *Chicago Tribune* believed that the Kennedys were actively shielding the UAW from 'a too searching inquiry into its picket line goon tactics'.

Republican senators noted their grievances in a report that attributed 'a clear pattern of crime and violence' to Reuther's union, while accusing Reuther of hiring 'professional hoodlums' who engaged in 'terroristic tactics' to win strikes. Senator Karl Mundt of South Dakota thought that Bobby practically acted as Reuther's defense attorney. When Senator Barry Goldwater of Arizona inquired as to how Bobby's chief forensic accountant, Carmine Bellino, was able to clear the UAW of any wrongdoing after a cursory check of their books, Bobby sprung to his feet and shouted at Goldwater for having the audacity to question his integrity while approaching the older man with fists clenched. 'Fortunately,' said Goldwater, 'Jack Kennedy leaped up from his chair, grabbed Bobby from behind, and prevented him from hitting a United States Senator.'

Bobby's hypocrisy did not escape Jimmy Hoffa, who already felt he was being singled out. Hoffa even compared himself to the Kennedy patriarch, saying, 'You take any industry and look at the problems they ran into while they were building up, how they did it, who they associated with, how they cut corners. The best example is Kennedy's old man.' As for his association with so many mobsters, Hoffa unapologetically told a reporter, 'Twenty years ago the employers had all the hoodlums working for them as strike-breakers. Now we've got a few and everybody's screaming.'

The competition between Hoffa and Bobby, who Hoffa referred to as 'Booby' or 'Bobby Boy' in order to get under his skin, continued outside the hearing room and, on one occasion, became physical. Bobby, who wanted to fistfight Joey Gallo and Senator Goldwater, seized hold of Hoffa from behind while the two were in a Capitol Hill restaurant. A shocked Hoffa, who was no stranger to violence, sprung to his feet and grabbed Bobby 'by the front of his jacket and bounced him up against the wall', ending Bobby's attempt to physically bully Hoffa and increasing his determination to antagonize him in the hearing room.

In July 1959, Hoffa and Bobby squared off again, this time before the American public: Hoffa made his case for innocence on the nationally syndicated popular news program *Face the Nation*, while Bobby went on the equally popular *Meet the Press*. Also in July, Bobby appeared on *The Tonight Show* where he let loose on Hoffa and the mob, telling the host, as well as millions of American viewers, 'Unless something is done, this country is not going to be controlled by the people but is going to be controlled by Johnny Dio and Jimmy Hoffa and "Tony Ducks" Corallo.'

By September 1959, after nearly three hundred days of public hearings, Bobby felt that he and Jack had received the national recognition they had sought to achieve. Bobby resigned from the Rackets Committee and went to work on his book about the hearings, titled *The Enemy Within*, a reference to the Teamsters and their mafia colleagues who were, unlike a foreign enemy, destroying the country from within. Critics of Bobby, however, believed that his true enemy lay deep within himself and a Berkeley professor suggested he call his new book *Profiles in Bullying*, a take on Jack's Pulitzer Prize-winning bestseller, *Profiles in Courage*, a montage of short biographies detailing acts of courage exhibited by past senators from John Quincy Adams to Sam Houston.

Bobby's new book was optioned for a movie by 20th Century Fox, with talk of actor Paul Newman playing the lead role of Bobby. But, to Bobby's utter dismay – while proving he was correct in theory, if not tactics – the movie could not get made in Hollywood where the mob and the Teamsters simply warned the studio against it, a warning backed not necessarily by violence, which is never off the table, but by the threat of a union shutdown that would cripple the studio.

*

On 2 January 1960, Senator Jack Kennedy entered the Senate Caucus Room in Washington DC and announced his candidacy for president of the United States. Bobby was tapped to manage the campaign. After the Kennedys had shown the public that the Teamsters were controlled by the mafia, Jack could now comment, 'I am extremely glad . . . Mr. Hoffa and his group are [not] supporting me.' Yet despite Bobby's recent and relentless assault on mobsters who could pose a serious threat to Jack's election given their sway over crooked politicians in highly populated cities, most mob bosses were curiously willing to support Jack's presidential run for a variety of reasons, one of which had to do with Frank Sinatra.

Chapter 5

Atypical Ambassadors

The last time we saw singer-actor Frank Sinatra was at the mob's Cuba conference held at Havana's Hotel Nacional in 1946. As you may recall, journalist Robert Ruark had written a hit piece on Sinatra which questioned his integrity by pointing out his presence in Havana, where he seemed pretty cozy with mobsters such as Lucky Luciano, who came from the same Sicilian village as Sinatra's family. Since then, Sinatra's career had sunk to an all-time low, while his domestic life fell apart. His dip in popularity was not attributable to the Havana hit piece, it was just a typical celebrity slump, and his family problems began when he started an affair with actress Ava Gardner while cheating on his wife and childhood sweetheart, Nancy Sinatra, who bore him three children. When mobster Willie Moretti read about the divorce, which was thoroughly covered by gossip columnists, he was concerned that Frank, whose career Moretti had helped start, was not making the proper family sacrifices and abiding by a man's duty to his wife and family. Moretti, who had no problem killing other men and was eventually killed himself, shot off a telegram to Sinatra that read:

I AM VERY MUCH SURPRISED WHAT I HAVE BEEN
READING IN THE NEWSPAPERS BETWEEN YOU AND
YOUR DARLING WIFE. REMEMBER YOU HAVE A
DECENT WIFE AND CHILDREN. YOU SHOULD BE VERY
HAPPY. REGARDS TO ALL. WILLIE

Unlike Moretti, who believed in marriages for life – whether to a woman or La Cosa Nostra – Sinatra represented a new breed of Americanized Italians who did not see anything wrong with a divorce, which he finalized with his wife of twelve years in October 1951 before marrying Ava Gardner, who eventually left him for a Spanish bullfighter. Between alimony, child support and unpaid taxes, and with no new musical hits topping the charts, Gardner said that Sinatra's money and glamour had run dry. 'Nobody wanted to be around him . . . He didn't amuse them anymore. He couldn't lift a check. There was nobody but me.' There was actually someone else who was prepared to help Sinatra – Johnny Roselli.

Johnny Roselli's birth name was Filippo Sacco. He was born on 4 July 1905, in Esperia, Italy, which is located about halfway between Rome and Naples. His father, Vincenzo, was a shoemaker who migrated to the States and settled in Boston, Massachusetts, then sent for his wife, Maria, and their six-year-old son, Filippo. In 1918, Vincenzo caught influenza and died a miserable death at the young age of thirty-three. Maria remarried an older man who turned out to be a deadbeat of a husband who still had a wife in Italy. He made an even lousier stepfather, so it was probably best when he walked out on them and returned to Italy. By his teens, Filippo was already headed down the wrong path, thieving with a gang of miscreants. He reconciled his new vocation with his staunch Catholic upbringing by saying, 'When

Johnny Roselli

Christ died on the cross, the closest man to him was a thief and that's good enough for me.' He was repeatedly arrested and finally took a serious pinch for heroin trafficking then murdered the informant before fleeing to Chicago where he fell in with the Capone mob. In need of a new identity, the fugitive leafed through an encyclopedia until he came across the name Cosimo Roselli, a Florentine painter during the time of the Medici family. The hoodlum assumed the surname of the Renaissance artist and replaced Filippo with Johnny, reinventing himself as Johnny Roselli.

In Chicago, Roselli was personally groomed by Al Capone, who took a shine to the clever young man who was also tough and 'did a lot of work', according to another bona fide hitman who was close with Roselli. At some point, the Chicago mob sent Roselli to California to look after their interests and help – or, more likely, keep an eye on – Jack Dragna. (It is quite possible that Roselli played a key role in Ben Siegel's murder since he replaced the late Siegel as the mafia's ambassador to Hollywood and Las Vegas, but on behalf of the Chicago mob as opposed to New Yorkers who were seen, out West, as outsiders.) In Los Angeles, where Roselli was known as 'The

Hollywood Kid', he frequented the finest restaurants and exclusive country clubs. He played golf with some of the most powerful men in Hollywood, including Joe Kennedy Sr and the head of Columbia Pictures, Harry Cohn, whose 'casting couch' was as worn out as an old dog's bed. Roselli helped Cohn secure a cash loan that made Cohn the majority owner of Columbia Pictures. He also helped Cohn avoid labor problems that could have halted movie productions. If diplomacy failed, carloads of thugs could be dispatched to beat back picket lines.

When Sinatra's agents at William Morris asked Cohn to give Sinatra the role of Angelo Maggio in the film *From Here to Eternity*, based on the bestselling James Jones novel of the same name, Cohn said, 'Who the fuck would want that skinny asshole in a major movie?' Johnny Roselli, that was who! According to a *New York Post* reporter, Sinatra contacted Frank Costello, who sent word to Roselli in Hollywood. After a nudge from Roselli, Cohn gave Sinatra the part which led to an Oscar in March 1954 for Best Supporting Actor, and ultimately to Mario Puzo's fictionalized account of a mob-connected actor, a stubborn movie producer and a horse's head in a bed. Hollywood publicist Joe Seide later said, '[Sinatra] got it through New York friends, and John Rosselli was the go-between. Johnny was the one who talked to Harry – he was the one who laid it out . . . it was in the form of look, you do this for me and maybe we won't do this to you. There was none of that stuff about a horse's head, but a lot of "juice" was directed.' And so, Sinatra's career was revived by Johnny Roselli, who was well liked by actors and actresses as well as author Edgar Rice Burroughs,

the creator of Tarzan, who invited Roselli over to his house every now and then for cocktails. Perhaps Burroughs was intrigued by the similarities between his fictional character and an actual man who grew up in a jungle and maintained control of the animals.

In 1960, the same year Jack Kennedy was running for president, Sinatra purchased part of the Cal-Neva Lodge, a resort and casino that was named Cal-Neva because it sat on the border of California and Nevada, with all the gambling equipment displayed on the Nevada side where

Frank Sinatra

gambling was legal. The resort, which overlooked Lake Tahoe, had fine dining, riding stables, pools, a golf course, a casino, and plenty of mobsters who not only stayed there but also owned a large piece of the place. Some suspect that Sinatra, who owned more than a third of the lodge, was fronting for Sam Giancana of the Chicago mob, and many believe that Joe Kennedy Sr, who spent a lot of time there, was also a partner. Actor Dean Martin (born Dino Paul Crocetti, which he changed to avoid Italian discrimination in Hollywood) also owned a piece and once joked, 'I'm the only entertainer who has 10 percent of four gangsters.' Martin was prudent enough not to name them.

Postcard of Cal-Neva Lodge

Before the Democratic convention in the summer of 1960, the FBI reported that the Kennedy patriarch was sequestered at the Cal-Neva Lodge where he was 'visited by many gangsters'. The report confirmed Joe Sr's close relationship to mobsters as well as Frank Sinatra, who, during the campaign, had become the mob's liaison to the Kennedy patriarch. Sinatra's daughter, Tina, said that her dad was approached by Joe Kennedy who said to Frank, 'I think that you can help me in Virginia and Illinois with our friends . . . So off to Giancana he went.' To be sure, Frank Sinatra was a staunch Democrat and his preference for Kennedy was genuine. 'Dad felt that Jack Kennedy was a breath of fresh air,' said Tina. 'He said he hadn't been as excited about an election since Roosevelt, whom he also campaigned for.'

The mob, always non-partisan, never ideological and forever wary of motives, were convinced that Sinatra was out to gain something or other in return for promoting Kennedy. Johnny Roselli thought Sinatra had 'big ideas . . . about being ambassador or something'. Still, the smooth-talking Sinatra was able to convince most mob bosses to back Kennedy, but he could not persuade Carlos Marcello of Louisiana or Santo Trafficante of Florida, both of whom distrusted the Kennedys, unwilling to forgive them for the heat they took during the Rackets Committee. They instead backed Lyndon Johnson in the Democratic primary. Jimmy Hoffa agreed with the Gulf Coast dons, as did the Chicago mob's consigliere, Murray 'The Camel' Humphreys.

Humphreys, a Welshman, was as close to the character of the non-Italian consigliere Tom Hagen, in Mario Puzo's bestselling novel *The Godfather*. Considered a criminal genius by mobsters and law enforcement alike, Humphreys was the premier strategist and political fixer for the Chicago mob for the better part of 30 years. As acting boss, Giancana had to run his decision to back Kennedy by the real don of Chicago, Anthony 'Joe Batters' Accardo, who, when making crucial decisions that affected the borgata, invited input from Humphreys and Paul 'The Waiter' Ricca. Although the Italians were smart enough, and tolerant enough of all ethnicities, to give Humphreys a permanent seat at the ruling table, the Welshman was sometimes in the minority when it came time to vote, only to be proven right later on. When Sinatra's request to back Kennedy in the 1960 election was put to a vote, Accardo, Ricca and Giancana were in favor, while Humphreys dissented. 'He hated having to go along with the outfit's vote to back Kennedy,' said Mrs Jeanne Humphreys. 'It was a constant source of aggravation for him. If he was outvoted on something, he was outvoted by the Italians. He'd say the spaghetti eaters and spaghetti benders stuck together.' As an aside, Jeanne Humphreys, who was well aware of her husband's power and place in the mob, admitted her surprise that he and his spaghetti-eating pals could sway a national election, something they easily did in Chicago for decades. But she imagined the national stage as more sacred. 'I didn't know then that a president could be elected on the whim of Chicago mobsters,' she said. 'In my ignorance, I thought majority ruled.'

Aside from the rigid holdouts – Marcello, Trafficante and the hot-headed Hoffa, who vented to Humphreys about his disgust with the Chicago mob's pledge to support Kennedy – Sinatra seems to have convinced the rest of the mob that their help in getting Jack elected would result in criminal leniency during Jack's tenure in office. Given the mob's experiences with Thomas Dewey and Estes Kefauver, both of whom used the mob as stepping stones to further their political careers then quickly moved on, most mob bosses assumed that the Kennedys would also forget the mob once they achieved their dream of being in the White House. They therefore funneled millions of dollars, via Sinatra, into the crucial West Virginia primary when Kennedy's coffers were running low.

Is it possible to redistribute that kind of cash in a political primary, and where did it go? The *York News-Times* called the West Virginia primary 'one of the most corrupt elections in . . . history', reporting that voter bribes 'ranged anywhere from $2 and a drink of whiskey to $6 and two pints of whiskey for a single vote'. One news correspondent from the *Baltimore Sun* said that he had personally witnessed cash changing hands in return for votes, while reporters from the *Wall Street Journal* dug up evidence that dirty cash had been circulating throughout the state; the editors decided against running the story, although one of the reporters later commented, 'We were fairly convinced that huge sums of money traded hands.' The thwarted investigative team had concluded that much of the money flowing into the state came from Chicago, which was Sam Giancana's home turf. There is evidence that money also came from Las Vegas, which was controlled by the Chicago mob along with their partners in New York. Paul 'Skinny' D'Amato, who was born in Atlantic City, New Jersey, and came up under Nucky Johnson, eventually became general manager and part owner of the Cal-Neva Lodge along with his partners, Frank Sinatra, Sam Giancana and Joe Kennedy Sr. After the election, D'Amato was overheard on a bug talking about how Joe Sr had asked him for help in West Virginia and how he had moved money there from Las Vegas, where cash was plentiful on account of the backroom skim.

The mob was also able to help on the ground with police and political pull in some of the state's fifty-five counties where crooked sheriffs had immense electoral power. In exchange for bribes upwards of $50,000, the sheriffs placed Kennedy's name at the top of their election slate, and could move polling places, making it easy or difficult for certain constituents to get to the polls. The executive assistant to the state's governor-to-be said that the Kennedys 'were spreading it around pretty heavy. I thought they spent two million dollars.' The political boss of McDowell County was seen receiving tens of thousands of dollars 'in a shoe box'. One political heavyweight in Harrison County actually considered himself principled for not being too greedy. 'All I had to do was tell him fifteen thousand or twenty thousand,' he said of his dealings with Bobby Kennedy, 'instead of five thousand, and I'd have got it.' Evelyn Lincoln, Jack Kennedy's loyal secretary and confidante until the day he died, summed up all of the above by saying, 'I know they bought the election.'

We are left to wonder if the Kennedy boys knew, or at least suspected, that their father was cutting Faustian bargains with Sinatra's tougher friends. To be sure, there was overwhelming evidence that the vines of their family fortune were entwined in the shadiest trees. Joe Sr's name had come up at the Kefauver Committee hearings which Bobby had followed closely. In a closed-door session, a Chicago bootlegger mentioned Joe's name and his company, Somerset Importers Ltd, but the committee quickly moved on without further inquiry. Although Kefauver took notes regarding the witness's testimony and connection to Joe Kennedy – still available in the voluminous Kefauver file stored at the University of Tennessee at Knoxville – the senator did not follow up, or call Kennedy before the committee. During the Rackets hearings, which Bobby oversaw, Joe's name popped up again. While Bobby's staff were probing for mafia links to New York City buildings that housed mob-connected Teamster locals, the investigators learned that Joe Sr owned one of the buildings. When Bobby found out, he was 'shocked'. When the superintendent was subpoenaed, he arrogantly said, 'I take my orders from the father, not the boys.' Senator Goldwater said that revelations such as this 'just killed' Bobby. In another instance, one of Bobby's prosecuting attorneys, Edwyn Silberling, was yanked from an assignment when the criminal trail he was following led dangerously close to Joe Kennedy. 'The reason being,' said Silberling, was that '[Bobby's] father was often mentioned in connection with the Mafia. [Bobby] was interested in crime-busting only to the extent that his family wasn't involved.' Bobby also had to know that the Cal-Neva Lodge, where his father hung out, was frequented by known mobsters. When a close friend of Joe asked him what he would tell his sons if they ever inquired about his shady past, Joe confidently replied, 'They won't ask me.'

'But,' asked his friend, 'suppose they do.'

'Well,' said Kennedy, 'if they do, I'll tell them to mind their own Goddamn business.'

Evidence that came to light before and after the 1960 election makes it abundantly clear that, had Bobby investigated his own father with half the zeal he displayed while dragging mobsters before the Rackets Committee, he would have disgraced the Kennedy name and likely landed the old man in jail. Why, then, was Bobby, whose father was so corrupt, fixated on rooting out corruption in America? The answer may be attributed to projection, feelings of self-doubt, daddy issues, and other insecurities best left to a psychologist, but for our story we need only know that the mob was well aware of Bobby's hypocrisy but concluded, in large part due to Sinatra's persuasion, that once Jack was in office, the Kennedy duo's attention would be drawn to much heavier issues like civil rights for African-Americans, slowing the nuclear arms race and halting the spread of communism in Latin America and Southeast Asia, while keeping the Soviets behind the Iron Curtain in Eastern Europe.

Chapter 6

Faustian Bargains

Judith Campbell

Back in 1934, while the mob was using its stockpiles of cash left over from Prohibition to colonize metropolitan areas across the country, Judith Exner was born into an affluent family. She grew up in a mansion in the upscale California coastal neighborhood of Pacific Palisades. At the tender age of eighteen, she married a second-rate actor, William Campbell, becoming Mrs Judith Campbell. In 1955, her husband landed a starring role as a death row inmate in San Quentin while, at the same time, their marriage went on death row. The couple divorced in 1958, and the beautiful 24-year-old became, by her own admission, a divorcée gone wild. 'I began dating the way most girls date when they're in high school,' she wrote in a memoir. 'Life became so good.' While enjoying this good life, Campbell attended a Hollywood party and met Johnny Roselli, who, like Campbell, was living the good life and, at fifty-five years old, was still dating like most boys date in high school. The two hit it off and may have carried on a short affair, with Campbell often crashing at Roselli's house after late-night partying. Roselli introduced Campbell to Frank Sinatra who also had a brief affair with Campbell before he introduced her to Jack Kennedy in February 1960, while Jack was staying at the mob-owned Sands Hotel and Casino during a campaign stopover in Las Vegas. Campbell said she began sleeping with Jack in March, and the only part of her story that raises any doubt is that it took him a month to close the deal, though it is quite possible that he was too busy with other women. A Justice Department memo reported that, 'Show girls from all over town were running in and out of the Senator's suite.'

While in Las Vegas, Jack, like Roselli and Sam Giancana, partied with Sinatra. 'Jack was mesmerized by Sinatra's swinging lifestyle,' said Campbell, referring to Sinatra's notorious 'girl-passing', which included regular passes to Jack *and* Joe Kennedy Sr. Campbell was also passed to Giancana who was faithful to his longtime wife until she died of a brain aneurysm in 1954, after which the balding middle-aged mobster frequented Las Vegas and lit up the Strip with Roselli while dating celebrities he was introduced to by Sinatra.

With the mob's help, Kennedy won the Democratic primary and was now pitted against Republican Richard Nixon in the general election. Jimmy Hoffa still broke with the majority of mobsters and had his executive board endorse Nixon for president while he simultaneously went on a public-speaking tour announcing that Kennedy 'presents a very real danger to our life as a nation if he is successful in buying our country's highest office'.

In order to grasp the mob's influence in the 1960 election, we must add a word about Nixon's connections to the mob just as we have traced the Kennedy family's connections. When the mob was still in control of Havana, Nixon was a frequent visitor to Cuba, where he would meet with Fulgencio Batista, making him one man removed from Meyer Lansky and Santo Trafficante, assuming he never met with them personally – which is not beyond the realm of possibility given Nixon's attraction to cash-filled suitcases. One of Nixon's closest friends, Bebe Robozo, was a wealthy and influential businessman of Cuban descent with strong ties to Miami's Cuban exile community as well as to Trafficante. To advance his political career, Nixon relied on influence peddler Murray Chotiner, who would one day serve as an advisor to Nixon. The Los Angeles mobster and former protégé of Ben Siegel, Mickey Cohen, was once asked by Chotiner to host a fundraising dinner for Nixon's 1946 congressional campaign. Cohen, who packed the affair with mob donors, said, 'There wasn't a legitimate person in the room.' Many years later, General Alexander Haig launched a secret probe into Nixon's connections to the mafia, and, according to the *Washington Star*, Haig concluded that, 'There were strong indications of a history of Nixon connections with money from organized crime.' Lastly, along with Jimmy Hoffa, Carlos Marcello and Santo Trafficante also funneled money into Nixon's 1960 campaign.

Suffice to say, the general election was a contest between rogues who were willing to play ball with the mob.

In addition to helping Kennedy win the Democratic primary, the New York and Chicago mobs also contributed to the general election and Judith Campbell, while carrying on affairs with both Kennedy and Giancana, became the perfect cash courier between the mob and the Kennedy campaign (although her amazed ex-husband said, 'They weren't dealing with some kind of Phi Beta Kappa'). In order for Kennedy to clinch the election, Illinois was a must-win state and Giancana controlled its largest and most corrupt city, Chicago.

Since the days of the Chicago mob's founding father, Johnny Torrio, and his prized protégé, Al Capone, the mob held tremendous sway over the state's notoriously corrupt Democratic machine with total control over certain electoral wards in Chicago that were densely populated with Italian-American residents. The mob had an especially tight grip over the 1st Ward, encompassing much of Downtown Chicago. 'Giancana rules the First Ward like a Tartar warlord,' wrote reporter Sandy Smith. 'He can brush an alderman off the city council with a gesture of his hand.' The 1st Ward's alderman, John D'Arco, in return for the mob's backing, handed out no-show jobs to violent mobsters left and right. Chicago hitman Samuel 'Mad Sam' DeStefano, whose imagination when it came to torturing victims would have made the Spanish Inquisitors blush, was hired by the Department of Streets and Sanitation. 'No one who knew him could ever imagine Sam sweeping the sidewalks or shoveling snow,' said one FBI agent, 'but they paid him handsomely for it.' When D'Arco left the city council, claiming poor health, the FBI concluded that Giancana had booted him out for his inability to deliver on one demand or another.

The mob also controlled the 28th Ward on Chicago's West Side and had put Richard Daley in as 11th Ward committeeman then lifted him into the mayor's office in 1955 when they backed him through the 1st and 28th Wards which he carried in a landslide. According to FBI files, Daley's childhood pal, Thomas Munizzo, 'collected vast sums of money from the hoodlum element for the Daley mayoralty campaign' and acted as 'the contact man . . . between the hoodlums and the mayor's office'. FBI agents said there were several other go-betweens besides Munizzo, and the FBI was aware of at least one favor the mob had gotten in return from Daley when they demanded that he replace an upright police captain in the 1st Ward with a more malleable one, which Daley promptly did. In 1960, the FBI overheard two mobsters talking about Daley on a bug. One said, 'This mayor has been good to us,' and the other replied, 'And we've been good to him.'

President Kennedy with Mayor Daley

Mayor Daley was also good to Jack Kennedy, telling him on the eve of the election, 'with a little bit of luck and the help of a few close friends, you're going to carry Illinois'. Although Daley did not define who his 'close friends' were, it was fairly obvious. On 8 November 1960, Daley and his close friends delivered Chicago, helping Kennedy become the thirty-fifth president of the United States by one of the slimmest margins in history. It may or may not have been lost on the Kennedys that Jack carried Chicago the same way Jimmy Hoffa carried Chicago when he was elected Teamster president – with the mafia's help. It was not lost on Sam Giancana, who was overheard telling Judith Campbell, 'If it wasn't for me, your boyfriend wouldn't even be in the White House.'

Beyond Frank Sinatra's role as a mob liaison and major fundraiser for the Kennedy campaign, he was also a top-tier celebrity influencer and, in that regard, was placed in charge of the inaugural gala in Washington that was to raise enough money to square up the Democratic Party debt incurred during the campaign. Radio commentator and columnist Fulton Lewis said there was 'something deeply shocking in the spectacle of Frank Sinatra . . . running the show on the entertainment end. Sinatra's associations and connections are scarcely in accord with the historic dignity of the occasion.'

Always angered but never altered by criticism, Sinatra jumped at the opportunity and 'devoted ten exhausting weeks to planning' an unprecedented entertainment extravaganza, the biggest in the history of the city. It included stars and performers such as Harry Belafonte, Ella Fitzgerald, Bette Davis, Leonard Bernstein, Sir Laurence Olivier, Jimmy Durante and Sinatra's own showbiz clique, known as the Rat Pack, which included Peter Lawford (who married the president's sister, Patricia), Dean Martin, Joey Bishop and Sammy Davis Jr, who was conspicuously absent from the gala, scratched from the list after

he announced his engagement to a blonde actress. Some said the decision to disinvite the African-American entertainer was made by Joe
Kennedy, while others blamed it on Jack, but no one disputes that it
was due to racial concerns.

As Jack's campaign manager, Bobby Kennedy had fought hard to get
him elected and was deserving of a reward in the new administration.
Most political observers thought that Bobby would become a senior
advisor to the president or be given a prestigious, however moot, role.
Family, friends and the media alike were therefore surprised to hear
that Jack was considering Bobby for attorney general, the absolute
highest law enforcement officer in the land. Florida senator George
Smathers told Jack, '[Bobby] never had a case in his life. He never
argued in a courtroom,' while Justice Department attorney Nicholas
Katzenbach said that Bobby was 'too young, too inexperienced, too
political, too brash, too immature in every way. All of these shortcom-
ings were obvious to everyone, including Bobby.'

When Jack announced the appointment, a reporter asked, 'Do you
know of any historical parallel to this?' to which Jack replied, 'No, we
are going to start one.' The press was universally aghast. *Newsweek*
called it a 'travesty of justice', while *The Nation* said it was 'the greatest example of nepotism this land has ever seen'. The American Civil
Liberties Union was in concert with the *Baltimore Sun* when it pointed
out Bobby's lack of regard for the constitutional rights of witnesses
who were dragged before the Rackets Committee where, according
to Yale Law professor Alexander Bickel, Bobby 'held hearings for the
sole purpose of accusing, judging and condemning people'. 'It's not
as if Bobby were against civil liberties,' a Kennedy insider told author
Gore Vidal. 'It's just that he doesn't know what they are.' Based on the
same conclusion, the *Chicago Tribune* believed Bobby 'could use his
powers vindictively'.

The mob was just as concerned as the press but was assured that Joe
Kennedy, who had made them promises, was behind the appointment
which meant that it would not amount to anything detrimental to
their interests. Igor Cassini, brother of fashion designer Oleg Cassini,
later wrote, 'I was in the room with old Joe when he picked up the
phone and told the president to put Bobby in as Attorney General.'
Reporter Charles Bartlett, who knew Bobby well, steered him away
from accepting the nomination, but was told by Bobby, 'Well, maybe

you'd like to call Dad.' A family friend, Clark Clifford, did just that, then visited Joe in his Park Avenue apartment. Joe allowed Clifford to lay out his argument then bluntly said, 'Bobby is going to be Attorney General.'

Back in 1957, *Parade* magazine wrote that Joe Sr's 'word is law' in the Kennedy clan. So, despite Jack's 'very serious reservations' about the appointment, the law had spoken.

Joe was infuriated by the press's accusations of nepotism, insisting that Bobby's exhaustive campaign work had earned him the nomination. But was that the true motive behind Joe's inflexible position? Not entirely. Joe was terribly concerned that allegations of voter fraud in places like Chicago and West Virginia would haunt the new president and possibly overturn the election in the wake of criminal indictments. Following the West Virginia primary, journalist Charles Bartlett wrote, 'The big hope is that a local grand jury may be induced to indict the Senator's brother, Robert Kennedy.' The only person Joe trusted to ensure that the Justice Department would turn a blind eye to whatever chicanery may have gone on was his own son.

After the election victory, Bobby's wife, Ethel, said, 'We were happy, but uncertain. Bobby had that awful gnawing feeling that it could be reversed. No one else seemed as conscious of this as Bobby, Jack and Mr. Kennedy.'

The state of Illinois had cast close to five million votes and Kennedy had won by less than ten thousand votes. This slim margin of victory, along with widespread accusations of voter fraud, led to local investigations. All three of Chicago's leading newspapers believed that the charges had merit, the *Tribune* writing that the election was rife with 'gross and palpable fraud'. Even London's *Economist* felt that the 'exquisite narrowness' of the election was a bit unsettling.

The FBI offices in Chicago and Washington DC were flooded with accusations that the election was stolen, something FBI director J. Edgar Hoover was already aware of through illegal eavesdropping devices planted in mafia hangouts across Chicago. G. Robert Blakey, who worked for the Justice Department and would one day draft legislation to decimate the mob, said that 'enough votes were stolen – let me repeat that – stolen in Chicago to give Kennedy a sufficient margin that he carried the state of Illinois . . . The surveillance in Chicago also establishes that money generated by the mob was put into the 1960 election.'

Hoover was also aware of the mob's help in West Virginia and briefly contemplated opening an investigation but was hogtied knowing that the Justice Department was going to be run by Bobby, who would never introduce the evidence into a courtroom. As one of the chief paymasters in West Virginia, Bobby was not about to investigate himself, nor would he follow leads in Chicago that led straight to his father. Hoover, moreover, could not expose evidence that was gleaned from illegal eavesdropping devices.

As for the defeated Richard Nixon, he chose not to contest the election, a move praised by some as magnanimous. In reality, Nixon knew the Democrats would be in charge of the recount in Chicago, and after the count was confirmed, he would be forever branded a 'sore loser', which would ruin 'any possibility of a further political career'.

Responding to a ceaseless stream of criticism from the press, the president-elect made light of Bobby's appointment as attorney general with his natural good humor, which only angered his thin-skinned brother. At a dinner event, Jack addressed Bobby's many detractors by saying, 'I can't see that it's wrong to give him a little legal experience before he goes out to practice law.' Bobby did not find this funny and later chastised Jack for making fun of him in public.

Lyndon Baines Johnson, who was chosen as Jack's running mate after the two battled during the Democratic primary, was still the Senate majority leader in Congress and therefore needed on the floor to help push through Bobby's confirmation. 'Well,' said Johnson, who knew the appointment truly came from Joe Kennedy, 'since the old bastard bought the office I guess he's got a right to get his money's worth.'

On 13 January 1961, Robert F. Kennedy entered the hearing room of the Senate Judiciary Committee in Washington DC, where senators had a chance to vet the new nominee. 'Mr. Kennedy,' observed the *New York Times*, 'who is 35 years old, looked even more youthful in the witness chair.' When Republican senator Roman Hruska of Nebraska grilled Bobby, saying, 'You have, as I understand it, never negotiated a settlement, for example, of a litigated civil case for damages or the breach of a contract or tort case,' Bobby snidely replied, 'I doubt if I am going to be doing that as Attorney General.' After the two-hour hearing, Bobby was unanimously approved and subsequently received a 99–1 vote on the Senate floor, the hold-out being Republican senator Gordon Allott of Colorado. The Harvard Law reject, who had never tried a case in court and was known for dispensing with civil liberties, was confirmed as the nation's youngest attorney general who would be working for the youngest president ever to be elected.

Bobby was sworn in by Chief Justice Earl Warren with Bobby's wife Ethel and a dozen or so Kennedy clan members looking on. Bobby, who had never managed anything so simple as a magazine stand, was now in charge of 30,000 employees across the many branches of the Justice Department, with an annual budget of over $300 million. He was also perfectly in place to head off the many inquiries into election fraud. One of Bobby's top lawyers at the Justice Department, who would go on to run Bobby's newly formed organized crime squad, said, 'we found substantial corruption in Democratic strongholds with people who had supported JFK strongly. And I was not reluctant to go ahead and prosecute, which caused problems with . . . Bobby.'

'A few months after the election,' wrote Seymour Hersh, 'allegations of vote fraud in Illinois were reported to Bobby Kennedy's Justice Department – and met with no response. The 1960 presidential election was stolen.' And the mob was expecting its reward, something J. Edgar Hoover was well aware of, via secret bugs and wiretaps.

Chapter 7

The Chairman and Leader

In 1675, the enigmatic Prince Frederick of Brandenburg, later known as Frederick I of Prussia, created an odd military regiment of 'big men', known as the *Potsdamer Riesengarde*, or the Giant Guard of Potsdam. In 'an obsession that would make him a laughingstock in later life', Frederick sought the tallest men from across Europe, sometimes gifted to him by other nations and states, to fill the ranks of this peculiar regiment which the king drilled every day. 'The most beautiful girl or woman in the world would be a matter of indifference to me,' said the king, 'but [tall] soldiers – they are my weakness.' Three hundred years later, another power-driven man with similarly peculiar ideas about appearances was FBI director J. Edgar Hoover, whose army of agents were not only expected to carry themselves a certain way, but also had to look a certain way. 'Weight–height rules . . . were enforced inflexibly,' wrote *Life* magazine, and 'bald-headed men', said FBI assistant director William Sullivan, 'were never hired as agents because Hoover thought a bald head made a bad impression'. Sullivan went on to reconcile the unavoidable fact that many men go bald as they age. 'Though a bald-headed man wouldn't be hired as an agent, an employee who later lost his hair . . . was kept out of the public eye.' There was also a strictly enforced conservative dress code that prohibited colorful attire and agents were fired for having pimples or sweaty palms.

During a 1961 trip to Washington DC, US attorney for the Southern District of New York, Robert Morgenthau, was hoping to meet Hoover and was given a few ground rules more consistent with a royal lawn party for the king of England. 'Don't shake Mr. Hoover's hand,' Morgenthau was told. 'Let him shake yours. And don't speak unless he speaks to you.'

John Edgar Hoover was born in Washington DC on 1 January 1895. As a young man, he worked as a file clerk at the Library of Congress where he took note of the card index used to keep track of publications, a filing system he would one day duplicate to keep track of radicals, communists and criminals. 'I'm sure he would be the chief librarian if he stayed with us,' noted a fellow clerk, which makes us shudder at the thought of what the penalties might have been for overdue books.

In 1924, President Calvin Coolidge's attorney general, Harlan Stone, appointed the 29-year-old Hoover as director of the FBI (originally, the Bureau of Investigation). Years later, when President Franklin Roosevelt considered replacing Hoover with another director, Hoover put the kibosh on his plans by calling on influential friends who intervened on his behalf. Having nearly lost his job, Hoover was spooked and embarked upon a private intelligence-gathering mission against politicians who might attempt to dethrone him in the future. To this end, Hoover compiled, as one columnist wrote, 'The greatest deposit of personal dirt ever amassed.' Hoover's vast collection of compromising material is believed to have contained, among other dirty little secrets, a litany of sexual escapades. If this were true, then President Kennedy, who once told a friend, 'I get a migraine headache if I don't get a strange piece of ass every day,' was the gift that kept on giving.

By 1960, Hoover had already compiled a fat file on Jack but hoped, as with past presidents, it would only collect dust. However, it was nearly dusted off after election day. On the night after the election, the president-elect had dinner with some close friends, one of whom said to Jack, 'There is just one thing I want you to do – fire J. Edgar Hoover!' Another thought it was more important to 'get Allen Dulles out of the CIA immediately', referring to Dulles as the 'godfather' of the intelligence community. Jack gave serious thought to both suggestions but ultimately decided to keep Hoover and Dulles in charge of his domestic and foreign intelligence agencies, not wanting to appear as if he were upending the old guard. William Sullivan believed that Jack kept Hoover on because he had won the election by such a slim margin 'that he felt he couldn't afford to alienate Hoover's considerable conservative following by getting rid of him'.

JFK, Hoover and RFK

*

After Bobby Kennedy was sworn in as attorney general, Hoover presented the much younger man with a mounted FBI badge, making him an honorary agent. That was where the niceties ended; they locked horns almost immediately thereafter. To start with, Bobby was bothered by the FBI's virtual autonomy; Hoover had always enjoyed direct access to the Oval Office so he could, according to William Sullivan, 'thumb his nose' at the attorney generals. Bobby wanted to remind Hoover that the attorney general was his boss, so he stood in the way of Hoover's access to the president while insisting that all FBI communication with the White House pass through the attorney general's office. Bobby further demanded that Hoover clear the FBI's frequent press releases with him first, and, to Hoover's dismay, Bobby would often edit the statements before approving them for release. Bobby, moreover, gave direct orders to FBI agents and dropped in on any one of the Bureau's fifty-four field offices across the country, unannounced, infuriating Hoover who did not want his Potsdam Giants reviewed by another king.

To make sure Hoover knew who was boss, Bobby, who was born a year after Hoover became director of the FBI, installed a loud buzzer on Hoover's desk so Bobby could summon him at will. According to Bobby's underling, William Hundley, Bobby would sometimes buzz the 65-year-old director just for kicks. On one such occasion, Bobby mischievously said to Hundley, 'Should I get Hoover over here?' Bobby buzzed and minutes later, Hundley saw an out-of-breath Hoover stomp into Bobby's office 'with a red face'.

RFK dressed leisurely at the Justice Department, which irritated Hoover

Even under normal circumstances, Hoover hated visiting Bobby's large, ornately decorated office where Bobby, whose 'reputation was that of an arrogant, narrow, rude young man', rolled up his sleeves, loosened his necktie, and kicked his feet up on the desk. 'It is ridiculous to have the Attorney General walking around the building in his shirtsleeves,' Hoover told an aide. Hoover was even more aghast when Bobby turned the office into a part-time playground where he tossed a football around with his pals and threw darts at a dartboard, sometimes while Hoover was speaking with him.

As Bobby tightened a figurative leash around Hoover's neck, he took a real leash off his 'large and ill-tempered Labrador' Brumus, who Bobby brought to work in defiance of federal code. The Ethiopian emperor, Haile Selassie, had a dog, Lulu, who sometimes sat on his lap during state ceremonies. Now and then, Lulu would hop down and urinate all over the feet of the emperor's dignitaries who sat in silence, afraid to shoo the dog away and risk offending the emperor, who did nothing to stop the dog. It became quite apparent that Bobby enjoyed the same thrill as Haile Selassie while letting Brumus mark territory, lick, fling spittle, and jump all over people with dirty paws. Everyone, including Hoover, had no choice but to suck it up. On one occasion, Brumus took a massive dump outside Hoover's office which infuriated Hoover who was already getting crapped on by Bobby.

Bobby and Hoover also clashed on issues of policy. Bobby considered the greatest threat to US national security to be organized crime, while Hoover insisted there was no such thing as a mafia in America. Hoover had carried on his dogged denial for decades and would have preferred to keep his head in the sand but was forced to lift it after the mass round-up of mobsters at Apalachin, which resulted in widespread media speculation about the existence of a national crime syndicate led by a tight-knit network of mafia families. The *New York Herald Tribune* had demanded that Hoover wage war on this 'invisible government' while Bobby, who was then still at the Rackets Committee, asked the Bureau for their existing files on the mobsters who were detained. Bobby was shocked to learn that Hoover had none; his thin file on the mafia consisted of 'some newspaper clippings'.

William Sullivan admitted that Apalachin 'hit the FBI like a bomb. The meeting proved beyond any doubt that organized crime existed on a massive scale in this country.' Hoover's trusted lieutenant, Cartha 'Deke' DeLoach, wrote, 'Incredible as it may seem, only after this meeting was reported did the FBI have sufficient proof to say that there was such a thing as La Cosa Nostra – a national crime syndicate.' Yet Hoover was still reluctant to take on the mob. After Apalachin, William Sullivan drafted a detailed report on the gathering. Hoover's reaction was to order the report and any copies of it destroyed, calling it 'baloney'.

Hoover was just as dismissive with former president Eisenhower's attorney general, William P. Rogers, who once formed a special group on organized crime, appointing Milton Wessel as its leader. Wessel never got very far and the reason was explained by the head of Wessel's Midwestern office, Richard Ogilvie, who said, 'Hoover was very cool to the whole idea of the Attorney General's special group. He ordered the FBI files, containing the very information we needed on organized crime, closed to us.' It took Hoover about two years to suffocate the group out of existence and Wessel may have unwittingly explained Hoover's reasoning for doing so when he said that the mafia was earning nine billion dollars a year in gambling, with 'fully half . . . earmarked for protection money paid to police and politicians'. How would Hoover explain this to the American people? If the mob was a threat to the nation, and the mob was in bed with the nation's elected officials, then the government was corrupt to its core. Were Hoover's FBI agents expected to surround the Capitol Rotunda and tell everyone to come out with their hands up?

In October 1960, the International Association of Chiefs of Police met in Washington DC, where they attempted to organize themselves on a federal level to tackle organized crime and make up for Hoover's lack of interest. Hoover responded by saying, 'Nothing could be more dangerous to our democratic ideals than the establishment of an all-powerful police agency on the Federal scene.' Did the irony escape the head of the largest federal police force in the world? Or, as Shakespeare said, 'The eye sees not itself.'

Regardless of Hoover's public stance and distaste for competitive agencies, the director knew he had to do something after Apalachin; he quietly ordered his agents to 'read over two hundred books on the Mafia' while also researching 'the New York Times coverage of organized crime for the last hundred years'. Next, in a way that meshed with his sneaky nature, Hoover had his agents plant secret listening devices in mafia hangouts; the covert operations were known as 'black bag jobs'. Within months of Apalachin, teams of FBI agents broke into mob hangouts across the country and installed bugs that overheard mobsters talking about their many political friends in high office. Mobsters who were never surveilled before, and had no reason to believe their words were being recorded, spoke openly about judges and politicians – local, state and federal – who were all on their payroll. Hoover's fear that mafia corruption went as high as the Capitol was confirmed. How many congressmen and senators in Washington were on the mob's payroll? Hoover did not care to know – beyond the purpose of blackmailing someone – and he had a hard time understanding why Bobby wanted to shake this beehive. Did Bobby really want Hoover to uncover that there was a direct link between the mafia's underworld government and the United States government? Would Bobby like Hoover to conduct a forensic accounting of the millions of dollars directed into his brother's presidential campaign, via Frank Sinatra? Did Bobby want Hoover to follow up on all the accusations of mob-induced voter fraud in Chicago, and probe the dirty underworld relationships of the president's close friend and supporter, Chicago's Mayor Daley? Would Bobby want Hoover to stake out the Cal-Neva Lodge (which Hoover actually did in secret) and publish photos of mobsters meeting with the president's father? Was this what the young, inexperienced attorney general truly wanted? Did Bobby really want Hoover to shake the American public's confidence in its own government?

In addition to black bag jobs, Hoover established the Top Hoodlum Intelligence Program, which trained agents to 'develop particularly qualified, live sources within the upper echelon of the organized hoodlum element who will be capable of furnishing the quality information required'. In time, approximately four hundred confidential sources, better known as informants, were recruited by the FBI. Their identities were kept so secret, even inside the Bureau, that they were indexed by numbers instead of names. Unbeknownst to Bobby, by the time he became attorney general in 1961, Hoover had had the program in place for several years already and was hardly in the dark about the mob. But because Hoover was not sharing his intelligence with the rest of the Justice Department, Bobby would have understandably seen Hoover as being derelict in his duties. And even if Bobby knew what Hoover was up to, he would have criticized him for not using the information to prosecute mobsters. Entirely unaware of Hoover's top-secret operations, Bobby publicly and privately attacked Hoover for his reluctance to take on the mob, determined to drag him into the fight, kicking and screaming if need be.

Despite Joe Kennedy's campaign promises to the mob, Bobby saw his role as attorney general as an opportunity to finish what he had started at the Rackets Committee. In his first speech after being sworn in, Bobby declared an all-out war on the mafia, telling an assembly of university students, as well as the American people, 'Organized crime has become big business. It knows no state lines; it drains off millions of dollars of our national wealth, infecting legitimate businesses, labor unions, and even sports . . . It promotes cynicism amongst adults. It contributes to the confusion of the young and to the increase of juvenile delinquency . . . This is a problem for all America . . . Unless the basic attitude changes here in this country, the rackets will prosper and grow.'

Back at the Justice Department, Bobby compiled a 'hit list' of top mobsters that started at forty and quickly exceeded 2,300. Using his immense power as the top lawman in the country, Bobby beefed up the Justice Department's racketeering section by 400 percent and 'centralized control of organized crime cases from the almost one hundred U.S. Attorneys' offices around the country'. To lead the fight, the man who was once likened to a Nazi by his own father prepared for a blitz on the underworld by mobilizing, according to the *Wall Street Journal*, a 'multi-agency drive', insisting everyone work together to bring down the mob.

The FBI, IRS, INS, Secret Service, customs bureau, narcotics bureau, labor department, treasury department, wildlife service and others were organized into a strike force and expected to participate in a coordinated attack on the mafia. Bobby was creating what Nicholas Katzenbach said was 'his own mini crime commission, of which he was the chairman and leader'.

For the first time in US history, the executive branch of the United States government had declared an all-out war on the mafia. The crusade Bobby had begun at the Rackets Committee was now fueled by the entire Justice Department.

The very first week Bobby started work as attorney general, Carmine Bellino, the brilliant forensic accountant who worked for Bobby at the Rackets Committee, visited the offices of the IRS (Internal Revenue Service) requesting income tax returns for suspected mobsters and mob-connected union leaders. Bellino's primary target was Jimmy Hoffa who, unlike the many mobsters who were fooled by Sinatra's promises, knew he would be 'in the soup' with the Kennedys in the Oval Office and had commented after Bobby was appointed attorney general, 'I'll have to hire 200 more lawyers to keep out of jail.'

To make sure he had a compliant IRS, Bobby appointed his former tax law professor from the University of Virginia, Mortimer Caplin, as its new commissioner. Sounding out Caplin, Bobby told him, 'One of the things that I, Bobby Kennedy, am going to do as Attorney General is to take on Organized Crime in this country . . . How do you feel about the Internal Revenue Service getting involved in that?' Caplin answered positively and was brought on board. On 24 February 1961, Caplin issued a confidential memo to regional IRS directors that read, in part, 'As part of the Government's drive against organized crime, the Attorney General has requested the Service to give top priority to the investigation of the tax affairs of major racketeers.' Any regional directors who did not comply, concerned that personal attacks were unconstitutional, were promptly replaced.

'The purpose of tax laws is to collect revenue,' said one tax attorney who frowned upon Bobby's misuse of the IRS. 'Once you bend them to catch criminals, you undermine the tax laws and ultimately destroy confidence in them. Justice has to be even-handed. It can't be personal.' Future attorney general Ramsey Clark further commented, 'What you're basically doing . . . is using tax law to justify judgments about people on other grounds.' The FBI's official liaison to the attorney general, Courtney Evans, said that the IRS's function was 'to collect taxes, not to put people in the penitentiary'.*

On 1 February 1961, Bobby appointed Edwyn Silberling to head up his new section on organized crime and racketeering, with a core staff of fifty attorneys. Silberling was no stranger to mobsters, having worked as an assistant district attorney under Frank Hogan, the man who once investigated Frank Costello for secretly appointing judges to the bench. In a stunning show of bigotry, the anti-mafia section was dubbed inside the Justice Department as the 'pizza squad'. Reducing men to pizza may have made it easier for Bobby to deprive them of their civil liberties which began with his attack on the Constitution's Fifth Amendment. The amendment, written into the nation's original Bill of Rights, seemed custom-made for *omertà* as it allowed individuals to remain silent in criminal matters as a protection against

---

* Ironically, Joe Kennedy Sr was widely believed to be guilty of tax evasion. In 1957, *Fortune* magazine estimated Joe's worth in the area of $200 to $400 million, and upon his death in 1969, the *New York Times* wrote that he was worth 'perhaps $500-million'. Seymour Hersh wrote, 'Joe spent his life making money – and hiding it.' Hersh's statement is supported by a close friend of the Kennedy family, Morton Downey, who said that Joe even used his connections to the Catholic Church to cheat the IRS. According to Downey, Joe would donate one million dollars to the Vatican and 'the Vatican, in turn, would give $500,000 back'.

self-incrimination. Bobby went before the House Judiciary Committee and requested a broader statute that would weaken the amendment's power and allow him to hold mobsters in contempt of court and imprison them for remaining silent under questioning. In response to legal experts who cited his blatant attack on civil liberties, Bobby responded in a way that shocked them all the more, stating, 'Although the Fifth Amendment is for the innocent as well as the guilty, I can think of very few witnesses who availed themselves of it who in my estimation were free of wrongdoing.'

Bobby pestered the INS (Immigration and Naturalization Service) to eject mobsters who had entered the country illegally or neglected to become naturalized citizens, used confiscation and forfeiture laws loosely, and worked on passing legislation that enlarged interstate commerce laws, allowing the federal government to apply the statute more broadly. Bobby also urged his old colleague, Senator McClellan, to enact conspiracy laws that would, according to Nicholas Katzenbach, 'make organized crime a federal offense'. When Bobby, in the presence of his colleagues, blurted, 'Can't we just make it a crime to be a *member* of the mafia?' the legal scholars 'squirmed at his suggestion . . . surprised by his legislative naiveté'. They were also surprised by his disregard for due process and habitual abuse of power.*

Bobby, a staunch Catholic who was friendly with cardinals – he was married by Cardinal Spellman while Jack was married by Cardinal Cushing – was determined to recruit the archdioceses in his crusade against the mob. In author Luigi Barzini's stunningly accurate portrait of Italians, he wrote: 'The great Mafia families of Sicily . . . are as intricately bound to each other by a network of old and recent marriage ties as old aristocratic families.' Of all the borgatas in the

---

* Bobby displayed little regard for freedom of the press. Quite a few reporters who were critical of the Kennedy administration were investigated. 'Under Robert Kennedy,' wrote columnist Victor Lasky, 'the freewheeling use of Federal agents to investigate leaks grew to menacing proportions. Some of the most respected Washington correspondents experienced "the treatment", which included visits by Federal agents to their homes, tapping of telephones, shadowing of reporters, investigations of their friendships, and other forms of intimidation.' When this same columnist wrote a bestselling book that was critical of President Kennedy, he, too, was investigated by Bobby. A number of journalists were mysteriously audited by the IRS, as was Richard Nixon and his campaign manager, following Nixon's loss to Kennedy. Attorney Roy Cohn, who Bobby once bumped heads with while the two worked for the McCarthy Committee, was indicted twice by prosecutors who were prodded by Bobby.

United States, that which most closely resembled Barzini's description was New York's Gambino crime family. 'The thing that's different about this group, that makes it different from any other Mafia group in America,' said a member of law enforcement who investigated the Gambino family, 'is the intermarriage tradition – the incest.' After hearing about this taboo, the obsessive Bobby began to dig through church records to see who was related to whom and is said to have spent hours studying the Gambino family tree. Quite ironically, Theodore Roosevelt's daughter, Alice, had once referred to Bobby as a 'revolutionary priest', while an attorney at the Justice Department said his 'zeal to break up the syndicates was reminiscent of a sixteenth-century Jesuit on the hunt for heresy'.

After federal agents 'drew up genealogical charts of the most notorious families of Sicilian extraction in the United States underworld and discovered that everybody was everybody else's son-in-law, grandfather, stepson, great-uncle, first, second or third cousin, godfather or godmother, and so forth', Bobby had the FBI contact the New York Archdiocese, alerting it to these unholy marriages it must have been unwittingly consecrating. Even this tattling was rife with irony since, although the Kennedy family marriages were lawful, the Kennedy men, father and sons alike, were known to share women and their extramarital affairs were often aided and abetted by wives and sisters. One family friend and aide to Jack said the Kennedy household was an 'almost incestuous atmosphere' where father and sons 'preyed off each other's dates [and] traded them like baseball cards'. The same man said of Jack, 'When he was finished with the girl, he usually gave her telephone number to his father or one of his brothers, and they did the same.'

With the Church looking into their marriages, Carmine Bellino and Mortimer Caplin sifting through their tax returns, and twenty-seven government agencies joined in a concentrated attack on organized crime, the mafia was not getting the return they expected from the contributions they had made to the Kennedy campaign. One mafia don, in particular, who was not persuaded by Frank Sinatra's assurances of sunny days ahead, and had backed Richard Nixon instead of Kennedy, became an intensely personal target of Bobby who was obsessed with destroying him.

Chapter 8

The Big Little Man

Calogero Minacore was born on 6 February 1910, in a Sicilian exile community in French Tunisia. When his parents heard that America needed immigrant labor, Calogero's father, Giuseppe, traveled to Louisiana, found a job and a place to live then sent for his wife, Luigia, who left for the States with her son, via Sicily.

In the autumn of 1910, the steamship *Liguria* weighed anchor in the Port of Palermo, slipped through the Strait of Gibraltar, and headed out into the rough waters of the Atlantic. Twenty-two days later, six hundred Sicilian immigrants arrived at the Port of New Orleans where they were welcomed by a crowd of Italian-Americans, some of whom had been there during the city's unapologetic 'dago' lynchings, only twenty years earlier. Despite the ongoing discrimination Sicilians were still subjected to in Louisiana, they were welcomed for one reason: their indefatigable work ethic.

Luigia disembarked with her eight-month-old son, Calogero. When questioned by immigration officials about the purpose of her trip, she said that her husband was currently working on a sugar plantation in New Orleans where she also planned to work. Luigia and her son were cleared for entry and greeted by Giuseppe, who was waiting on the dock. Although immigration officers searched the ship for mafiosos, we cannot fault them for overlooking the tiny eight-month-old boy in Luigia's arms who would grow up to become one of the wealthiest, most powerful mafia dons in American history.

To facilitate their assimilation into American society, Giuseppe and Luigia changed their names to Joseph and Louise, and their son's name to Carlos. Joseph's boss on the sugar plantation was also named Minacore so he asked Joseph to change his surname so that the two men would not be confused at work. He did, and little Carlos Minacore became Carlos Marcello.

Over the years, the immigrant couple added another six sons and two daughters to the family. They worked hard and saved every penny

A young Carlos Marcello

until they could afford to purchase a small patch of land in the bayou country where they grew vegetables for the French Market. By age fourteen, Carlos Marcello quit school and began to cart the family's produce to market. By his late teens, he became acquainted with other local criminals and drifted into crime. At age nineteen, he was pinched for a bank robbery in New Orleans and given a nine-to-twelve-year sentence in Angola State Prison. While he was in jail, his father, who was arrested as an accessory to the crime but released for lack of evidence, bribed Governor O.K. Allen, who was apparently okay with releasing bank robbers early for the right price. Marcello was pardoned after serving only four years.

Upon Marcello's release from prison, the 25-year-old returned to crime, pulling local capers and trafficking in drugs. He also opened a bar that catered to Black patrons, naming it the Brown Bomber in honor of his favorite heavyweight champion, Joe Louis. Inside the bar, Marcello loaned money to Black people who could not stroll into a white bank on Main Street and walk out with a loan. Over the next several years, Marcello racked up a long record of assaults, robberies and narcotics convictions, and was suspected of murder.

While building his street résumé, Marcello came to the attention of Silvestro 'Silver Dollar Sam' Carollo, who had succeeded Charles Matranga as boss of the Louisiana borgata in 1922. Carollo's under-boss, Frank Todaro, was especially fond of Marcello and allowed the young man to court his niece, Jacqueline. The two fell in love and were married on 6 September 1936. Because Todaro wanted the best for his niece, Marcello was given one of the best rackets in the borgata, the distribution of jukeboxes and pinball machines which he installed in business establishments throughout the state.

After the 1932 Democratic National Convention, where Frank

Costello had struck a deal with Louisiana senator Huey 'Kingfish' Long to move his slot machines into the state, Costello reached out to his fellow mafia don, Silver Dollar Sam Carollo, who agreed to give Costello the local police and political protection he needed in New Orleans in return for access to Senator Long, something Silver Dollar Sam needed. To distribute Costello's slot machines, Carollo recommended Marcello, who had already secured numerous locations for his jukeboxes and pinball machines. Marcello swung into action, spreading thousands of Costello's slot machines across the state. Costello was so impressed with Marcello's speedy output and reliability that when he and his partners, Meyer Lansky and Dandy Phil Kastel, decided to build a plush casino on the East Bank of Jefferson Parish, the trio asked Marcello if he would become their managing partner. Marcello accepted the offer and also signed up bookmakers for Costello's race wire in New Orleans, which Marcello also managed.

Marcello and Costello's profitable relationship proved especially advantageous to Marcello when Silver Dollar Sam Carollo was deported as an illegal alien in April 1947. Carollo's natural successor should have been his underboss, Frank Todaro, but Todaro was challenged by Carollo's son, Anthony, who had a cadre of loyal friends,

Frank Costello, who stood firmly behind Carlos Marcello's ascension to the throne in Louisiana

mostly flunkies who kissed up to him because he was the boss's son. To avoid bloodshed, the borgata's capos called for an election. Besides citing his blood-claim to the throne, Carollo portrayed Todaro as a pre-war relic, unfit to lead the borgata into the future. But the wily old Todaro outfoxed the young, spoiled thug by arranging for his 38-year-old nephew through marriage, Carlos Marcello, to emerge as the leading candidate in his stead. Marcello was also endorsed by the Prime Minister of the Underworld, Frank Costello. (Costello's endorsement was unofficial since he did not want to appear to be meddling in another family's affairs, but it still carried weight. And Marcello's multiple partnerships with Costello, resulting in various streams of trickle-down revenue for other members of the borgata, further played to Marcello's advantage.)

The election was scheduled for 5 May 1947, at the mob-owned Black Diamond nightclub in New Orleans. Marcello arrived at the club with Frank Todaro, and four of Marcello's six brothers – Peter, Vincent, Joseph and Anthony Marcello – and cousins Jake and Nick Marcello; and several powerful capos who were also throwing their weight behind Marcello. The men made their way to the back room that had been used for mob meetings in the past. The Creole waiters and musicians who were employed at the club and were regularly privy to high-echelon mafia talks could tell right away that something much bigger than the usual sit-down was afoot.

At the table, the smaller Carollo faction lobbied for the 25-year-old's candidacy but his claim was knocked down on account of his youth and inexperience; he was thirteen years younger than Marcello. Carollo then endorsed an older mobster, but everyone saw it as a ploy by Carollo to rule by proxy. After a show of hands, Marcello was crowned as the new don of the New Orleans mafia.

The next day, Marcello's neighbors witnessed a steady stream of fancy cars rolling up to his Italianate mansion as men entered his house, paid their respects, then drove away. Even Sheriff Frank 'King' Clancy, who 'ruled the delta flats and neon jungles of Jefferson Parish', paid homage to Marcello at his home. Frank Costello did not show up but was quick to send a congratulatory note which certified the election and eliminated any opposition from the bitterly dejected Carollo faction. After Costello made his voice heard, Silver Dollar Sam sent his blessing from Sicily.

As Louisiana's new don, the five-foot-two semi-literate Marcello, who spoke in a strange English-Sicilian-bayou drawl, became known as 'The Little Man' or, more accurately, 'the big little man'. He built an empire that grossed over a billion dollars a year while shifting money from the rackets into real estate, restaurants, hotels, motels, bars, petrol stations, electrical appliance stores, liquor stores, linen supply services, wholesale beverage distributorships, truck dealerships, shipbuilding firms, mortgage companies, taxi and bus companies, tour guide companies, a fleet of shrimp boats, and a tomato canning factory that supplied the United States Navy, allowing Marcello to portray himself as a 'tomato salesman'. It was virtually impossible to reside in or visit Louisiana without somehow putting money into Marcello's pockets.

Like most wealthy businessmen, Marcello understood the import-
ance of political clout and became, according to one newspaper, 'an old
hand at buying politicians, a breed he despises but cultivates because
of their influence'. Marcello was known to hand out suitcases filled
with cash to politicians from both parties and would one day boast to
an undercover agent that he would drive around and dish out $50,000
in cash on any given day. In one gubernatorial election, Marcello liked
both candidates so he backed both.

Former FBI agent and managing director of the Metropolitan Crime
Commission of New Orleans, Aaron Kohn, investigated Marcello but
never got anywhere, believing his power and immunity from prosecution were largely due to the corrupt political climate in New Orleans
which Marcello exploited to the fullest. For an idea of how corrupt
the climate was, which had not changed since the lynchings in 1891,
we need only look at one of Kohn's first endeavors in his new post
as managing director, which was to accuse the New Orleans Police
Department of corruption. Kohn produced a list of mob-connected
gambling houses that were regularly paying off the police. To Kohn's
bewilderment, the district attorney was only interested in where Kohn
got the list. When Kohn refused to give up the cop who slipped it to
him, *Kohn was jailed for contempt*!

To expand his reach into politics, Marcello hired political fixer Jack
Halfen, whose clientele included a future president, a future Supreme
Court justice, and Frank Costello. Halfen's payoffs were sometimes
disguised as ordinary campaign contributions while stacks of cash
were also passed along to politicians, via their bagmen. Investigative
journalist Michael Dorman said that Marcello would pick up 'virtually the entire tab for a campaign for governor or other statewide
office'. When the dogged Dorman tracked down Marcello later in
life, the still active mob boss denied being a mafia don, saying, rather
comically, 'I don't come from Italy, much less Sicily, where the Mafia's
supposed to have started. I was born in Tunisia. And I wouldn't know
a Mafia or a Cosa Nostra from a Congolese tribesman.' Beyond this
blanket denial, Marcello was forthcoming about his involvement in
politics, believing it was his right, perhaps even his duty, as a United
States resident – he was not a citizen – to be involved in the political
process. 'Sure, I've got plenty of political connections,' said Marcello.
'I don't deny that. I've been helping put people in office for years. I've
spent a whole lot of money on campaign contributions and I've spread

the word to people to support my candidates. What's wrong with that? I thought it was everybody's duty to take part in politics. I hear talk all the time that it's terrible that Carlos Marcello is supporting so-and-so for office. You don't hear that it's terrible that the banks or the utilities or the oil companies are supporting so-and-so. Hell, many of the big companies operating in Louisiana are run by outsiders. I'm a local fellow. I provide a lot of people with jobs. Why shouldn't I have the same right as these big companies to try to elect my friends to office?'

Dorman also interviewed a racketeer who worked with Marcello for decades. Like Marcello, the man denied any knowledge of a mafia but candidly explained the environment from which he and Marcello sprouted. 'When Carlos and I were starting out in the rackets,' he said, 'just about the only money available for political campaigns in Louisiana and other Southern states was rackets money. These were poor states. There were no "fat cats" around to finance political campaigns. If a guy wanted to run for any important office, the only place he could get enough money was from us. So we got control of the political machinery. We picked the candidates; we paid for their campaigns; we paid them off; we told them what to do. We even provided the poll-watchers and vote-counters. It didn't really matter how many votes a candidate got. What counted was how many votes we tallied for him.' The man went on to explain how complex their approach was when supporting one particular candidate. 'We didn't ask for wide-open gambling or anything like that. What we wanted was the power to name the next state conservation commissioner. Sounds innocent, right? You'd think the conservation commissioner would be an unimportant guy – supervising parks and fishing and hunting licenses and crap like that. But this election was in an oil state, and the conservation commissioner had the power to approve or reject the drilling of every oil and natural gas well in the state! After the election, we named the commissioner – and there were millions made through that appointment. With a deal like that, who the hell needs gambling?' That is not to say that Marcello did not control the state's gambling as well, which he did, nor did it suggest that Marcello's means of achieving his end was not sometimes violent. But although Marcello ordered murders, he was not one to litter the streets with corpses, which would have resulted in public pressure on his political pals. Reliable informants told Aaron Kohn that Marcello's victims were never found because they were first decomposed in a tub of lye before being dumped in one of Louisiana's many alligator swamps.

The headquarters for Marcello's illegal rackets and legitimate businesses was a stand-alone cinder block office on the property of Marcello's Town and Country Motel, located at 1225 Airline Highway. On his neat desk were two telephones, a large flame-throwing cigar lighter, and a sculpted gladiator's head with helmet. On the walls were maps and aerial photographs of his real estate and construction projects. The only indication that the office was occupied by an unusual proprietor was a sign that hung on the door above the exit so visitors could see it on their way out: THREE CAN KEEP A SECRET IF TWO ARE DEAD.

Postcard of Marcello's Town and Country Motel

In a much fancier office back in Washington DC, Attorney General Bobby Kennedy was probing every known detail of Marcello's life in an attempt to bring him up on criminal charges, or deport him from the United States. It is important to note that, although Bobby went after the entire mob, he reserved a special hatred for Marcello, Trafficante and Hoffa, the three men who backed Lyndon Johnson in the primary and Richard Nixon in the general election.

Chapter 9

The Jungles of Central America

When Senator Estes Kefauver's traveling circus passed through Louisiana, Carlos Marcello, referred to by a local newspaper as the 'crime czar' of New Orleans, was summoned before the committee. Marcello pled the Fifth one hundred and fifty-two times, resulting in a contempt of Congress charge for which he was sentenced to six months in prison. An appellate court reversed the conviction before Marcello stepped foot in a cell. At the same time, Kefauver prodded the Justice Department to deport him. Deportation proceedings began in 1953 and dragged on throughout the remainder of the decade. When a senator asked Marcello to explain how he had managed to stay in the country so long after being ordered to be deported, Marcello honestly replied, 'I wouldn't know.'

Bobby Kennedy wanted an answer to this same question and countless others when he called Marcello before the Rackets Committee in March 1959. Marcello aggravated Bobby by repeatedly pleading the Fifth. Shortly after Bobby became attorney general, he instructed the Immigration and Naturalization Service (INS) to review the old deportation order and told them to figure out a way to eject Marcello.

If Marcello was sent far away to Sicily where his parents were born, or to his original birthplace of Tunisia, he feared he would lose control of his empire so he looked around for a closer country where he could claim a birthright. He settled on Guatemala for its corrupt political climate and because it was a relatively quick airplane ride from Louisiana. Next, Marcello sent for Carl Noll, a notorious con man with a long criminal history, and asked him to broker a deal with the Guatemalan minister of the interior, Eduardo Rodriguez Genis, and Genis's law partner, Antonio Valladares, both of whom were close with the country's prime minister. Using an official state car with a government-paid chauffeur, Valladares took Noll on a tour of the countryside in search of birth records until they found a village outside of Guatemala City with an original birth ledger that had a blank space for an entry on the day Marcello was born. They matched the ink and handwriting with that of the older entries as best they could and filled in the space with Marcello's genuine birth name, Calogero Minacore. Genis then issued an official birth certificate and gave it to Noll. A forged Guatemalan passport followed, along with citizenship papers bearing an authentic Guatemalan seal. At the risk of committing a couple of relatively trifling crimes, and for a total cost of $100,000, Marcello was now born in San José Pinula, just across the Gulf of Mexico, which would allow him to receive regular visits from his capos and maintain control of his empire in the event he was deported. We should pause for a moment to reflect on this complicated scheme which shows off Marcello as a calculating man willing to spend lots of money and to go to great lengths in order to keep what was his, and prevail over Bobby Kennedy.

When Bobby's lawyers at the Justice Department got wind of Marcello's Guatemalan forgery, they urged the FBI to dispatch agents to Guatemala and dig up evidence of his crime. Hoover, however, wanted no part in this assignment and sat on his hands. Frustrated by the FBI's inactivity, Bobby personally sent a prosecutor, John Diuguid, to Guatemala, where Diuguid was able to find the exact ledger with Calogero Minacore's name added. Diuguid had a professional FBI chemist examine the ink, and the chemist concluded that it was much newer than the other entries on the old turn of the century paper. Bobby brought this to Hoover's attention but the crotchety old director was still uninterested in pursuing criminal charges against Marcello, so Bobby pressured the commissioner of the INS, General Joseph Swing, to immediately deport Marcello. Swing must have known that Hoover had already deflected this hot potato since Swing contacted Hoover for advice on how to proceed. Other than an FBI memo that read, 'General Swing is under pressure from the AG to deport Marcello,' Hoover made no comment and avoided Swing by passing him off to an assistant director, who also eluded him. With no guidance from an unusually silent Bureau, Swing caved in to Bobby's demand and prepared to deport Marcello.

Bobby briefly considered dumping the Louisiana don in Europe or even farther away in Asia, but Marcello's phony birth certificate was too good an opportunity to pass up. Bobby contacted the Guatemalan authorities and knowingly misrepresented Marcello's forged papers as authentic. The Guatemalan government issued the INS a permit of re-entry for Marcello, and the moment the permit was processed, Bobby gave General Swing the order to deport him.

Since Marcello had been under a soft deportation order for the better part of a decade, he was regularly required to check in at the INS offices located inside the New Orleans Masonic Temple building. On 4 April 1961, Marcello entered the building and paid a routine visit to his case officer, where he would typically exchange a few niceties, sign his name in a logbook, then run off. This time, the case officer instructed Marcello to take a seat. Marcello instantly knew there was trouble. As the case officer informed Marcello about an official order to deport him to Guatemala, two INS agents suddenly appeared and handcuffed Marcello. The case officer, who was normally cordial to Marcello, denied his request to speak with his attorney, or his wife. According to the laws of the United States – which Bobby Kennedy had solemnly sworn to uphold – Marcello was being unlawfully abducted by armed men.

With no toothbrush, no change of clothing and only some pocket cash, Marcello was marched outside and shoved into a waiting automobile. A mini-convoy with sirens blaring sped him over to Moisant International Airport, where a seventy-eight-passenger airplane was idling on the tarmac with only a pilot and co-pilot on board. Given the blatant unlawfulness of this procedure, and the burly men who shoved Marcello onto an empty airplane while refusing to answer any of his questions, Marcello, who was well-acquainted with violence, felt it was a setup to kill him and may have considered a sky-fall as his possible fate. When Augusto Pinochet took power in Chile and wanted to eject his enemies from the country, he said, quite candidly, to Admiral Carvajal, 'My view is that we grab all these gentlemen and we send them out of the country, anywhere they want. And then, in midflight, we begin throwing them out of the plane.' In hindsight, historians might argue that Bobby Kennedy and General Swing were more principled than Pinochet and Admiral Carvajal, but Marcello could not have known this at the time, and a kidnapper is an impulse away from a murderer.

After a 1,200-mile flight in silence with no food or drink, the airplane landed at a military base in Guatemala City. The colonel in charge of the base did not know what to do with Marcello, so he sent him home with his own personal secretary, Ms Jinks, who displayed traditional Latin American hospitality by telling the mob boss he was welcome to sleep on the other side of her bed. The prudish mob boss would later comment, 'I didn't have no pajamas. I was ashamed.'

Displaying the gritty resilience that catapulted him to the top of the underworld, Marcello quickly got his bearings and checked into Guatemala City's Biltmore Hotel. He got in contact with his wife and family who were relieved to learn that he was alive. Along with attorney Mike Maroun, Marcello's wife and daughter flew south to visit Marcello at the hotel, where they found him already holding court. After Marcello's brothers flew in with airline luggage filled with stacks of cash and clothing, he was back to his normal self, meeting with Guatemalan businessmen and discussing various opportunities in industries such as hospitality, legal gambling and shrimping. Felice Golino, who once owned one of the largest shrimp-boat fleets in the Gulf of Mexico, was thrilled to talk business with Marcello, as were Guatemala's aristocracy, who rolled out the red carpet for their unexpected visitor whose yearly income of a billion dollars equaled the small country's gross domestic product. Marcello was even flown around on the president's private plane and became a regular visitor to the VIP section of the Guatemala City racetrack.

While Marcello was making the best of his forced vacation and striking new deals with business leaders, the double farce played on the Guatemalan people was brought to the attention of President Miguel Ydígoras Fuentes. At first, Fuentes did not wish to interrupt the festivities being held around the country's strange guest, but after a political thunderstorm he was forced to dismantle Marcello's satellite office at the Biltmore Hotel and ordered him expelled from the country. Marcello's wife and daughter, who had been spared from witnessing his abduction at the Masonic Temple building, were now witnesses to his arrest by a foreign government. He was tossed into the city jail. After being released on house arrest, Marcello was separated from his family who were permitted to leave the country by airplane while Marcello was seized by police and driven to the El Salvadoran border along with attorney Mike Maroun, who refused to leave his side.

Marcello was quickly jailed in El Salvador, while, back in the States, Bobby told the press he was 'very happy Carlos Marcello is no longer with us'. Although Bobby insisted the deportation order was executed 'in strict accordance with the law', his minions at the Justice Department were not as convinced, nor were they willing to risk their hides for Bobby's personal vendetta. Within forty-eight hours of Marcello's deportation, Edwyn Silberling, chief of the Organized Crime Section, shot off a communiqué to the assistant attorney general of the Criminal Division, Herbert J. Miller Jr, expressing the following concern:

> In light of the information contained in our intelligence file the United States Government may be placed in the embarrassing legal position of having made certain representations to the Guatemalan government about Marcello's birth record while it was in possession of information indicating that the birth record was a forgery.

In addition to Bobby lying, committing a felony and revealing how little he thought of the small nation of Guatemala, he had also ignored a United States Supreme Court ruling that explicitly mandated a seventy-two-hour notice of departure be given to every deportee. Canadian columnist Jack Wasserman called Bobby's deportation of Marcello 'persecution, revenge and blind justice' as well as 'bureaucratic tyranny', later adding that it was the 'darkest and foulest chapter in deportation history'.

Marcello sat in the clink for a week, until an El Salvadoran military commander, who wanted no part of these hot *tamales*, directed Marcello and Maroun onto an old bus that drove them into neighboring Honduras, where they were 'dumped off the bus like baggage thrown in the dust, left to fend for themselves on a forested hilltop with no signs of civilization in sight'. In the mafia's tropical version of Ernest Shackleton's grueling journey from Elephant Island, the middle-aged Marcello and Maroun, dressed in silk suits and alligator shoes, struggled over jungle trails, up and down hills, and beneath the sweltering heat of a burning sun with nothing to eat or drink. The short, chubby mob boss was dangerously dehydrated when he repeatedly collapsed into the dirt while cursing Bobby Kennedy, who was in Washington with his feet up on his desk, playing darts in an air-conditioned office. 'If I don't make it, Mike,' Marcello said through gasping breaths that warned of a heart attack, 'tell my brothers when you get back, about what dat kid Bobby done to us. Tell 'em to do what dey have to do.' In mob lingo, that means whack Bobby.

With Maroun's help and inspiration, and a burning desire to enact his own revenge on Bobby, Marcello dug deep and found the strength to carry on. The lost and exhausted men were at the end of their rope when they came upon two local boys who they recruited as guides to lead them to civilization. Using machetes, the boys hacked through thick brush as Marcello and Maroun followed closely behind. At some point, Marcello, who had killed men and disposed of them in the bayous of Louisiana, got it in his head that the boys were leading them deeper into the brush where they planned to machete him and Maroun to pieces before picking through their pockets, which were stuffed with cash. Marcello signaled to Maroun that they should hang back and escape. As soon as some distance grew between them and the boys, the men flung themselves down a steep hill, rolling over rocks and thorns. They lay at the bottom, bruised and bleeding; Marcello had three broken ribs from the fall. The boy-guides, who probably were not out to kill them since they'd already had ample opportunity to do so, but had not, must have wondered why two crazy old gringos had suddenly thrown themselves down a hillside for no apparent reason. Marcello continued to curse Bobby as he labored on in pain.

Through a combination of luck and determination, the men endured a seventeen-mile trek in 100-degree heat and eventually spotted civilization, where they asked if anyone had an airplane. They were directed to a small airfield where a private pilot flew them to the Honduran capital, Tegucigalpa. Marcello booked a hotel room and slept for two days straight then sought medical attention, while Maroun flew back to Louisiana on a passenger plane and informed the Marcello family that their patriarch was injured but alive.

After much needed rest and healing, Marcello was back to his old, spunky self, but his family was not faring so well in Louisiana. Once Bobby had Marcello out of the way, he personally directed the IRS to file tax liens of close to a million dollars against Marcello's innocent wife, Jacqueline. The family's bank accounts were frozen, preventing them, according to Marcello's attorney, from 'purchasing the necessities of life'. When news of Jacqueline's harassment reached Marcello, he flew into a rage. Since Bobby was out to destroy Marcello's family, Marcello had no choice but to meet the challenge head-on, even if that meant destroying Bobby's family. But first he needed to get home.

Isaac Irving Davidson worked as a lobbyist on Capitol Hill for clients such as Coca-Cola, the Teamsters, the CIA, Latin American dictators, Arab sheiks and Carlos Marcello, who Davidson referred to as 'the boss' when in his company and 'Uncle Snookums' behind his back. Davidson, who was well-acquainted with power, said that

Marcello 'controlled things in Louisiana', and called him the 'best-connected man in America'. Using Davidson as his liaison, Marcello paid General Rafael Trujillo, dictator of the Dominican Republic, to have an air force jet fly him to Miami where he caught a domestic flight home to Louisiana. An FBI memo written in June 1961 reported that a 'high-ranking U.S. government official may have intervened with the Dominican Republic on Marcello's behalf'. The memo noted Louisiana Senator Russell Long's interest in Marcello's situation. The dots were not hard to connect – Senator Russell Long was the son of Senator Huey 'Kingfish' Long. Marcello would later boast that he funded Russell Long's political campaigns and *Life* magazine once wrote, 'Two generations of the Long family have coexisted with the Mafia.'*

Upon his return to Louisiana in early June, Marcello went into hiding while he assembled a battery of attorneys to contest Bobby's illegal deportation. When Bobby heard that Marcello was back in the States, it was his turn to fly into a rage. Anticipating a new wave of public scrutiny for casually dispensing with Marcello's civil liberties and subverting justice by deceiving the Guatemalan authorities, Bobby had little choice but to double down. He ordered two dozen federal agents to Louisiana with orders to turn over every rock in search of Marcello and arrest him for illegal re-entry. To relieve the immense pressure put on his immediate family, Marcello surrendered to the INS and

---

* There are a number of stories about how Marcello returned home to Louisiana. One version has him returning on a flight with an enigmatic private pilot, David Ferrie, who we will meet in this book. Another version has him leaving Central America on one of Felice Golino's shrimp boats which transported him home to New Orleans, via the Mexican port of Chetumal. There is no evidence to support these or other versions, while a wiretap later confirmed that Marcello returned on a Dominican Republic air force jet which points to Trujillo.

Two days after Marcello landed on US soil, Trujillo was on his way to visit his mistress when he and his chauffeur were ambushed in a CIA-backed hit. 'Trujillo was wounded but he was still walking,' said one of the shooters, 'so I shot him again.' It so happened that the CIA's plot to murder Trujillo had the go-ahead from Attorney General Bobby Kennedy who, in addition to realpolitik, saw the Trujillo hit as a chess move against his mafia enemies who had gotten cozier with Trujillo after they had lost Cuba to Fidel Castro. 'The Kennedy White House knew in a general way ... and approved,' wrote Arthur Schlesinger. If Marcello needed any proof that the concern for his life on that empty airplane was warranted, or that Bobby was playing for keeps, he now had it; the dictator Marcello had bribed to rescue him was dead and stinking on a road outside of San Cristóbal after ruling his Caribbean nation for more than thirty years.

was placed in a detention center until he was able to post bond. The clever J. Edgar Hoover, who stayed far away from this debacle from the start, could now snicker as the attorney general ducked under a hailstorm of criticism.

In October 1961, Bobby directed federal prosecutors in Louisiana to charge Marcello with perjury, fraud and illegal re-entry. Marcello's brother Joseph, who allegedly dealt directly with Carl Noll, was charged alongside Marcello who viewed Joseph's arrest as yet another spiteful and unwarranted attack on his immediate family. That was not enough for Bobby, who also increased the pressure on Marcello's extended family. One day before Marcello was scheduled to appear in court and plead 'not guilty' to re-entering the country illegally, members of his borgata were swept up in raids targeting gambling dens across the state that were connected to bookmaking operations across the country. It was apparent that Bobby's goal was to have Marcello's fellow mobsters blame him for their problems and, with a little luck, dispose of Marcello, which would instantly dissolve the messy situation Bobby had gotten himself into.

From the night Carlos Marcello came to power in the Black Diamond nightclub until the day Bobby Kennedy was appointed attorney general, Marcello's legal troubles in Louisiana had ranged from negligible to non-existent. Now, as 1961 came to a close, he was fighting a federal indictment, a deportation order, his brother was facing prison time, his wife was suffocating from tax liens, his family's bank accounts were frozen, and his broken ribs were still hurting after an unlawful abduction that left him fighting for his life in the jungles of Central America. As we leave Marcello in a most desperate situation that called for the most desperate measures, let us turn to the CIA, which felt the United States had been thrust into a similarly desperate situation that called for the most desperate measures.

Chapter 10

A Strategic Alliance

In the wake of Fidel Castro's seizure of power in Cuba, a wave of Cuban immigrants settled in Miami, Florida. They were very much like the Sicilian immigrants who had arrived in the United States before them, in the sense that most were hard-working, law-abiding people. But, unlike the Sicilian exodus to America that brought shiploads of poor manual laborers, the Cuban immigrant community, being forced into exile as opposed to searching for a better life, was a perfect cross-section of society from top to bottom: professors, doctors, lawyers and laborers. Some had never cared for Castro while others had cheered him on or fought alongside him but were disenchanted with his Marxist policies, Soviet-style trials, halting of free elections and erosion of civil liberties. With lightning speed, the Cubans picked up with their lives in America and contributed to every stratum of society while many still longed for home, fourteen hundred of whom became part of the Cuban Brigade, a CIA-trained military unit that was eager to oust Castro in a counter-revolution.

The brigade had come about in March 1960 when former president Eisenhower permitted the CIA to mobilize the exiles into a fighting force, only about 10 percent of whom were professional soldiers. The goal was to have the brigade invade Cuba and replace Castro with a moderate regime that would return previously confiscated US assets on the island, break ties with the Soviets, and revive Washington's former relations with Havana, a lopsided relationship Castro viewed as colonialist. When Eisenhower left office, the CIA hoped that his vice president, Richard Nixon, would succeed him in the Oval Office and execute the invasion plan. But Nixon was defeated by Kennedy, leaving it up to Eisenhower's CIA director, Allen Dulles, to brief the incoming president.

Allen Welsh Dulles was the brother of Eisenhower's secretary of state, John Foster Dulles, resulting in the 'first and only time in American history that siblings ran the overt and covert arms of foreign

Allen Dulles with his brother John Foster Dulles

policy'. When Eisenhower took office in 1953, the spread of communism was the CIA and State Department's primary concern; the Soviets were flexing their muscles beyond the Iron Curtain, Mao's Red Army had seized power in China, and American military forces had suffered over fifty thousand casualties at the hands of communist North Korea. John Foster Dulles died in 1959, leaving it up to Allen to deal with the communist threat in Cuba, located only ninety miles off the tip of Florida.

During the presidential campaign, Jack Kennedy was briefed by Allen Dulles who visited him at Hyannisport on 23 July 1960, and again on 19 September. Although Cuba was mentioned on both occasions, Kennedy was not fully briefed about the planned invasion until he received a visit from Dulles and his deputy director of plans, Richard Bissell, who flew to Palm Beach, Florida, on 18 November, ten days after Kennedy was elected to office. Although there is still a debate as to how much classified information Kennedy was told while campaigning against Nixon, it is fairly safe to say that the Palm Beach visit is when most of the invasion plans were laid out before the incoming president. Kennedy listened silently, and Dulles interpreted his silence as a nod to proceed with a land invasion launched by the disaffected Cubans, coinciding with an internal uprising sparked by the planned assassination of Castro. Bissell told Kennedy that they believed 'Castro would be dead before the landing', and Senator George Smathers, the man who had visited Cuba with Kennedy when the latter allegedly engaged in a ménage à quatre before the eyes of Santo Trafficante, said that, following the briefing, Kennedy told him, 'There is a plot to murder Castro. Castro is to be dead at the time the thousand Cuban exiles trained by the CIA hit the beaches.' In 1988, Smathers reaffirmed this, telling author Michael Beschloss that Kennedy was in the know. 'Someone was supposed to have knocked [Castro] off,' said Smathers, 'and there was supposed to be absolute pandemonium' across the island. It is unclear and remains the subject of intense debate as to how much Dulles told Kennedy, then or later, about this assassination plot which was to be carried out by – the mafia.

The CIA's director of security, Sheffield Edwards, was the first to suggest that the CIA recruit the mob to murder Fidel Castro. Back in August 1960, Edwards approached Richard Bissell and told him the mafia wanted Castro dead as much as the CIA did; they wanted their billion-dollar casinos back and supposedly had bundles of cash still buried on the island. Since the mob regularly killed people for less, Edwards believed they would happily kill Castro, if asked. Bissell agreed with Edwards but the former economist who once worked on the Marshall Plan 'had no desire to become personally involved', so he tapped Robert Maheu, a former FBI agent who was trusted to handle 'delicate or clandestine matters' for the CIA and was known to have mob connections in Las Vegas.

When Edwards and Bissell told Maheu what they were thinking, he was reluctant to take part in a murder, even under the banner of patriotism. The agents were sympathetic to Maheu's concern and told him that they had grappled with the same moral dilemma but rationalized that it was okay to kill for national security. Maheu soon came around and agreed to reach out to his mafia contact who he had met through Washington attorney Edward Bennett Williams.*

Robert Maheu was once on a business trip to Las Vegas where he was to serve the owner of the El Rancho Hotel with a subpoena. Maheu said the mission 'seemed like a walk in the park' until he and his wife tried to book a room. After being turned away from the El Rancho, the Flamingo, the Desert Inn 'and every other hotel in town', Maheu called his pal, Edward Bennett Williams, who had powerful connections on every level of society, including the underworld. According to

---

* Maheu was not the first person who was approached by the CIA and, while researching a different subject, I came across at least one more individual. Deputy director of the Federal Bureau of Narcotics, Charles Siragusa, who pursued mobsters like Lucky Luciano, spoke of a strange encounter he'd had with a friend from the CIA. They were sitting in Siragusa's Washington DC office 'just shooting the breeze' when the agent said, 'We are forming an assassination squad . . . since you have a lot of contacts with the underworld, we'd like you to put together a team to conduct a series of hits . . . There's some foreign leaders we'd like dead . . . We're prepared to pay a million dollars per hit.' A startled Siragusa offered a diplomatic reply, telling his friend and colleague that he would consider this proposition if it were a time of war while politely reminding him that they were in a state of peace.

Maheu, Williams 'told me to sit still. Ten minutes later, a man called back and asked what I needed in Las Vegas. I told him a room at the El Rancho, and he said it was a done deed.' The caller then told Maheu he would drop by the following evening to formally introduce himself. 'I'll be wearing a dark suit and I have gray hair,' said the caller, 'and my name is Johnny.'

After Johnny got involved, Maheu said the El Rancho 'rolled out the red carpet' and lodged him and his wife in 'a beautiful bungalow, filled with flowers and fruit. And they told us everything was on the house.' The next evening, Maheu met the mysterious Johnny, who was Chicago mobster Johnny Roselli. Impressed by his new acquaintance, Maheu decided to tear up the subpoena he had intended to serve.

Maheu was in awe of Roselli's power, calling him the 'key to the city' and 'the ultimate mob fixer in the desert'. He remained friendly with Roselli, figuring he was a good person to know if he ever wanted a complimentary room or steak dinner in Las Vegas, never imagining he would need him for a hit on a Caribbean dictator.

Following Maheu's unusual meeting with the CIA, he invited Roselli to his home in Arlington, Virginia, where Maheu was in the habit of throwing 'big Maine-style clambakes' in his backyard. Roselli had already become a regular guest at Maheu's house, where Maheu's children 'took to calling him Uncle Johnny', but the reason for this particular invitation was so Jim O'Connell, who had previously worked as Maheu's CIA case officer, and O'Connell's boss, Sheffield Edwards, could size up Roselli at the party before recruiting him for an assassination plot on a world leader. While watching Roselli interact with people in the backyard, the agents took note of his polite manners and quiet demeanor; he was a perfect gentleman with no *bada bing* in his style, which reassured them of his serious nature.*

After the party, the agents told Maheu to go ahead and recruit

---

* One day, the co-founder and president of Columbia Pictures, Harry Cohn, who relied on Roselli to avoid labor disputes in Hollywood, told actor Marc Lawrence to go out with Roselli and observe him as a character study for an upcoming movie in which Lawrence would be playing the role of a mobster. 'So that night I go to the fights with Roselli,' Lawrence reflected on the evening. 'And I'm *studying him*, like Harry said. He talks. He watches the fight. He eats a hot dog. And he's great. Good conversation. He pays for everything. He laughs at my jokes. What the fuck was I going to do with any of this? I'm playing a vicious gangster, and this guy's a sweetheart.' The CIA agents reached a similar conclusion but knew there was a Mr Hyde inside Johnny Jekyll.

Roselli into their plot, but to pretend that he would be working not for the CIA, but on behalf of 'big business organizations which wished to protect their interests in Cuba'.

In the autumn of 1960, Maheu invited Roselli to lunch at the Brown Derby, a Hollywood hot spot for actors, directors and producers. While sipping coffee after a meal, Maheu started to recite the CIA's cover story about big business interests which Roselli immediately sniffed out as hogwash; he told Maheu to come clean. Maheu spat out the truth, telling Roselli the CIA wanted the mafia to assassinate Castro. This was so unexpected and contrary to what Roselli thought of the United States government that he wondered if Maheu was setting him up. Were the feds, knowing Roselli was a killer, trying to entrap him by getting him to accept a murder contract?

'Me?' asked a startled Roselli, who was relentlessly targeted by Bobby Kennedy. 'You want *me* to get involved with Uncle Sam? The Feds are tailing me wherever I go. They go to my shirtmaker to see if I'm buying things with cash. They go to my tailor to see if I'm using cash there. They're always trying to get something on me. Bob, are you sure you're talking to the right guy?'

Maheu convinced Roselli that the pitch was legit. Roselli then gave Maheu a lesson in the mafia's chain of command: the same way Joe Socks Lanza had once needed an okay from Lucky Luciano to collaborate with Naval Intelligence during the Second World War, Roselli told Maheu that he would need to clear this with his boss, Sam Giancana, who was not expected to be a hard sell. Once, when Giancana's daughter, Antoinette, expressed admiration for the macho Cuban revolutionary leader, Giancana shouted, 'That son of a bitch . . . do you have any idea what he's done to me . . . to our friends?' Antoinette said that she 'thought he was going to have a stroke. The veins in his neck and forehead swelled and pulsed as he continued to shout at me.' Not surprisingly, when Roselli approached Giancana with Maheu's proposal to whack Castro, Giancana said, 'That rotten bastard. He stole millions of dollars from us. I can't wait to kill the fucker.'

Because Giancana and Roselli would be running the operation out of Miami where the CIA had built a sprawling intelligence facility near their exiled Cuban colleagues, they had to clear it with Santo Trafficante, who controlled Florida and was also crucial to their plot since his borgata was deeply immersed in the Cuban exile community. (As fellow dons, Giancana and Trafficante were already well-acquainted. Roselli was also on excellent terms with Trafficante, having represented Chicago's interests at Trafficante's Sans Souci Hotel and Casino in Havana.)

In late 1960, Roselli, Giancana and Trafficante met with Maheu and Jim O'Connell in Miami's Boom-Boom Room, a lounge located inside the well-known Fontainebleau Hotel. After some small talk, the party retired to a private suite where everyone, except Trafficante who prudently listened without comment, openly discussed various ways to kill Castro. Maheu, who was initially hamstrung by ethical concerns, now suggested they cut Castro to pieces in a hail of gunfire. (We tend to sprint after we reluctantly cross our moral lines in the sand.) Giancana, who had executed his share of mob hits, knew how difficult it would be for a hit team to pop Castro and escape alive, so he steered the group away from the idea of a traditional mob hit and suggested they poison Castro instead. O'Connell liked this idea and said he would talk to his superiors about it.

O'Connell spoke with Director Allen Dulles and Deputy Director Richard Bissell, who were also keen on the idea and wanted to use an undetectable poison, hoping that an untraceable murder would avoid a possible showdown with Castro's Soviet backers which could lead to a nuclear war. To concoct the perfect poison, they turned to Sidney Gottlieb, a man known as 'the Borgia of the CIA' for his expertise at poisoning people.

Sidney Gottlieb was born in New York in August 1918. He had deformed feet like his future mentor, Allen Dulles, who was born with a clubfoot, creating what one writer described as 'a strong but never mentioned bond between them'. As a boy, Gottlieb needed leg braces to walk until the age of twelve, when, like Forrest Gump, he tossed them aside. But the similarities to the innocent Gump ended there. In 1943, as war engulfed the globe, Gottlieb earned a doctorate in bio-chemistry from the California Institute of Technology. Unfortunately for his future victims, he would use this degree and his extraordinary intelligence in ways that would make author Stephen King cringe.

During the Second World War, the United States launched its first bioweapons program and, upon Germany's defeat, some of the worst Nazi doctors were not only spared from the gallows but hired by the Office of Strategic Services, which was the forerunner to the CIA. Men like the brilliant German rocket scientist, Wernher von Braun, who went on to work for NASA and became the chief architect of the Apollo Saturn V rocket, were actively sought out and recruited by American agents. Von Braun helped the US win the space race, but the very same program that gave him and other Nazi scientists blanket immunity also forgave plenty of evil scientists who were guilty of the most horrendous atrocities carried out on innocent victims, such as the concentration camp inmates at Auschwitz, Dachau and Buchenwald. In many cases, crimes were expunged and biographies rewritten in the interests of 'national security', which looked ahead to future wars and how they could be won by the United States.

By the mid-1950s, the great power that defeated the Nazi menace was conducting or underwriting a variety of inhumane experiments on patients, prisoners and prostitutes, and at least one experiment in which 'mentally handicapped children were fed cereal laced with uranium and radioactive calcium'. Allen Dulles eventually ended up in charge of Bluebird, a mind control program to make Cold War enemies 'sing like birds'. Dulles worked with Sidney Gottlieb, who had joined the CIA six months after Dulles. One CIA employee from those early days remarked that 'it was fashionable among that group to fancy that they were rather impersonal about . . . human life'.

After exhibiting little to no regard for human life, Gottlieb eventually became the head of the recently formed Chemical Division of the Technical Services Staff, also known internally with dark humor as the 'Health Alterations Committee', where Dr Gottlieb developed 'everything from mind-control drugs to very efficient exotic poisons'. One study of this regrettable period in American history recounted how, in '1951, a team of CIA scientists, led by Dr. Gottlieb, flew to Tokyo. Four Japanese suspected of working for the Russians were secretly brought to a location where the CIA doctors injected them with a variety of depressants and stimulants . . . Under relentless questioning, they confessed to working for the Russians. They were taken out into Tokyo Bay, shot and dumped overboard.' The same study went on to report that in '1952, Dulles brought Dr. Gottlieb and his team to post-war Munich in southern Germany. They set up a base in a safe house . . . Throughout the winter of 1952–3, scores of "expendables" were brought to the safe house. They were given massive amounts of drugs . . . to see if their minds could be altered. Others were given electro-convulsive shocks. Each experiment failed. The "expendables" were killed and their bodies burned.' Gottlieb also tested his poisons on laboratory monkeys, knowing he had something worth pursuing when enough monkeys dropped dead. The London *Times* later wrote, 'What Gottlieb and his CIA henchmen did was only in degree different from the activities which had sent a number of Nazi scientists to the gallows at Nuremberg in 1946.'

Much like the superintendents of Nazi death camps and murderous mafiosos, both of whom possessed an uncanny ability to separate murder from domestic life, Gottlieb carried on a seemingly normal home life with his wife and four children while believing himself to be spiritual. Like any other father, Gottlieb sometimes told his children what he was up to at work; his seventeen-year-old son told a girl-friend, 'You know, my dad has killed people. He made toothpaste to kill someone.'

Gottlieb also experimented with hypnosis, hoping that an induced killer ordered to commit a political murder would obey without question, be unaware of who ordered the murder, and even forget, after awakening from the hypnotic trance, that he had committed the act. Until that breakthrough was achieved, however, the agency carried on with more traditional methods of murder for which they needed men like Roselli, Giancana and Trafficante.

After being tapped by Dulles and Bissell, Dr Gottlieb developed a poison for Castro and it was given to Trafficante who passed it on to his contacts in Miami's Little Havana. They, in turn, were to deliver it to operatives in Cuba who would somehow get the poison into Castro's bloodstream at the same time as the Cuban invasion was underway.

Chapter 11

The Bay of Betrayal

Since President Kennedy's inauguration, CIA strategists had been searching for the perfect beachhead to land the Cuban Brigade. By April 1961, they settled on a landing strip named *Bahía Cochinos*, or Bay of Pigs. Because the bay butted up against the swamps of the Zapata Peninsula, which once supported guerilla activities during the Spanish-American War of 1898, the CIA believed it was ideal for an invasion force to move inland from the beach. But the terrain had changed since then and the exact opposite was true. The next blunder was the CIA's decision to launch an amphibious landing at night. Throughout the Second World War, amphibious landings were never attempted in darkness, nor were the 1950 Incheon landings in Korea which turned the tide of war in favor of the United States military. It does not take a genius to figure out why; darkness hides the shoreline, the surf can be frightening for soldiers loaded down with heavy gear, and the enemy cannot be seen inland, intensifying an already dangerous situation. Yet fourteen hundred Cuban exiles known as Brigade 2506 (named in honor of an early recruit who was accidentally killed and whose identification number was 2506) and made up of 'peasants and fishermen as well as doctors, lawyers, and bankers' of all ages 'from sixteen to sixty-one' were to disembark from 'hulking old cargo vessels' and secure a beachhead in the dead of night. Once the exiles accomplished this seemingly impossible mission, they were assured that several hundred Cuban guerillas operating in the vicinity would link up with them before they all moved on toward Havana.

The invasion force was split into three groups that would land on three different sections of beach along a forty-mile coast. Each group wore different-colored scarves: the Blue Brigade, White Brigade and Red Brigade. Unfortunately, they were as doomed as Britain's ill-fated Light Brigade since Castro knew exactly when they were coming.

Castro had his own spy agency, G-2, which was modeled after the Soviet KGB and reliant on a massive informant network. The spies were trained by Soviet agents and had no problem infiltrating the counter-revolutionary groups in Miami who 'don't know how to keep secrets', according to Richard Bissell. One former chief of the CIA's Miami office said, 'To a Cuban, a secret is something you tell only one hundred people.' By 1960, Little Havana was crawling with G-2 spies who even infiltrated Miami's sprawling CIA station, staffed by over three hundred Americans and located on a 1,571-acre parcel of land adjacent to the University of Miami.

The press had also tipped off Castro. For months, Latin American newspapers openly wondered about the curious training activities taking place in Guatemala where the exiles were housed and an airstrip had been constructed. Back in October, a Guatemalan newspaper, *La Hora*, broke the story that an invasion of Cuba was imminent. That same month, the *Hispanic American Report* disclosed the presence of an anti-Castro guerilla training camp in Guatemala. By November, when Dulles was briefing the president about so-called classified intelligence, *The Nation* ran the story in the United States, calling it a 'dangerous and hare-brained project'; it was picked up by the *Washington Post*, *Miami Herald*, *Los Angeles Times* and other American news outlets, some sources actually detailing the invasion plans. Kennedy told Arthur Schlesinger, 'I can't believe what I'm reading! Castro doesn't need agents over here. All he has to do is read our papers.'

Castro was indeed reading the reports and receiving regular updates from Ramiro Valdés, the creator of Castro's Stasi-like security services, who said, 'We knew who everybody was, what weapons they carried, how much ammunition they had, where they were going to be, how many of them, at what time, and what they proposed to do.' Valdés confirmed that the invasion was 'an open secret' in Miami's 'Little Havana'. According to journalist Tad Szulc, the 'operation was conducted with such astonishing indiscretion that Castro in Havana was as aware of what was happening as if he himself had sat in on the meetings in the bars and hotels along Biscayne Boulevard and Flagler Street'.

Concerned that the invasion could trigger an insurrection, on 1 April 1961 Castro ordered his state security services, or secret police, into action, having them round up anyone suspected of being a counter-revolutionary. Thousands of people, including Havana's Roman Catholic bishop, were detained as wholesale arrests were carried out across the island. The hapless Cubans were held in prisons, a large sports arena and the massive Blanquita Theatre. In some places, five or six thousand people shared two bathrooms. Any hope the CIA had of an internal uprising was snuffed out.

On 9 April, as the invasion neared, Castro appeared on a Havana television station, telling the world, 'The extremely vigilant and highly prepared Cuban people would repel any invasion attempt by the counter-revolutionaries now massing in Florida and Guatemala who are sponsored and financed by the United States.'

President Kennedy was aware of the press coverage, the round-ups and Castro's dire warning, and should have called off the invasion but his hands were tied. The president of Guatemala, who had welcomed then kicked out Carlos Marcello, was experiencing the same cycle of emotions with regard to the exiles. In March, he had sent a letter to Kennedy, asking that their camp be evacuated by April. Kennedy said, 'If we decided now to call the whole thing off, I don't know if we could go down there and take the guns away from them.' Kennedy was right, and the exiles would not be inclined to give them back. The *Washington Post* reported that the CIA, referred to by the exiles as the 'Cuban Invasion Authority', had told the brigade to mutiny if Kennedy called off the invasion. There were also political concerns. If Kennedy stopped the planned invasion, he would have no choice but to let the brigade loose in Miami where they would denounce him for presidential betrayal and land him in a political quagmire; Kennedy's Republican opponents would pounce, accusing him of being soft on communism. With a restless brigade and the Guatemalan president issuing an eviction notice, Kennedy felt he had no choice but to launch the invasion.

On 10 April, the brigade was moved from their Guatemalan camp to Puerto Cabezas in Nicaragua, where they would prepare to board a fleet of old ships, some left over from the Second World War while others were, quite literally, banana boats, old freighters once used to carry bananas from Central America. Despite the small and shabby armada, the courageous Cubans were in good spirits, cheering and singing *vivas*. According to their leader, José Pérez 'Pepe' San Román, the CIA promised them, 'If you fail, *we* will go in.' This CIA pledge was made despite Kennedy making it ultra-clear to Allen Dulles that American forces would *not* participate in the invasion. Kennedy's firm decision was made with the international chess board in mind; although the entire world would know exactly who was behind the invasion, Kennedy wanted to deny America's hand in it and avoid Soviet retaliation in places like Berlin, where the American military was in a constant standoff with the Red Army.

On 12 April, while the invasion force was making its way toward Cuba, Kennedy reaffirmed his pledge to stay neutral at a news conference where he stated, 'There will not, under any conditions, be an intervention in Cuba by United States armed forces.' Having tied his own hands, the knot was tightened on the 17th when Secretary of State Dean Rusk reiterated the same pledge. In stark defiance of the president's public pledge and expressed command to Dulles, CIA agents assured the brigade that US forces would indeed back them up, certain they could twist the president's arm when push came to shove. Brigade member Manuel Ray said that he and his comrades were 'told that ten to fifteen thousand men would be available'.

Two days before the flotilla set sail for Cuba, eight US B-26 bombers, left over from the Second World War and painted with Cuban air force markings, took off for Cuba to knock out Castro's air force, while a ninth flew straight to Miami, pretending to defect. The pilot recited a rehearsed story of how he and the other pilots had left Cuba together and some decided to bomb the island on their way out. When no one believed his cover story, concluding that the US was behind the ruse, Kennedy choked and called off a second wave of airstrikes that were to be directed against Castro's more lethal Soviet-supplied MiG jets.

Before dawn on the 17th, the brigade was greeted inside the Bay of Pigs by a wall of machine-gun fire from Castro's little red army who were stationed nearby. Landing crafts ran into coral reefs and many of the soldiers were massacred as they stood knee-deep in the surf. Others made it to land but were thrown back into the sea like the Persians at Marathon. Castro, who had taken to sleeping during the day and staying up nights to await the attack, was alerted in Havana. He sped to the scene along with his Soviet-trained army which shelled the beachhead with artillery. Soviet T-34 tanks, outdated but still known for the great tank battle of Kursk, encircled the brigade as Castro's jets – which should have been knocked out – pounded them from the air.

After two days of heroic fighting, it was clear that the brigade could not secure a beachhead. News from the front was bleak as Kennedy's Joint Chiefs of Staff told him the exiles could not hold out without adequate air support. The Joint Chiefs wondered, since Castro had Soviet tanks and jets, why Kennedy was so concerned with appearances. The chief of naval operations, Arleigh Burke, pleaded with the president to allow an aircraft carrier to destroy Castro's air force and evacuate the survivors but Kennedy refused. 'Fifteen hundred men's lives were not as important as his political purposes,' said Colonel Jack Hawkins, one of the invasion's architects, adding, 'It was one of the most disgraceful things I ever had to be part of. I've regretted it all my life.' Kennedy's chairman of the Joint Chiefs of Staff, General Lyman Lemnitzer, called Kennedy's inaction 'absolutely reprehensible, almost criminal'.

Allen Dulles, who may have suspected the good chance of a debacle after Kennedy publicly pledged that US forces would not intervene, was conveniently out of town; it was left to Richard Bissell and CIA deputy director General Charles Cabell to try to persuade Kennedy to reconsider. In a last-ditch attempt to change the president's mind, they raced over to the State Department and impressed upon Secretary of State Dean Rusk the need for immediate air support, the absence of which would mark the betrayal of the stranded brigade and the entire Cuban exile community who were biting their fingernails. Rusk, a former Rhodes Scholar, who had made the same pledge as the president, understood the dilemma and telephoned Kennedy, asking him for an airstrike. Kennedy refused to budge. As the hours wore on, the situation became worse. By 4 a.m., 'Cabell drove through the darkened capital to Rusk's hotel' where the deputy director again asked Rusk to telephone the president. This time, Cabell got on the line, practically begging for air cover. Kennedy still said no.

Pepe San Román radioed the Americans from the beach: 'Do you people realize how desperate the situation is? Do you back us up or quit? All we want is low jet cover . . . I need it badly or cannot survive. Please don't desert us.' The brigade leader may as well have been talking to a crab in the sand. Before twilight on the 19th, the invasion was finished, less than forty-eight hours after it had begun. The final signal dispatched from the beach was picked up by a ham radio operator in faraway New Jersey. 'This is Cuba calling. Where will help come from? This is Cuba calling the free world. We need help in Cuba.'

The surviving exiles, bereft of food and medical supplies, crawled inland through swamps where they ate birds, insects, snakes, lizards, bark and weeds to survive. Vultures and land crabs picked at the dead and dying. When Castro's troops captured one group of exiles, they cried out, 'Shoot us, but in the name of humanity, give us water first!'

The prisoners were loaded onto trucks bound for Havana where the anticipated uprising had never occurred and where Santo Trafficante's poison had never reached a very alive and animated Castro whose voice, given the victorious occasion, was a few octaves higher than usual. In his typical exaggerated rhetoric, Castro called the invasion 'Cuba's Pearl Harbor' and erected a sign on the battle-scarred beach that read: 'Welcome to the Site of the First Defeat of Imperialism in the Western Hemisphere.' The debacle unified the tiny island nation behind Castro, who liked entertaining his people by putting on show trials followed by public executions. But in this case, he miraculously spared most of the exiles, not out of any sudden spark of compassion for his former countrymen, but due to geopolitical concerns: mass executions could disgust the international community and embolden Kennedy to unleash the marines. (It was further revealed in 2021, through a Freedom of Information Act request, that Kennedy passed a message to Castro through Brazil's president, João Goulart, to spare the prisoners while 'dangling a pledge of strict nonintervention' in Cuba from then on.) Although Castro did refrain from mass executions, he could not fully restrain himself and did, in fact, execute five prisoners after a sham trial. The rest were marched before television cameras for five days as a live audience chanted 'to the wall'. Some of the prisoners repented, or were, more accurately, forced to apologize for their 'crimes', while others exhibited courageous defiance, asking Castro why, if he was so popular, he had banned opposition parties and was afraid to hold free elections.

When not being used as political pawns, the captives were confined to a sports arena where they endured unimaginable inhumanities and humiliations. Many of the men were wounded, most were still bloodied from the battle, and all were dirty, but none were permitted to shower or shave, and had to beg to use the lavatory. They were constantly interrogated and only permitted a few hours' sleep each night, which proved nearly impossible on hard floors, beneath bright stadium lights. After two weeks of this torture, a young woman swept through the crowd of broken men, handing out yellow T-shirts and yelling, 'Yellow, yellow, yellow' – a taunting reference to their supposed cowardice, an especially degrading insult given their sublime courage which never faltered in the course of combat. As an indication of how heroically they had fought, they lost 114 soldiers while it is estimated that Castro lost somewhere in the region of 2,000 men. The rest were captured after they had been treacherously abandoned. Pepe San Román later said, 'I hated the United States, and I felt that I had been betrayed. Every day it became worse and then I was getting madder and madder and I wanted to get a rifle and come and fight against the U.S. . . . I felt that if they had organized us and taken us through a whole year of that training, even if the world was going to fall to pieces, they should not have forgotten us.'

While President Kennedy took public responsibility for the debacle and was criticized as weak, soft on communism and anti-American, he lashed out behind the scenes, saying, 'I've got to do something about those CIA bastards' who had misled Kennedy by assuring him that the brigade could independently reclaim Cuba, that Castro would be dead upon their arrival, and that a national uprising would accompany the landings. Kennedy swore to 'splinter the C.I.A. in a thousand pieces and scatter it into the winds'.

By the end of April, Kennedy appointed Bobby and a team of investigators to find out what led to the brigade's defeat. The investigation was billed as a postmortem in order to avoid the same mistake twice but was, in fact, grounds for a shake-up of the CIA. Bobby targeted Allen Dulles, telling him he could take up to twelve months to resign but no longer. He also dumped Richard Bissell and Deputy Director Charles Cabell, both of whom had pleaded with Kennedy and Rusk to provide air support. Bissell and Cabell's genuine distress over the betrayal of the brigade was lost on the president, whose competitive win-at-all-costs attitude, instilled in him since childhood, was misdirected. Instead of viewing the ordeal as a challenge between him and Castro, he saw it as a test of wills between him and his CIA advisors, which was made apparent when he commented to Dave Powers, 'They were sure I'd give in to them and send the go-ahead order . . . They couldn't believe that a new President like me wouldn't panic and try to save his own face. Well, they had me figured all wrong.'

In late 1961, Allen Dulles, the longest-serving director of the Central Intelligence Agency, whose old American family had produced two secretaries of state before his brother became a third, resigned under a black cloud. Like the disappointed Moses, who was permitted to see but prohibited from entering the Promised Land, Dulles had conceived and developed the sprawling CIA headquarters at Langley, Virginia, but never got to work there. The president briefly considered replacing him with his brother Bobby, but Bobby was quite happy in his mob-chasing role as attorney general so they settled on John McCone, a shipbuilding mogul who had chaired the Atomic Energy Commission under Eisenhower. Bissell was replaced by Richard Helms, and since Director McCone allowed Helms to run clandestine operations with little, if any, oversight, the plot to assassinate Castro, involving Roselli, Giancana and Trafficante, continued unabated.

In December 1962, after twenty months in Castro's rat- and cockroach-infested prisons, the abandoned exiles were ransomed in return for tens of millions of dollars in much needed farm equipment and pharmaceuticals. Many, if not all, felt they had the president to thank for their long captivity; the last four months of imprisonment were especially galling given that Bobby had deliberately held off the exchange that could have been accomplished back in September because he was concerned about how their ignominious return to the States might taint the mid-term elections held in November.

The president welcomed the brave men home at the Orange Bowl in Miami despite the fact that many of his advisors, including Dave Powers, Kenny O'Donnell, Dean Rusk and McGeorge Bundy, urged him not to appear there, fearing that his presence would be misconstrued by the exile community as a wink that the US was planning another invasion. But the advisors were overruled by Bobby, who told Jack to attend. Before a crowded stadium, Kennedy was presented with the brigade's battle flag before he went off script and pledged that the flag would one day fly over a liberated Havana. Just as Kennedy's pledge disguised his unfaithfulness to their cause, the stadium's loud applause hid their bitter resentment toward him; they were hopeful, the reason they showed up and applauded, but skeptical. Their desperate situation might best be likened to Dorothy searching for home in the classic novel by Frank Baum, *The Wizard of Oz*. 'No matter how dreary and gray our homes are, we people of flesh and blood would rather live there than in any other country, be it ever so beautiful. There is no place like home.' Despite Florida's bright sunshine, white sandy beaches, exotic birds and breezy palm trees, the abandoned Cuban Brigade felt the same way as Dorothy; they still longed for home and, although they blamed President Kennedy for abandoning them on a beach and delaying their release from captivity, they had no one else to put their hopes in. There were, however, a number of Cuban militants who would turn to others for help.

The Cuban Revolutionary Council (CRC) was a CIA-sponsored conglomerate of smaller exile groups created with the hope of maintaining some overall control and oversight of the larger network of militant groups. After the Bay of Pigs fiasco, the CRC and some of their CIA handlers became sworn enemies of the president. In their hatred of him, the CRC formed a natural alliance with mobsters across the country who also felt betrayed by the Kennedys. They fanned out across the Southern states, opening training camps for snipers, guerilla fighters and saboteurs, primarily in Florida where they worked closely with Santo Trafficante, and even larger camps in Louisiana where they were funded by Carlos Marcello, a man whose nefarious abduction by Bobby Kennedy had occurred only weeks before the Bay of Pigs betrayal. Besides wanting Cuba back and hating the Kennedys, the two groups – the mob and the CRC – did not have much in common but, as the ancient proverb goes, 'The enemy of my enemy is my friend.'

Chapter 12

James Bond, Three Stooges and a Comedian

Johnny Roselli, who had been killing people since he was a teenager, was wondering if he was dealing with fraternity gags when, in November 1960, his CIA project officer, Jim O'Connell, showed him a cigar and said, 'When Castro smokes this, it will make his beard fall off.'

'How soon does he die?' asked Roselli, who came from a world where men were punished with more than hair remover.

'This doesn't kill him,' answered O'Connell. 'It makes him a laughingstock. He'll be afraid to go outside.'

'I thought we were here for a legitimate hit,' Roselli replied, incredulous. 'You want us to play a . . . joke?'

Other ideas Roselli would have considered comical were a 'death ray' aimed at Castro from afar, and a plan to contaminate Castro's broadcasting studio with mind-bending hallucinogens that would distort his long speeches. (Given Castro's already long and scattered diatribes, the drug may have inadvertently made his next speech clear and incisive.) Dr Gottlieb eventually made a box of fifty poisonous Cohiba cigars meant to kill Castro when he smoked one, and a poisonous ice-cream cone, hoping Castro would lick himself to death. More wacky plots included poisoning Castro's scuba diving suit, contaminating his air tanks with foot fungus, and an exploding seashell planted by a midget submarine – they hoped Castro would pick up the shell while diving, a favorite hobby of his.

President Kennedy may or may not have been aware of the approximately two dozen ridiculous James Bond-style plots to murder Castro, but we do know that he was enthralled with intrigue and a loyal fan of every James Bond novel, with signed copies sent to him directly from British author Ian Fleming. Bobby did not read as much as Jack but he, too, was enamored with Bond. Undersecretary of State George Ball said Bobby 'was fascinated by all that covert stuff, counterinsurgency, and all the garbage that went with it', while CIA agent Samuel Halpern wondered if the 'weird ideas – exploding seashells, poisoned wetsuits, etc.' originated with Jack and Bobby. When Halpern questioned his superior about one of these absurd plots, he was told, 'The president wants this.'

Before the president took office, Ian Fleming was invited as a Sunday dinner guest at Jack Kennedy's house in Georgetown. After dinner, while coffee was being served, the conversation turned to Cuba and what to do about Castro. Fleming was asked how his character, James Bond, would handle him. Fleming said that Cubans only cared about sex and money, then laid out a plot which sounded like his latest spy novel pitch to his publisher, Jonathan Cape. He said that leaflets should be dropped from the sky informing Cubans that an atomic test had released radioactivity into the atmosphere which tends to linger in thick beards and leads to impotence. As a result, said Fleming, the hot-blooded horny revolutionaries, starting with Castro, would shave their beards to spare their sex lives. Once the beards were gone, Fleming fantasized, the romanticism surrounding the macho revolutionaries would fade.

The next day, one of Kennedy's dinner guests related Fleming's highly imaginative plot to Allen Dulles, who was also a big fan of James Bond. Dulles was silent – because his agency was, at that very moment, working on a more preposterous plot to remove Castro's beard, leaving us to wonder if it would have mattered if Dulles wrote fiction and Fleming was in charge of the CIA.

While the CIA was inadvertently mimicking Ian Fleming's comical advice, they had assigned the operation to eliminate Castro to their very own 007. Quite consistent with the European view of Americans, the man billed as 'America's James Bond' was not the suave gentlemanly Sean Connery or Roger Moore but an uncouth, foul-mouthed, belching, portly drunk – William Harvey, who was known to spin the cylinder of his revolver during meetings with top brass, trim his dirty fingernails at the conference table with a pocketknife, or lift his ass and blow a fart in an expression of contempt. He always carried a gun, sometimes two, and once said, 'If you ever know as many secrets as I do, then you'll know why I carry a gun.'

William King 'Bill' Harvey was born in Danville, Indiana, on 13 September 1915. He graduated from Indiana University with a law degree in 1937 and went to work for the FBI in 1940. Before the end of the decade, he left the Bureau to join the newly formed CIA. Some say that Harvey left the FBI after a big blow-out with J. Edgar Hoover, while others suspect that Hoover planted Harvey inside the agency as his personal mole.

As a CIA agent, Harvey was the first to sniff out Britain's Kim Philby of the infamous Cambridge Five spy ring. After exposing Philby, Harvey was tapped to head the CIA's Berlin station, where he was responsible for the 1,500-foot-long Berlin spy tunnel, an underground passageway that reached into the divided city's Soviet zone. Although the tunnel, nicknamed 'Harvey's hole', was quickly discovered by the KGB and collected close to nothing in the way of intelligence, Allen Dulles called the operation 'one of the most valuable and daring projects ever undertaken' and awarded Harvey the Distinguished Intelligence Medal which, together with spotting Philby, contributed to Harvey's legendary status inside the agency.*

Harvey returned to Washington DC in 1959, the same year Castro came to power in Cuba. By the end of 1961, he was placed in charge of foreign assassinations and told to kill Castro. By April 1962, he had replaced Jim O'Connell as the CIA's direct link to Johnny Roselli. The two tough guys hit it off. Harvey's wife would later say of his relationship with Roselli, 'My husband always used to say that if I had to ride shotgun, that's the guy I would take with me. Much better than any of the law enforcement people.' Roselli, who Harvey referred to as a man of 'integrity as far as I was concerned', regularly dined at Harvey's home and the two were known to have 'secret, martini-fueled rendezvous' in Miami and the Florida Keys, where they cursed Bobby Kennedy. Like Roselli, Harvey 'hated Bobby Kennedy's guts with a purple passion', referring to him as the 'little fucker'. He thought of both Kennedys as 'rich boys who were playing with the nation's security', and considered the president's inaction during the Bay of Pigs as tantamount to treason.

When not drinking and cursing the Kennedys, Roselli and Harvey worked on ways to murder Fidel Castro. Harvey, who believed that Dr Gottlieb 'enjoyed his work a little too much', had little faith in poisons; he instead wanted a team of snipers to take out Castro during a public appearance then escape amidst the ensuing pandemonium.

---

* It was later learned that the Soviets knew about the tunnel all along, exposed by British spy George Behar, who served a short stint in Wormwood Scrubs before escaping to Moscow, where the Order of Lenin was pinned on his chest.

Santo Trafficante,
who may have been a
double agent

To this end, Roselli acquired long-range rifles from an underworld source, but the snipers who were sent to Cuba disappeared without a trace and were presumed dead, forcing Harvey to return to schemes that involved poisons.

The poisons were again given to Santo Trafficante whose Cuban assassins always failed, leaving Harvey to wonder if the Florida don was truly dedicated to the plot or working both sides of the fence, which may have explained why the snipers disappeared so quickly. Harvey knew that Castro's G-2 spies had infiltrated Miami's exile community and suspected Trafficante of aiding and abetting them. Ricardo Canete, a Cuban who worked for the Florida don, later confirmed Harvey's suspicion when he reported that the chief G-2 agent in Miami 'took orders from Trafficante'. Those who believed that Trafficante was intentionally foiling the CIA plots traced his alleged betrayal to his detention in Cuba during the summer of 1959. After Trafficante ducked Castro's firing squad and fled the island, he told everyone that he had escaped by bribing Fidel Castro's brother, Raúl, with a pile of cash. Many wondered if Trafficante had bought his freedom, as he claimed, or if he had offered the Castro brothers something much more valuable than a lump sum of cash. Rumor had it that Trafficante, known as the 'kingpin of narcotics in the Caribbean', had struck a deal with Castro to distribute Cuban narcotics throughout the United States, with his home turf in Florida as the entry point, while agreeing to assist Castro's secret agents in Miami. The US narcotics bureau confirmed that the Cuban drug pipeline into Florida, begun decades earlier by Trafficante's father, was uninterrupted by Castro who needed the illicit revenue stream to bolster his lagging economy. A bureau memo, dated July 1961, considered the possibility that Castro 'kept Santo Trafficante Jr in jail to make it appear that he had a personal dislike for Trafficante, when in fact Trafficante is an agent of Castro'. The massive and steady flow of illegal drugs from Cuba to Florida was evidence pointing toward Trafficante's motive to betray the CIA in favor of the Beard, with whom he would have been making millions of dollars each month.

Trafficante may have been rooting for Castro's survival for another personal reason: a liberated Cuba would allow the vast majority of Cuban exiles to return home, drying up the majority of Trafficante's Miami rackets which he had to himself, unlike Havana, a city he shared with every mob boss in America – why slice up a pie he was eating alone? Surely, Trafficante could not tell any of this to CIA agents or his fellow mobsters when they recruited him into their plot to kill Castro, and it may have been why Trafficante was the only person who quietly listened and did not speak as the mob and the CIA chatted at the Fontainebleau. Although Trafficante took Dr Gottlieb's poison pills, pledging to use them on Castro, he later told his attorney that he 'flushed them down the toilet'.

Sam Giancana's dedication to the assassination plot was just as dubious but for different reasons. Giancana saw his involvement with the CIA as an opportunity to pickpocket the government for a few bucks and ask them for personal favors. As far as the money was concerned, CIA budgets are classified, but most historians estimate the annual budget spent on Operation Mongoose, the CIA's covert name for the plot to kill Castro, somewhere in the area of $100 million, offering Giancana plenty of opportunities to skim, the same way he would in a Las Vegas casino. As for personal favors, after being appointed Chicago's acting boss, Giancana began dating singing sensation Phyllis McGuire of the McGuire Sisters. 'His wife had passed away and he was very nice to me,' said the talented, innocent-looking McGuire. 'And if he had done all those things they said he did, I wondered why in God's name he was on the street and not in jail.'

When the McGuire Sisters began touring with comedian Dan Rowan, a jealous Giancana suspected that Phyllis and Rowan were having an affair. Giancana asked Robert Maheu to bug Rowan's room in Las Vegas to see if his hunch was true. Instead of talking some sense into Giancana, Maheu approached Sheffield Edwards and asked if the CIA would install a microphone on the wall of the suite next to Rowan's room in the Riviera Hotel. 'Since it wouldn't penetrate the wall,' said Maheu, 'it would not be breaking and entering, and would therefore be legal.' Edwards did not want to get involved in these adolescent antics, so he gave Maheu $1,000 to hire an outside party. Maheu turned to a private investigator who illegally entered the hotel room and went about attaching a bugging device to the telephone, contrary to Maheu's instructions. Believing he had all the time in the world, the private eye left his tools and electronic equipment in the room and ran off to catch a show. When a maid entered the room and saw tools and electronics, she called security. Security called the sheriff, and the sheriff arrested the private eye who called Maheu from the clink. 'What the hell were you doing with a wiretap instead of a bug?' a confused Maheu yelled into the receiver. 'I don't know of anyone who makes love while talking on the telephone.' The sheriff referred the matter to the FBI, and Hoover, who had internal radar for spotting juicy incidents, became personally involved.

As Hoover tried to figure out why someone would want to tap a comedian's telephone, Rowan dumped McGuire, telling her he was afraid to end up 'in the bottom of Lake Mead'. By then, Hoover had connected the incompetent private eye to Robert Maheu, and summoned the ex-FBI agent, demanding to know what this debacle was all about. Maheu later said, 'Hoover wanted to debrief me about what I might have learned concerning Johnny and Sam's "business ventures",' but Maheu claimed that he 'turned [Hoover] down flat', which strains belief. It is more probable that Maheu cringed before the all-powerful director and coughed up the whole story, including the CIA's clandestine work with Roselli, Trafficante and Giancana, since Hoover suddenly knew everything and the FBI's inquiry into the Rowan bugging fiasco was dropped now that Hoover had a bigger fish on the line.

Without revealing Maheu as his informant, Hoover contacted the CIA's Richard Helms and told him he was hip to the assassination plot against Castro. Hoover, who liked to amass dirt on private individuals, felt he had the entire agency by the balls. In the words of William Sullivan, 'Hoover was jealous of the CIA's power and he had been bitterly disappointed when the new agency was formed to dominate the field of worldwide intelligence.' Hoover was especially concerned that the CIA could morph into a domestic agency that rivaled or replaced the FBI at home.

Helms must have known that Hoover was waving a gun around with no intention of firing a shot since he did not call off the operation to kill Castro. He did, however, instruct Bill Harvey to cut contact with the reckless Giancana and Maheu while permitting him to carry on with the more discreet and reliable Johnny Roselli, who had expressed disgust at the charades of Giancana and Maheu, and swore to Harvey that, had he known about it, he would have put a stop to it. But it was too late; Hoover was connecting more dots and digging like a mole. He found out that Roselli was close friends with Judith Campbell, and Campbell was placing regular telephone calls to the White House in search of her lover, President Kennedy. White House telephone logs recorded at least seventy calls between Campbell and the White House, some of which were placed from Johnny Roselli's West Hollywood apartment. Hoover also had access to wiretaps in Giancana's bugged Chicago headquarters which bore other fruit. 'You sure get your rocks off fucking the same broad as the brothers, don't you,' Roselli was overheard telling Giancana after the latter had slept with Marilyn Monroe, who was also sleeping with Jack *and* Bobby. Before the election, and around the same time Jack had begun having an affair with Judith Campbell, he had started seeing Marilyn Monroe. Like Campbell, Monroe was also sleeping with mobsters who she would rendezvous with at the Cal-Neva Lodge. Genovese family capo Vincent 'Jimmy Blue Eyes' Alo was once a guest at the lodge when he witnessed a drunk and drugged 'Monroe on all fours being straddled by Giancana' with Frank Sinatra laughing along. The old-world Alo called their behavior 'disgusting'.

Feigning serious concern for the survival of the Kennedy adminis-tration which would be mired in scandal if this leaked out, Hoover sent a memo to Bobby with a copy forwarded to Kenny O'Donnell: 'I thought you would be interested in learning of the following informa-tion which was developed in connection with the investigation of John Roselli, West Coast hoodlum.' Hoover went on to inform Bobby about a mafia probe that uncovered an affair between Judith Campbell and the president. (Hoover must have got a kick out of showing Bobby where investigations into the mafia inevitably lead.) Bobby was also informed about the Castro assassination plot, which some suspect Bobby had already known about.

Bobby let Hoover know that he would speak to his brother about Campbell, but he did not halt any of the Justice Department's ongoing investigations into the very same mobsters who were deeply entwined with the CIA. Johnny Roselli complained, 'Here I am, helping the government, helping the country, and that little son of a bitch is break-ing my balls.' As for Sam Giancana, whose mutual dating of Jack's girlfriends must have annoyed Bobby, the attorney general 'pushed to get Giancana at any cost', said William Hundley. 'That rat bastard, son-of-a-bitch,' Giancana ranted to Santo Trafficante, 'we broke our balls for him and gave him the election and he gets his brother to hound us to death.'

Distrusting that Bobby would convey the correct message (or warning) to his brother, Hoover managed to bypass Bobby and asked to have lunch with the president on 22 March 1962. Hoover, who must have excitedly skipped along Pennsylvania Avenue on his way to the White House, informed the president that he was sleeping with a woman who had current ties to mobsters Sam Giancana and Johnny Roselli. Jack played it cool, knowing exactly what Hoover was up to. At the time Hoover broke this news to Jack, there were rumors that Jack and Bobby wanted to get rid of Hoover by easing him out of office, as they had recently done with Allen Dulles. Hoover was well aware of the rumors and was now letting Jack know that this dirty little secret could leak out should Hoover lose his job; it was typical *Hooverian* blackmail.

Following Bobby's visit from J. Edgar Hoover, he ordered Richard Helms to brief him about the agency's work with the mafia. On 7 May, Helms sent Sheffield Edwards and the CIA's general counsel, Lawrence Houston, to visit the attorney general and inform him about Operation Mongoose. No notes of the meeting exist and there are some who question what is reported to have occurred. According to later testimony from the CIA, Bobby was informed that the agency had worked with mobsters in an attempt to kill Castro before the Bay of Pigs invasion but had since ceased any further contact with them. Of all that this startling revelation entailed in terms of illegalities, immoralities and breach of trust, Bobby was stuck on the fact that Johnny Roselli had declined to be paid for his services. It did seem like a trivial detail but it contradicted Bobby's world view that Roselli represented the 'enemy within', while Bobby was wrapped in the American flag. Robert Maheu, who eventually had a falling-out with Roselli, had no reason to lie when he said, 'Many people have speculated that Johnny was looking for an eventual deal with the government, or some sort of big payoff. The truth, as corny as it may sound, is that deep down he thought it was his "patriotic" duty.' A number of CIA agents would later testify that they had reached the same conclusion, one agent adding that, unlike Giancana and Trafficante, he had never caught Roselli lying. Bobby is reported to have closed the meeting by saying, 'I trust that if you ever try to do business with organized crime again – with gangsters – you will let the Attorney General know.' The CIA said that they would, forgetting to mention to Bobby that Harvey and Roselli were still, at that very moment, trying to whack the Beard.

As Johnny Roselli continues to work with the CIA to assassinate Castro and reverse the Cuban revolution, a crazy mobster in Brooklyn will ignite the first mafia revolution in America, and although no historian has ever made the connection, it stemmed directly from the Gallo brothers' appearance before the Rackets Committee.

Part Two

Rebellion

Chapter 13

A King's Ransom

Giuseppe 'Joe' Profaci was born in Villabate, a village in the province of Palermo, Sicily, in October 1897. He quit school in his early teens and began working with his father who sold cheeses and olive oil. As a young adult, Profaci begrudgingly served in the Italian army during

Joe Profaci

the First World War. After his discharge, he was caught stealing a horse and spent a year in jail. He migrated to the United States in 1921 and became known as the 'Olive Oil King' for his Brooklyn-based import company, Mamma Mia, which was one of the largest distributors of imported Italian olive oil in the United States. He also owned a food packing company named after his daughter, Carmela Mia, and owned or controlled more than twenty other successful companies while overseeing his borgata, which was christened by Lucky Luciano in 1931, upon the creation of New York's five

families. After the Kefauver hearings, where Profaci remained mute in the face of relentless questioning, he avoided a deportation order and dodged a federal tax lien of close to $1.5 million by slyly transferring his assets to relatives.

Profaci's residences included a modest two-story brick house in Bensonhurst, Brooklyn, where he lived with his immediate family, a winter getaway in Miami Beach, Florida, and a 328-acre, thirty-room hunting lodge in Hightstown, New Jersey, once owned by a cousin of President Theodore Roosevelt. Known as Twelve Pines, the estate had an airstrip and a private chapel so that the boss who ordered dozens of murders could pray for forgiveness at his own convenience. According to Profaci's niece, Rosalie, the chapel's altar 'was a hand-carved replica of St. Peter's Basilica in Rome'.

Profaci thought of himself as genuinely religious, and he came from a religious family: two of his sisters were nuns and a brother was a priest. He had a lifelong quest for Vatican knighthood, which was almost realized in 1949. Brooklyn priests who were the recipients of Profaci's generous donations petitioned Pope Pius XII, who had personally dealt with the likes of Mussolini and Hitler, each of whom made Profaci look like a saint. The Pope was seriously considering their petition until a Brooklyn prosecutor shot off a letter to Rome, informing His Holiness of Profaci's Luciferian side, which was later exhibited in an incident related to the Church in 1952.

Whenever he was in Brooklyn, Profaci attended daily Mass at St Bernadette's Church, which one detective called 'his only predictable public appearances'. Another nearby church, Regina Pacis – or Queen of Peace – had asked its parishioners to donate gold, silver and jewels so the clergy could have two crowns made that were to be worn by statues of the Madonna and Child inside the church. Hundreds of parishioners contributed to the project and the crowns were blessed by the Pope in Rome then returned to Brooklyn where, in January 1952, two thieves made off with them. When Profaci heard about the robbery, he said to his men, 'I want one ball from each of those guys brought to me.' An FBI agent said the jeweled crowns were returned to the church in just over a week, and the thieves' bodies were found dead. The *Brooklyn Daily Eagle* reported that one of the thieves, 33-year-old Ralph 'Bucky' Emmino, told a female friend, 'I have to meet somebody – I'll see you later.' Emmino's 'bullet-pierced body' was later found dumped on a 'weed-grown sidewalk' in Brooklyn for everyone to see. (Numerous accounts report that the men were strangled with rosary beads, a falsehood since rosary beads are not made strong enough to strangle anyone.)

By 1961, Profaci was a balding man with sharp features and a thin, delicate nose. He wore tortoiseshell eyeglasses, conservative suits with fedoras, and did not appear tough. He was, moreover, possessed of a typical Himmleresque nature: abusive and arrogant toward underlings while meek and sycophantic toward men of power, like the clergy and high-ranking officers of the law. But, also like Heinrich Himmler, Profaci was extremely dangerous and displays of his brutality, an example of which was the fate of the jewel thieves, kept him feared and free from challenges to his throne – until Bobby Kennedy called the Gallos before the Rackets Committee.

Larry and Joey Gallo were already well-known in their Brooklyn neighborhood when Bobby summoned them to appear before national television cameras in Washington DC, which enlarged their fame back home, inflated their egos and made them seem much stronger than they actually were. They returned to Brooklyn convinced that they were powerful enough to replace Profaci by way of a complicated coup that began at Cardiello's Tavern on the evening of 4 November 1959.

At around 8 p.m., Frank 'Frankie Shots' Abbatemarco, who was a capo in Profaci's borgata, walked into the tavern and greeted everyone, including the bartender, Tony Cardiello, who poured him a drink. Frankie Shots drank while chitchatting and glancing outside every now and then; he seemed to be awaiting someone's arrival. At around 8:30 p.m., Frankie Shots spotted whoever he was waiting for and said goodnight to everyone at the bar. He buttoned his overcoat and was halfway out of the door when two men outside lifted red bandanas over their faces, drew handguns and pumped four bullets into him. The force of the bullets pushed Frankie Shots back into the tavern where he staggered then crashed to the floor. As the bartender dropped behind the bar for cover and patrons ducked under tables, the hitmen entered the bar and stood over Frankie Shots; one leaned down and reached under the injured capo's coat, removing a .38 Smith and Wesson from a shoulder holster. He stood up and fired four more bullets into him with this gun then placed the gun barrel under Frankie Shots' chin and fired a coup de grâce that exited through his left ear. Both hitmen looked at one another and nodded, as if to say, 'He's done,' then left as calmly as they had entered. The sixty-year-old capo lay on his back, one eye open, the other filled with blood. He was hit a total of nine times, five from his own gun which was later found on the sidewalk outside the bar.

Detectives arrived at the scene and questioned bartender Tony Cardiello, who claimed he had not seen anything. Other patrons described one shooter as a short, chubby man in his early thirties. The detectives had a hunch that this short, well-fed shooter was Joseph 'Joe Jelly' Gioielli, one of Larry Gallo's best friends and a lead suspect in the Albert Anastasia hit. When brought into the station house and questioned by detectives, Joe Jelly said he had never even heard of

Frankie Shots. When asked about the Gallos, who he was seen with on a daily basis, he said, 'Who are they?'*

Historians tell us that the Gallo brothers carried out the hit on Frankie Shots, along with Joe Jelly, on orders from Profaci after Frankie Shots withheld $50,000 in tribute money from his Brooklyn policy racket. This does not add up and I will explain why. Frankie Shots' gambling operation netted over ten thousand dollars a day, amounting to nearly four million dollars a year, a generous piece of which was kicked up to Profaci who made Frankie Shots a capo and brought him into his inner circle, which qualified Frankie Shots for invitations to the don's private estate at Twelve Pines, the equivalent of receiving a royal invitation to Balmoral Castle. (Joey Gallo was known to complain, 'When you want somebody hit' – meaning Profaci – 'we're good enough. But not good enough to come to the house' – meaning Twelve Pines where the Gallos were never invited.) Does it make sense that Profaci would whack a major earner over a lousy late fee that amounted to less than one week's worth of profits? Especially when Profaci could have broken Frankie Shots down to a soldier, stripped him of his racket and shelved him as adequate punishment. Given these inconsistencies, I was naturally confused and reluctant to repeat that Profaci ordered him killed, so I dug deep and eventually found a clue that pointed elsewhere. In an out-of-print autobiography written by Peter 'Pete the Greek' Diapoulas, one of Joey Gallo's closest friends since childhood, Greek said that he and the Gallos were planning to use Frankie Shots' policy bankroll to fuel an open rebellion against Profaci. When Frankie Shots got cold feet and withdrew from the plot, the Gallos decided to kill him, steal his racket and, according to Greek, they 'threw it on Profaci'. There you have it, straight from a conspirator's mouth.

With Pete the Greek bringing the story into focus, we can easily imagine the Gallos, who collected receipts for Frankie Shots, holding back the $50,000 *from Frankie Shots* before they killed him and keeping the money, as opposed to Frankie Shots withholding the money from Profaci for no apparent reason. Further evidence pointing toward this version of events was Profaci's conspicuous absence from Frankie

---

* In both the Anastasia and Abbatemarco hits, the shooters pulled bandanas over their faces and discarded the murder weapons near the murder scenes, which is uncommon. Historians have failed to connect these two pieces of evidence that point to the same men.

Shots' funeral service, while, at the same time, he permitted everyone else in the borgata to attend. When a boss orders a hit, he either
shows up along with everyone else to throw the scent off himself, or he
does not show up and prohibits everyone else from attending, letting
everyone know the victim had broken a cardinal rule. Profaci's blatant
inconsistency – him skipping the service while encouraging everyone
else to attend – can only mean that Profaci did not immediately know
what happened to Frankie Shots, and, as such, stayed away for his
own safety, but saw no reason to keep everyone else away. In fact, he
would have sent spies to poke around and see what they could glean
from the chatter.

A final piece of evidence pointing toward the Gallos also comes
from Pete the Greek, who further said that, after Frankie Shots was
dead, he and the Gallos ended up in a tug-of-war with Profaci over
Frankie Shots' large gambling and policy books. As mere runners, the
Gallos had no rightful claim to this racket which belonged to the borgata, i.e. Profaci, who could do with it as he pleased. Unless, of course,
the Gallos were trying to steal it, which they were. To this end, they
convinced Frankie Shots' son, Anthony 'Tony Shots' Abbatemarco,
that Profaci whacked his father, then played themselves off as Tony's
defenders who only wanted to help him reclaim his underworld inher-
itance which was being unlawfully confiscated by Profaci, so they
claimed. The Gallos spread rumors that Profaci was a greedy pig who
not only killed Frankie Shots over a few bucks, but disinherited his
loyal and loving son, Tony Shots.

By the autumn of 1960, the Gallos were seeking out alliances in
other families. By December, Larry Gallo was seen by detectives meeting with Genovese family heavyweight Anthony 'Tony Bender' Strollo
at Luna's restaurant on Mulberry Street in Manhattan's Little Italy.
Tony Bender was Vito Genovese's underboss when Genovese went to
prison. But Genovese must have been a bit wary of his ambition since
he put Bender on a triumvirate with Jerry Catena and Tommy Eboli,
both of whom allowed Bender to oversee the Gallo rebellion. A few
weeks after the first meeting, in January 1961, Larry, Carmine Persico,
Joseph 'Joe Yak' Yacovelli and Nicholas 'Jiggs' Forlano, all young
up-and-comers in the Profaci borgata, met again with Tony Bender
at the White Turkey restaurant in Manhattan. Tony Bender's involvement with this group of Young Turks signaled to Larry that they had a
nod of approval from the imprisoned Vito Genovese which paved the

way for Carlo Gambino and Tommy Lucchese to stand behind Larry. In case you are wondering why Genovese, Gambino and Lucchese would back a coup against their fellow don, Profaci, it is necessary to understand Commission politics at this time.

In 1961, Joe Profaci and Joe Bonanno had ruled over their respective borgatas for three decades. They both married traditional Sicilian women and arranged the marriages of their children to combine and strengthen their dynasties. Joe Bonanno's son, Salvatore 'Bill' Bonanno, married Profaci's niece, Rosalie Profaci, who said, 'Our fathers were not only friends but allies in their world.'*

On the other side of the Commission table sat Carlo Gambino and Tommy Lucchese, who arranged a dynastic marriage of their own: Gambino's son, Tommy, married Lucchese's daughter, Frances. (Salvatore 'Bill' Bonanno married Rosalie Profaci in 1956. Tommy Gambino did not marry Frances Lucchese until 1962. Although we are currently in the year 1961, the latter marriage was already ordained by the parents and is therefore relevant to the politics at hand.) These marital arrangements spoke to the larger political alliances at play when Larry Gallo sounded out Tony Bender, who tapped Gambino and Lucchese by appealing to their natural inclination to break the Profaci–Bonanno bond by removing Profaci from power.

With a nod from three titans on Mount Olympus, Larry Gallo was ready to make a sanctioned move on Profaci. In February, he dispatched five separate teams to kidnap Joe Profaci, his brother Frank, his underboss and brother-in-law Joe Magliocco, and capos John Scimone and Joe Colombo. (Some sources have Sally 'The Sheik' Musacchia in place of Colombo. It was Joe Colombo.) Four out of five men were taken from their homes and social clubs, but the slippery Olive Oil King eluded his abductors. As the other kidnappings unfolded, Profaci must have been spooked and high-tailed it to Miami where he checked into a hospital. He was rumored to be suffering from the early stages of cancer but the hospital visit was seen as a ruse to duck a round of questioning from law enforcement who were sniffing around, confused by the string of abductions.

---

* Rosalie's father had died in a boating accident so her uncle, Joe Profaci, assumed the role of her father. In a traditional sense, the marriage was equal to Bill Bonanno tying the knot with Joe Profaci's daughter. Joe Profaci's biological daughters were also married off to consolidate alliances. One daughter married the son of Detroit don Joe Zerilli, and another daughter married the son of Vito 'Black Bill' Tocco, who co-ruled with Zerilli.

The kidnappings were a rather odd departure from the traditional mob hit and some detectives were convinced that, had the Gallos seized Profaci, they would have executed all five men, removing any obstacles to the throne in one fell swoop. An alternative theory later came from informants who told police that, while the Gallos were in the process of planning a coup, they became aware that they were marked for death by Profaci and took the hostages as collateral so they could negotiate for their own lives. The message was, if one Gallo is even touched, the hostages will be killed. Whichever motive was behind the kidnappings, it quickly became apparent that Larry Gallo did not know how to play the rotten hand he had dealt himself, so he decided to use the hostages as bargaining chips in an attempt to negotiate a fairer share of Profaci's pie. When Profaci received an invitation to negotiate, he sent word back to Larry that there was nothing to discuss until the hostages were released, unharmed.

As Profaci mustered his forces of some two hundred soldiers who were still loyal to him and swung open his bloated war chest, Larry, with only thirty men behind him, asked Tony Bender if he could appear before the Commission to argue his case. When Bender, Gambino and Lucchese agreed to give Larry a hearing instead of automatically condemning his actions, Profaci knew that all three were behind the rebellion and decided that it was unsafe to attend, sending word through Joe Bonanno that he had no obligation to sit at a round table with a man who was not his equal.

At the Commission hearing, Larry denied that he'd had any intention to kill Profaci and argued that the kidnappings were a reaction to Profaci's insatiable greed which was well-known in the underworld. Besides complaining that Profaci disinherited Tony Shots after Frankie Shots was killed, Larry pointed out Profaci's $25-a-month tax on all family members, which supposedly went into a slush fund reserved for the attorney fees of anyone in the borgata who was arrested. This monthly payment plan was seen by the Gallos as a soft shakedown of the lower ranks, who had to steal for their daily bread.

After Larry laid his case on the table, the bosses were poker-faced until Tony Bender pierced the silence and came out in favor of Larry without even hearing Profaci's side of the story. Bonanno, as expected, stood firmly behind Profaci, while Gambino and Lucchese, who were behind the coup when it was expected to succeed, now straddled the fence, concerned that an approval of Larry's actions could encourage revolts in their own borgatas. With Tony Bender behind Larry, Bonanno behind Profaci, and Gambino and Lucchese on the sidelines, Larry could not dethrone the old don by decree. 'Settle it yourselves,' Larry was told, as was Profaci, via Bonanno.

That Larry was able to appear before the Commission and return alive with a stalemate was a major achievement in itself; it raised the morale of his rebel gang and brought new men into his camp. But Larry still had to figure out what to do with those darned hostages who were unsure of their fate. Their dispositions under pressure varied. Joe Magliocco was always 'whimpering' and 'whining'. Frank Profaci and John Scimone were visibly nervous but able to contain themselves, while Joe Colombo alone displayed rare courage similar to that of Julius Caesar when the latter was kidnapped by pirates. '[Colombo] was the coolest of the lot,' said Pete the Greek, 'saying he feared dying like any other man. He asked that it be done quick and without torture, as that would be silly since he was nothing but a bookmaker with lousy action at that.'

Thirty-one-year-old Crazy Joe Gallo, who let his older brother take the lead, was frustrated by the stalemate and told Larry to murder the hostages and dump their bodies on the street for everyone to see. Larry, however, knew he could not kill them now, for the same reason Fidel Castro was unable to kill the interned members of the Cuban Brigade – it would turn people's opinions against him. On the other hand, if Larry freed them, he would look weak and appear to be caving in to Profaci's demand.

While Larry wondered what to do with the hostages, Profaci sent a carefully chosen delegation to the Gallo camp which included part-time consigliere Calogero 'Charlie The Sidge' LoCicero, a man in his fifties with a long, violent criminal history; he was respected by the Young Turks, who viewed him as an old warrior. LoCicero was accompanied by Don Lorenzo, a highly successful businessman in his seventies who was known for his sound advice. Though both men had everything to gain from Profaci remaining in power, they were considered fair-minded and therefore welcome inside the Gallo camp on President Street in Brooklyn, a strongly defended insular world we will take a peek at before the delegation arrives.

Chapter 14

Sleeping with the Fish

Amidst all the tension, the Gallo faction went on a war footing. They stockpiled guns and ammunition and set up bunks and cots on the second floor of two attached brick buildings at 49 and 51 President Street in Brooklyn, both owned by the Gallos' grandmother, Mama Nunziato, who was hip to the streets. Once, when detectives were searching for Larry, Mama asked them why and was told that he was suspected of shooting someone who had miraculously survived. She chased them away and later scolded her grandson, telling him, 'Whatsa matter, Larry? You can't shoot straight?'

Of the thirty-odd men holed up inside President Street, half were unemployed while the other half claimed some form of sketchy employment, like no-show jobs or ownership of a pet supply store where the entire inventory consisted of a single dog leash displayed in the front window, or a delicatessen with only cardboard pictures of various meat products propped up in a dusty display case. Eighteen of the men were married, many with children. Nearly everyone had long criminal records and some also had distinguished military records, having served in the Second World War. Their combat experience on the Pacific islands taught them to nail chicken wire across any open windows to stop someone from hurling in a hand grenade. Some of the cops assigned to surveil the mobsters on President Street had served overseas with them. Detective Vincent Kelly, for example, had fought alongside Tony Shots Abbatemarco during the 3rd Marine Division's heavy fighting on the island of Guam. Shots and Kelly knew exactly which side of the street they were on in Brooklyn, but in the South Pacific they were brothers and still felt a special comradery only combat veterans can understand. Now and then, one man or the other would cross the street to discuss the heroic battle they had survived together.

The Gallo crew, known as the United Nations of the Underworld, spoke to the changing composition of the mafia's growing network of associates as well as the exceptionally broad-minded outlook of

Italian-Americans who bonded with everyone, without prejudice. Besides Pete the Greek, Joey Gallo's other best friend was Ali Hassan 'Ali Baba' Waffa, an Egyptian with a wife in Cairo. Larry Gallo's unofficial consigliere was Louis 'Louie the Syrian' Hubela, who also fought heroically in the Second World War and handled the Arab neighborhoods in Brooklyn for sports betting and loansharking. Louie the Syrian was related to another trusted Gallo crew member, Samuel 'Sammy the Syrian' Zahralban. There were also two Jews, Sydney and Hyman, an African-American named Wesley, an Irishman, a Puerto Rican, and plenty of Italians, one of whom had Asian-Italian-American children with his Japanese wife. Rounding out the Gallo crew was their faithful mascot, a four-foot-tall dwarf, Armando 'Mondo' Illiano, who was the cousin of certified tough guy and crew member, Frank 'Punchy' Illiano. Mondo owned the Longshore Rest Room, a club where the gang played cards and billiards. He was a personable guy who made a huge impression on everyone he met, including the six-foot-tall blondes he was known to date. Mondo cared for the crew's female ocelot, known as Cleo the Lion. Joey purchased Cleo from an illegal animal trafficker who sold big cats, chimps and monkeys. Cleo lived in Mondo's basement, which became known as the Lion's Den. Rumors that loanshark victims were dragged before her cage were untrue since Cleo was domesticated, but she did grow fast and they gave her away when she outgrew Mondo.

While the men were holed up in the buildings, wives and girlfriends regularly dropped off food and necessities, and smuggled in extra weapons, covered in plastic wrap and buried inside trays of lasagna and macaroni. Guns and ammunition were hidden in the basement, on the roof, and inside ceilings and walls. On a warm summer evening, passers-by on President Street could hear the music of Verdi or Puccini drifting from an open window. The music buff listening to the grand composers of Italian opera on his stolen phonograph was Larry Gallo, described by one FBI agent as 'the smartest hood I ever met'. While Larry appreciated classical music and read the Great Books, Joey read Sartre, Nietzsche, Kafka and Camus. Others in the crew liked poetry, painted, and one sculpted indoor and outdoor statues. Between the poets, painters, sculptors and musicians, the cops might have wondered if they were staking out a mafia stronghold or the French salon of Gertrude Stein.

Umberto 'Papa' Gallo enjoyed cooking for everyone, often making big pots of macaroni sauce (or gravy, as we used to call it), with sausage, meatballs, pig's feet, pig's skin and pig's knuckles. He sometimes sent heaping plates of food to the cops assigned to stake out the street; the cops trusted the Gallos enough to indulge and return the plates with a hearty thank you.

Now that we have an idea of what the 'barracks' on President Street were like, as well as the hybrid crew that resided there, we can return to Charles LoCicero and Don Lorenzo as they arrive on their diplomatic mission to get the hostages released.

The older men patiently listened to Larry's grievances and appeared sympathetic, always speaking in a friendly tone without condescension. When they finally asked about the hostages, Larry assured them that they were all alive and well, and that no one would be killed if his list of demands was met: he wanted the gambling racket that once belonged to Frankie Shots restored to Frankie's son, Tony Shots (which meant the Gallos would co-own it), and he wanted to install vending machines in Profaci-owned or -controlled businesses like restaurants and bowling alleys. He also demanded an immediate cash settlement of $150,000. Seasoned mobsters like Profaci, LoCicero and Lorenzo were masters of artifice, able to disguise the impurity of their intentions behind platitudes such as honor and duty; they would never have demanded money in the midst of such a delicate situation, which made the Gallos look like two-bit kidnappers in need of a ransom. It was a cheap move but with thirty mouths to feed on President Street, Larry was hard up for cash. His ransom demand, poorly disguised as a settlement, was a major blunder as it revealed his desperation to Profaci, who needed only to stall and wear them down, which was what the wily old-timer decided to do.

The delegation departed, having made no commitments. When none of Larry's demands seemed forthcoming, he began to argue with Joey about the fate of the hostages. Joey wanted to kill them off, one each week, until their demands were met. Larry was against this and became so concerned that Joey might murder the hostages on his own that he released them prematurely, squandering any leverage he had over Profaci.

The Profaci and Gallo factions settled into a state of eerie quietude that prevailed into the summer months and resembled Great Britain's 'phony war' with Germany, a tense period of diplomatic and military inertia that both sides knew would end in fireworks.

*

While John Scimone was still in captivity, he told the Gallos that he had considered their grievances and decided that they were in the right. At the time, Scimone knew the miserly Profaci would never fork out a ransom, so his change of heart may have been based on survival. After his release from captivity, Scimone fell back in with Profaci but led Larry to believe that he was still sympathetic to the Gallo cause.

On Sunday afternoon, 20 August 1961, Scimone telephoned Larry and told him he had hit on a horse and wanted to share his winnings with him. Gamblers seldom boast of their winnings or offer to share any of it, but Larry trusted Scimone and was too strapped for cash to smell a trap. After Scimone handed Larry a few bucks, he invited him for a drink at the Sahara Lounge on Utica Avenue in the Flatbush section of Brooklyn, telling him, 'Some of the boys will be there.'

Larry and Scimone entered the dimly lit lounge and were greeted by bartender Charles 'Charlie Brown' Clemenza, who poured them drinks. Minutes later, Carmine Persico and Salvatore 'Sally D' D'Ambrosio, both of whom were on the Gallo side during the hostage crisis, walked in and greeted Larry and Scimone at the bar. As the four men chitchatted, Persico slid behind Larry and looped a garrote around his throat. With Sally D's help, Persico was strangling the life out of the five-foot-nine, 125-pound Larry when, at approximately 2:50 p.m., Sergeant Edward Meagher of the NYPD poked his head in the side door and said hello to Clemenza. Surprised to see a cop, the hoods dropped Gallo to the floor as the badge asked Clemenza, 'How are things?'

'Everything's fine,' said Clemenza, pretending to spot-clean glasses in the dark. 'Everything is great.'

Meagher heard Gallo moaning and stepped inside for a better look around. 'Is that something on the floor?' he asked Clemenza.

'Take him!' yelled Sally D.

'Not here!' Clemenza yelled to his pals, fearing they would kill the cop.

Scimone, Persico and Sally D darted for the door, bulldozing Meagher who was thrown to the floor. Outside the bar, Meagher's partner, 35-year-old Officer Melvin Blei, sprang from his squad car and was reaching for his gun when he was shot in the face by Sally D. As the injured Blei tumbled over the hood of his car, the three men piled into a white Cadillac and sped away. Meagher got up, ran outside, squeezed off two rounds at the Caddy then tended to Blei and radioed for help.

The Sahara Lounge was soon crawling with cops as Blei was rushed to the hospital in stable condition. A purple-faced Larry, who had blacked out, came to gasping for air. He struggled to his feet then rubbed the rope burn around his neck. He was relieved to be alive but terri-

bly embarrassed when he realized he had soiled his pants. A cop assured him that it was a bodily reaction to the trauma, not a measure of his manhood. The cop helped him to the men's room where Larry ditched his dirty underwear and washed up.

Larry Gallo in a squad car with a rope burn around his neck

When questioned, Larry had nothing to say. Asked about the bruise around his neck, he said it was from shaving. He was arrested, charged with assaulting himself and held on $100,000 bail. *New York Newsday* ran a headline: Cop Halts 'Rub Out' of Gallo, Gets Shot, while the *New York Daily News* accurately reported that Larry was 'still slated for murder by the underworld'. The following day, newspapers wondered if Joey Gallo would be targeted, too; the *Daily News* ran a photo of Joey with a caption that read, 'Still alive, as of yesterday,' meaning they were uncertain if he would make it through the night.

As Larry sat in the clink planning his revenge, the cops launched a series of raids on President Street in search of weapons. One detective found several guns under a dummy floor in a closet. He pointed to them and asked Kid Blast what they were.

'It looks like guns,' answered Blast.

'Whose guns?' asked the detective.

'Gee,' Blast shrugged, 'the former occupants of this apartment must have been some kind of malefactors.'

As it turned out, the guns were legal. Another raid turned up rifles, a carbine and a shotgun with more ammunition, but these were also legal. During a third raid, the cops discovered four handguns in the basement of one of the buildings. Papa Gallo, who was caught in the basement next to the guns, said he had no idea who had put them there and that he was not hiding from the cops but had gone into the cellar for some quiet time.

Frustrated by all the excuses, the cops felt it was time to shake everyone up so they dragged eleven members of the Gallo gang, including Joey, Papa Gallo and Mondo the Midget, to the Raymond Street jail where they spent the night. Kings County judge, Samuel Leibowitz, was asked to hold Joey with no evidence of a crime having been committed. Leibowitz spurned the request as unlawful then said, resignedly, 'They're going to settle it their own way, under their own rules. You can expect other murders.' The judge added that, 'Even the members of Murder Inc. never shot a policeman,' referring to Officer Blei, who had recovered from his injuries.

The next morning, the crew was released on bail. On Joey's way out of the courtroom, reporter Gabriel Pressman asked him if he had anything to fear. Joey leaned down, threw an arm around Mondo and said, 'How can I be afraid when my bodyguard is with me?' Right on cue, Mondo the Midget growled at the reporter. Everyone seemed to get a laugh out of this – except Bobby Kennedy, who was closely following the rebellion from Washington. He put pressure on the Brooklyn cops and prosecutors to make more arrests and pushed the INS to deport Papa Gallo who was born in southern Italy.

Joseph ('crazy Joe') Gallo is followed from court by dwarf Amando Illiano after they were freed on bail.

Joey Gallo and Mondo leave the courthouse together

Larry's lawyer bargained his bail down to $25,000. When the judge asked the assistant district attorney if he opposed the lower bail, he said, 'If I were in his shoes and my bail was down to twenty-five dollars, I'd stay in jail. But if he wants to walk the streets, that's his business.' Larry posted bail and returned to President Street where Joey threw him a party but bluntly told him, 'You should have done it my way,' meaning Larry should have murdered the hostages. The next morning, the Gallo brothers, along with Pete the Greek, the Syrians and Ali Baba, held a war council to discuss their next move. Larry's *compare*, Joe Jelly, was conspicuously absent from this high-echelon gathering which was extremely odd since Larry and Jelly were like peanut butter and jelly. As it turned out, Jelly was, as the expression goes, underwater with his own problems. In this case, the expression was quite literal.

On the Wednesday before Larry was garroted, five men, including Sally D, Carmine Persico and John Scimone, all of whom had ambushed Larry inside the Sahara Lounge, had invited Joe Jelly on a fishing trip. As Sally D's cabin cruiser headed out to sea over the choppy waters of Sheepshead Bay, Joe Jelly was asked to set up Larry Gallo. We can guess what his answer was since he was shot, cut into pieces, stuffed into a weighted drum and dumped overboard. Days later, a dead fish wrapped in Joe Jelly's jacket was tossed on the sidewalk in front of the Gallo family restaurant, Jackie's Charcolette. The package contained Joe Jelly's ring finger and the message was that Joe Jelly sleeps with the fish.

Between Joe Jelly's gruesome death and the recent attempt on Larry's life, it was apparent that Joe Profaci had split the Young Turks in a classic divide and conquer. Persico, who Larry nicknamed 'The Snake' after his betrayal at the Sahara Lounge, was now at the head of a splinter group that had broken off from the Gallo gang and was taking orders from Profaci.

Carmine John Persico was born in Brooklyn on 8 August 1933, two years after Profaci officially founded the borgata. His parents were Carmine Persico Sr and Assunta, known as Susan. The couple married young; he was twenty and she was eighteen and pregnant. One night, Carmine gave Susan a black eye. She called the police on him. When brought before a judge, Carmine admitted to hitting his wife and said, 'I believe in curfews for wives, Your Honor. Ten-thirty. On the dot. She got home late so I hit her.' The couple had three sons. The oldest was Alphonse, who the underworld would come to know as 'Allie Boy'.

The next child was Carmine Jr, known as 'Junior' or 'The Snake', after he double-crossed Larry at the Sahara Lounge. And then there was Theodore, known as 'Teddy'. All three brothers became made men in Profaci's borgata.

Not long after the hostages were released, Profaci had convinced Carmine Persico that although the Commission was entertaining the Gallo revolt, they would never approve Larry as his replacement, so it was best to turn on Larry now in return for a reward. Had the Gallos been paying closer attention, there were early signs that Persico was working as a double agent in the weeks leading up to Joe Jelly's death and Larry's neck being squeezed like a wine press at the Sahara Lounge. Before Joe Jelly went missing, Persico was seen around the neighborhood looking for him, and had asked a couple of guys to call Joe Jelly. The guys smelled trouble and did not want to get involved. At one point, Persico approached Marco Morelli, who said he could not betray anyone from the Gallo crew before Morelli was taken for a ride and never seen again.

Larry felt especially snubbed by Persico's betrayal and wanted revenge for his pal, Joe Jelly. The American mafia had a strict ban on explosives since the shrapnel could kill innocent people, but Larry ignored it and dispatched a demolition expert who planted a pipe bomb under Persico's car. When Persico got into the driver's seat, it was detonated. The explosion lifted the car off the ground, shattering glass and swinging the doors open. Like a scene from *The Terminator*, Persico somehow got out, staggered around in a circle for a minute or so then brushed himself off and walked away like nothing had happened. Some said he was lucky while others claimed he was indestructible.

Two months later, Larry took another shot at the Snake. This time, a hit team hid in the back of a panel truck that cruised around Brooklyn in search of Persico. When the truck finally pulled alongside him and stopped, two gunmen opened the side door and unloaded their weapons, hitting Persico in the hand, arm, shoulder and face. The truck sped off, but once again, the Terminator was alive. Surviving this second murder attempt worked wonders for Persico's reputation as word spread that he had spat a bullet out of his mouth. In truth, the bullet was lodged in Persico's cheek and fell out at the hospital; what else could he have done with it, swallow it? Persico refused to tell detectives who shot him, and he left the hospital with a paralyzed arm. This permanent war injury and his second Purple Heart in two months contributed to his growing fame and another nickname, the 'Immortal'.

On 4 October 1961, Gallo loyalist Joseph 'Joe Mags' Magnasco was cruising along a Brooklyn street when he spotted Profaci loyalists Harry and Sal Fontana. When Magnasco grabbed Harry by the collar, Sal drew a .32 caliber revolver and shot Magnasco in the chest three times. Like his cousin, Tony Shots Abbatemarco, Magnasco was a highly decorated war hero; he had survived Japanese banzai attacks on the bloody sands of the Pacific only to die on a dirty sidewalk in Brooklyn. Tony Shots' wife, Lucy Abbatemarco, happened to be emerging from a subway station as Magnasco was bleeding out on the pavement. 'My God,' she yelled, 'that's my cousin Joe.'

With a war underway and frustrated cops unable to make a collar, prosecutors subpoenaed Joey Gallo who, over the years, had been served with dozens of subpoenas from the same assistant district attorney, Walter Buchbinder. Joey told him, 'Walter, someday I'm going to give *you* one of these things. I've had about a hundred from you, and you haven't solved a crime yet.' When the Gallo crew was rounded up for a photo line-up and asked if they could identify Magnasco's killer, Mondo the Midget told detectives, 'I saw his belt buckle. Show me a lineup of belts and I might be able to recognize it.'

Two weeks after Magnasco was murdered, the Gallos decided to take another shot at knocking off the chief. Word had it that Profaci was slipping in and out of Brooklyn while remaining holed up at his hunting lodge in New Jersey which was patrolled by shotgun-carrying soldiers. When Larry found out that Profaci would be at a country club, he dispatched a hit team, but Profaci was either tipped off or spooked and easily escaped, unscathed, continuing his incredible lucky streak.

On 11 November, two Gallo men stormed into a lounge and killed two Profaci associates. Three weeks later, on 2 December, Persico and Sally D dressed as women and drove around Brooklyn in search of Larry, who had left the barracks on President Street for a secret meeting with Tony Bender. When they spotted Larry, they fired at him with a shotgun, but missed.

Next, Crazy Joe was taken out – by the law. Joey was a professional extortionist but the gang was desperate for money and Joey got sloppy. He was shaking down a legitimate businessman who begged Joey for some extra time to cough up the dough. 'Sure, take time!' said Joey. 'Take three months in a hospital on me!' Unbeknownst to Joey, the victim had alerted the bulls who were staked out nearby; they made a quick arrest. After a three-day trial, Joey was convicted on all counts and was given a seven-to-fourteen-year sentence. Bobby Kennedy, who was still following the war from afar, was thrilled with the verdict and the stiff sentence, as was Profaci, who called for a ceasefire now that the hot-headed Joey was taken off the street.

The expense of war taxes a mafia family as it would a nation and, by 1962, the FBI filed a report stating that Profaci's policy business was taking a beating on account of the war, while the Gallos' street income had completely evaporated. Beyond Larry's financial woes, Tony Bender, who had been Larry's staunchest advocate, was ordered by Genovese to set the Gallos adrift. Once it became clear that Profaci had rallied the troops and the Gallos had no clear path to victory, the crew became a liability. Let us not forget that Genovese was an imprisoned boss who was vulnerable to an insurrection and did not find it politically expedient to support a failed rebellion. Bender, who was blamed for betting on the wrong horse, had even bigger problems than Gallo. Rumor had it that Bender, who oversaw the importation of drugs along the New Jersey waterfront, had somehow contributed to Genovese's imprisonment which conveniently left Bender in charge. Genovese further believed that Bender was thinking about making a power grab.

During the first week of April, the 62-year-old, bespectacled Tony Bender started spending more time in his palatial Fort Lee, New Jersey, home built on a bluff overlooking Manhattan. Knowing Genovese was suspicious of him, he tried to get his mind off the rackets by preparing his garden for spring and filling up his swimming pool. On Sunday, 8 April at around 10:40 p.m., he told his wife of thirty years, Edna, that he was running out for a pack of cigarettes.

'You'd better put on your coat,' said Edna, 'it's chilly.'

'Well, I'm only going to be a few minutes,' Bender replied. 'Besides, I'm wearing my thermal underwear.' He should have been wearing armored underwear. Bender pulled away from the house in his black Cadillac sedan and was never seen or heard from again. His wife told police, 'I'm sure something awful must have happened to him.' She was right. It was believed that he was cut up into little pieces, and his *gumare*, described by the press as an 'attractive brunette sports clothes designer', disappeared the following day, almost certainly as a precautionary measure in case Bender had engaged in too much pillow talk.

No one could escape Genovese's wrath – except one soldier who happened to be under Genovese's nose, doing time with him in Atlanta Penitentiary.

Chapter 15

Mistaken Identity?

Joe Valachi

As a teenager, Joseph Michael Valachi, known as 'Joe Cago', ran with a gang of petty thieves and did a short stint in Sing Sing where he met a few wiseguys who took a liking to him. By his own admission, he was a Neapolitan who fell in with the Sicilian mafia during the Castellammarese War when Salvatore Maranzano needed recruits. After Maranzano was killed, Lucky Luciano and Vito Genovese assigned Valachi to Tony Bender's crew, where he led a rather undistinguished career as a soldier.

In 1962, Valachi was serving a fifteen-year stretch in the same penitentiary as his don, Vito Genovese, when another inmate labeled Valachi a snitch. Since historians contend that Valachi was *not* a snitch at this point, it is incumbent upon me to correct the record while pointing out their ignorance of La Cosa Nostra law *and* universal prison rules. Valachi was serving time for drug trafficking. In order to get a lighter sentence, he informed on several drug dealers who were not part of the Italian-American mafia. Because Valachi did not snitch on his fellow mobsters, he did not consider himself a rat, and historians have accepted his distorted opinion of himself as accurate. But according to La Cosa Nostra, anyone who tells on anyone else is a rat, and for those of us who have served hard time, the rules in prison are just as strict. If, for example, an Italian mobster informs on Black or Hispanic drug dealers but spares his fellow Italians, he is still a rat to us Italians who have stood up and are serving time alongside those same Black and Hispanic convicts who have also stood up. Not surprisingly, Genovese saw it this way, too. Valachi therefore knew, once he was outed as a rat, he was in serious trouble with Genovese.

Fearing for his life, Valachi 'checked in', meaning he asked the prison guards to take him into protective custody. In prison, a 'check-in', in and of itself, is considered a 'rat move' since real men are expected to confront threats and accusations, not run from them. Another fear factor behind Valachi's check-in, overlooked until now, was Tony Bender's recent disappearance. Bender was labeled a rat before taking his final ride. Since Valachi was in Tony Bender's crew, he would have known that Genovese was examining that particular bushel for more rotten apples.

While relatively safe in protective custody, Valachi asked to speak with narcotics agents, which meant he was now prepared to open up about his fellow mobsters. Unfortunately for Valachi, the agents never arrived and prison officials released him back onto the compound where Giuseppe 'Joe Beck' Di Palermo was waiting with orders from Genovese to kill Valachi. Between the snitch label and the check-in, which only confirmed the label, Valachi knew he was a dead man. Before Joe Beck could get the jump on him, Valachi ran up to inmate John Joseph Saupp and beat him to death with an iron pipe. Valachi later claimed that he mistook the 52-year-old Saupp, described as a 'weasel-faced postal thief', for the hardened mobster Joe Beck, and historians have taken him at his word, yet again, and repeated this story ever since. Let us presently unravel this fallacy and put it to rest, once and for all.

To start with, Valachi knew exactly who Joe Beck was. They had been in the same borgata and the same damn crew for the past thirty years! Joe Beck was, moreover, a major heroin trafficker who regularly supplied Valachi with drugs. They were not only lifelong friends and business associates but were squeezed into the same prison together where they would have passed each other a dozen times a day and eaten at the same 'Italian table' three times a day. I can tell you from experience, in a maximum-security penitentiary where life hangs by a thread, every one of us knew every single face in our cramped environment so well that if a newbie entered the yard, we all turned to look at him. Why then did Valachi claim to mistake Joseph Saupp for Joe Beck, a bespectacled man with long arms and legs whose appearance was unmistakable?

The unmistakable 'Joe Beck' Di Palermo

After Valachi was ejected from protective

custody, the only way to get back into the safety of an isolation unit was to commit an assault on another inmate, which warrants an immediate trip to the hole and is often followed by a transfer to another prison. Contrary to Valachi's claim that he had accidentally killed the wrong guy, excusing himself by saying, 'They're both ugly. They're both skinny,' Valachi had looked around the prison yard for the weakest animal in the herd and had piped over the head a non-violent forger in order to escape Vito Genovese and Joe Beck, and save his own life. He may not have intended to kill Saupp, who clung to life for three days, but he needed to remove himself from the compound by way of an assault and he confirmed this when he said, 'I told the warden to just lock me up,' giving away his motive since convicts never volunteer for punishment. I am so sure that Valachi *did not* mistake Saupp for Beck that I would bet *my own life* on it.

After the death of Joseph Saupp, who had no mafia ties whatsoever, Valachi faced the death penalty from the law instead of the mob – but he could talk his way out of this mess, and he had plenty to say. Once again, Valachi asked to speak with federal agents and this time, with blood on his hands, he was taken more seriously. Narcotics agents rushed to visit him in Atlanta Penitentiary but they did not have Valachi long before he was taken away from them. Deputy director of the Federal Bureau of Narcotics, Charles Siragusa, said, 'Bobby Kennedy called me in Washington, and asked me if the Justice Department could question Valachi. So we gave him access to Valachi, who was turning out to be one of our best sources of information. Then, before you knew it, Bobby Kennedy, because of his hatred of the mob, had completely taken possession of Valachi. Frankly, we were pretty upset about it.'

On Bobby's orders, the FBI spirited Valachi to an army barracks at Fort Monmouth, New Jersey, where Agent James Flynn was assigned the trying task of picking through Valachi's demented mind. Flynn also had to deal with Valachi's whiny complaints, the first of which lends insight into his deep-seated resentment toward his don, Vito Genovese, who had never raised Valachi above the rank of soldier: Valachi bitched about being confined to the quarters of a mere enlisted man and demanded that he be housed in an officer's suite. The FBI obliged and, each morning, Agent Flynn showed up at Valachi's heavily guarded suite with food and cigarettes.

As Valachi ate Italian specialties like Genoa salami, pepperoni and provolone, and puffed through three packs of cigarettes a day, he recounted for Flynn his involvement in thirty-three homicides. In order to get the most mileage out of Valachi's tongue, Flynn sympathized with him, complimented him, learned how to react to his mood swings, and allowed him to blame his crimes on everyone else, resisting the temptation to point out Valachi's failure to accept any responsibility for his own actions. In addition to recounting a seemingly endless catalog of crimes, Valachi told Flynn who the FBI should target as potential informants based on who he felt was embittered, like him. The FBI followed Valachi's advice and was able to recruit a number of new informants. Flynn and Valachi usually wrapped up their debriefings before lunchtime, just as Valachi became too irritable to handle.

As Vito Genovese tried to figure out if there was still a way to kill Joe Valachi, Carlo Gambino, Tommy Lucchese and Joe Bonanno called for a second Commission meeting to try to bring an end to the Profaci–Gallo war, which was causing heat across the New York underworld and taxing all of their wallets. The meeting was held in the basement of a Long Island restaurant. Larry Gallo showed up but, once again, Joe Profaci did not. This time, Profaci's absence was genuinely on account of his illness, the severity of which he hid from the other bosses, knowing the vultures would circle the injured prey. Gambino, Lucchese and Bonanno were joined by Vincent 'Jimmy Blue Eyes' Alo who represented the Genovese family. Gambino opened the meeting by suggesting to the other dons that Profaci gracefully ease into retirement. As expected, Lucchese agreed with Gambino and, according to Bonanno who defended Profaci, they 'made it sound as if Profaci would be doing himself a favor if he retired'. Bonanno's firm stance behind Profaci contained an element of self-defense. If Profaci was knocked off the round table, Bonanno would be isolated and they would attempt to retire him next; it was the only way to delay an expected attack on himself.

Although it may have appeared that Gambino and Lucchese were standing behind Gallo by pushing for Profaci's retirement, this was not the case. They went on to say that the war needed to end and that could only happen when Profaci *and* Gallo stepped aside and allowed for a new boss who was acceptable to both factions. Naturally, Gambino and Lucchese wanted to choose Profaci's replacement so they could exert some influence over the fractured borgata. As for Jimmy Blue Eyes, he remained neutral, which confirmed that the Genovese family had abandoned Larry Gallo.

When Profaci heard a recap of the meeting's minutes from Bonanno, he was enraged and adamantly refused to step down. He probably would have held out forever but life does not offer that luxury. On 6 June 1962, Profaci died of liver cancer at Long Island's South Side Hospital. At the time of his death, he was still delinquent to the tune of $1.5 million in unpaid government taxes, and detectives estimated his net worth somewhere in the region of $100–200 million. The Olive Oil King, who had once stolen a horse in Sicily, galloped into Valhalla, laughing.

No sooner had Larry Gallo been set adrift by the Commission, and Joe Profaci been buried, than Tony Shots Abbatemarco walked out of the front door of President Street, followed by half of the Gallo crew. The group exited the barracks so abruptly that some of the men left behind their personal belongings. Tony Shots' defection came as a complete surprise to Larry Gallo, who learned that Shots had been wooed away from him by Carmine 'The Snake' Persico. (I have been told that Tony Shots had begun to suspect that the Gallos were behind his father's murder, and the whispers came from Persico.)

For most of Profaci's reign, his brother was his consigliere, and his brother-in-law, Joe Magliocco, was his underboss. Back in Sicily, the Profacis were long-standing friends and allies of the Maglioccos. Profaci's wife, Ninfa, was a Magliocco, and after Profaci's death, Joe Magliocco quickly stepped into Profaci's shoes. Since Magliocco was close with Joe Bonanno, his elevation, in the eyes of Gambino and Lucchese, was unacceptable. But unlike Profaci, who Gambino and Lucchese could not force into retirement, they had a rightful say in the matter of Magliocco's ascension. By rule, the Commission had the authority to sanction whoever claimed Profaci's old seat at the table, suddenly empowering Gambino and Lucchese as kingmakers. They immediately rejected Magliocco, asserting that he was only a dumber, fatter version of Profaci. Bonanno, who was fast to recognize Magliocco, worked behind the scenes to keep him in place while Gambino and Lucchese looked around for a malleable replacement.

Larry Gallo was not in the running but that did not stop him from trying. He and Carmine 'The Snake' Persico, each with a rival crew of young toughs, jockeyed for position, creating renewed tension until hostilities resumed in June 1963, one year after Profaci's death. Gallo loyalist Emilio Colantuono was gunned down, followed by the murders of Vincent DiTucci and Alfred Mondella. The next month, the still imprisoned Joey Gallo took a personal blow when Ali Baba was shot to death in New Jersey.

Following Profaci's death, Ali Baba had taken to sea as a chef on a cruise ship. He was a known hashish trafficker and his job on the ship may have been a cover for international drug smuggling. In mid-July, Ali Baba disembarked on a pier in Hoboken, New Jersey, and was probably waiting for a ride to arrive when two men in a car rolled up and shot him with a .45 automatic. He clung to life for a couple of days in critical condition then died, leaving Joey Gallo heartbroken. Ali Baba had been the best man at Joey's wedding and Joey's wife said, 'He was part of Joey and me.' Pete the Greek said of Joey and Ali, 'They loved each other.'

In August, Joseph 'Joe Bats' Cardiello was shot to death as he sat in his car. That same day, 'Johnny Moose' Batista and 'Tony Fats' Regina murdered 'Cadillac Louie' Mariani.

Gambino and Lucchese were quick to blame Magliocco for the latest outbreak of violence and were planning to relocate him to a nearby cemetery when Magliocco figured he should get the jump on them. Magliocco gave Salvatore 'Sally the Sheik' Musacchio a contract on Gambino and Lucchese. History is replete with lessons that escaped Magliocco. In AD 204, Plautianus, commander of Rome's notorious Praetorian Guard, ordered a double hit on Septimius Severus and his son, Caracalla, but the man Plautianus entrusted with the contract went straight to the targets and alerted them, resulting in Plautianus's ignominious death. In this case, Sally the Sheik recruited Joe Colombo who went straight to Gambino and alerted him to the plot, which thickened when Gambino found out that Joe Bonanno's son, Bill, was with Magliocco when the latter gave the contract to the Sheik. Gambino and Lucchese concluded that Joe Bonanno must have sent Bill to feed the idea of a double hit to the dimwitted Magliocco. Bonanno the elder vehemently denied the accusation, insisting that Bonanno the younger was having marital problems with Rosalie Profaci and was staying at Magliocco's heavily guarded Long Island estate to seek his marital advice. That Magliocco, who could not keep his own crime family together, was a sought-after marriage counselor sounded absurd to Gambino and Lucchese who summoned Magliocco before the Commission, where he was questioned, broke under pressure and confessed to the conspiracy. He begged for his life, proving how terribly unfit he was for the job anyway.

As a reward for betraying the plot, the Commission anointed the forty-year-old Joe Colombo as the new boss of the old Profaci borgata with orders to stabilize the warring factions. Gambino and Lucchese had found their puppet.

Chapter 16

He is Going to be Hit

Joseph Anthony Colombo was born in Brooklyn on 16 June 1923. His father, known as 'Tony Durante' and 'Tony Two Guns', was a Calabrian-born immigrant and member of the Profaci borgata who was garroted to death in 1938 on orders from Profaci after Colombo was caught cheating with a married woman who was found dead alongside him. Fourteen-year-old Joe Colombo began thieving to help care for his widowed mother and his sister. During the Second World War, he served in the Coast Guard. After the war, he went to work on the Brooklyn waterfront as a longshoreman where he stole pallets of merchandise and took numbers on the side. He eventually got a sales job with a wholesale meat company controlled by Carlo Gambino, who'd known him since he was a boy. Later in life, Colombo became a real estate broker for Cantalupo Realty in Brooklyn. A stand-in took the realtor exam for him and the local realtor's office was suddenly transformed into a hub of mob activity. To establish a legitimate income of approximately $35,000 a year, other realtors transferred their sales commissions to Colombo, who would repay them with cash under the table. The brokers were happy to save on taxes which Colombo was happy to pay in order to create seemingly lawful income. The steps Colombo took to maintain the appearance of a legitimate business-man, combined with his subdued lifestyle, appealed to the low-key Gambino who maneuvered him into place at the head of Profaci's borgata after Colombo betrayed Magliocco's plot. Colombo was so low-key that some members of the borgata had no idea where he had emerged from when he was suddenly elevated to the throne. In fact, the FBI did not even have a current surveillance photo or mugshot of him on record.

Not everyone in the borgata was happy with how Colombo had achieved power. One mobster said of his betrayal of the plot, 'He sold out his outfit. He played position.' Because Colombo was never a huge earner, Gambino loaned him a million dollars so he could push it onto the street in smaller loans as a sort of mini Marshall Plan to help boost the war-torn economy that had ravaged the Profaci borgata over the last several years. In return, Colombo was expected to vote with Gambino at Commission meetings which he faithfully did, essentially giving Gambino two votes at the table.

To appease the Gallo crew, Colombo promised to 'spread the bread', and raised Larry to a capo to prove his sincerity. He also made Carmine 'The Snake' Persico a capo in light of his chest full of Purple Hearts and in deference to the mighty crew he had built up in Park Slope, Brooklyn. With everyone momentarily placated, the borgata appeared to be one big happy family. We cannot say the same for their extended family of mobsters across the country, who were still scrambling to survive Bobby Kennedy's personal jihad to dismantle organized crime.

Within two years of Bobby becoming attorney general, 'Indictments secured [against mobsters] rose from zero to 683, and the number of defendants convicted went from zero to 619.' While exerting unprecedented pressure on the mob, Bobby continued to criticize FBI director J. Edgar Hoover, openly and privately, for withholding the full might of the FBI. Throughout 1963, Bobby repeatedly told people around him at the Justice Department that Hoover, who was approaching seventy years old, the government's mandatory retirement age, would not be the director for Jack's second term in office. Bobby's vow to retire Hoover from office is incomprehensible given Hoover's ever-fattening files on the Kennedy family and his not-so-subtle threats to use them, if forced. Numerous witnesses have expressed Hoover's dire fear of being pushed out of office which may have reminded him of his own father's downfall – the man suffered a nervous breakdown and was institutionalized after losing his government job. The 'very idea of retirement terrified him', said Deke DeLoach, who also revealed that, once a year, Hoover would invite him and Clyde Tolson to his house for dinner. 'It was not his birthday he was celebrating,' wrote DeLoach, 'but usually the anniversary of the day he was named director of the FBI, as if at that moment his life had really begun.' If the directorship was the beginning of Hoover's life, then Bobby was literally threatening to end it. Not surprisingly, Bobby's intention to retire Hoover got back to the director, who was secretly listening in on everyone's conversations, including mobsters, who expressed feelings toward the Kennedys that Hoover would have shared.

Hoover's secret listening devices, planted in mob hangouts across the country, picked up a ceaseless stream of threats made toward the Kennedy brothers from a number of high-ranking mobsters. As early as the summer of 1962, Michelino 'Mikey' Clemente told Joe Profaci's brother, Sal, 'Bob Kennedy won't stop today until he puts us all in jail all over the country. Until the Commission meets and puts its foot down, things will be at a standstill.'

Around the same time, an unidentified Genovese family mobster was overheard saying, 'I'd like to hit Kennedy. I would gladly go to the penitentiary for the rest of my life, believe me.' That same year, Philadelphia don Angelo Bruno, who was a close friend and ally of Carlo Gambino, was overheard discussing President Kennedy with mob associate Willie Weisberg, who said, 'With Kennedy, a guy should take a knife . . . and stab and kill the fucker, where he is now. Somebody should kill the fucker, I mean it. This is true. Honest to God. It's about time to go. But I tell you something. I hope I get a week's notice, I'll kill. Right in the White House. Somebody's got to get rid of this fucker.'

On another occasion, Angelo Bruno was talking with his in-laws, wiseguys Mario and Peter Maggio (though it is unclear which Maggio is speaking):

> Maggio: [President Kennedy] wants Edgar Hoover out of the FBI because he is a fairy, you know he is a fairy, I heard that.
> Bruno: Who?
> Maggio: Edgar Hoover is a fairy.
> Bruno: Who would ever listen to that bullshit?

Hoover, that's who! The lifelong bachelor, who lived with his mother until her death, was taking it all in, reading every transcript that crossed his desk as he also learned that Bobby referred to him as a 'fucking cocksucker' and wondered if he had to 'squat to pee'. Bobby also disparaged Hoover's right-hand man, Clyde Tolson, whose 'rapid rise would go unmatched in the entire history of the Bureau'. Hoover and Tolson ate meals together, spent weekends and holidays together, and took vacations together, leading to whispers in Washington. Bobby often referred to Tolson as 'J. Edna' and once, when Tolson was hospitalized for a medical procedure, Bobby mused aloud that it was for a hysterectomy.

Back when Bobby was working with Joseph McCarthy, the notorious senator who hunted American communists, one of Bobby's tasks was the investigation of homosexuals inside the State Department. Reminiscent of those outdated days, Bobby now ordered his organized crime chief, William Hundley, to compile a dossier *on Hoover*. 'We tried to prove that Hoover was a homosexual,' Hundley later confessed. As for the Kennedy brothers' plan to boot Hoover out, Hundley confirmed that 'Bobby mentioned [it] to too many people . . . And it got back to [Hoover].'

The man who was in power for decades, the man who was obsessed with his image, the image of his agents and the reputation of his bureau, the man who annually celebrated the day he became director, was about to be smeared as a homosexual – which was socially and institutionally unacceptable in the 1960s – and forced into a shameful retirement. Hoover's very survival was on the line and the only thing that could save him from total ruin was if the Kennedys went first. Was this why Hoover was attentively listening to the mob's death threats toward the president but did nothing about them?

In July 1962, Carlos Marcello invited friends and family to his Grand Isle fishing camp and vacation lodge in the Mississippi Delta. While Marcello was drinking a Scotch, a friend of his commented about the Supreme Court's recent decision to uphold Marcello's deportation order. Marcello spat out his Scotch and shouted, 'Don't worry, man, 'bout dat Bobby. We goin' to take care a dat sonofabitch!' Marcello was asked if he meant that Bobby would be whacked. 'What good dat do?' answered Marcello. 'You hit dat man and his brother calls out the National Guard. No, you gotta hit de top man.'

On another occasion, Marcello made a similar remark about the Kennedys, saying, 'the dog will keep biting you if you only cut off its tail', meaning that Bobby was the tail and Jack, the dog's head, needed to be cut off in order for the dog to die. A witness said that Marcello had 'already thought of using a "nut" to do the job'.

In September, Marcello made another ominous outburst, this time at Churchill Farms, his 6,400-acre estate on the outskirts of New Orleans. Marcello was drinking with some pals at a picnic table when a caretaker heard someone bring up Bobby's name, which was off limits unless you wanted to watch steam rise from Marcello's ears.

'Don't worry about that little Bobby son of a bitch,' Marcello screamed across the table. 'He's driving my wife fuckin' crazy. All Jackie do is cry all night thinkin' Kennedy is goin' to throw me outa the country again . . . She can't sleep. Bobby is drivin' my daughters crazy, too. They don't want to lose their Daddy . . . Well, I'll tell you boys they ain't goin' to lose their ole man. No, sir. 'Cause I gotta plan . . . wait an' see if that son of a bitch Bobby Kennedy is gonna take me away from my wife an' kids.'

The very same month that Marcello was threatening the Kennedys in Louisiana, Santo Trafficante met in Florida with Cuban exile leader and criminal associate, José Aleman, the son of 'an incomparably corrupt' Cuban cabinet minister who, when asked how he had stolen millions of dollars from the Cuban treasury, replied 'in suitcases'. Upon arriving in Miami, Aleman, who inherited his father's vast real estate holdings in Miami, sought out the Florida don who helped him acquire construction loans through the Teamster pension fund. While sitting in Miami's Scott-Bryant Hotel, where they met to discuss a $1.5 million real estate loan that had 'already been cleared by Jimmy Hoffa', Trafficante, who was an avid reader, 'spoke almost poetically', according to Aleman, 'about democracy and civil liberties' that were being trampled upon by Bobby Kennedy. Finally, Trafficante said to Aleman, 'Mark my words, this man Kennedy is in trouble, and he will get what is coming to him.' Aleman, who did not understand the extent of what Trafficante meant, told him he should sit tight and wait Kennedy out until he was voted out of office.

'No, José,' answered Trafficante, 'he is going to be hit.'

It was abundantly clear to Aleman that Trafficante was privy to an assassination plot against the president, if not personally involved. Unbeknownst to Trafficante, Aleman was an active informant for the CIA and the FBI, regularly reporting to the latter about Trafficante's underworld rackets, including Bolita, loansharking and drug trafficking. He left the meeting and went straight to the FBI field office in Miami to report Trafficante's unsettling remarks to his FBI handlers. The agents on duty, Paul Scranton and George Davis, listened carefully, then reported Trafficante's remarks to their superior, Special Agent-in-Charge Wesley Grapp. Grapp forwarded a report to Hoover in Washington where the information died on his desk. Hoover did not launch an investigation, nor did he ask to speak with the attorney general, the head of the Secret Service, or request an audience with the president as he had quickly done after the Judith Campbell affair had come to his attention.

On 27 September, another wiseguy was overheard saying that all of the mafia's problems were 'instigated by Robert Kennedy' who was 'murdering the Italian name'.

Two days later, Ed Partin, an inmate at a Baton Rouge, Louisiana, jail, told his keepers that Jimmy Hoffa had once asked him to assassinate Bobby Kennedy. According to Partin, Hoffa told him, 'I've got to do something about that son of a bitch Bobby Kennedy. He's got to go.' Hoffa further told Partin that Bobby 'drives alone in a convertible and swims by himself. I've got a .270 rifle with a high-power scope on it . . . It would be easy to get him with that.' As another option, Hoffa suggested that Partin throw a plastic bomb into Bobby's house, assuring him that Bobby had 'so many enemies now they wouldn't know who had done it'. The warden contacted the FBI who gave Partin a lie detector test, which he passed.

To recap, in the month of September alone, threats from Teamster leader Jimmy Hoffa and mafia chieftains Santo Trafficante and Carlos Marcello were made in Washington, Florida and Louisiana, and attested to by multiple witnesses.

In October, Marcello took one last shot at avoiding violence when he asked Sam Giancana to have his pal Frank Sinatra, considered 'the ambassador between the U.S. government and the mob', visit the president and ask him to reel Bobby in a few notches. While hanging out with Johnny Roselli and Sam Giancana, Sinatra was, at the same time, a regular guest at the White House and frequent visitor to the Kennedys' Hyannisport and Palm Beach homes. But although Sinatra had gotten the mob into this mess by striking a deal with Joe Kennedy Sr, the patriarch had since become incapacitated and unable to exert influence over his sons.

On 19 December 1961, the 74-year-old Joe Sr played a round of golf at the Palm Beach Golf Course. After the sixteenth hole, he felt faint and, by 2 p.m., he was admitted to St Mary's Hospital. He had suffered a stroke caused by a blood clot in the brain. From then on, he was paralyzed and unable to speak. 'There were moments when he was desperate to communicate,' said Oleg Cassini, 'but he couldn't.' It was only eleven months into Jack's presidency and the man who had made the mob so many promises was an invalid. Although his sons may have been free of his tyranny, they were also freed from the promises he had made to mobsters, and devoid of his guidance. 'The tragedy was Joe Kennedy getting a stroke,' said Gore Vidal. 'He could have settled the problem with the Mafia in two minutes.'

Charles Bartlett, a family friend who became the Washington bureau chief of the *Chattanooga Times*, said that Joe 'was very strong; he'd done things for the kids and wanted them to do some things for him. He didn't bend. Joe was tough.' Not anymore. According to one biographer, Joe Kennedy 'was in an instant transformed from the most vital, the smartest, the dominant one in the room to a gnarled, crippled, drooling, speechless, wheelchair-bound, utterly dependent shell of a man ... He could not dress himself, feed himself, shave or shower, or communicate his thoughts, desires, fears, or hopes in spoken or written language.' This meant that the mob and Sinatra were out of luck.

Still, Giancana and Roselli talked to Sinatra, who was fairly confident he could get Bobby to ease up, or have Jack yank the stick out of Bobby's ass. Sinatra visited the Kennedys, but his diplomatic mission backfired: Bobby was incensed by the intrusion and wanted Jack to cut ties with Sinatra, which he did after being shown a Justice Department report linking Sinatra to Cosa Nostra bosses around the country. While this was happening, Sinatra was looking forward to having Kennedy as a guest at his Palm Springs estate and had built a helicopter pad for Marine One. Kennedy canceled at the last minute while also scratching Sinatra from the guest list of a White House dinner.

Thanks to Bobby, the man who helped Jack into office and had arranged the inaugural gala was *persona non grata*. And instead of turning down the heat on the mob, Bobby turned it up. Around the same time, the Soviets turned up the heat on President Kennedy in Cuba, resulting in another mismanaged debacle that would drive an already embittered group of Cuban exiles – who were trained to kill by the CIA – even closer to Carlos Marcello and Santo Trafficante.

Part Three

Conspiracy and Cover-up

Chapter 17

Missiles and Whistles

Following the failed Bay of Pigs invasion, the Soviet Union supported the Cuban economy by increasing economic and military aid to the tiny island nation, in turn propping up the already popular Castro regime. But Fidel Castro still feared that a second US-led invasion was imminent and Soviet leader Nikita Khrushchev did not think, if that were to happen, that the US would fumble the ball a second time. To neutralize this possibility, Khrushchev took a drastic measure that brought the world to the brink of nuclear war.

Early on the morning of 16 October 1962, President Kennedy summoned Bobby Kennedy to the White House to tell him he had just been informed by the CIA that the Soviets were constructing an atomic missile base in Cuba. Back in September, President Kennedy had halted reconnaissance flights over Cuba after an American surveillance pilot was shot down in Soviet airspace. During the surveillance gap that went on for forty-five days, the Soviets had slipped nearly one hundred nuclear warheads into Cuba. After CIA director John McCone pushed the president to resume surveillance, following a tip from a Soviet spy, the alarming high-altitude photographs were taken.

For the next thirteen days, the White House was thrust into the worst Cold War crisis to date. Unlike the Bay of Pigs, when Kennedy wanted to hide America's complicity in the invasion, the United States was now provoked with every right to defend itself. This was the ideal pretext for a military invasion that many in the administration, the Joint Chiefs of Staff and the CIA had dreamed of – US marines would not look like the imperialist mercenaries Castro painted them as, but patriotic defenders of a nation threatened with nuclear holocaust.

As the Joint Chiefs urged the president to strike at Cuba, news of the crisis leaked out and the Cuban exile community felt a sudden renewal of hope, convinced that Kennedy had no choice but to invade the island. But the majority of Kennedy's cabinet, including Bobby, were of the opinion that a blockade, allowing no Soviet vessels in or out of Cuban waters, would be most effective and less provocative toward the Soviets who could launch a nuclear strike on the United States or retaliate with military aggression in Berlin.

While the president mulled over his options, military reserves were activated, soldiers and tanks were moved down to Florida, missile crews and tactical air squadrons were placed on maximum alert, B-52 bombers were loaded, and the navy deployed some two hundred ships into the Caribbean. With his small nation squeezed between two superpowers, a reckless Castro urged the Soviets to launch a nuclear attack on the United States. Khrushchev, who sometimes feigned lunacy on the world stage, sanely reminded Castro that his little island would be 'crushed into powder'.

At the height of the crisis, McCone ordered America's 007, William Harvey, to desist from his usual sabotage missions into Cuba, which could aggravate the situation. True to character, Harvey ignored McCone's orders to stand down and sent raiding parties into Cuba to pave the way for a full-scale military invasion. A number of CIA witnesses later said that Johnny Roselli accompanied Cuban exiles on dangerous missions along the island's coastline. 'For all of his tailor-made clothing and careful Hollywood-style grooming,' wrote one author, 'Johnny had guts, pure and simple.' In one incident, Roselli's boat was shot out from under him. The fit, 58-year-old wiseguy, who frequented golf courses and yacht clubs, courageously swam in the choppy dark sea until he was rescued by a friendly vessel.

US allies were in favor of an invasion of the island. After being informed of the crisis, Britain's prime minister, Harold Macmillan, advised Kennedy to invade and be 'done with it', while France's Charles de Gaulle, who had Khrushchev pegged as a bluffer, demanded that Kennedy stand up to him. This was in sync with Kennedy's Joint Chiefs of Staff, who felt the Soviets were dead wrong and would suck up a good clobbering. Kennedy's foreign relations committee chairman, J. William Fulbright, agreed with the Joint Chiefs, telling the president, 'I'm in favor . . . of an invasion, and an all-out one, and as quickly as possible.'

On the flip side, Bobby Kennedy argued against an invasion 'with a vehemence that startled most of the men in the room'. Bobby believed that an attack on the small island would smear America's reputation on the world stage and 'blacken the name of the United States in the pages of history'.

After intense discussions with his cabinet, President Kennedy leaned toward a blockade, feeling that if it were broken, the US could then retaliate. The Joint Chiefs warned the president that the blockade could allow the Soviets more time to arm the missiles. As with the Bay of Pigs, the president stood his ground against the experts and, on the morning of Saturday, 20 October, he opted for a quarantine of the island with close to 200 warships and eight aircraft carriers deployed into the Caribbean. Soviet ships en route to Cuba were stopped by US naval vessels while Soviet submarines were forced to surface and turn around.

Soviet nuclear missile reach from Cuba

Meanwhile, Kennedy opened a secret diplomatic channel to Khrushchev, who admitted the Soviets had already installed enough missiles to 'destroy New York, Chicago, and other huge industrial cities, not to mention a little village like Washington'.

During back-channel diplomatic discussions, Khrushchev agreed to remove the Soviet missiles in Cuba if Kennedy would remove US missiles in Turkey where they were pointed at the Soviet Union, thus striking a side deal that would be hidden from the American public for twenty-five years. Khrushchev also wanted an assurance 'that the United States would not invade Cuba either directly or through proxies', the proxies being the CIA-trained exiles. 'It would be foolish to expect the inevitable second invasion,' said Khrushchev, 'to be as badly planned and as badly executed as the first.' Kennedy, desperate to avoid a nuclear holocaust, agreed to Khrushchev's demands, frustrating members of NATO who viewed Kennedy as a Chamberlain. The CIA was especially furious over Kennedy's second failure to liberate Cuba, and the Pentagon felt he had 'missed the big bus' by not using the crisis as an excuse to invade the island.

Once again, as at the Bay of Pigs, the Cuban exiles suffered the most. They had not only lost this ideal opportunity to reclaim their homeland but Kennedy, in order to live up to his promise to Khrushchev to forgo a second invasion, 'terminated CIA financial support' to the exiles and ordered a halt to any raids or sabotage missions conducted from US soil. On orders from the White House, via the Justice Department, the FBI began raiding training camps, confiscating weapons and charging the exiles with criminal offenses. In a startling overnight shift, the exiles had gone from the universal mascots of liberty to criminal targets of the Kennedy administration. Many believed that Kennedy was being harder on the exiles than he was on Khrushchev and Castro, both of whom he was getting closer with through secret correspondences that bypassed the normal intelligence channels. To be sure, Kennedy's motives were patriotic and inspired by the desire for a peaceful world, but the intelligence community did not want a young president, who had already erred twice, exchanging love letters with a red czar.

In light of Kennedy's recent change of heart, a growing number of Cuban *fanáticos* became convinced that 'only . . . one development' could hasten the return of their beloved island: 'if an inspired Act of God should place in the White House within weeks a Texan known to be a friend of all Latin Americans'. Kennedy's vice president, Lyndon Johnson, was from Texas and an explanation is required as to why he seemed preferable to Kennedy.

Lyndon Baines Johnson was born in Stonewall, Texas, on 27 August 1908. He grew up poor and rode a donkey to school, got into politics early in life, and was suspected of stealing elections since high school, directing the stuffing of ballot boxes and the miscounting of votes. A ninth-grade schoolmate remembered the twelve-year-old Johnson once blurting, 'Someday, I'm going to be President of the United States.' According to the same schoolmate, the other children laughed at Johnson, who said, 'I won't need your votes.'

By 1948, the forty-year-old Johnson was elected United States senator from Texas, a seat that he was also suspected of stealing, a pattern that prompted cries from other politicians, such as 'He stole that election' and 'that damn Johnson stole some votes again'. Johnson's pre-eminent, Pulitzer Prize-winning biographer, Robert Caro, wrote: 'The first time the suspicions were checked, the result proved to be precisely what Johnson's opponents had charged it would be.' In another volume of Caro's multi-volume masterpiece on Johnson, the author called his subject 'Manipulative, a schemer . . . unprincipled and unscrupulous', adding that, 'For years men had been handing him . . . checks or sometimes envelopes stuffed with cash – generally plain white letter-size envelopes containing hundred-dollar bills.'

The governor of Texas said of the 1948 election, 'if the District Attorney here had done his duty, Lyndon Johnson would now be in the penitentiary instead of the United States Senate'. One man who attempted to investigate the election was murdered, gangland style. That is not to say that Johnson ordered the hit, but it did indeed happen and most people believe that the death was connected to the probe, later confirmed by one of the lead suspects.

During the 1960 Democratic primary in which Johnson and Jack Kennedy battled for the nomination, Johnson's team hurled damaging insults at the Kennedy clan which Bobby took to heart. After one of Johnson's aides compared Joe Kennedy to a Nazi, Bobby told the man, 'You Johnson people are running a stinking damned campaign, and you're gonna get yours when the time comes!' The man said that Bobby was 'leaning forward, clenching his fists, thrusting his face into mine', before Bobby angrily stomped off.

After an especially bitter and contentious primary, Bobby despised Johnson, but Joe Kennedy wanted Johnson on the ticket, and Joe always got his way. 'Obviously, it was not [Johnson's] qualifications that put him on the ticket,' wrote the St Louis Post-Dispatch. 'He was put there to carry Texas and persuade the South.' Newsweek wrote that Johnson 'will help keep the bulk of the South in the Democratic column in November'.

Few people expected Jack to offer Johnson the bottom half of the ticket, and even fewer thought that Johnson would accept it. Those who knew Johnson knew he was never content to play second fiddle. His aunt said that, even as a boy, 'Lyndon was in the forefront . . . Whatever they were doing Lyndon was the head. He was the main one'; and an old friend said of his sportsmanship, or lack thereof, 'if he couldn't lead, he didn't care much about playing'. Why, then, was Johnson prepared to abandon his role as 'Master of the Senate' to play second fiddle to Kennedy? Texas oil tycoon Haroldson Lafayette 'H.L.' Hunt, who was reported to be the richest man in the country 'worth an estimated $700,000,000, give or take a few oil wells', backed Johnson during the primary and was actually with him in his hotel suite when Johnson lost to Kennedy. Hunt was in favor of Johnson accepting the vice presidency, saying, 'I began to advance the idea that it was his duty to do so two days before the presidential balloting.' Hunt felt that anything could happen, perhaps a twist of fate, that could put Johnson in the Oval Office.

When Johnson accepted Kennedy's offer, a confused *Miami Herald* wrote, 'Few men in American history have given up so much for so little.' After Johnson was installed on the ticket and the election was won, Johnson believed he would have an active role in the administration but Bobby, who held a bitter grudge against him, convinced his brother to sideline Johnson. Jack sent him on unimportant trips abroad and, according to the president's secretary, began 'sending him fewer memos and giving him fewer assignments'.

During the missile crisis, Johnson sided with the hawks but his input was not taken into account, nor was he invited to the meeting where Jack made his final decision. Bobby said of that tense time, '[Johnson] had the feeling that we were being too weak, and that we should be stronger.'

Bobby was physically and verbally abusive toward Johnson and once told Johnson's closest friend in the Senate, 'They're supposed to make 'em tough down in Texas, but Big Lyndon doesn't look so tough to me.' Once, while Johnson was talking with a group of civil rights leaders, Bobby, who was pressed for time, told an aide, 'Can you tell the Vice President to cut it short?' The aide felt it was disrespectful to convey that message so he did not. Bobby then snapped at the aide, saying, 'Didn't I tell you to tell the Vice President to shut up?'

On rare occasions when Johnson and his wife, Lady Bird, were invited to Bobby and Ethel Kennedy's Virginia estate, Hickory Hill, the couple were seated at Ethel's 'losers' table'. At cabinet meetings, it was said that Bobby and Johnson 'literally couldn't look at each other'. Doris Kearns Goodwin, who worked for, penned a biography of, and interviewed Johnson, wrote of his implacable anger toward Bobby, and Robert Caro wrote that, 'Johnson found himself increasingly dealing with – increasingly in confrontation with – the President's brother.' Nicholas Katzenbach, who knew both men well, said, 'Bobby saw LBJ's success as the product of sleaze and manipulation, maybe even corruption. And LBJ saw Bobby's success as that of a spoiled little rich boy.'

In Washington DC, others picked up on the feud and, since the Kennedys held power, they also started to beat up on the beleaguered vice president. Once, at a cocktail party, Johnson, who had trouble finding anyone to talk with, dropped in on a conversation between two mid-level government employees but found himself shunned. As he despairingly walked away, one of the men said, 'I think we just insulted the vice president,' and the other replied loudly, 'Fuck 'im.' Johnson turned back but was at a loss for words.

By the end of the missile crisis, Johnson was a broken man whose fortunes had plummeted and whose future was bleak. According to Kenny O'Donnell, 'Johnson blamed his fallen prestige on Bobby Kennedy.' But the Kennedys had created enough enemies to make Johnson a few important friends. The Cubans now wanted him in office. J. Edgar Hoover, who Johnson had lunch with at least once a week, preferred him to the Kennedys. Hoffa wanted to see Kennedy replaced by Johnson. And Carlos Marcello, as one might expect given his long reach into the world of politics, had been funding Johnson for many years. In Houston, Texas, alone, where gambling was controlled by Marcello, Marcello's political fixer, Jack Halfen, was said to dish out between $50,000 and $100,000 a week in political bribes and was a major contributor to Lyndon Johnson's House and Senate campaigns. In return for Marcello's money, Johnson killed anti-rackets legislation in committee that would have otherwise decimated Marcello's gambling empire in the Lone Star State, and he curbed congressional investigations into the rackets.

Lyndon Johnson chats with Richard Nixon. Numerous witnesses have accused both men of taking money from the mob

In a word, some of the most powerful men in the country, who all hated the Kennedys, happened to like Lyndon Johnson.

Just as the Kennedy brothers had turned on Allen Dulles after the failed Bay of Pigs invasion, they now went after John McCone over the missile crisis. When the *Washington Post* wrote a story crediting McCone's foresight, Bobby went bananas, certain it was a CIA leak designed to save McCone from criticism and discredit the president. Jack agreed with Bobby, calling McCone a 'real bastard'.

Next, Bobby went after William Harvey, who denied that he had received an order to stand down during the crisis. Bobby browbeat him, calling his unauthorized sabotage missions with Johnny Roselli 'half-assed', and accusing him of being indifferent to people's lives. Not one to back down, Harvey got into a 'screaming match' with the attorney general in which they called each other 'liars and sons-of-bitches'. Before Bobby left the room in a huff, Harvey yelled, 'If you fuckers hadn't fucked up the Bay of Pigs, we wouldn't be in this fucking mess!' Director McCone was certain Harvey had 'destroyed himself', but Harvey's CIA protectors worked fast to get him out of Bobby's sight, transferring him across the ocean where he picked up as the new station chief in Rome. Before departing for Italy, the FBI observed Harvey – who now hated Bobby as much as the disgraced Allen Dulles, the humiliated J. Edgar Hoover, the persecuted Jimmy Hoffa, and the recently kidnapped Carlos Marcello – carousing with his pal Johnny Roselli. Harvey and Roselli went deep-sea fishing together, shared dinner in Miami, then traveled to the Florida Keys where they drank and lodged at the Plantation Yacht Marina. I think we can accurately imagine what they talked about.

In January 1963, Bobby buzzed J. Edgar Hoover to his office and all but scolded the elderly director for the Bureau's lax attitude toward Carlos Marcello. The next month, Hoover sent a teletype to New Orleans, directing his field agents to intensify their efforts against the bayou boss. Hardly anything was done in response to Hoover's directive, leaving us to wonder why. Did the field agents know the directive was only sent to placate the attorney general, or had Marcello corrupted the agents along with everyone else in Louisiana? Even if the agents were not corrupted, how far would they get with an investigation when Marcello controlled the state's political machinery, including the governor and New Orleans district attorney's office?

While hoping to retire Hoover or indelibly smear him as a homosexual, Bobby seized an opportunity to disgrace him in public by parading a real-life mobster before America's television sets. The Rackets Committee, where Bobby had first launched his attack on organized crime, was dissolved in March 1960, but a permanent Subcommittee on Investigations was kept open. Bobby worked closely with his old colleague, Senator John McClellan, to bring about televised hearings that featured Genovese family turncoat, Joe Valachi, as the government's star witness. Hoover was not happy about this development,

Joe Valachi testifies before Congress

nor were other heads of law enforcement who felt that Bobby was using Valachi for his personal agenda.

In August 1963, Valachi was transferred to a jail in Washington in preparation for his congressional testimony which began on 26 September, when Valachi walked into the Senate Caucus Room dressed in a black suit and silver tie. In a garbled, hoarse voice that made Sylvester Stallone sound like an Oxford professor, Valachi told a panel of shocked senators about his mafia induction ceremony in 1930, then went on to outline the structure of a borgata, including its chain of command, and the larger framework of La Cosa Nostra, which included multiple crime families spread out across the country with the bulk of its members – 50 percent of an estimated five thousand soldiers – in the lower boroughs of New York.

When Valachi named the five New York bosses who were in power at the time, the press ran with it, giving the borgatas the names by which they are still known today. The Profaci borgata was now the Colombo family. Lucky Luciano's borgata, after some years with Frank Costello in charge, was now the Genovese family. The Mangano borgata, after a brief turn with Albert Anastasia in charge, was now the Gambino family. The Reina borgata, after being led for a time by Tom Gagliano, was peacefully bequeathed to Tommy Lucchese, thus the Lucchese family. The Bonanno family alone maintained the name of its original patriarch, as Joe Bonanno was still in charge.

Valachi, whose testimony was supported by local and federal law enforcement officers, spent a week on the witness stand recalling his forty-year criminal career. Sounding a lot like his puppeteer Bobby Kennedy, Valachi said that he wanted to destroy La Cosa Nostra. When asked why, he did not attribute the need for its immediate demise to its many victims or the dire economic consequences to society but said it was because the bosses 'have been very bad to the soldiers and they have been thinking for themselves'. When one senator asked the loquacious thug what would happen to him if he went back to prison, Valachi replied that he would be 'dead in five minutes'. (Or, more likely, he would kill another random inmate in four minutes and be placed back into protective custody.)

Although Joe Valachi was the first member of the American mafia to openly expose the secret society, his congressional testimony led to no major prosecutions and amounted to a publicly broadcast introductory lecture on organized crime in America. There is some evidence to suggest that the FBI, which was already gathering intelligence from its black bag jobs and Top Hoodlum Intelligence Program, spoon-fed Valachi some of the information Hoover wanted transmitted to the American public now that he had no choice but to confront the problem. To be sure, Hoover had, at first, taken the news of Valachi's decision to inform as if he himself was being fingered on a homicide. He now came up with a cover story to head off criticism that he had been asleep at his desk for thirty years. He penned a piece for *Parade* magazine that read, in part, 'La Cosa Nostra, the secret murderous underworld combine . . . is no secret to the F.B.I.' Although the statement was factually true, it contradicted decades of public denials.

Bobby Kennedy knew that Hoover was making up for lost time while dodging accusations of ineptitude, but between the well-publicized Apalachin conference and the nationally televised Valachi hearings, Bobby now had all the public support he needed to annihilate the mafia and drag Hoover out of the Dark Ages. As for the mob, they found themselves in the same position as the Cuban exiles: nothing short of a miracle could save them. That miracle arrived when Carlos Marcello was introduced to David Ferrie.

Chapter 18

Master of Intrigue

David William Ferrie was born in Cleveland, Ohio, in 1918. As a young man, he had ambitions of becoming a Catholic priest but was thrown out of seminary school for 'erratic personal behavior'. He ended up becoming an ordained bishop in the Orthodox Church of North America, which was not recognized by the Vatican. In 1941, Ferrie graduated from Baldwin-Wallace College with a BA in Philosophy, and earned a PhD from an unaccredited college in Bari, Italy.

Besides philosophy and religion, Ferrie studied Latin and Greek and had an interest in psychology, medicine, chemistry, hypnosis and the occult. One of his many scientific pursuits was a cancer research program headquartered in his small, book-filled New Orleans apartment where hundreds of research mice scurried around in cages. A woman who knew and worked with Ferrie said that tumors were implanted in the mice and that Ferrie was working this program in concert with the CIA, which was interested in the possibilities of infecting people with cancer – something we can easily imagine Dr Gottlieb being interested in as he searched for untraceable ways to kill people. The CIA may have also been interested in Ferrie's experiments with hypnotism, a major focus of the agency's Operation Bluebird.

In 1951, Ferrie became a proud pilot for Eastern Airlines and he eventually flew covert missions for the CIA, delivering weapons to Castro's small band of guerillas in the Sierra Maestra Mountains. Although the CIA backed Batista, it was hoping to curry favor with the rebels in the event of Castro's victory. After Castro seized power and established closer ties to the Soviet Union, eventually declaring himself a Marxist, Ferrie felt personally betrayed and often spewed profanities at the Cuban leader.

In his blanket hatred of communists, Ferrie once worked himself up to the point of writing a letter to General Hale, commanding officer of the First Air Force, that read, in part, 'There is nothing that I would enjoy better than blowing the hell out of every damn Russian,

Communist, Red, or what-have-you . . . Between my friends and I we can cook up a crew that can really blow them to hell . . . I want to train killers, however bad that sounds. It's what we need.'

Leading up to the Bay of Pigs invasion, Ferrie flew CIA-backed bombing raids over Cuba and helped set up a military training camp outside of New Orleans for Cuban exiles who referred to him as the 'master of intrigue' because he 'delighted in weaving elaborate plots'. Ferrie put a lot of time and effort into preparing for the invasion, but after President Kennedy abandoned the Cuban Brigade on the beaches, he felt personally betrayed, once again, and now spewed profanities at the president, calling him more dangerous than Castro given Kennedy's premier position on the world stage. The FBI later said that Ferrie had occasionally stated that Kennedy 'ought to be shot'.

David Ferrie

Ferrie did not tone down his threatening rants while working as a pilot for Eastern Airlines, where he was suspected of luring underage boys onto airplanes he was piloting, then encouraging them to have sex with him. The experience must have been especially horrifying for the boys on account of Ferrie's physical appearance. He suffered from alopecia, which, in itself, does not detract from human beauty, but Ferrie wore a homemade red mohair wig that looked like a stray cat's bed which he mounted on his scalp with plastic cement. He also wore false eyelashes and thick, uneven greasepaint eyebrows. Beneath this creepy mess of his own doing were two beady eyes, narrow windows into a strange soul.

After being arrested for having sex with minors, Eastern Airlines conducted an internal investigation of Ferrie in September 1961 and decided to fire him. With the help of New Orleans attorney G. Wray Gill, Ferrie filed a lawsuit against the airline. Curiously, and perhaps attributable to Ferrie's connections with the US government, an Eastern Airlines memorandum stated that the airline's attorneys were contacted by two US congressmen who 'wanted to express to Eastern their interest in the Ferrie case and to explore the possibility of a compromise . . . the Congressmen indicated that they did not believe that Captain Ferrie and Mr. Gill would be interested in a resignation as a compromise'.

Eastern Airlines was unmoved by the high-powered push to rein-state Ferrie and stuck with their decision to fire him, but Gill was so impressed with Ferrie's private investigating skills and legal research abilities during the course of the case that he hired Ferrie at his law office to help him with other cases. One particular case Gill assigned Ferrie to work on was the defense of his most prominent client, Carlos Marcello, who was fighting the federal fraud indictment brought against him at the instigation of Bobby Kennedy. Even before Ferrie was introduced to Marcello, he would have certainly known about the don's raging anger toward Bobby Kennedy, since the Kennedy–Marcello feud was a highly publicized feature in the New Orleans press.*

We can only imagine, given Marcello's venomous rants against the Kennedys in Guatemala, Honduras, Grand Isle and Churchill Farms, and given Ferrie's loud, violent, well-documented threats toward the president, that the two were in good company, with nothing to curb their orgy of profanities but sheer oral exhaustion. Both men would have, moreover, found a large chorus among the Cuban exile com-munity of Louisiana, which was, in terms of sheer numbers, second only to the Cuban exile community in Miami. According to Layton Martens, a friend and ally of David Ferrie and active supporter of Cuban militants, 'Cuban refugees were arriving in New Orleans at the rate of as many as five thousand per day.' This presents us with a question that has not, to date, been asked but begs to be answered. Of all the places to settle in the United States, was it by chance or design that the most violent Cuban paramilitary groups in existence ended up in Florida and Louisiana, smack in the center of territories controlled by Santo Trafficante and Carlos Marcello?

Marcello's early funding of the more radical Cuban exiles was not born of any nefarious intent and can even be considered patriotic as it perfectly aligned with America's national security interests. Like the CIA, the US military and the State Department, Marcello wanted Castro dead so he could reclaim what he had lost in Cuba. An FBI report from April 1961 noted that Marcello pledged a 'substantial donation' to the New Orleans Cuban exile leader Sergio Arcacha

---

* There is speculation that it was Ferrie who flew Marcello home from his Central American exile; however, there is no solid evidence to support this theory, while circumstances point toward the two men meeting, at least officially, through G. Wray Gill, the attorney who represented them both.

Smith, who headed the Cuban Revolutionary Council (CRC) in New Orleans, and whose purpose was 'to establish a democratic government in Cuba through the use of military force'. Arcacha Smith was described by the FBI as 'one of the more conspiratorial Cuban exile leaders', which placed him in excellent company with the master intriguer, David Ferrie. According to Arcacha Smith, Ferrie 'had just shown up at my door one day offering to help'.

When Marcello began donating to the CRC, he was fairly confident that the CIA and the US military would help the exiles reclaim Cuba, and he expected, in return for his investment, favorable treatment in the way of gambling concessions, real estate development opportunities and wholesale tomato sales for his Pelican Tomato Company – which already supplied the US Navy – once Castro was ousted. When these hopes were dashed at the Bay of Pigs, and again during the missile crisis, Marcello was clearly out his investment, yet he continued to generously donate to the CRC. The question is: why? What was the savvy mob boss expecting in return for his money?

By February 1963, Kennedy's State Department launched a concerted effort to halt Cuban exile activities in accordance with the president's promise to Khrushchev. In March, the Coast Guard, Secret Service and FBI teamed up with British authorities in the Bahamas where they raided an exile training camp. By April, the Coast Guard sent more ships into the Florida Straits to cut off sabotage raids into Cuba; they boarded vessels and arrested exiles at gunpoint.

After the US government's funding of the CRC was abruptly halted, Sergio Arcacha Smith was in desperate need of money, as were other exiles, most of whom were poverty-stricken. One historian wrote: 'For all the business community's desire to help liberate Cuba, the New Orleans locals, suffering from a depressed economy, had very little money to donate to the cause.' A CIA officer who founded a fundraising organization, the Friends of Democratic Cuba, lamented, 'I got 2,000 empty cans to use for collecting contributions. But there was no interest. I think we made five dollars.' Suddenly, however, Arcacha Smith found funding. According to exile Carlos Quiroga, David Ferrie, who was now officially working as part of Marcello's legal defense team, was seen walking around with crisp hundred-dollar bills, handing Arcacha Smith money whenever he needed it. Ferrie was never known for having extra money which, the consensus believed, was coming directly from Carlos Marcello.

When Ferrie was not working out of the office of G. Wray Gill, he was usually hanging around the office of Guy Banister, where he also performed investigative work.

Born in Louisiana in 1901, Guy Banister was a special agent for the FBI for twenty years and had headed up the Bureau's Chicago office. Following his retirement in 1954, he was hired by the mayor of New Orleans, deLesseps 'Chep' Morrison, who was practically owned by Marcello, to address growing complaints of police corruption throughout the city. An honest investigation would have begun and ended with Marcello, but curiously went nowhere near him.

Banister later founded Guy Banister and Associates, a private detective agency located at 544 Camp Street where, among other functions, Banister ran background checks on Cubans who wished to join Sergio Arcacha Smith's CRC, which was backed by the CIA and which was headquartered in the same corner building as Banister's office. For Banister, the work was not just business but ideological. He belonged to the right-wing militia group, the Minutemen, and was a firm believer in the communist domino theory, which posited that if one Latin American country became communist, the rest could follow. His detective agency published one report called 'The Louisiana Intelligence Digest', self-described as a 'militantly conservative publication . . . devoted to the exposure of the operations of the Socialist and Communist organizations in Louisiana, and the dupes, fellow-travelers, and do-gooders who give them aid and comfort'.

When Castro declared his revolution Marxist and cozied up to the Soviets, Banister linked up with the Cuban underground in New Orleans who were determined to oust the Beard. Driven by shared goals and a mutual hatred for President Kennedy based on real or perceived notions of betrayal, Banister became fast friends with David Ferrie, who had recently become fast friends with Carlos Marcello. Another young man often seen with Ferrie inside Banister's office was Lee Harvey Oswald.

Lee Harvey Oswald was born in New Orleans on 18 October 1939. His father, Robert, dropped dead while Lee was still in his mother's womb. With three sons and no father, Lee's mother, Marguerite, struggled to survive until she dropped the boys off at the Bethlehem Children's Home. Lee was rejected because he was underage, so he went to live, on and off, with his mother's older sister, Lillian, and her husband, Uncle Charles 'Dutz' Murret, who was a known bookmaker in Carlos Marcello's borgata. Dutz answered directly to capos Nofio Pecora and Salvador 'Sam' Saia, who Aaron Kohn of the New Orleans Crime Commission called 'the biggest and most powerful operator of illegal handbooks and other forms of illegal gambling in the city'. Kohn also confirmed that Sam Saia was 'very close to Carlos Marcello'.

In December 1942, Marguerite reapplied for Lee's admission into the children's home; this time he was taken in, but Marguerite soon removed him and they relocated to Dallas, Texas, with her new fiancé. The rest of Lee's childhood is a bleak catalog of domestic instability; he regularly moved between Dallas and New Orleans and attended twenty-two different schools. Throughout this trying time, the only balance in Lee's life seems to have been the Murrets, who were always ready to take him in when Marguerite was unable or unwilling to care for him.

In 1954, the fifteen-year-old Oswald joined the New Orleans Civil Air Patrol as a cadet. One of its founders was David Harold Byrd, owner of the large Texas School Book Depository building and a cousin of Senator Harry F. Byrd. Both Byrds were very close to Lyndon Johnson, and one of the Civil Air Patrol's captains and pilots was David Ferrie, who was present in at least one photograph with the young Oswald.

Ferrie (second left) and Oswald (far right) together at the Civil Air Patrol

Although we do not know much about Oswald and Ferrie's relationship during this early period, we do know that Ferrie was a hypnotist and inveterate pedophile who was fired from Eastern Airlines for preying on young men, and that Oswald's fatherless and erratic domestic background made him the poster child for vulnerability.

In 1955, Oswald quit school for the last time and tried to enlist in the Marine Corps but was turned down because of his youth. The next year, he tried again and was accepted with the help of his mother, who signed a parental waiver for her underage son. From July 1957 to October 1958, Oswald was stationed at the highly secret Atsugi Naval Air Station near Tokyo, Japan, where he curiously learned to read and speak Russian. Oswald seems to have been highly intelligent and, since ancient times, there has been a belief in the link between genius and madness, which may explain why, in 1958 alone, Oswald was court-martialed twice and suffered a nervous breakdown.

In 1959, Oswald requested a special hardship discharge so he could care for his mother who became ill. He was granted a discharge in September and defected to the Soviet Union in October, via Finland. That same month, a friend presented him with a copy of Fyodor Dostoyevsky's *The Idiot* for his birthday. The gift would prove incredibly prescient given that the novel's protagonist, Lev Myshkin, was a brilliant young man who the world mistook for an idiot.

In 1960, while living in the Soviet Union, Oswald married a Russian woman, Marina Nikolayevna. He eventually became disenchanted with Russian communism and returned to the United States with his new wife. In June 1962, they settled in Fort Worth, Texas. Oddly, the US State Department not only permitted Oswald's return but even extended him a loan, as if he had embarked upon a harmless hiking trip across the Alps that left him short on cash. We are left to wonder if he had truly defected or was working as a double agent for the United States government. Upon his return to the States, the FBI interviewed Oswald and opened a file on him, which probably means they were not privy to any State Department secrets but were eager to find out more.

On 24 April 1963, Oswald was living and working in Dallas when the White House announced that the president would visit the city in November. That same day, Oswald boarded a bus for New Orleans where he crashed at Aunt Lillian and Uncle Dutz's home in the mob-run French Quarter. Uncle Dutz put Oswald to work as a runner for his bookmaking operation, which meant that Oswald was essentially working for Carlos Marcello. In late April, Oswald was seen accepting money from one of Marcello's soldiers inside the restaurant of Marcello's Town and Country Motel. It is quite possible that this was a normal gambling transaction related to his job as a runner, or was it something more sinister?

A short distance up the highway from Marcello's Town and Country

Motel was a bar owned by Bernard 'Ben' Tregle. Tregle ran a gambling book for Marcello and also displayed Marcello's slot machines and jukeboxes inside his establishment, which is believed to have been part-owned by Marcello. In April 1963, Eugene De Laparra, who was close with Marcello's brothers and worked at Ben Tregle's bar, was present for a conversation between Tregle and several other Marcello associates. Tregle was viewing an advertisement for a rifle in a detective magazine when he suddenly looked up at the group and said, 'This would be a nice rifle to buy to get the President . . . [there is] a price on the President's head . . . somebody will get Kennedy when he comes down South.' De Laparra, who was an ex-marine and a reliable FBI informant, reported the conversation to his handlers. Once again, as in the case of José Aleman who had reported Santo Trafficante's similar remark in Florida, nothing was done about it.

In July 1963, Guy Banister printed up a box of leaflets that urged people to join the Fair Play for Cuba Committee which was supposedly sympathetic to Castro's communist cause. The address printed on the back of the leaflets was the office of Banister, who was, ironically, an ardent *anti-communist*. It seems that Banister was attempting to ferret out communist sympathizers who would unwittingly show up at his door. The leaflets were distributed on the street by Oswald and when Banister's secretary asked Banister why Oswald, who she knew from Banister's office, was distributing pro-Castro leaflets, Banister replied, 'He's with us.' Besides uncovering communists, Banister may have had an additional motive to distribute the leaflets, which had to do with reinforcing Oswald's reputation as an active leftist since Banister or someone else arranged to have Oswald photographed and filmed.

Oswald hands out leaflets in what many believe to have been a staged event

Adding more mystery to this already strange situation, Oswald got into a street fight with Cuban exiles who were offended by his public recruitment drive, though skeptics believe that the fight was staged. After being arrested, Oswald made an unusual request to speak with the FBI then used his one telephone call to dial Uncle Dutz, asking him to call on his underworld connections to spring him from jail. Oswald was soon bailed out by Emile Bruneau, who also paid Oswald's fine. Bruneau, besides being a close associate of Uncle Dutz, was also close with Nofio Pecora and Joe Poretto, both of whom were high-ranking members of Marcello's borgata.

Also in July, a group of Cuban exiles traveled from Miami to New Orleans, where they practiced guerilla warfare at a training camp constructed on a sprawling property owned by a known mafia associate who was directly connected to Carlos Marcello. By the summer of 1963, there were at least six Cuban exile training camps that doubled as munitions depots near or around Louisiana's Lake Pontchartrain. One of the main camps was located on the property of William McLaney, who once owned a tourist agency in Havana, Cuba, but was run out of town by Castro. William's brother, Michael McLaney, was partners with the mob in Havana where he had owned a large share of Meyer Lansky's Hotel Nacional, the site of the mob's 1946 conference. After Castro took power and locked up a number of mobsters, Michael McLaney was briefly detained in a Havana jail, like Santo Trafficante, and later escaped the island, also like Trafficante. But unlike Trafficante, whose loyalties were questionable, McLaney, upon his return to the States, became a true believer in the Cuban exiles' bid to repatriate to their homeland. He put a steep bounty on Castro's head and lined up a fleet of private planes to bomb Cuba's confiscated oil refineries – but was talked out of it by American oil companies who, anticipating Castro's demise, hoped to reclaim the structures intact.

On 31 July, the FBI launched a raid on William McLaney's Lake Pontchartrain property in accordance with the Kennedy administration's merciless crackdown on Cuban exile paramilitary groups. Agents confiscated over a ton of dynamite, napalm and other explosives 'crated for shipment to Cuba'. The FBI took eleven men into custody, including Sam Benton, who was a close associate of Santo Trafficante and Johnny Roselli. New Orleans newspapers reported the raid and detailed the curious cache of explosives it had turned up, but for some reason that has never been explained all of the men were promptly released without being charged with a single crime and despite being in possession of enough illegal explosives to launch the island of Cuba into outer space. It seems that CIA agents, who were still working with these men, had intervened on their behalf.

Although David Ferrie was not at the McLaney property during the raid – assuming he did not hide or escape – he is believed to have trained exiles there, taught them how to fly and use various weapons, and helped finance the training camp. Anyone familiar with the expenses required to run a single household can only imagine the costs involved in just feeding an entire camp such as this one. As noted earlier, when the government cut off the exiles' funding, men like Sergio Arcacha Smith, David Ferrie and Guy Banister, whose office was referred to as 'Grand Central Station' for militant Cuban exiles, were in desperate need of money. Also, as noted earlier, Marcello's empire was reported to rake in over a billion dollars annually. If any one man in New Orleans had the financial means to replace lost government funding, it was Carlos Marcello.

Although the hidden details of exactly what was happening in New Orleans may never come to light, here is what we do know. In the summer and fall of 1963, David Ferrie, who despised the Kennedy brothers as much as Carlos Marcello did, was regularly meeting with the Louisiana don at his Town and Country headquarters to supposedly strategize for his upcoming trial. At the same time, Ferrie was also meeting with angry Cuban exiles who felt treacherously betrayed by President Kennedy and were somehow transformed from cherished symbols of freedom to criminal targets of the Kennedy administration. Ferrie was, moreover, regularly meeting with a retired FBI agent and right-wing militant with obvious ties to the CIA, Guy Banister, who despised President Kennedy for his disloyalty to America's Cold War values. And Ferrie and Banister were seen in the company of Lee Harvey Oswald, who was supposedly infatuated with communism, even though it is quite difficult to imagine him expressing this political passion in the presence of Ferrie and Banister, who, if they believed him, would have beaten him to death with a hammer and sickle. Whatever we choose to make of this bizarre confluence of strange individuals, nothing binds men more powerfully than mutual hatred of a common enemy. A perfect storm was brewing in Louisiana.

Chapter 19

Sparky from Chicago

No sooner were the Bay of Pigs prisoners ransomed from Castro and back in Miami than Bobby Kennedy said to one of his employees who asked for a day off, 'What about Hoffa?' While overseeing the Rackets Committee, Bobby had failed, 'despite 1500 witnesses and 20,000 pages of testimony', to pin anything on Jimmy Hoffa. Bobby took it personally and promised his colleagues, 'the game isn't over'. After becoming attorney general, it was time for a rematch.

Bobby instructed Walter Sheridan, an ex-FBI agent who had also worked for the National Security Agency, to set up a special unit to combat labor racketeering, with a particular focus on Jimmy Hoffa; the squad would become known as the 'Get Hoffa Squad'. Head of the Organized Crime Section, Edwyn Silberling, thought that Bobby's choice of Walter Sheridan was 'rather odd, you know – Sheridan wasn't a lawyer – he didn't have any legal training but he was handpicked by Bobby'. There was actually nothing odd about it: Sheridan was a dogged investigator who was not afraid to skirt the boundaries of the law and, if need be, cross the line. He was known to lean on witnesses and even threaten the wives of potential witnesses with imprisonment if their husbands did not testify. Sheridan was also as reckless as Bobby when it came to targeting powerful enemies. In an April 1961 internal memo, Sheridan wrote that, in addition to mobsters, his squad would go after 'so-called legitimate people both in the business world and in government service without whose cooperation these people could not operate. This would include employees of the Federal investigative and regulatory agencies who are being paid off, Congressmen and Senators who are collaborating, bank officials and businessmen.'

Edwyn Silberling, who thought 'Bobby just wasn't cut out to be a lawyer', was uncomfortable with the direction the Justice Department was taking and no longer wanted to pursue Bobby's personal vendettas; he resigned after two years. But most of Bobby's attorneys went along for the ride. 'Sure we had a vendetta,' a member of the Get Hoffa

Squad later commented. 'But you have to understand how terrible this guy was . . . We weren't Nazis . . . But I guess in this day and age I'd have problems if other people organized a squad like this specifically against some other guy.' William Hundley, who was Walter Sheridan's boss at the Criminal Division, said, 'I'd hate to see a group like the Hoffa squad become any sort of precedent. I think in our case it wasn't abused, only because of the people involved.'

Whether or not Hundley and Sheridan were able to responsibly persecute someone, as they believed, we cannot blame Hoffa for feeling singled out. He complained, 'They go to school and investigate my kid . . . They go around to his friends and say, "How many suits of clothes has Jim Hoffa got? How much money does he carry in his pocket?" They gave orders to every airline office in the country – when Hoffa makes a reservation, call the nearest FBI office and give the time he takes off and the time he arrives. You wouldn't believe some of the creepy stuff they are pulling.'

Hoffa purchased thousands of copies of George Orwell's 1984 and sent them to union locals across the country, telling them that Orwell's grim prediction was already happening under Bobby Kennedy, whose treatment of potential witnesses did nothing to assuage Hoffa's concerns. Joe Franco was suspected of knowing something about Hoffa's corrupt practices in Detroit. Franco said that the Get Hoffa Squad illegally broke into his home, cuffed him and brought him to Bobby, who told him, 'I want information from you. I don't care whether it's hearsay or fantasies or what. I want anything you can give me that I can use to bring Hoffa to trial.' Bobby promised to put Franco in prison for a long time if he did not comply, telling the recent widower, 'What I'm going to do is take your four children away from you and put them in an orphanage and have you declared an unfit father.'

Once, when Walter Sheridan was pressuring a Hoffa loyalist into testifying against him in return for a pass on pending criminal charges, Sheridan said, 'We need some help, and you can help us.'

'Well, what the hell do you mean, I can help you?' asked the loyalist. 'Do you want me to phony up a charge to get out of the trouble I'm in?'

'You're a big boy,' answered Sheridan, meaning he could figure it out for himself.

Bobby and his Get Hoffa Squad also launched investigations into Hoffa's attorneys, violating Hoffa's civil rights, specifically his Sixth Amendment right to counsel. The investigations, beyond being spiteful, were used as a scare tactic to dissuade attorneys from representing Hoffa in court. Attorney Edward Bennett Williams had anticipated this injustice when he said, 'If Jack Kennedy is elected president, I guess I'd better apply for a passport.' Bobby defended his mistreatment of attorneys, telling one reporter, 'Lawyers who take their money from the Teamsters are legal prostitutes.'

In search of powerful allies, Hoffa drew closer to Carlos Marcello and Santo Trafficante, whose innocent wife was also subpoenaed by Bobby, placing her in the company of Marcello's wife who was still under a suffocating tax lien.

Attorney Frank Ragano, who represented Trafficante for the better part of four decades, was often asked by Trafficante to deliver messages to Marcello and Hoffa, both of whom Ragano also represented, though less frequently. In February 1963, Trafficante was complaining about the Kennedys when he told Ragano, 'Somebody is going to kill those sons-of-bitches. It's just a matter of time.'

Ragano, who had also heard Marcello and Hoffa curse the Kennedy brothers, felt that his clients had every right to feel angry but assumed they were just hot-tempered men blowing off steam. Then one day, as Ragano wrapped up a case with Hoffa and was leaving to visit Marcello and Trafficante in New Orleans, Hoffa said to Ragano, 'Something has to be done. The time has come for your friend [Trafficante] and Carlos [Marcello] to get rid of him, kill that son-of-a-bitch John Kennedy.' Knowing how worked up Hoffa would become over the Kennedys, Ragano thought nothing of it. When he arrived in New Orleans and was seated at a dinner table with the southern mob bosses, he relayed Hoffa's message, thinking he would give them a laugh. '[Hoffa] wants you to do a little favor for him,' Ragano said, cueing up the punchline, 'you won't believe this, but he wants you to kill John Kennedy.' Ragano waited for them to laugh and was shocked to see them exchange icy glances across the table. According to Ragano, 'I had blindly intruded into a minefield that I had no right to enter: that without my knowledge the thought of killing the president had already seriously crossed their minds.' Ragano was relieved when the waiter appeared, offering him an opportunity to change the subject.

On 27 May, the US Supreme Court declined to review Marcello's appeal, allowing Bobby to deport Marcello the moment he found another nation willing to accept him. Unless fate intervened and Bobby was somehow removed from office, Marcello would be booted out of the country and permanently separated from his borgata as well as his immediate family. It was apparent that one man or the other needed to be destroyed.

On 16 August, a local television crew filmed Lee Harvey Oswald handing out more pro-Castro literature, this time in front of the New Orleans International Trade Mart.

At the beginning of September, Bobby again tore into J. Edgar Hoover for accepting that Marcello was just a tomato salesman. Also in September, David Ferrie began meeting more often with Marcello, while New Orleans newspapers reported that the president's visit to Dallas, Texas, would be on 21 or 22 November.

The state of Texas, which shares a roughly 370-mile border with Louisiana, was under Marcello's control. 'Next to New Orleans,' wrote author John H. Davis, who was a cousin to the Kennedys, 'the most important city in the invisible empire of Carlos Marcello was Dallas. The Marcello gambling syndicate in Texas numbered several hundred bookmakers handling gross revenues in the hundreds of millions of dollars. In 1963, the Marcello slot machines could be found in almost every city in Texas, especially in Dallas.'

In Houston alone, Marcello's race wire fed information to hundreds of bookmakers, each paying $250 to $500 per day for the service. Marcello also funded the policy banks, and distributed jukeboxes across the state. He used Teamster loans to build motels in Dallas, and invested in bars, strip clubs and restaurants, all of which displayed

Texas don Joe Civello

his slot machines. The staggering cash flow derived from this leviathan led to the usual corrupting of police and politicians, a talent Marcello had perfected in Louisiana. But unlike Louisiana, where Marcello personally ran the operation, his satellite state of Texas was overseen by his pal and proxy, Don Joe Civello.

Joe Civello was born in 1902 and was originally from Louisiana, where he answered directly to Carlos Marcello. After Marcello became the boss of Louisiana, he slowly expanded his empire into Texas and sent Civello there to distribute his slot machines and expand his race wire. With Marcello's cash and influence, Civello, a convicted drug trafficker who was once arrested for murder, grew strong and easily took over the Texas borgata in 1956 while pretending to be the humble proprietor of Civello's Fine Foods & Liquor.

In 1957, Marcello, who held a seat on the Commission but shied away from national politics, sent Civello to Apalachin as his representative. After Civello returned to Dallas, the media referred to him as one of a number of 'anonymous officers of an invisible government'. A number of people who had read about Civello's trip to Apalachin in the newspapers, spotted him having dinner with Sergeant Patrick Dean of the Dallas Police Department, who was on record stating that the Dallas police 'had no trouble with the Italian families'. Civello's long reach into the law enforcement community was evidenced by a crime condition report filed in Dallas on 1 March 1962, that read, in part, 'No evidence of illegal activity by Joseph Francis Civello.' Apparently, no one was looking very hard, which bothered Bobby Kennedy. By early 1962, Bobby went after the Civello borgata, knowing it was connected to Marcello. He launched gambling raids throughout the state's major cities and, by October, the *Wichita Falls Times* called Bobby's onslaught 'a full-scale investigation into gambling and racketeering' in Texas.

Joe Civello's underboss was another Marcello crony, Joe Campisi, who, along with his brother Sam, ran a multimillion-dollar bookmaking operation. The Campisi headquarters was the Egyptian Restaurant, a Dallas eatery open to the public that doubled as a mafia hangout.

Egyptian restaurant – note the concrete parking curb that reads 'Campisis only'

The Campisi brothers were extremely tight with the Marcello brothers; they all did business together and mingled socially, including rounds of golf in Texas and Louisiana, depending on who was visiting whom. For many years, telephone toll records went back and forth on a daily basis between Marcello, Civello and Campisi, while Civello and Campisi were regularly seen in the company of another Dallas hoodlum, Jack Ruby.

Born Jacob Rubenstein in Chicago in 1911, Jack Ruby was raised in the West Side ghetto, a two-mile-wide, three-mile-long stretch of the city where Yiddish-speaking immigrants lived in overcrowded conditions, similar to New York's Lower East Side. The Chicago ghetto was ridden with Jewish street gangs and part of its boundary bordered 'Dago Town', where young Jewish and Italian gangsters formed life-long alliances.

The fifth of eight surviving children, Ruby grew up in a dysfunctional home. His father was a drunk who beat his mother until the couple separated when Ruby was ten years old. At eleven, Ruby was already getting into trouble on the streets. The Institute for Juvenile Research 'recommended that he be placed in a new environment, one that would stimulate his interest and keep him off the street'. Given his subsequent trajectory in life – operating a chain of titty bars – one might argue that the adolescent Ruby followed this directive to a T.

Ruby quit school after the fifth grade and joined a street gang, eventually becoming a *schlammer*, or enforcer, for the unions. He was later recruited for muscle by the Scrap Iron and Waste Handlers Union in Chicago, controlled by mobster Paul 'Red' Dorfman, who had taken over the union after its founder and president, Leon Cooke, was murdered. Ruby was picked up by police for questioning but quickly released.

In 1937, Ruby's 61-year-old mother was committed to an insane asylum, and in 1947 the Chicago mob sent Ruby to Texas. Exactly what sparked the transfer remains unclear. An associate of Ruby's said he 'had been run out of Chicago by the mob', while another associate said he was sent to Texas to plant a flag. The two are not inconsistent. The mob knows how to kill and, if you screw up, you're dead. But you can also be 'chased' or run out of town for a variety of reasons that do not warrant death. Ruby could have been told to lie low and stay out of someone's sight for a while but instructed to pick up with mob action elsewhere. It is possible that Ruby, who was close with Leon Cooke, could not get along with Paul Dorfman who then complained to the bosses and had Ruby transferred.

In Texas, the high-energy Ruby, known as 'Sparky from Chicago', got right down to business, becoming involved in slot machines,

Jack Ruby with his employees at the Carousel Club

gambling and strip clubs. As the Chicago mob continued to invest heavily in Las Vegas hotels and casinos, it cared less about Texas and ceded its interests to the Civello borgata, which fell under the umbrella of Marcello's Gulf Coast kingdom. Though Ruby would have still answered to Chicago, he would have been on loan to Civello who admired the tough transplant – Ruby bounced at his own bars and nightclubs where 'he beat with his fists, blackjacked, or pistol-whipped unruly patrons'. One of Ruby's business competitors, Barney Weinstein, said, 'Jack had seven fights a week. I've had three fights in thirty years.' Besides managing strip clubs, Ruby distributed Marcello's slot machines, via Civello, and hung out at the Egyptian Restaurant where he became especially close with the Campisi brothers.

Notwithstanding his short temper, Ruby must have been a personable guy since police officers took to him as easily as mobsters did, and groups of both mingled together at his strip clubs. Ruby's Carousel Club, in particular, catered to off-duty cops and held 'Officers' Night' once a week so the men in blue could enjoy themselves in their own private setting. Bartender James Rhodes said that Ruby would not let the cops pay for anything and gambler Jack Hardee would later tell the FBI that anyone looking to set up a casino or run numbers in Dallas had to run it by Ruby first, so he could get an okay from the cops. To be clear, the mafia does not allow men to maintain close ties to the police *unless the men are corrupting the cops on behalf of the mob*. In Ruby's role as a mafia–police liaison, he was the most valuable asset of the Civello borgata which was, as we have thoroughly established, an extension of Marcello's empire.

Given Marcello's anaconda grip over the state of Texas, which included its police and politicians, when he heard that the president was traveling to Dallas in November, he must have been as thrilled as if he had heard Kennedy would be lodging in one of the abandoned cabins on his bayou property. With an entire infrastructure in place, Marcello needed only to prepare for the president's visit, a task taken up by the mafia's Clausewitz, David Ferrie.

Chapter 20

The Hit Heard Round the World

By September 1963, at least six witnesses in Louisiana had seen David Ferrie in the company of Lee Harvey Oswald. On one occasion, they were taking part in a training maneuver in a bayou outside of New Orleans. As we have already established, by all appearances Ferrie was a right-wing zealot and Oswald was a left-wing communist. Since both men were known to get into heated arguments with anyone who disagreed with their point of view, how did they get along so well? The answer to this question is in the National Archives.

Toward the end of September, Oswald, or someone impersonating him, left for Mexico City where he tried to obtain a Cuban visa at the Cuban embassy. Oswald, or his impersonator, was denied a visa and directed to the Soviet embassy where he also struck out. He left Mexico on 2 October, arriving in Dallas on the 3rd. On the 5th, Dallas newspapers confirmed the president's visit as 22 November. The presidential motorcade would wind its way through Dealey Plaza, passing beneath the Texas School Book Depository building where Oswald, after a brief job-hunting expedition, began working on the 16th.

Also in October, Ferrie visited Marcello's Town and Country headquarters, presumably to prepare for Marcello's upcoming trial. During this same month, FBI listening devices picked up a new stream of death threats toward the Kennedys made by mobsters across the country. Joe Bonanno's uncle, Buffalo don Stefano Magaddino, told his brother, Peter, 'They should kill the whole family, the mother and father too.' The father was already halfway there.

On Sunday, 20 October, President Kennedy visited the family compound at Hyannisport, where his paralyzed and mute father sat in a wheelchair on the porch of the main house and watched the president's helicopter, Marine One, land on the sprawling front lawn. Before leaving the next day, Kennedy threw an arm around his dad and kissed his forehead. As President Kennedy was walking toward his awaiting helicopter, he turned back and gazed at his father, then returned to kiss him again. That evening, Dave Powers, who was present for the affectionate farewell, remarked that he had never seen Jack Kennedy act that way before and felt 'as if the President had a feeling that he was seeing his father for the last time'. As Marine One took off, Powers also noted that the president's eyes welled up with tears as he looked down at his father and said, 'He's the one who made all this possible, and look at him now.' Though I would not think that Kennedy's range of thought at that touching moment included what Joe Sr had done for him in the way of mafia help during the campaign, his father did indeed make it all possible, but his invalidity made it impossible to rein in Bobby and follow through on promises made to mobsters who were working, at that moment, to undo the error.

Following White House confirmation that the president would indeed be visiting Dallas in late November, Jack Ruby, who was a well-known associate of the Campisi brothers, 'suddenly felt compelled to phone Mafia pals from all over the country he hadn't been in touch with for years, others he didn't know at all'. Ruby's long-distance telephone records are revealing. In May, June, July, August and September, he averaged approximately thirty calls per month. This steady number of calls suddenly jumped to seventy-five in October, and ninety-six during the first three weeks of November. Why was Ruby making so many more long-distance telephone calls and who was he speaking with? In October and November, Ruby made seven calls to Lewis McWillie, a murderer who was directly connected to Santo Trafficante, the Florida don who had told an FBI informant that Kennedy would be hit. McWillie worked at Trafficante's casinos in Cuba and later as a pit boss at the Cal-Neva Lodge, partly owned by Sam Giancana.

Ruby also placed a call from his Carousel Club in Dallas to Irwin Weiner in Chicago, who was connected to mob-run casinos and the Teamsters Union, and was described by the *Chicago Daily News* as 'the mob's favored front man' and by the *Washington Post* as the 'underworld's major financial figure in the Midwest'. Weiner, a regular recipient of Teamster pension fund loans, would later be indicted along with Paul Dorfman. The main witness against them was shotgunned to death in front of his own family and the case fell apart.

Ruby placed another call to the ex-wife of Russell Matthews in Louisiana. Matthews, who had a long criminal record that included armed robbery and murder, was tight with Ruby, Carlos Marcello,

Santo Trafficante and Joe Campisi. Days later, Ruby called the Sho-Bar, a New Orleans strip club owned and operated by Carlos Marcello's brother, Peter. The call was followed by a trip to the French Quarter, where Ruby visited the Sho-Bar. While in New Orleans, Ruby was seen with Vincent Marcello and Frank Caracci, who *Life* magazine described as a 'Marcello mobster'.

Ruby also spoke with Robert 'Barney' Baker, a Teamster organizer who was jailed for racketeering in 1961 because of Bobby Kennedy, who referred to Baker as Jimmy Hoffa's 'Ambassador of Violence'. Around the same time, Baker made telephone calls to Victor Emanuel Pereira, whose favorite crime partner was Eugene Hale Brading, a man with a rap sheet that included gambling arrests in Miami, Florida, where he worked under Santo Trafficante. In September, Brading changed the name on his California driver's license to Jim Braden and asked his parole officer for permission to visit Dallas during the week of 22 November. Permission was granted.

Ruby also telephoned Teamster official Murray 'Dusty' Miller, who had close ties to both Jimmy Hoffa and Santo Trafficante; and Harold Tannenbaum, a strip show booker who displayed Marcello's slot machines inside strip clubs he co-owned with Marcello. Ruby's communication with Tannenbaum is particularly interesting since Tannenbaum answered directly to one of Marcello's most trusted capos, Nofio Pecora, who was close with Emile Bruneau, the man who had bailed out Oswald from the local jail after the street fight (that may have been staged). Back in early August, Ruby had received a direct call from Nofio Pecora and, on 20 October, Ruby placed a one-minute call to Pecora. Since Pecora was one of the very few men who had the authority to speak with Marcello's tongue, Ruby was practically speaking with Marcello on these two occasions.

On Saturday, 2 November, President Kennedy was scheduled to arrive at Chicago's O'Hare International Airport so he could attend the Army–Air Force football game at Soldier Field. The Wednesday before, while Secret Service agents were preparing for the president's arrival, an informant named 'Lee' tipped the Secret Service about a plot to kill the president in Chicago, to be carried out by 'rightwing para-military fanatics'. According to the informant, four sharpshooters with high-powered rifles and telescopic sights would be staked out along the presidential motorcade route.

The Chicago branch of the Secret Service foiled the plot, found four rifles with telescopic sights inside of a rented apartment, and took two of the four suspects into custody on Friday. Neither of the men was cooperative and both were mysteriously released. For some inexplicable reason, we do not know who they were, and have never been told. What we do know is that, after the president was to be killed in a crossfire from the four men positioned along the motorcade route, an ex-marine and 'disaffiliated member of the John Birch Society', considered a far-right group with a distaste for President Kennedy, was to take the fall; his name was Thomas Arthur Vallee.

Vallee was a wounded Korean War veteran, discharged in 1956. Like Lee Harvey Oswald, he was somehow connected to US intelligence agencies, had once been stationed at a base in Japan, and was involved with Cuban militants. In August 1963, as Oswald was about to move from New Orleans to Dallas where he got a job in a building overlooking the planned presidential motorcade route in Dallas, Vallee left New York for Chicago where he suddenly landed a job as a printer in a tall building overlooking the planned presidential motorcade route in Chicago. The view of the presidential limousine Vallee would have

Thomas Arthur Vallee, who just missed being Lee Harvey Oswald

had from his window was ten times better, and three levels lower, than the view of the passing presidential limousine from the School Book Depository building where Oswald happened to land a job. The motorcade route in Chicago was to make a sharp turn in front of Vallee's building, slowing it down to a crawl for an easier target. Less than three hours before Kennedy had been scheduled to arrive in Chicago, Vallee, the would-be scapegoat, was taken into custody and history has spared his three-word name from eternal ignominy, exchanging it for another.

Carlos Marcello's trial was scheduled to begin on Monday, 4 November. The day before the trial opened, Bobby Kennedy telephoned the chief prosecutor of New Orleans to wish him luck. Given the media buzz and the notoriety of the lead defendant, the courtroom was packed. Sitting among Marcello's support group was David Ferrie,

Marcello's wife and children, his brothers, and the seventy-year-old Louise Marcello, who had cradled the eight-month-old future mob boss in her arms as she walked down the gangplank of the *Liguria*, fifty years earlier.

On the same day Marcello's trial opened, Ron Skelton, a member of the Texas Democratic National Committee, told Bobby Kennedy that he would 'feel better if the president's itinerary did not include Dallas'. Stanley Marcus told Vice President Johnson, 'I sure wish to hell you'd persuade Kennedy not to come. It is a grave mistake to come to Dallas.' These warnings, which were not conveyed to the president, echoed that of Senator J. William Fulbright of Arkansas, who told the president, 'Dallas is a very dangerous place. *I* wouldn't go there. Don't *you* go.' The US ambassador to the United Nations, Adlai Stevenson, had visited Dallas on 24 October. Waiting for him at his hotel was an angry crowd of protestors who rushed past security then spat on him and slammed a sign over his head. Stevenson also warned the president to stay away from Dallas, and Ann Brinkley, wife of newscaster David Brinkley, warned Kenny O'Donnell to keep the president far away from Dallas. Other warnings came from concerned citizens who wrote letters to the White House. Despite all this concern, the trip was not canceled.

On 9 November, William Somerset, who was a police informant in Miami, recorded a conversation he'd had with a racist right-wing extremist, Joseph Milteer, who was a suspect in the 1963 church bombing that claimed the lives of four young Black girls in Birmingham, Alabama. Milteer and Somerset discussed Kennedy's upcoming visit to Florida with its planned presidential motorcade traveling through downtown Tampa on 18 November.

> Somerset: I think Kennedy is coming here on the 18th . . . He will have a thousand bodyguards.
>
> Milteer: The more bodyguards he has, the easier it is to get to him.
>
> Somerset: Well, how in the hell do you figure would be the best way to get him?
>
> Milteer: From an office building with a high-powered rifle.
>
> Somerset: They are really going to try to kill him?
>
> Milteer: Oh yeah, it is in the working . . . They will pick up somebody within hours afterwards . . . Just to throw the public off.

The Miami Police Department relayed Milteer's death threat to the FBI and the Secret Service, who, from 9 November onward, not only knew of a serious plot to kill the president, but exactly how it would be carried out. Incredibly, no action whatsoever was taken to warn the president even though the plot was foiled by Miami police.

The common denominator between right-wing militants like Joseph Milteer, Cuban exiles like Sergio Arcacha Smith and mafia dons like Santo Trafficante and Carlos Marcello was the master of intrigue, David Ferrie, who also worked for the CIA and had connections to the FBI through Guy Banister.

Furthermore, it is rather curious that the three traps laid for President Kennedy in November were in Chicago (a trip canceled for political reasons), Tampa and Dallas, three cities under the complete control of Giancana, Trafficante and Marcello. With Chicago and Tampa now off the table, it had to happen in Dallas, where the city's mayor, Earle Cabell, had been helped into office by the Campisis and just happened to be the brother of the disgraced CIA deputy director, General Charles Cabell, who Kennedy had forced to resign in disgrace after the failed Bay of Pigs invasion. Both Cabells, whose father and grandfather had been mayors of Dallas, felt that Kennedy's inaction during the Bay of Pigs was tantamount to treason.

On the weekend of 9–10 November, Ferrie shacked up with Marcello at his Churchill Farms estate, the place where Marcello had once sworn to cut the head off the dog – Jack Kennedy – to stop the tail – Bobby – from wagging. What were two men – one an 'aggressive homosexual with a penchant for teenagers', the other a traditional family-oriented mob boss who was too ashamed to sleep in the same bed with a woman in Guatemala because he 'didn't have no paja-mas' – doing together in a remote farmhouse for an entire weekend? Supposedly discussing Marcello's trial defense strategy even though it was rather strange that Marcello's well-paid attorneys, who would argue the case before a jury, were not invited, never showed up, and could not be reached by telephone since the isolated dwelling had no outside lines of communication.

On Veterans Day, 11 November, President Kennedy visited Arlington National Cemetery with his two-year-old son, John Jr. The little boy who hugged his father's legs in front of the crowd would return to Arlington in three weeks to tug at the nation's heartstrings. Leaving Arlington, Kennedy commented to Louisiana senator Hale

Boggs (another man whose campaigns were funded by Marcello), 'This is one of the really beautiful places on Earth. I could stay here forever.' Marcello and Ferrie had just spent an entire weekend together, presumably planning to make that happen sooner rather than later.

President Kennedy spent the weekend of 16–17 November in Florida, touring Cape Canaveral, while Marcello and Ferrie, *for the second weekend in a row*, shacked up in Marcello's lodge at Churchill Farms. That same weekend, the Secret Service arrived in Dallas to plan their upcoming security detail in conjunction with the Dallas Police Department.

On 17 November, Jack Ruby continued making mysterious telephone calls to mob-connected hoodlums around the country, some of whom he had not spoken with in decades.

On Monday morning, 18 November, as Marcello and Ferrie emerged from their second straight cloistered weekend together, the president awoke at his family's oceanfront estate in Palm Beach, Florida, boarded Air Force One, and took the short flight to Tampa, the plane landing just before 11:30 a.m. at MacDill Air Force Base which was, incidentally, about six miles from Santo Trafficante's home in Tampa. After Tampa, it was on to Miami, Trafficante's second home and where Joseph Milteer had made the ominous threat Kennedy had not been informed of.

That same day, 62-year-old Forrest Sorrels, who had been with the Secret Service for forty years and was in charge of its detail in Dallas, was instructed by his visiting superior to implement a slight change to the motorcade route: the presidential limousine would now turn right onto Dealey Plaza before making an abrupt left turn, bringing the long automobile to a crawl and placing the president between the Texas School Book Depository building where Oswald worked and a stockade fence at the top of a grassy knoll that peered down onto Dealey Plaza.

On Wednesday, the 20th, police officers spotted a curious gathering of men standing just beyond the stockade fence at the top of the grassy knoll. In itself, this may not have been concerning, but the men were aiming rifles over the fence as though running a mock drill for an ambush. As the cops ran up the hill to confront the men, they piled into a car and sped off. Incredibly, the cops failed to report this incident and only brought it to the attention of the FBI days later. Over the next two days, more suspicious activity was observed in the area of the grassy knoll.

Since the Giancana–Rowan bugging affair, Johnny Roselli had been under close surveillance by the FBI. According to FBI agents who tailed Roselli, they observed him on two occasions meeting with Jack Ruby, who Roselli considered 'one of our boys'. On 20 November, the agents then lost sight of Roselli, or claimed they had lost sight of him. He did not surface again until 27 November, a curious lapse in surveillance that has never been explained.

On 20 November, Bobby celebrated his thirty-eighth birthday. Following a birthday bash at the Justice Department where he proudly hopped onto a desk and boasted about the immense pressure he was putting on organized crime, he was briefed about the status of Marcello's trial in Louisiana which was expected to result in a conviction. Later that evening, Bobby's wife Ethel threw him a party at their sprawling estate, Hickory Hill, in McLean, Virginia, where they toasted the president. Bobby then attended a White House reception with his brother, who was preparing to depart for Texas.

That same day, the 20th, a stripper who worked for Jack Ruby was thrown out of a car on a highway near the town of Eunice, Louisiana. Melba Christine Marcades, whose stage name was Rose Cheramie, had been beaten up and ditched by the men she was traveling with, then grazed by a car while hitchhiking. Cheramie was rescued by Lieutenant Francis Fruge of the Louisiana State Police who took her to the East Louisiana State Hospital in Jackson where doctors could tend to her injuries.

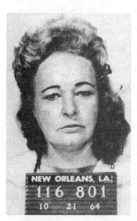

While Fruge was driving Cheramie to the hospital, she told the trooper she had been on her way to Dallas to 'pick up some money, pick up her baby, and to kill Kennedy'. Cheramie went on to tell Fruge that she was accompanying two Italian men who were making a drug run from Miami to Houston. The men told her that, after Houston, they were heading to Dallas to murder the president. She added that Kennedy's imminent assassination was common knowledge in the underworld.

Rose Cheramie, who forewarned police of the president's assassination

Besides Cheramie's physical injuries, she

was experiencing heroin withdrawals, leading Fruge to conclude that her story was a drug-induced fantasy. If we can add some pieces to this puzzle, we already know that Santo Trafficante was a major drug trafficker in Miami, where the men were traveling from. And informants have linked Jack Ruby to drug trafficking between Florida and Texas, where the men were traveling to. Were these men sent to Texas by Trafficante?

On 21 November, President Kennedy flew into San Antonio, Texas. The plane touched down at 1:30 p.m. Kennedy, along with the first lady, was greeted by Vice President Lyndon Johnson who, like his weekly lunch pal, J. Edgar Hoover, was under the dark shadow of Bobby's axe.

Throughout November, Jack and Bobby had talked about forcing Johnson off the ticket before the next election. When Kennedy's secretary, Evelyn Lincoln, asked her boss who his running mate would be in 1964, he replied, 'It will not be Lyndon.' With intent to compromise Johnson so he could get rid of him, Bobby had his Justice Department target Johnson's crooked friends, beginning with Billie Sol Estes, a Texas businessman with ties to organized crime. When a state Agricultural Stabilization and Conservation Service officer began investigating Estes with regard to a multimillion-dollar agricultural scandal that was linked to Johnson, the officer was brutally murdered, gangland style. The death was ruled a suicide without an autopsy, which meant the man somehow managed to shoot himself in

the chest five times with a bolt action rifle. The coroner's report was later corrected, and two decades later Estes linked Johnson to the murder, eventually accusing him of complicity in several other homicides having to do with dirty Texas business deals involving political influence in Washington DC.

Bobby put together a solid case against Estes then offered him his freedom in exchange for testimony against Johnson. 'I didn't take that deal,' Estes told the *Houston Chronicle*. 'I'd have been free for thirty minutes. Then I'd have been dead. There were already some others who had gone that route.'

Billie Sol Estes in hot water. He would accuse Lyndon Johnson of conspiracy to murder

Bobby Kennedy also targeted Johnson's political advisor and favorite influence peddler, Bobby Baker, who Bobby referred to disparagingly as 'Little Lyndon Johnson'. Baker started out as a teenage page in the Senate and became secretary to the Senate Democrats while still in his twenties. According to historian Doris Kearns Goodwin, 'Baker knew as much about the workings of the Senate and the habits of individual Senators as any staffman twice his age' – which made him extremely valuable to then Senate majority leader Johnson, who made Baker his personal secretary, stating that Baker was his 'right arm . . . the last man I see at night, the first one I see in the morning'. This proximity to Johnson made Baker a prime target of Bobby Kennedy who launched an aggressive investigation into Baker that picked up even more speed in early 1963. Baker, a mil-

lionaire who earned less than $20,000 annually, lawyered up with the high-priced attorney Edward Bennett Williams, who was a close friend and longtime counsel to Carlos Marcello. But a mutual attorney was not all Baker had in common with the Louisiana don. Author Richard Mahoney, who was the secretary of state for Arizona, wrote, 'LBJ's ties to Marcello through Bobby Baker . . . went back to the early 1950s. Marcello's Texas "political fixer" Jack

Bobby Baker, who Bobby Kennedy referred to as 'Little Lyndon Johnson'

Halfen reportedly arranged to siphon off a percentage of the mobster's racing wire and slot machine profits for LBJ's Senate campaigns.'

Bobby Kennedy's colleague, Nicholas Katzenbach, said that most people at the Justice Department viewed the attack on Baker 'as an effort on Bobby's part to dump [Johnson] from the ticket in 1964', while future White House press secretary George Reedy said, 'Of course there was no question that Johnson felt they, Bobby Kennedy in particular, used Bobby Baker to get at him.' Johnson confirmed this himself when he bluntly said the president's 'snot-nosed brother's after my ass'.

In October, because of all the legal and political pressure, Baker resigned in disgrace, but his resignation did nothing to slow the probe as nearly every major news source in America took it as proof that there was more to see. A nine-member *Life* magazine investigative team was assigned to the Baker–Johnson story and, by November, *Life* ran a headline: CAPITAL BUZZES OVER STORIES OF MISCONDUCT IN HIGH PLACES. THE BOBBY BAKER BOMB SHELL. *Life* began to expose to its thirty million readers that Johnson, a supposedly humble civil servant on the public payroll, was in fact a 'millionaire'. The investigative team's leader, Associate Editor William Lambert, concluded that Johnson 'looks like a bandit to me', and was convinced that Johnson 'had used public office to enhance his private wealth'.

Since any scandal involving Johnson could easily metastasize into a full-blown Democratic Party disaster, we again see Bobby's recklessness on full display, confirmed by Baker himself, who said, if he'd decided to talk, 'many senators would have found themselves in highly embarrassing circumstances, to say the least'.

On 21 November, as Marcello's two-week trial was starting to wrap up, a light rain fell on the capital as US attorneys from around the country converged on Washington for a two-day conference devoted to the complete destruction of organized crime in America.

That same day, over in Texas, Eugene Hale Brading – who was the crime partner of Victor Pereira, the man who, in early November, had spoken with Barney Baker immediately after Jack Ruby's conversation with Baker – visited the offices of Texas oil tycoon H.L. Hunt, at the same time as Ruby was visiting Hunt's offices. Brading was a hardened criminal with connections to the mafia and right-wing militia groups – very much like David Ferrie – and, as we will recall, mysteriously changed the name on his driver's license before flying from California to Texas.

That evening at around 10 p.m., Ruby enjoyed a late steak dinner with Texas underboss Joe Campisi, then left for the Cabana Motel at around midnight to supposedly meet for drinks with some friends from out of town inside the motel's Bon Vivant Room. Eugene Hale Brading was, when Ruby arrived, staying at the motel. Brading's room was registered under the name of his traveling companion, Morgan Brown, who can be best classified as a functioning lunatic with a firearm. Once, when police tried to arrest Brown for fraud, he beat up the cop, took his gun, then tied him up and was only taken into custody after a shootout with a dozen police officers. Why were Brown

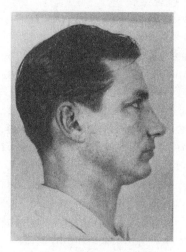

Eugene Hale Brading

and Brading in Texas, and what were they doing with Ruby at the Cabana Motel? There was, moreover, a woman in Ruby's company that evening who had received a telephone call, just two months earlier, from David Ferrie.

Just after midnight on the 22nd, President Kennedy landed in Fort Worth, Texas. By 1 a.m., he and Mrs Kennedy had checked into their suite at the Hotel Texas.

As the president and first lady slept, nine agents of Kennedy's Secret Service detail were in the mood for late-night drinks and headed over to the Fort Worth Press Club, located on the top floor of the nearby Blackstone Hotel. Just after 1 a.m., the club closed for the night, so the agents moved to an after-hours joint that served drinks with the added attraction of strippers who were sent over by Jack Ruby. The place did not have a liquor license but the owner, Pat Kirkwood, was on good terms with officers of the Dallas Police Department, also thanks to Kirkwood's pal, Jack Ruby.

Even when not on duty, Secret Service agents were prohibited from drinking while assigned to the president since they had his life in their hands at all times and could be called for an emergency at any moment. It is part of a stripper's job to encourage patrons to drink – i.e. spend money at the bar – so we can easily imagine the ladies encouraging the agents to drink up, which they did. Three more agents who were working the midnight shift just outside the president's hotel suite got wind of the bash and took turns leaving for Kirkwood's illegal bar. The cellar's manager later said, 'Those guys were bombed.' Some of the bombed agents left at around 3 a.m., while at least one stayed until 5 a.m., all having to report for duty at 8 a.m.

By 10 a.m., President Kennedy spoke at a Chamber of Commerce breakfast held in the Grand Ballroom of the hotel as the first lady readied herself upstairs. As Jacqueline Kennedy sat at her dressing table, Jacqueline Marcello was in New Orleans preparing for her husband's final day in court and bracing herself for the verdict that would decide her and her children's fate. Photographs of Jacqueline Marcello

Jacqueline Marcello accompanies her husband to court

accompanying her husband to and from court show a woman as tastefully dressed and stylish as the first lady, who decided on a pink Chanel skirt suit with matching pillbox hat and white gloves.

At 11:30 a.m., as the president and first lady prepared to depart Fort Worth for Dallas, the president walked over to a window in their suite and mused aloud in the presence of Mrs Kennedy and Ken O'Donnell. 'We're in nut country today,' said Kennedy. 'It would not be a very difficult job to shoot the president of the United States. All you'd have to do is get up in a high building with a high-powered rifle with a telescopic sight, and there's nothing anybody could do.' Kenny O'Donnell said that the president 'often talked about how easy it would be for somebody to shoot at him with a rifle from a high building', even telling his fearful wife, 'If somebody wants to shoot me from a window with a rifle, nobody can stop it, so why worry about it?'

Around the same time Kennedy made this eerie remark, a 23-year-old Dallas housewife, Julia Ann Mercer, was driving west through Dealey Plaza when she had to stop behind a Ford pickup truck that was halted in her lane, blocking traffic. While Mercer waited for the truck to move, she watched a young man exit the passenger side and remove a long paper bag from the truck's tool compartment. Mercer believed that the bag concealed a rifle. The young man carried the package to the top of the grassy knoll, where he disappeared from sight. When Mercer was finally able to merge into an outer lane and drive around the pickup truck, she 'locked eyes with the driver' and would later identify him as Jack Ruby.

Back in Washington, Bobby Kennedy had a busy morning as he began the second day of his two-day conference on organized crime. John Diuguid, who Bobby had previously sent to Guatemala to investigate Marcello's fraudulent birth certificate after J. Edgar Hoover refused to get involved in the affair, was monitoring Marcello's trial on behalf of Bobby. After hearing closing arguments, Diuguid reported back to Bobby that the jury had gone out and he felt confident they would return with a conviction. Bobby hoped to hear the news during the conference so he could make a formal announcement to the attendees and lead them in a hearty cheer. He left word with his secretary, Angie Novello, to interrupt the conference should the jury reach a verdict.

At the same time, Bobby was waiting for word to leak from a closed-door hearing before members of the Senate Rules Committee where a witness against both Bobby Baker and Vice President Johnson began offering incriminating evidence at 10 a.m. The witness provided the committee with actual documents, including checks and invoices, that would incriminate both Baker and Johnson, whose finances were heavily entwined. That same morning, *Life* magazine's investigative team carried on with their work as the story grew 'bigger and bigger' and they considered breaking the abundance of material into a multi-part series titled 'Lyndon Johnson's Money'. The scandal also involved sex, but knowing that President Kennedy could be linked to numerous sex scandals, Bobby Kennedy asked the Senate investigators to omit any sexual allegations from their inquiry.

Just after noon (Washington DC time, which was one hour ahead of Texas time, where it was just after 11 a.m.), the senators were getting such shocking testimony and physical evidence that they decided to forgo the usual lunch break and instead sent out for sandwiches.

At 11:20 a.m. in Texas, the president and first lady took a thirteen-minute flight from Carswell Air Force Base in Fort Worth to Love Field, a public airport six miles northwest of downtown Dallas. A large crowd awaited the president as his plane landed. After seeing the many cheering supporters, one of whom handed the first lady a bouquet of red roses, the president said, 'This trip is turning out to be terrific . . . it looks like everything in Texas is going to be fine for us.'

It had rained that morning and although Air Force One had touched down on a wet tarmac, the skies were bright and sunny. Whether it was the Protestant Wind that battered the Spanish Armada, the heavy rains that muddied the fields of Waterloo, or the thick fog that grounded Allied aircraft over the Ardennes, weather has repeatedly decided the course of human history: the sudden sunshine meant that the bubbletop on the president's midnight blue 1961 Lincoln convertible limousine would be removed.

At 11:55 a.m., the motorcade left Love Field with the president and Mrs Kennedy traveling in a car along with Texas governor, John

Connally, and his wife, Nellie. Dealey Plaza would be the final leg of the motorcade before the limousine drove under a triple underpass and entered Stemmons Freeway for a five-minute drive to the Dallas Trade Mart which was hosting the president's next event.

In Washington, following a lengthy discussion on Sam Giancana and a newly planned attack on Las Vegas, which had become the Chicago mob's bread basket, Bobby's crime conference broke for lunch. Bobby, who was in the habit of bringing colleagues home for lunch, invited New York district attorney Robert Morgenthau and the chief of Morgenthau's Criminal Division, Silvio Mollo, back to Hickory Hill for tuna fish sandwiches and clam chowder soup. Once again, Bobby left word with Angie Novello to interrupt his lunch without delay if Marcello's jury returned with a verdict.

In Dallas, a quarter of a million people jammed the sidewalks to

Presidential motorcade in Dallas

see the president pass. In one of the motorcade's cars, Kenny O'Donnell turned to Dave Powers and said, 'There's certainly nothing wrong with this crowd.' The president was just as thrilled with the size and enthusiasm of the cheering crowd, which would have strengthened the resolve of his sworn enemies who would have viewed the massive turnout as an indication of his popularity.

At 12:29 p.m., the president smiled and waved to his admirers as the limousine followed the mysterious last-minute alteration in the motorcade route, making a sharp turn on to Elm Street, which slowed the vehicle to fewer than ten miles per hour, and placed it between the Texas School Book Depository building and the grassy knoll which was now a stone's throw from the president. Beneath the din of deafening cheers, Texas first lady Nellie Connally said to Kennedy, 'Mr President, you can't say Dallas doesn't love you.' Mrs Connally said that Kennedy's 'eyes met mine and his smile got even wider' before a gunshot was fired, hitting Kennedy in the throat; the president clutched at his neck with both hands as another shot hit Governor Connally, who cried out, 'My God, they are going to kill us all.' A third shot was fired from behind the limousine before another shot, fired from the grassy knoll, took off a chunk of Kennedy's head and blew out a piece of his brain. Kenny O'Donnell, who was in one of the follow-up cars, said, 'We saw pieces of bone and brain tissue and bits of his reddish hair flying through the air.' Dallas police chief Jesse Curry said 'a red sheet of blood and brain tissue exploded backward from Kennedy's head into the face of Officer Hargis', a motorcycle cop who was trailing behind the left rear fender of Kennedy's limousine. Hargis was sure the shot came from the front right side of the limousine; he dropped his motorcycle and took off on foot toward the grassy knoll.

Pieces of President Kennedy's brain and skull, with tufts of hair attached, were splattered across the first lady who screamed, 'I have my husband's brains in my hand.' With a horrified look that defies description, Mrs Kennedy crawled onto the trunk of the car to try to retrieve a stray chunk of her husband's skull as though she might puzzle-piece it back into place.

Most of the Secret Service agents responded, according to Senator Ralph Yarbrough who was riding in another car with Lyndon Johnson, 'very slowly, with no more than a puzzled look'. The exception was Agent Clint Hill, who raced to the limousine and courageously climbed aboard the trunk, placing himself in grave danger as there was still the possibility of more bullets being fired at the car. Hill took one look at the hole in the president's head and saw chunks of brain and skull on the seat and floorboards, then looked back at his fellow agents and flashed them a thumbs-down, conveying that the president was, or would be, dead from his injuries.

In New Orleans, the press was gathered in the courtroom as newspaper editors, certain the Marcello verdict would dominate the news cycle, mulled over various headlines for the next morning. But a very different verdict arrived from Dallas. A bailiff entered the courtroom, briskly walked over to the judge, and handed him a note. As the judge read the message, a 'look of shock and consternation spread over his face'. After the judge recovered from his initial shock, he announced the grim news that President Kennedy had just been shot in Dallas. While courtroom spectators gasped and broke into nervous chatter, Carlos Marcello and his brother Peter remained stone-faced. (History has not provided us with the reaction of David Ferrie, who was also present in the courtroom.)

Back at Hickory Hill, where Bobby Kennedy was enjoying a

poolside lunch with his colleagues, a painter who was working on an extension to his white antebellum house ran toward the men with a transistor radio in hand. As Robert Morgenthau tried to discern what the painter was yelling about, a telephone next to the pool rang and Ethel Kennedy took the call. She told Bobby that J. Edgar Hoover was on the line. Just as the painter's words became clear to Morgenthau, Hoover said to Bobby, 'I have news for you. The President's been shot.'

'What?' said Bobby. 'Is it serious?'

'I think it's serious. I'll call you back when I find out more.'

Bobby clapped a hand over his mouth then yelled, 'Jack's been shot! It might be fatal.' As Bobby hung up the phone, Morgenthau saw

an expression of 'shock and horror' cross his face as Ethel rushed to comfort him. About a half-hour later, Hoover called back and said, 'The President's dead.' 'Not quite as excited,' Bobby would later recall, 'as if he was reporting the fact that he found a communist on the faculty of Howard University.' Bobby told Nicholas Katzenbach that same day, 'I think Hoover enjoyed giving me the news,' and William

Hickory Hill, where Bobby received word that the president was dead

Sullivan later noted 'Hoover's cold-blooded attitude when Kennedy was murdered'.

Allen Dulles took the news as dispassionately as Hoover had conveyed it. Dulles received a telephone call in his study from a former colleague at the CIA. With no expression on his face, he listened to the news then hung up the phone and said to the gentleman in his presence, 'Let's call it a day, shall we . . . The President's been shot in Dallas.'

CIA director John McCone was at Langley when he heard the president had been shot. He telephoned Bobby at Hickory Hill then raced there to be with him. When Bobby saw McCone, he asked him, point-blank, 'Did you kill my brother?' McCone assured Bobby that the CIA had nothing to do with the president's death. But McCone was, in fact, less informed than Bobby when it came to his own agency's intrigues.*

Later in the afternoon, as Bobby nervously paced the grounds of Hickory Hill, he told his press secretary, Ed Guthman, 'I thought they would get one of us . . . I thought it would be me.' The dog's tail had apparently confused itself with the head.

At 12:40 p.m., the television soap opera quite appropriately named *As the World Turns* was interrupted by a CBS News bulletin, reporting that shots had been fired at the president's motorcade.

By 1 p.m., the president was pronounced dead at Parkland Hospital. CBS News anchorman, Walter Cronkite, removed his black horn-rimmed eyeglasses and choked up as he delivered the news to a stunned nation.

In Texas, Lyndon Johnson, who was being investigated by the Senate Rules Committee that very morning, summoned Texas judge Sarah Hughes, whose judicial appointment was proposed by Johnson but initially obstructed by Bobby Kennedy, who felt the mature woman was 'too old for the appointment'. Hughes quickly arrived and swore Johnson in as the nation's new president aboard Air Force One. (Bobby's relentless prosecutions of members of the Civello borgata subsequently petered out inside the courtroom of the Honorable Sarah Hughes.)

Back in Washington, behind the closed doors of a hearing room where a witness presented documented evidence of Lyndon Johnson's complicity in relation to Bobby Baker's many crimes, senators were informed that the president was dead. The astute witness, realizing Johnson was now president, reached across the table to retrieve his documents, saying, 'You won't need those.' But the committee took possession of the evidence, refusing to give it back, not out of any noble pursuit of justice but because they knew that Johnson was now top dog and the evidence should be buried like a bone. The Senate investigation died, as did the upcoming multi-part *Life* magazine articles. *Life*'s editor, James Wagenvoord, said, 'It was going to blow Johnson right out of the water. We had him. He was done . . . Johnson would have been finished and off the 1964 ticket, and would have probably been facing prison time.'

---

* William Harvey said that he and Richard Helms had kept McCone in the dark about the CIA–mafia plot to kill Fidel Castro. 'There was a fairly detailed discussion between myself and Helms,' said Harvey, 'as to whether or not the Director should . . . be briefed . . . We agreed that it was not necessary or advisable.'

Just after 3 p.m., the jury in Marcello's trial informed the judge that they had reached a verdict. Marcello and his brother, Joseph, were acquitted on all counts – it would later surface that they had bribed a juror.

Bobby canceled the afternoon session of his crime conference held at the Justice Department. An underling, Thomas McBride, later recalled, 'About forty of us were at the long round-up meeting on assassination day. [Bobby] never met the section again.' Robert Morgenthau, who was poolside with Bobby when he received the tragic news, said, 'He never mentioned organized crime to me again.' Another Kennedy underling, Ronald Goldfarb, said, 'Every reasonable presumption was that we would continue our work indefinitely. Certainly into President Kennedy's next term. The future was unlimited.' Goldfarb went on to say that, after the assassination, 'Everyone knew it was over. Everyone knew the mafia had won.'

Future attorney general Ramsey Clark said of the Justice Department, 'It was a quiet and sleepy place until January of '61 . . . Then it came *alive.*' Now, it was dead again, and G. Robert Blakey explained why when he said, 'Suddenly, it occurred to me, it all depended on Robert Kennedy. And Robert Kennedy depended on John Kennedy. And the day the assassination went down, all that was over.' Blakey continued, 'After the President's assassination, the steam went out of the organized-crime program. Whatever was intended, the mob proved to be the principal beneficiary of Dallas.' Justice Department attorney William Hundley echoed Blakey's conclusion when he said, 'The minute that bullet hit Jack Kennedy's head, it was all over. Right then. The organized crime program just stopped.' When Hundley was finally able to tell Bobby that Marcello had been acquitted in New Orleans, Bobby just stared at him, blankly, leaving Hundley to wonder if the news had even registered.

Within the space of six seconds in Dallas and as shockwaves were rippling across the globe, Carlos Marcello was no longer going to prison, no longer being deported, and no longer worried about tax liens or undue pressure on his wife and family. In doing what he had to do to protect himself and his family, Marcello had exhibited the epitome of *omertà*. The short, squat mob boss, whom Bobby had vowed to destroy, had destroyed Bobby.

With the president's passing, the emotionally distraught Bobby abandoned his work at the Justice Department. When Walter Sheridan asked him when he planned to return, even pleading, 'We need you,' Bobby responded, 'I know, but I don't have the heart for it right now.' Toward the end of January, Bobby tried to resume his official duties as attorney general, but he was utterly demoralized. He was thinner, his eyes were baggy, likely from crying and loss of sleep, and he was not cutting his hair. His friend Lem Billings said, 'He didn't know where he was.' Nicholas Katzenbach, who would succeed Bobby as attorney general, echoed Billings, saying Bobby 'looked like the ghost of his former self', adding, 'he could not focus on matters beyond his broken heart . . . he was withdrawn, pale, somehow diminished, with none of the energy he had brought to the office'. White House press secretary Pierre Salinger said, 'He was the most shattered man I had ever seen in my life. He was virtually non-functioning.' Author and Kennedy cousin John H. Davis said, 'Bobby was destroyed. He mumbled, walked in circles and, in my opinion, seemed consumed by guilt.' Bobby's friend Dave Hackett said, 'It was as though someone had turned off his switch.' Justice Department attorney G. Robert Blakey said, 'He was a walking zombie.' Bobby's assistant on civil rights cases, William vanden Heuvel, said, 'I never saw anyone so grief-stricken over anything as Bobby was after the assassination. His face was all pain, filled with an anguish that never left him for the rest of his life.'

When Jimmy Hoffa was finally convicted of conspiracy in 1964, Nicholas Katzenbach said that Bobby 'could not bring himself even to celebrate the downfall of his archenemy'. Journalist Murray Kempton said the guilty verdict had zero effect on Bobby. 'I think he lost all interest in Hoffa,' said Kempton. 'I never heard him say anything about Hoffa that really indicated much more than boredom with the subject.' Bobby summed up his own apathy when he said, 'I'm tired of chasing people.'

In contrast, the mob had plenty of reason to celebrate. On the evening of the assassination, Santo Trafficante met for dinner with his attorney, Frank Ragano, telling Ragano, 'The son-of-a-bitch is dead . . . This is like lifting a load of stones off my shoulders . . . Our problems are over . . . Now they'll get off my back, off Carlos's back, and off [Hoffa's] back.' Trafficante raised a glass for a toast. 'For a hundred years of health and to John Kennedy's death.'

Jimmy Hoffa dialed Frank Ragano in Tampa (which was equal to calling Trafficante) and said, exuberantly, 'Have you heard the good news? They killed the sonofabitch. This means Bobby is out as Attorney General. Lyndon will get rid of him.' (Note that Hoffa was on first-name terms with Johnson.) When Hoffa was later asked about the attorney general during a television interview, he said of his arch-nemesis, 'Bobby Kennedy is just another lawyer now.'

J. Edgar Hoover, who had been bullied by Bobby for three long years and was about to be booted from the Bureau and possibly smeared as a homosexual when the shots rang out over Dealey Plaza, must have felt the same way. An attorney with the Organized Crime Section told the *New York Times*, 'Within a month the FBI men in the field wouldn't tell us anything. We started running out of gas.' William Sullivan said that Bobby had continually pestered Hoover for results, 'until President Kennedy was killed and the whole Mafia effort slacked off again'. A Kennedy staffer said of the Bureau's agents, 'Starting at 1:10 on November 22 [minutes after Kennedy was pronounced dead], they began pissing on the attorney general.' The loud buzzer Bobby had installed on Hoover's desk so he could taunt the director with the press of a button was buried in a closet. Hoover was again communicating directly with the Oval Office, just as he had done since Bobby's first teeth had grown in.

Chapter 21

Silenced

Carlos Marcello no longer had Bobby Kennedy to worry about, but he had other immediate problems. Following his acquittal, Marcello's family wanted to celebrate the verdict, but Marcello told them to go ahead and celebrate without him. He then headed straight to his office at the Town and Country Motel, appearing to have 'something urgent on his mind'. David Ferrie seemed just as perturbed as Marcello after the two men heard news reports that Dutz Murret's nephew had been taken into police custody.

After the last shot was fired at the president, Officer Marion Baker of the Dallas Police Department entered the Texas School Book Depository building. On the second floor, Baker crossed paths with Lee Harvey Oswald, who was seated at a lunch table, 'calmly sipping a Coca-Cola'. Oswald's calm demeanor gave Baker no cause for concern, so the officer passed him by. When Oswald finished his soda, he casually left the building. A short while later, Dallas police officer J.D. Tippit was shot dead, presumably by Oswald, though there is eyewitness testimony and conflicting evidence that challenges this allegation. Soon after, Oswald was apprehended inside of a movie theatre. It was only ninety minutes since the assassination, and already someone in Ferrie's inner circle was in police custody. If law enforcement picked up on the scent, they could easily trace Oswald to Marcello, via Ferrie, who was seated with Marcello when the president was killed and had spent two long weekends with Marcello leading up to the assassination.

When Ferrie heard that Oswald had been arrested, he flew into a panic then telephoned the Alamotel in Houston, Texas, which was owned by Carlos Marcello. Ferrie reserved a room for that evening then called the Winterland Skating Rink in Houston to find out the rink's hours of operation. At about 9 p.m., Ferrie, along with two companions, piled into a 1961 blue Comet station wagon and drove 350 miles non-stop, through a thunderstorm, pulling into the motel's parking lot at approximately 4 a.m. on Saturday morning. By then, Oswald had been charged with the murder of police officer J.D. Tippit, and was subsequently charged with the murder of President Kennedy.

Alamotel, where David Ferrie raced to after
Oswald was taken into custody

Ferrie was not the only man who was visibly disturbed by Oswald's arrest. It also threw Jack Ruby into a panic. After the shooting, Ruby raced to Parkland Hospital where the president had been taken. He was seen by Seth Kantor, a reputable Dallas journalist turned White House correspondent. Ruby then left the hospital and drove to his Carousel Club, where he made and received telephone calls throughout the afternoon. According to witnesses, 'Ruby seemed to become progressively agitated by the calls he was receiving.' After his last phone call, Ruby put a revolver in his right front pants pocket and drove to the police station where Oswald was being held. Since Ruby was the mob's police liaison and was friendly with most of the cops on duty, he easily entered the station house.

At approximately 7 p.m., Ruby, who was packing a concealed weapon, was somehow seated just outside room 317 where Oswald was being interrogated by Captain William Fritz, chief of the Dallas Police Department's Homicide Division. News reporter Victor Robertson, who was present, watched Ruby attempt to enter the interrogation room; he was stopped by an officer posted outside the door. For the next several hours, Ruby, an armed mobster with a criminal record who had absolutely no valid reason to be anywhere near the president's alleged assassin, who had no official duties with either press or law enforcement, loitered around the station house, without being questioned, told to leave or escorted outside.*

Having failed to get at Oswald, Ruby eventually left the station house and mimicked the plight of a condemned man; he bid adieu to friends and relatives, some of whom he had not seen or spoken with in years, others he had not been getting along with. He seemed to be a man who wanted to tie up the loose ends of his life before departing this world. He cried, talked about leaving town, and suffered from an upset stomach before heading to Temple Shearith Israel, where the Sabbath service had begun at 8 p.m. Ruby, who had never been an observant Jew, arrived toward the end of the service, at around 10 p.m. Rabbi Hillel Silverman found it strange that, as he conversed with Ruby, the latter never mentioned the assassination.

Oswald in police custody

After services, Ruby went to the Ritz Delicatessen and ordered sandwiches for the cops at the station house. He re-entered police headquarters, delivered the sandwiches, then moved around the station house with the ease of an invisible man. By 11:30 p.m., Chief of Police Jesse Curry announced to the press that they would be given their first look at the president's alleged assassin, Lee Harvey Oswald, in the basement's assembly room. With no press credentials, whether real or fraudulent, Ruby inserted himself into the tight huddle of excited reporters as they hustled down the corridor and into the basement.

---

* Although Oswald was interrogated for a total of twelve hours, no audio, video or steno-graphic recordings were made throughout the interrogation, an extremely odd omission for an investigation into one of the most important and consequential murders in human history. If, as a researcher, I was able to derive any amusement from this unspeakable tragedy, it was from the numerous historians who have bent themselves into pretzels in their attempts to cover up the most obvious investigative errors, including this one. One prominent historian said that the police had no reason to turn on a tape recorder or summon a stenographer because Oswald just shrugged a lot. For twelve hours? And even if this were true, are we not entitled to a record of the questions?

At 12:05 a.m., Oswald was trotted out before the press corps. We can almost feel Ruby's grip tightening around the cold steel of his pocket revolver, but he refrained from drawing the weapon; according to Seth Kantor, who was present, 'Ruby simply could not have gotten off a clean shot at Oswald . . . Oswald was bunched in the midst of detectives and obscured by a herd of photographers nudging and elbowing each other in front of the puny prisoner.'

DA Henry Menasco Wade informed reporters that Oswald was part of the Free Cuba Committee. Almost incredibly, Ruby craned his neck and yelled out, 'The Fair Play for Cuba Committee,' correcting the district attorney and assisting reporters who were scribbling notes. No one present wondered how a mob-connected strip club owner with no official purpose at a press conference was aware of the one-member committee Oswald belonged to, and why he felt it his duty to correct the record. Nor did Wade openly wonder why Ruby was even present.*

Thus far, Ruby had missed his chance to kill Oswald in interrogation room 317, and again in the assembly room. Time was running out, and it showed as Ruby became increasingly unhinged. In the hours since the assassination, Ruby was witnessed vomiting, pacing nervously and searching for God at shul. After a long night of anxiety, Ruby returned home to his apartment at around 6 a.m. Saturday.

Besides Jack Ruby and David Ferrie, another man who had lost his composure following Oswald's arrest was Ferrie's pal, former FBI agent, loyal member of the Minutemen and faithful friend of the Cuban exiles, Guy Banister. While Ruby was stalking Oswald in a police station with an unlicensed gun, and Ferrie was barreling through an overnight thunderstorm on his way to Texas, Banister, whose offices at 544 Camp Street were frequented by Oswald, Ferrie and plenty of militant Cuban exiles, was putting away a few drinks

---

* Henry Wade was a friend of mobsters and Lyndon Johnson. After the 1959 primary that Johnson lost to Kennedy, Johnson thanked Wade for his unfailing help, telling him, 'It is most rewarding for a man in public life to be able to count on friends like you.' According to one defense attorney, Wade had also 'known Ruby on a first-name basis for 10 years', and Ruby told one reporter, 'I am a pretty good friend of Henry Wade's.' As recently as early November, Wade had come under fire when he was attacked by the president of the Dallas Crime Commission, who said, 'We have reason to raise some serious questions relative to gambling and narcotics cases, some of which have not been tried since 1958.' Wade did not respond but once told the Dallas Morning News, 'I don't think there's much organized crime in Dallas. I think the whole idea of the mafia is overrated. I think it's just sort of a romantic thing for reporters to write about.'

inside of a New Orleans bar with a friend of his, Jack Martin. At some point, Banister and Martin got into a heated argument that continued in Banister's office where a frustrated Martin blurted out, 'What are you going to do – kill me like you all did Kennedy?' Banister's secretary, Delphine Roberts, witnessed Martin's outburst then watched in horror as Banister pistol-whipped Martin with a .357 Magnum while warning him to keep his mouth shut. After a trip to Charity Hospital, Martin filed a police report and told a New Orleans assistant district attorney that the president's suspected assassin, Lee Harvey Oswald, was known to pal around with Banister and Ferrie. Martin said that Ferrie was 'a longtime colleague and tutor of Lee Harvey Oswald' and was repeatedly overheard threatening to assassinate the president.

With Martin's tip, the New Orleans Police Department, FBI and Secret Service launched a manhunt for Ferrie, who was now in Texas, staying at a motel owned by Carlos Marcello, while also communicating with Marcello by telephone. According to an FBI report, on Saturday afternoon, 23 November, Ferrie made a collect call to Marcello at his Town and Country Motel in New Orleans. Ferrie then traveled to the Winterland Skating Rink where he used the rink's public telephone to make and receive mysterious phone calls throughout the afternoon.

While Ferrie was in Houston, another strange character had just arrived there, Eugene Hale Brading, the man Ruby was in close proximity to on the day and night of the 21st. After the shots rang out in Dealey Plaza, police scoured the area searching for culprits; they came across the 48-year-old Brading who they believed was acting suspiciously. They took him into custody, leading him out of the Dal-Tex building, which was adjacent to the School Book Depository and offered an even better shot at the president's limousine than the school-book building. Brading was dressed in 'a black leather jacket and black gloves', and although he told police he had run into the Dal-Tex building after the president was shot in search of a public telephone, Deputy C.L. Lewis of the Sheriff's Department said that Brading 'was in building when [president was] assassinated'. After Brading presented the cops with his phony story and pseudonymous driver's license, they mysteriously released him (in 1976, the National Archives admitted that the documents relating to his arrest had somehow gone missing).

After being released from police custody, Brading hopped on a flight and was en route to Houston just as Ferrie was on his way there, too, which returns us to our story and begs the following question: Did Brading, who was obviously connected to Ruby, also know Ferrie? Brading was a frequent visitor to New Orleans, did regular business with men in Marcello's borgata, and rented office space on the same floor of the Pere Marquette building where Ferrie worked on Marcello's case inside the offices of attorney G. Wray Gill. On one parole document, Brading listed his office as 1706 – one door away from where Ferrie worked at 1707.

After Ferrie learned that he was wanted for questioning, he contacted Gill, who in turn reached out to the district attorney's office, assuring them that Ferrie was planning to surrender himself upon his return to New Orleans.

While Ferrie was glued to a public telephone in Houston, Jack Ruby was bouncing around between several public telephones in the Dallas area, also making mysterious phone calls.

Ferrie and his pals left the skating rink, checked out of Marcello's Alamotel in Houston and drove to Galveston, Texas, where they checked into another motel. They arrived in Galveston around the same time as did another Marcello–Trafficante associate, Breck Wall, a nightclub comedian and sketchy character who referred to Jack Ruby as 'a real Chicago thug'. Wall claimed that he had watched the motorcade then went to Galveston 'to stay with some friends'. While there, Ruby telephoned Wall, perhaps while Ferrie was with Wall.

On Sunday morning, 24 November, while mourners across the country filled church pews to listen to sermons about the president, Dallas police and the FBI received strikingly similar warnings from anonymous callers, informing them that Lee Harvey Oswald would be murdered during his transfer from the police station to the county jail. The security measures law enforcement took in response to these threats were about as effective as if they had told Oswald to skateboard over to the jail himself and call them when he got there.

That morning, Jack Ruby sat around his apartment in his underwear while flipping through the Sunday newspaper, watching television and eating scrambled eggs. After he showered, shaved and dressed, his roommate, George Senator, observed a jittery Ruby awaiting an important telephone call. After the call came in at around 9:30 a.m., Senator said that Ruby was overcome by a surge of nervous energy; he began feverishly pacing back and forth across the room, mumbling to himself.*

Also, at around 9:30 a.m., Oswald was led from his cell on the fifth floor of police headquarters to the third floor where Captain Fritz was waiting to question him one last time, though it is hard to believe, if Oswald was as silent as we are told, that anyone saw a reason for it. Yet again, there is no record of the interrogation.

At 10:19 a.m., a stripper nicknamed Little Lynn telephoned Jack Ruby asking him for an advance on her salary. Ruby promised to send her a wire through Western Union. He then dressed in standard mafia uniform – dark suit, fedora, gold cufflinks, pinky ring and a black .38 Colt revolver – and headed out of the door. Just after 11 a.m., Ruby entered Western Union and sent money to Little Lynn, as promised, then went to police headquarters where he walked down an automobile ramp that led into the underground parking garage. As usual, Ruby was unmolested by police. Captain C.E. Talbert had assigned the basement security detail to Sergeant Patrick Dean, the same policeman who was once observed, just six years earlier, happily dining with Texas don Joe Civello, after the latter had returned home from Apalachin where he had attended the infamous mafia conference. Dean was also the same policeman who publicly stated that he and the police 'had no trouble with the Italian families'. Had Dean permitted Ruby into the basement? As one investigator later said, 'You have to suspect the possibility that Dean at a minimum had seen Ruby enter the basement and had failed to do his duty.'

At 11:30 a.m., Dallas County sheriff J.E. Decker was expected to assume custody of Oswald. As bizarre as this might seem, Decker had once appeared before a federal parole board to serve as a character witness for Texas don Joe Civello when Civello had applied for a pardon after serving six years for drug trafficking. To anyone without blinders on, it is clear that Officers Dean and Decker were two of the mafia's inside men.†

---

* The telephone call is widely believed to have been from Jack Ruby's tipster inside the police department, telling Ruby what time Oswald would be leaving police headquarters through the basement parking garage. Although I have not read it anywhere, it seems natural to me to also wonder if Ruby's inside man had told him that Oswald was not as quiet as we have been led to believe, contributing to Ruby's anxiety.

† In 1964, Sgt Patrick Dean was given a polygraph test and failed. The test results, like so much else relating to the Kennedy investigation, mysteriously disappeared. But Dean had enough honesty left in him to admit that he had failed the test when he was interviewed in 1978 by a House Select Committee.

As Ruby waited for the police to emerge with Oswald, he had to know that it was a tough hit with immediate consequences since there was no way to deny guilt or avoid capture. Once resigned to this inevitability, it was a hitman's dream: every eye in the room would be focused on Oswald, allowing Ruby to draw his gun and take aim as dozens of flashbulbs lit up his target who would be handcuffed and bookended by cops with nowhere to run.

Following Oswald's final interrogation at 11:15 a.m., he was escorted from Captain Fritz's office in handcuffs. Chief Jesse Curry was to be present for the transfer but was suddenly distracted; he later said, 'As Capt. Fritz was leaving his office I mentioned that I would go on down to the basement to watch the transfer. As I was walking down the corridor, I was called to take a phone call from Dallas Mayor Cabell in my office . . . I stayed in my office.' Was Mayor Earle Cabell, who hated the Kennedys and whose brother was General Charles Cabell, the disgraced CIA deputy director, luring the incorruptible Curry away from the transfer so he could not innocently interfere with a plan? It is strange that the mayor was not glued to a television set, like millions of Americans, waiting to watch the transfer on live TV. It is strange that Cabell, who was a former police chief, would bother Chief Curry at that precise moment, well aware of Curry's immediate duties.

Oswald was led into an elevator with his right wrist cuffed to Detective J.R. Leavelle's left wrist. At 11:21 a.m., a smirking Oswald stepped off the elevator in the basement as a newsman yelled, 'Here he comes!'

Ruby was standing amidst seventy-seven police officers and fifty or so newsmen (and Breck Wall, who had viewed the motorcade, curiously left for Galveston following the assassination, and was already back in Dallas to witness the transfer in the basement). Ruby, who is believed to have been permitted to enter the garage by Sgt Patrick Dean, was now standing behind Officer Blackie Harrison, who many believe was the mysterious caller who alerted Ruby to the details of the transfer. A retired police captain said of the Dallas police force, 'Man, it was a dangerous place to work in. You never knew which side your boss or partner was on. There was plenty of money floating around.'

Oswald emerged without the most standard protection of a human police shield. He was bookended by only two police officers with no security in front of him, making him as easy to shoot as if he had been brought before a firing squad. A reporter for the London *Daily*

Ruby shoots Oswald

Telegraph who was on the scene wrote, 'If anyone had wanted to silence Oswald the police could not have helped them more.' Ruby wrapped his sausage fingers around his .38 Colt revolver, broke through the crowd like a running back, and lunged forward while extending his right hand to close the distance. 'You son of a bitch,' he blurted while squeezing off a single round that cut into Oswald's abdomen. Oswald cried out like a wounded animal as he clutched at his stomach then slumped to the ground. Police tackled Ruby who yelled, 'Hey, you all know me! I'm Jack Ruby!'

The single bullet that was fired into Oswald damaged his aorta, spleen, kidney, liver, vena cava and a rib before coming to rest in his gut. This was the first mafia hit in history to be broadcast on live television before an audience of over a hundred million people (except Mayor Cabell, who was chitchatting with Chief Curry, though we must wonder if Cabell was mischievously watching the transfer at the same time).

As 300,000 mourners lined the funeral procession route that carried the president's body from the White House to the Capitol Rotunda, bystanders, who were also monitoring news broadcasts with transistor radios, heard that Jack Ruby had shot Lee Harvey Oswald. Regardless of what the future cover-up would purport, the FBI, CIA and Secret Service were initially certain that there was a direct link between Ruby and Oswald. Gerald Behn, head of the Secret Service in Washington, called Forrest Sorrels, head of the Secret Service in Dallas, and said, 'It's a plot.' Sorrels replied, 'Of course.' General Maxwell Taylor, who helped Bobby Kennedy purge the CIA after the failed Bay of Pigs invasion, was convinced that Ruby was out to 'suppress something', which is also what J. Edgar Hoover privately expressed, believing Ruby had committed a typical mob rub-out of a potential informant.

Oswald was taken to Parkland Hospital where the president had been rushed only forty-eight hours earlier. At 1:07 p.m,, he was pronounced dead. Within hours of his murder, it was announced that the case was closed. Ruby's mission was accomplished.

After hearing that the 24-year-old Oswald had been shot, the crowd outside police headquarters erupted in loud applause. But no one was happier than Carlos Marcello, except perhaps David Ferrie, who now felt it safe enough to return to New Orleans and face law enforcement agencies, who were waiting to question him. It was now also safe to face Marcello, who may have otherwise had to relocate Ferrie to an alligator swamp in order to erase the trail that led back to him.

On Monday, 25 November, Ferrie turned himself in and was booked as a fugitive. He was interrogated by the New Orleans Police Department, the Secret Service and the FBI. At the center of their inquiry was how he knew Oswald, how he knew Marcello, and why he so suddenly took off for Texas following the assassination (more accurately, following the news of Oswald's arrest). Under FBI questioning, and memorialized in a report, Ferrie admitted that he had 'been working on a case involving Carlos Marcello' and that he had spent the weekends of 9 and 16 November at 'a farm owned by Carlos Marcello, mapping strategy in connection with Marcello's trial'. He denied knowing Oswald, in contradiction to witness testimony, and later confirmed by a photograph of them together, and said that he had traveled to Houston in search of rest after working tirelessly on Marcello's trial defense. Ferrie's traveling companions refused to answer questions about the trip and 'it was not until an attorney on the payroll of Carlos Marcello showed up to represent Ferrie's friends that they agreed to respond to questioning', which, in terms of value, amounted to more silence.*

In a bizarre twist that underscores the Shakespearean notion of being hoisted by one's own petard, Marcello and Ferrie's perfect alibi as to why they were isolated together in the bayou for two straight weekends leading up to the president's assassination was provided by Bobby Kennedy. Had Bobby not deported Marcello on the basis of a

---

* Recall that David Ferrie was in Houston as Eugene Hale Brading arrived there from Dallas. Ferrie had now returned to Louisiana, to where Brading had curiously traveled after his trip to Houston and before he flew back to California, where the California attorney general referred to him as 'a real bad guy' with 'Mafia connections'.

forged birth certificate he knew to be phony, then tried to cover his tracks by indicting Marcello afterward, the case that brought Marcello and Ferrie together would never have happened.

When questioned about the specifics of his trip to Texas, Ferrie claimed to have spent Saturday afternoon skating around a rink while taking some time to inquire with the rink's owner, Chuck Rolland, about operating a rink of his own in New Orleans. When Rolland was questioned by FBI agents who wished to verify Ferrie's story, Rolland told them that Ferrie was lying and that Ferrie had spent the afternoon making and receiving telephone calls from the rink's public phone. Ferrie's blatant lie warranted further investigation, yet he was oddly cleared of any wrongdoing and released. J. Edgar Hoover had already cracked the case, so there was no need to look any further.

Chapter 22

The Exhaustive Report

From the moment Lee Harvey Oswald was charged with the president's murder, J. Edgar Hoover set out to prove that Oswald was a man 'in the category of a nut' who had acted alone. Just one day after the assassination, the cover-up that continues to this day began to take shape when Hoover, together with President Johnson, told Captain William Fritz of the Dallas Police Department to quell any rumors of a conspiracy. Given the Dallas Police Department's relationship with Joe Civello, Joe Campisi and Jack Ruby, who inexplicably roamed around police headquarters on Friday evening and strolled past security on Sunday morning, they were happy to oblige.

On 24 November, less than three hours after Oswald was killed, Hoover told Walter Jenkins, a top aide to President Johnson, 'The thing I am most concerned about . . . is having something issued so we can convince the public that Oswald is the real assassin.' (Note that Hoover did not say 'lone' assassin, but 'real' assassin.)

On 26 November, Hoover told his assistant FBI director, Alan Belmont, to bury any talk of a conspiracy along with Oswald's body. Belmont would later say that Hoover sent FBI supervisors to Dallas 'to set out the evidence showing that Oswald is responsible for the shooting that killed the President . . . that Oswald was an avowed Marxist, a former defector to the Soviet Union and an active member of the FPCC [Fair Play for Cuba Committee], which has been financed by Castro'.

Hoover began to leak his version of events to the press which dutifully, if perhaps unwittingly, reported every bit of it. Hoover also told the deputy attorney general, Nicholas Katzenbach, who stepped in for a vegetative Bobby Kennedy, to silence any talk of conspiracy. Katzenbach obeyed, sending a memo to President Johnson's assistant, Bill Moyers, on the 25th that read, 'The public must be satisfied that Oswald was the assassin; that he did not have confederates who are still at large; and that the evidence was such that he would have been convicted at trial . . . Speculation about Oswald's motivation ought to be cut off.' And it was, beginning the greatest cover-up of all time which is ongoing today, more than sixty years later. Luckily, we have a record of news broadcasters who reported the event in Dealey Plaza as it unfolded. With a billboard behind him that read 'Was There a Second Sniper?' anchorman Walter Cronkite reported on a national news broadcast, 'Parkland Hospital doctors were quoted as saying they thought at least one bullet entered Mr. Kennedy's neck from the front.' Journalist Dan Rather also reported that there was an entry wound to the president's neck, based on the initial examination performed by Dallas doctors at Parkland Hospital, one stating at a press conference that 'there was an entrance wound below [the president's] adam's apple', meaning Kennedy was shot from the front. On 23 November, the early edition of the *Dallas Morning News* reported 'a single shot through the right temple took the life of the 46-year-old Chief Executive', and the *Dallas Times Herald* wrote that a 'witness . . . explained the President did not slump forward as he would have after being shot from the rear'. The Zapruder film, a twenty-six-second home movie recorded by bystander Abraham Zapruder, confirmed what this witness saw but the film was hidden from public view after it was purchased by Henry Luce, owner of *Life* magazine, for $150,000. Luce, who was friends with the Dulles brothers, did not purchase the film to enlighten the public as we might expect from a reputable news organization, but to bury it in a bin, hoping the public would never see it. Dan Rather was the only news reporter to view the Zapruder film on the day it was recorded, yet he reported that Kennedy's head 'could be seen to move violently forward' as opposed to violently backward, which is obvious to anyone who has seen the film.

While this cover-up took shape in the highest corridors of power, honest members of the law enforcement community, who were not yet clued in, were hard at work on the ground. Following the assassination, a rattled and remorseful Lieutenant Francis Fruge of the Louisiana State Police returned to the hospital in Jackson to look for Rose Cheramie, the woman who had been slapped around and thrown out of an automobile before telling Fruge that the men she was traveling with would murder the president in Dallas. (After Kennedy's brain was blown out of its shell, it became quite apparent that the men had treated Cheramie rather gently.) At the hospital, Fruge learned that Cheramie had repeated the same warning to Doctors Bowers and Weiss. After Fruge spoke with these doctors, he took Cheramie into custody and contacted Captain William Fritz, who already had his marching orders from Washington. Fritz told Fruge he 'wasn't interested'.

Once the president was pronounced dead, FBI agents from the Miami field office were suddenly interested in the September 1962 report made by José Aleman. On the morning of 23 November, agents showed up at Aleman's door, digging deeper into the ominous remarks that were made to him by Santo Trafficante. Aleman was cooperative and rehashed the conversation, hoping it would provide a crucial lead in the investigation. But, once again, no one followed up on it. Aleman later told the *Washington Post* that he had reported Trafficante's boast to the FBI *before* Kennedy was shot, and at least twice afterwards. The *Post* reporter contacted the FBI agents involved, neither of whom denied or confirmed Aleman's allegation. One of the agents bluntly told the reporter, 'I wouldn't want to do anything to embarrass the FBI.'

Assuming Hoover was not already aware of Eugene De Laparra's tip to the FBI that Marcello's underling, Ben Tregle, had said, '[There is] a price on the President's head ... Somebody will get Kennedy when he comes down South,' by 28 November the report was sitting on Hoover's desk. De Laparra added that it was Marcello's brother, Anthony, who had informed Tregle of the open contract Carlos Marcello had put on the president's head. Hoover ignored the report, just as he had disregarded the many transcripts of mobsters who were overheard threatening the president's life *before* the assassination.

On 29 November, President Johnson signed an executive order that created what would become known as the Warren Commission, named after its chair, Chief Justice Earl Warren of the United States Supreme Court, the same justice who had administered Kennedy's oath of office on inauguration day. Johnson formed the commission to keep the investigation away from others, like the Texas police and Congress, where he feared a congressional inquiry would be difficult to control. 'You take care of the House of Representatives for me,' Johnson told Speaker of the House, John McCormick.

'How am I going to take care of them?' asked McCormick.

'Just keep them from investigating!'

Former CIA director Allen Dulles, who had approved the CIA's recruitment of Johnny Roselli, Santo Trafficante and Sam Giancana, and was forced to resign in shame after the Bay of Pigs disaster which Dulles blamed on Kennedy, volunteered to join the Warren Commission and was, quite astonishingly, given a leading role. A former marine who worked for Dulles said that he 'lobbied hard for the job', while CIA historian Tim Weiner called Dulles a 'duplicitous man . . . not above misleading Congress or his colleagues or even his commander in chief'. The appointment afforded Dulles the opportunity to dupe all three, plus the American people, as he worked to obstruct justice and hide the CIA's involvement with the mafia when attempting to kill Castro and, the evidence suggests, while helping to kill Kennedy. Warren would later say, 'I don't think Allen Dulles ever missed a meeting.'

Future president Gerald Ford, who has been described by numerous sources as the CIA's reliable friend in Congress, was appointed to the commission. Hoover also had faith in Ford to 'look after FBI interests', and William Sullivan, the third ranking member of the FBI, referred to Ford as 'our man, our informant, on the Warren Commission'. While Dulles would steer the investigation away from any clues that led back to the CIA, and Ford would keep the FBI in the clear, Louisiana congressman Hale Boggs, whose district included New Orleans and who had received an unending stream of campaign contributions from Carlos Marcello for many years, according to Special Agent Aaron Kohn, was also appointed to the Warren Commission. President Johnson and Congressman Boggs, each having received political funding from Marcello in their respective states

The Warren Commission with former CIA director Allen Dulles (far left), Louisiana representative Hale Boggs (second from left) and representative Gerald Ford (far right)

of Texas and Louisiana, had zero interest in pursuing any trail that led to Marcello, knowing that a forensic accounting of Marcello's finances could easily lead to them. In a word, the CIA, FBI and the mafia each had a trusted representative on the Warren Commission.

Since the FBI was the Warren Commission's investigative arm, Hoover ultimately decided what evidence the commission would and would not see. His power to withhold, suppress or destroy evidence allowed him to manipulate the final verdict which he had rendered within twenty-four hours of the assassination. In case anyone on the Warren Commission caused Hoover a problem and needed to be compromised, he had Clyde Tolson prepare secret files or 'derogatory dossiers' on members of the commission.

Why Hoover would not want a proper investigation has been the subject of intense debate. FBI assistant director William Sullivan later testified that Hoover feared a thorough investigation 'would discover important and relevant facts that we in the FBI had not discovered'. This was a gross understatement when, in fact, there was a mountain of evidence Hoover intentionally ignored prior to the assassination. A proper investigation would have revealed the steady flow of mafia death threats – most of which were overheard illegally through Hoover's black bag jobs – that crossed Hoover's desk in 1962 and 1963, all of which he failed to pass on to the attorney general, the president or the Secret Service, which was required by law. Although we all know that no criminal charges would have been brought against the FBI director, there would have been a public outcry for his removal or resignation. Just about everyone in Washington was aware that the Kennedys wanted to retire Hoover at the start of Jack's second term; how long would it have taken before someone suggested that Hoover ignored the threats for want of them to succeed?

Hoover had more to hide than just threats. Lee Harvey Oswald's connection to David Ferrie, and Ferrie's connection to Carlos Marcello, would have been extremely uncomfortable for Hoover, who, until recently, was on record denying the existence of a national crime syndicate. First, Hoover was faced with Apalachin, then Joe Valachi, now he would have to explain to the American people how the mafia was somehow connected to the president's assassination. Hoover would have been doomed, once again accused of chasing communists while allowing the mafia to run wild. As luck would have it, he now had communists to blame for the president's death. Oswald's Soviet defection and Marxist background, whether genuine or contrived, allowed Hoover to boast that the communist threat was real while mafia concerns were overblown. Whether by chance or design, everything fit perfectly into Hoover's world view.

Then there was Guy Banister. How would Hoover explain Ferrie's close relationship to a retired twenty-year veteran of the FBI without calling the entire Bureau into question? Oswald and Ruby also had connections to the FBI. There is plenty of evidence that both men were federal informants. Of course, Hoover denied that Oswald had been an FBI informant, but a total of ten FBI agents had some form of contact with him prior to the assassination. Two days after the assassination, Agent James Hosty took a note pertaining to Oswald, which was written before the assassination, and flushed it down a toilet after being advised by his superior, Agent Gordon Shanklin, to get rid of it. The notes taken by Agent John Lester Quigley, who met Oswald in a New Orleans jail, were also destroyed. Aside from FBI files on Oswald, there were also files on him inside the State Department and the Office of Naval Intelligence, none of which have seen the light of day.

As for Ruby's connection to the FBI, the Bureau opened him as an informant in 1959 on account of his 'knowledge of the criminal element in Dallas'. Special Agent Charles Flynn met with Ruby on eight separate occasions but shut him down as an informant after concluding that his information was unhelpful. Was Ruby truly unhelpful, or perhaps misinforming Flynn while acting as a double agent for the mafia? Or was Ruby's information *too* helpful to an agency with its head in the sand? None of these questions are beyond the realm of possibility.

By 26 November, less than one week since the president had been killed, at least a hundred tips had poured into FBI field offices linking Oswald to Ruby. Patrons, strippers and employees of Ruby's Carousel Club said that Oswald and Ferrie had both frequented the club prior to the assassination. One stripper said that Ruby had introduced Oswald to her as 'Lee Oswald of the CIA'. The same woman said that Ferrie was at the club so often that she thought he was the assistant manager. Raymond Cummings told investigators that he drove Ferrie and Oswald to Ruby's Carousel Club in early 1963, and Dallas police chief Jesse Curry later wrote: 'Witnesses to the shooting [of Oswald] wondered if there wasn't a gleam of recognition in Oswald's eye when Ruby stepped out from the newsmen.'

Surely, Hoover knew of Ruby's extensive connections to organized crime, the reason the Bureau had enlisted him as an informant. Aside from Ruby's links to Joe Civello, Joe Campisi, Carlos Marcello and

Santo Trafficante, let us not forget that Ruby was observed by FBI agents on two separate occasions as he met with Johnny Roselli in a Miami motel.

Lastly, Hoover had a good idea that Oswald was a patsy and that others had created a trail of artificial evidence that pointed to him as the assassin. In a memo dated 3 June 1960, over three years *before* the assassination, Hoover warned the State Department that 'there is a possibility that an imposter is using Oswald's birth certificate'. Within a day of the assassination, Hoover sent a top-secret memorandum to Secret Service chief James Rowley, regarding Oswald's alleged trip to Mexico City: 'The Central Intelligence Agency advised that on October 1, 1963, an extremely sensitive source had reported that an individual identified himself as Lee Oswald, who contacted the Soviet Embassy in Mexico City . . . Special Agents of this Bureau, who have conversed with Oswald in Dallas, Texas, have observed photographs and have listened to a recording of his voice. These Special Agents are of the opinion that the above-referred-to individual was not Lee Harvey Oswald.' Hoover also told President Johnson, 'We have up here the tape and the photograph of the man who was at the Soviet Embassy using Oswald's name. That picture and the tape do not correspond to this man's voice, nor to his appearance. In other words, it appears that there is a second person who was at the Soviet Embassy down there.'

Why would anyone be impersonating Oswald while trying to obtain a Cuban visa? After President Kennedy promised Nikita Khrushchev that he would never invade Cuba or support an invasion of the island, bitter exiles and rabid anti-communists across the country became Kennedy's sworn enemies. It seems that, whoever set up Oswald, wanted it to look like he was planning to escape to Cuba after the assassination, just as he was killed, possibly by Officer J.D. Tippit, who would have been hailed as a national hero for having snuffed out the president's assassin when Oswald 'resisted arrest'. Or perhaps it was Ruby's job to dispose of Oswald in a way in which his body was never found, and it would look as though he had fled to Cuba. If Castro appeared to be harboring the fugitive assassin, the American public would demand an invasion of the island, the exiles would get their homeland back, the CIA would halt the spread of communism in the Western Hemisphere, and the mob would get back their billion-dollar-a-year Havana casinos. Everyone would be

happy, thanks to the master intriguer, David Ferrie. Unfortunately for
the conspirators, Oswald was taken into custody, monkey-wrenching
the plan. Now that Oswald was dead and Hoover had labeled him
a 'lone nut', President Johnson was able to wiggle free of a dreaded
replay of the 1962 missile crisis when two superpowers sat on the
brink of nuclear war. Shortly after the assassination, Khrushchev
said that Johnson assured him 'he would keep Kennedy's promise
not to invade Cuba'. Unlike anti-communists and Cuban exiles who
were distraught over Johnson's failure to invade the island, Carlos
Marcello's primary goal was to knock out Bobby Kennedy, which succeeded. Marcello may have been the only conspirator who got exactly
what he wanted out of the plot. After Bobby's departure from the
Justice Department – in spirit, immediately after the assassination,
and officially on 1 August 1964 – Marcello's Gulf Coast empire was
again running at full steam, revving up to an estimated gross annual
income of well over a billion dollars according to the *Saturday Evening
Post*.

To further bolster the argument that the plot was intended to result
in an invasion of Cuba, after being arrested Jack Ruby commented
to Dallas police officers that the United States would now invade the
island – an astute geopolitical prediction for the owner of a topless bar
– and his only concern was whether Oswald was dead or not. When
Ruby was told that Oswald had indeed died, which meant that he
would now face the electric chair as opposed to an attempted murder
charge that could allow him to walk free in a few years, Ruby smiled
and seemed like a load had been lifted off his shoulders. Newsman Vic
Robertson, who observed Ruby in the station house, said he 'appeared
to be anything but under stress or strain. He seemed happy, jovial, was
joking and laughing.' Why was Ruby so happy? According to mafia
rules, if you blow a hit, you die. As noted earlier, it seems Ruby's job
was to get rid of Oswald, maybe with the help of dirty officers inside
the Dallas Police Department, which meant he initially blew the hit
and his own life was, as a result, jeopardized. He was now off the
hook as far as the mob was concerned, which was good reason to joke
and laugh, rather than vomiting all over the place as he was doing
before the hit. As for the law, it was better to be charged with the
murder of the president's assassin, which was already earning Ruby an
outpouring of public sympathy and would perhaps lead to an acquittal in court, than be charged, if Oswald talked, with a conspiracy to

Jack Ruby in custody

Ruby's revolver

assassinate the president. Ruby was smart enough to figure out on his own what two notable law professors had proven when they polled two hundred Dallas citizens and learned that an overwhelming majority felt that Ruby deserved no more than a light sentence for killing Oswald. A tough guy like Ruby could do that standing on his head.

On 27 November, a Dallas grand jury indicted Jack Ruby for the murder of Lee Harvey Oswald. The case would be prosecuted by DA Henry Wade, who knew Ruby well and had been corrected by him in the basement assembly room. Wade, who had been privy to the Zapruder film on the day of the assassination, had initially believed that the president's death was the result of a conspiracy, then he suddenly changed his mind, meekly forfeited his jurisdictional authority to investigate the assassination and persuaded Chief Jesse Curry to hand over all the evidence to the FBI.

On 30 November, Texas underboss Joe Campisi, a man who golfed with Carlos Marcello, frequented the racetrack with Marcello's brothers and sent Marcello 260 pounds of Italian sausage every Christmas, visited Ruby in jail for ten minutes. When later questioned about this visit, Campisi said he had gone to see Ruby in response to a telephone call he had received from Sheriff Decker, 'a one-eyed, chain-smoking ex-bootlegger turned sheriff', who had once acted as a character witness for Don Joe Civello. Decker was also the same sheriff who had placed Sgt Patrick Dean in charge of the basement security detail before Dean presumably allowed Ruby into the underground garage. When later questioned by law enforcement, Campisi admitted to dining with Ruby at the Egyptian Restaurant on the evening before the president's death. What did Ruby, the murderer of the president's assassin, discuss with the Texas underboss as they sat across from one another, chewing steak? What did they talk about during the prison visit? The world may continue to wonder but Hoover did not care to know. Nor did Hoover care that Don Joe Civello admitted to knowing Ruby 'for about ten years'.

When questioned by Dallas police, Ruby said that he killed Oswald to save Jacqueline Kennedy the anguish of having to endure a trial, and to prove that Jews had guts.

As for the Jacqueline part, while discussing his case with defense attorney Joe Tonahill, Ruby, who thought that the prison visiting room was bugged, asked for a legal pad on which he wrote: 'Joe, you should know this. Tom Howard told me to say that I shot Oswald so that Caroline and Mrs. Kennedy wouldn't have to come to Dallas to testify. OK?' Tom Howard, who was Ruby's first attorney, represented mobsters, was a close friend of Joe Campisi, and had a conviction of his own for income tax evasion. It is likely that Howard was retained by Campisi since Ruby was in steep financial debt at the time. Another attorney who would be brought on to the case said that Ruby's 'story of trying to protect Mrs. Kennedy from a harrowing court appearance at a trial for Oswald did not add up . . . I am sure the story was false because it didn't square with everything else we knew.' Even though Ruby insisted he loved the president enough to shoot his alleged assassin, during brief moments of candor he would drop the patriotic façade and say, 'It's strange that perhaps I didn't vote for President Kennedy, or didn't vote at all, that I should build up such a great affection for him.'

As for the bit about Jews having guts, Ruby was reacting to horrid Holocaust reels of naked and emaciated Jews being led to the slaughter as if they were the stuff of some cowardly race. Most people fail to consider that they were unarmed, being pushed around by machine guns, with their sons and daughters, mothers and fathers held hostage before their eyes. On New York's Lower East Side or in Chicago's West Side ghetto, where Meyer Lansky, Ben Siegel, Lepke Buchalter or Jack Ruby could pick up a gun, their matzah balls grew to the size of watermelons. Had Hitler visited Manhattan in the 1930s, there may not have been a world war or a Holocaust, just a page six headline that read: Mustachioed Male Found Cut in Half and Rotting in a Barrel Beneath the South Street Wharf.

At some point, the local Texas attorney, Tom Howard, was relieved by the more prominent California attorney, Melvin Belli. How did Ruby, who was broke and in debt with the IRS, afford a lawyer whose clientele included A-list celebrities and top mobsters? Belli claimed he represented Ruby *pro bono* with the hope of a future book deal; the truth is less charitable. Seymour Ellison, who worked with Belli, received a telephone call from a friend who said, 'Sy, one of our guys just bumped off the son of a bitch that gunned down the President . . . There's a million bucks net for Mel if he'll take it.' Mel took it. Who would put up a million dollars for Jack Ruby? Marcello and Trafficante come to mind.

While preparing for trial, Ruby expressed concern to his attorney that he could be linked to Marcello and Trafficante. The many links to Marcello have already been established. As for Trafficante, on 26 November, just two days after Ruby shot Oswald, British journalist and Oxford University graduate John Wilson informed the American embassy in London that in 1959, while he was being detained in Cuba's Triscornia Detention Camp along with Trafficante, 'Santo was visited frequently by an American gangster type named Ruby.' Wilson naively believed that his revelation would be welcomed and that he might contribute to one of the biggest investigations of all time. After all, a grieving British public took the news of the president's death as hard as the American public, with hordes of people riding buses and trains to the American embassy in Grosvenor Square, once occupied by the Kennedy family, to express their sympathy and show their support. Naturally, the Brits were eager to pass on this information, so London cabled the news to the US State Department. But the reaction was quite different from the one Wilson expected. Within days, the CIA labeled Wilson a 'psychopath' and invalidated his allegation without looking into it. It was left to another British journalist, Anthony Summers, to at least confirm with Triscornia's superintendent that Wilson was indeed detained at the same time and in the same holding area as Trafficante. It has since been established that Ruby visited Cuba on at least two occasions, though probably more. Besides running guns to the island, there is evidence to suggest that he may have been sent with bribe money to bail out mobsters, like Trafficante, who were being held in Castro's jails, and Johnny Roselli once said, 'Ruby was hooked up with Trafficante in the rackets in Havana.'

On 3 December, three days before the Warren Commission held its first executive session, United Press International, acting on a leak from the FBI, ran the following story: 'An exhaustive FBI report . . . will indicate that Lee Harvey Oswald was the lone and unaided assassin of President Kennedy, Government sources said today.' The FBI's so-called 'exhaustive report' was so lacking and misleading that it has exhausted conspiracy theorists for the past sixty years. The Bureau concluded that Oswald was a 'lone nut', a theory effectively destroyed when Ruby murdered Oswald since no one would need to silence a lone nut. Hoover then doubled down and painted Ruby as a second 'lone nut'. Had someone shot Ruby, the shooter may have been labeled a third 'lone nut', and so on as the lone nuts piled up in the Dallas morgue like Monty Python's seduced milkmen.

The Warren Commission would not dare deviate from Hoover's report, so they went through the motions which included a trip to Dallas to visit Jack Ruby who begged to speak with them. Ruby, however, did not feel safe in Dallas where men like Sheriff Decker were close with men like Joe Campisi. When Earl Warren and a small retinue of commission members met with Ruby in jail, Ruby asked Sheriff Decker to leave the room before he pleaded with Warren to bring him to Washington. 'I want to tell you the truth,' Ruby said to Warren, 'and I can't tell it here . . . I have been used for a purpose.' Incredibly, the highest judge in the land and the head of the Warren Commission was utterly uninterested in Ruby's 'purpose' and did not think to ask Ruby, even out of simple curiosity, who had used him and to serve what purpose.

At one point, Ruby asked, 'Is there any way to get me to Washington?' 'I beg your pardon?' said Warren.

'Is there any way of you getting me to Washington?'

'I don't know of any,' answered Warren, who turned down Ruby's offer to spill his guts in Washington eight consecutive times and defended his inaction by later insinuating that Ruby was just looking for a free trip and he was not going to pay for it. I am sure the American taxpayers would have happily paid for the trip. During the Berlin airlift, 2.3 million tons of food, fuel and supplies were flown into West Berlin by way of 189,000 flights – yet Warren refused to transport a 175-pound knish from Dallas to Washington in economy class.

By 15 December, not quite a month since the president's death, a dozen or so known members of organized crime who were directly connected to Carlos Marcello were questioned by the FBI, including Marcello's brothers, Anthony and Vincent, capos Nofio Pecora and Joe Poretto, soldiers Frank Caracci and Nick Graffagnini, associates Ben Tregle, Eugene De Laparra, Harold Tannenbaum, and the executive branch of Marcello's Texas franchise, Joe Civello and Joe Campisi, not to mention the master of intrigue, David Ferrie, who was with Marcello during the assassination and the weeks leading up to it. With nearly everyone around Marcello under a cloud of suspicion, Marcello must have felt a noose tightening around his neck. But any concerns quickly evaporated as the government's cover-up unfolded before his eyes. Had Marcello gotten lucky? Or had he shrewdly anticipated that the CIA and FBI's own dirty deeds would result in an investigative paralysis?

On 24 September 1964, after a mere ten months of receiving carefully handpicked 'evidence' from Hoover, the Warren Commission delivered its 888-page report to President Johnson, who was not known 'to look for more than a minute or two at any printed matter less timely than a news magazine'. The report was released to the public on the 27th. The American people immediately showed their distrust in its findings by flooding CBS News with 'thousands of letters asking the network to further investigate the suspect claim that Oswald had acted alone'. Most Americans believed that a conspiracy had been covered up and, although the more vocal Americans would be attacked as conspiracy theorists, it is interesting to note that the first conspiracy theorists were the Texas governor, John Connally, and First Lady Jacqueline Kennedy. When the bullets were fired into the presidential limousine, one hitting Governor Connally, he yelled, 'Oh no, oh my God, *they* are going to kill us all.' After President Kennedy was shot, the first lady cried, 'My God, what are *they* doing? My God, *they've* killed Jack, *they've* killed my husband.' Later, while Johnson was being sworn in aboard Air Force One, it was suggested that Jacqueline Kennedy change her suit which was 'caked with blood' so she could be present for the brief ceremony that would be photographed. Jacqueline said, 'No. Let *them* see what *they've* done.' When Lee Harvey Oswald was shot by Jack Ruby, Earl Warren was in his study preparing a speech for the ceremony inside the Capitol Rotunda where Kennedy's body lay in state. Warren's daughter, Dorothy, ran into his study and said, 'Daddy, *they* just killed Oswald.' Warren brushed her off, telling her not to pay heed to rumors. 'But Daddy,' Dorothy continued, 'I saw *them* do it.' Although some people may tend to say *they* and *them* when confused and traumatized, Governor Connally and Mrs Kennedy continued to believe in a conspiracy.

The next group of conspiracy theorists were *actual members of the Warren Commission* who were convinced that there had been at least one other shooter besides Oswald, while some wondered if Oswald had even fired a shot. The commission ignored the vast majority of witnesses who insisted that shots came from the grassy knoll, as well as the many witnesses who said that they saw snipers standing in other windows on other floors in the Texas School Book Depository building.

Then there was the ridiculous 'single-bullet theory' which defied the laws of physics and bothered certain members of the Warren Commission. Given the abundance of evidence that more shots were fired at Kennedy's limousine in too short a time than Oswald, using a bolt-action rifle, could have squeezed off by himself, and that two shots were almost simultaneous, meaning there was at least one additional shooter in Dealey Plaza, the commission explained this away by claiming that the bullet that struck Governor Connally had first traveled through Kennedy who was seated directly behind Connally. This 'magic bullet', fired from a sixth-floor window, supposedly entered Kennedy's back, turned upward and exited through his throat, then turned downward and entered Governor Connally's back, bore through his torso, nicked two ribs, exited his chest cavity, then hit his wrist bone and settled in his thigh, with the bullet later appearing on a gurney at Parkland Hospital as if it had just been purchased from a local gun store, neither smashed nor distorted, and without any traces of either victim's blood, bone or tissue.

In a television interview with Dan Rather, Governor Connally said of the single-bullet theory, 'To me, it's just inconceivable that the first shot that went through his throat, his neck, entered my back. I don't believe that. I never will believe that. They can't run enough tests to make me believe that.' Senator John Cooper, who sat on the Warren Commission, later said, 'I heard Governor Connally testify very strongly that he was not struck by the same bullet, and I could not convince myself that the same bullet struck both of them.' To be sure, without this single-bullet theory, the Warren Commission's final conclusion that Oswald had acted alone falls apart, making the commission's report one of the lengthiest works of fiction ever written, surpassing *War and Peace*, which is probably more factual.

The *National Review* reported that panel member Senator Richard Russell of Georgia was 'disgusted by the conduct of the investigation'.

Russell believed that a conspiracy was being covered up, saying of Oswald, 'I think someone else worked with him.' Russell had serious 'doubt that [Oswald] planned it all by himself'. The senator refused to sign off on the Warren Commission's final verdict, asking Earl Warren to consider him in dissent. Warren, in turn, refused to acknowledge Russell's request; he needed the members to appear united. At one point, Senator Russell telephoned President Johnson and told him, 'They are trying to prove that the same bullet that hit Kennedy first was the one that hit Connally . . . Well, I don't believe it.' Johnson, who was two cars behind Kennedy's limousine, replied, 'I don't either.' (In 1969, Johnson joined the growing list of conspiracy theorists when he said, 'I never believed that Oswald acted alone.')

And what was Oswald's motive? Warren Commission attorney Burt Griffin, who went on to become a judge, said, 'Everybody who has read the report knows we ducked the question of motive.' Griffin further said of Ruby, 'I had and continue to have very great skepticism that Ruby did this on the spur of the moment.'

Bobby Kennedy went along with the Warren Commission's final verdict, sending the commission a letter that read, 'I know of no credible evidence to support the allegations that the assassination of President Kennedy was caused by a domestic or foreign conspiracy.'

From the start, Bobby was against any investigation into his brother's death and expressed this to a number of friends and colleagues. Why wouldn't a loving sibling want to know who murdered his own brother? Why would the most powerful and driven law enforcement officer in the land, who could not bear to see Carlos Marcello get away with spitting on the sidewalk, accept the murder of his own brother? To many around Bobby, his inconsolable despair and brooding following Jack's death revealed lacerations to his heart that were deeper than those typically endured by men who have experienced the loss of a brother, even an iconic brother, but suggestive of a man who had caused or contributed to his brother's death which may form part of the answer. 'My own feeling,' said Nicholas Katzenbach, 'was that Bobby was worried that there might be some conspiracy, and that it might be his fault . . . It might very well have been that he was worried that the investigation would somehow point back to him.'

In addition to Bobby's own culpability, another plausible reason had to do with the Kennedy name. Even in his grief-stricken state on assassination day, Bobby began to protect his brother's legacy when he contacted national security advisor McGeorge Bundy and told him to secure his brother's confidential files inside the White House and transfer them under guard to the Old Executive Office Building, just across the street.

There were other crucial moments in which Bobby put aside his anguish and despair in order to destroy or hide evidence that would have tainted the image of Camelot, including but not limited to Jack's reckless philandering and his knowledge of the CIA's program to assassinate world leaders. Investigative journalist Seymour Hersh wrote, 'Bobby Kennedy understood that public revelation of the materials in his brother's White House files would forever destroy Jack Kennedy's reputation as president, and his own as attorney general.' Senator Harris Wofford, a friend to the Kennedy family, said, 'There was no way of getting to the bottom of the assassination without uncovering the very stories [Bobby] hoped would be hidden forever. So he closed his eyes to the coverup . . . and took no steps to inform the Commission of the Cuban and mafia connections that would have provided the main clues to any conspiracy.' One evening, Bobby said to presidential advisor Dick Goodwin, 'If anyone was involved, it was organized crime. But there's nothing I can do about it. Not now.' Goodwin talked about the subject at length with Bobby and later said of their conversations, 'We know the CIA was involved, and the mafia. We all know that. But how you link those to the assassination, I don't know.'

In order to protect his brother's posthumous reputation, and safeguard his own future political ambitions, Bobby accepted the Warren Commission's bogus report without question. It took Jack's death for Bobby to finally understand the balancing act the wily old Hoover had desperately tried to teach him through example.

Unlike Jack, who was an avid reader throughout his life, Bobby had little interest in books. His mother, Rose, once said of him, 'He didn't read very much when he was young. He was one of the ones I had to keep urging to read.' Beset with guilt, Bobby now dove into the classics of Greek literature. In one book, he underlined a passage by Aeschylus that read, 'All arrogance will reap a harvest rich in tears. God calls men to a heavy reckoning for overweening pride.'

Beyond being humbled, Bobby also learned to cry, an emotional response that was unacceptable in the Kennedy household, and something he had forbidden his own children from doing, telling them, 'Hush now, a Kennedy never cries.' On the day after the assassination, as Hoover went to gamble at the racetrack, Bobby locked himself inside the Lincoln bedroom of the White House where he was heard sobbing in his sleep while chanting, 'Why, God, why?' Should we be so audacious as to answer for the Almighty, we might respond, 'Why, Bobby, why did you pick fights with Allen Dulles, J. Edgar Hoover, Lyndon Johnson, Jimmy Hoffa, Santo Trafficante, Sam Giancana, William Harvey, Johnny Roselli, Carlos Marcello, and five thousand sworn mafia killers across the country, with another five thousand CIA-trained Cuban militants?' For years to come, whenever bottled-up anger erupted from inside him, Bobby would blame his brother's death on 'those Cuban cunts' and the 'guy from New Orleans', never Oswald, who, at best, was a pawn if not a patsy.

At the opening of the Valachi hearings back in September 1963, Bobby was called as an expert witness to provide a basic understanding of the mafia. In his testimony, which was given at the same time New Orleans was buzzing with conspiratorial activity, Bobby unwittingly explained exactly how Carlos Marcello expected to get away with the murder of a president. Mafia dons, said Bobby, 'have insulated themselves from the crime itself . . . If they want to have somebody knocked off, for instance, the top man will speak to somebody who will speak to somebody else who will speak to somebody else and order it. The man who actually does the gun work . . . does not know who ordered it. To trace that back is virtually impossible.'

Chapter 23

It Ain't Goin' Nowhere

Jack Ruby's trial opened on 4 March 1964. Joe Campisi was sometimes seen in the courtroom which almost certainly meant that Carlos Marcello was receiving trial updates since Campisi spoke with Marcello on a daily basis. Melvin Belli, who was retained by the mob if we are to believe his partner, Seymour Ellison, may have also been updating the bosses. Despite Ruby's pleas to testify on his own behalf, Belli kept him off the witness stand, which is probably why the mob hired the half-Italian, Rolls-Royce-driving attorney, not necessarily to get Ruby off, but to clam him up. When Frank Ragano, longtime attorney and house counsel to Santo Trafficante, was suing *Time* magazine for libel, Ragano hired Belli to represent him. Before Ragano met with Belli to discuss his lawsuit, Trafficante warned Ragano, 'Whatever you do, don't ask him about Jack Ruby. Don't get involved. It's none of your business.'

By 14 March, Ruby's hope of getting off lightly was upset by a jury that convicted him of murder. He was sentenced to die in the electric chair. In a jailhouse interview, Ruby said, 'The same people who want me to get the electric chair are [the] ones who wanted President Kennedy killed.' Perhaps it was time to get rid of Ruby just as it had been time to get rid of Oswald. Oddly enough, Sgt Patrick Dean, the man believed to have allowed Ruby into the underground parking garage, was a key prosecution witness who contributed to Ruby's demise; if Dean's last assignment was to help Ruby dispatch Oswald, his latest assignment may have been to send Ruby to the chair. Even more oddly, Ruby must have understood Dean's dilemma and did not take it personally; he inscribed a copy of the Warren Commission report for Dean with the words 'Your buddy, Jack Ruby'.

In October 1966, Ruby's conviction was overturned on appeal and a new trial was scheduled for February 1967, but he conveniently died of cancer in January. He expired at Parkland Hospital where President Kennedy and Lee Harvey Oswald had both died. Ruby's corpse was tagged M-67-007, shortened to 007 on some of the medical records. In an age when fact is becoming increasingly indistinguishable from fiction, we must wonder if, perhaps with a sense of humor, history has left us a small clue as to how this national tragedy began. Allen Dulles, who James Bond author Ian Fleming referred to as 'Agent 008', attempted to drag Fleming's spy fiction into the realm of reality, evidenced by poison cigars, death rays and exploding seashells. Dulles, who said, 'President Kennedy and I often talked about James Bond,' befriended Fleming and once wrote, 'I kept in constant touch with him. I was always interested in the . . . secret gadgetry Fleming described from time to time . . . They did get one thinking and exploring.' Jack Kennedy was also an avid reader of Bond novels and, in March 1961, *Life* magazine listed *From Russia, with Love* as one of the president's top ten favorite books. When *Dr. No* premiered as a movie, Kennedy had it shown at the private family theatre inside the White House. According to Andrew Lycell, Fleming's biographer, President Kennedy was reading a Bond novel on the night before his assassination, as was his alleged assassin, Lee Harvey Oswald, whose favorite television program as a teenager was *I Led 3 Lives*, based on a book of the same name – it was about an FBI informant who posed as a communist spy in order to infiltrate the movement. 'Lee watched that show every week,' said Oswald's brother. 'When I left to join the marines, he was still watching the reruns.' As for Jack Ruby, during his brief stint as a federal informant, he purchased a 'microphone-equipped wristwatch, a bugged tie clip, a telephone bug and a bugged attaché case'. Is it possible that Ian Fleming's novels, created as light entertainment for a sober British audience, had an unexpected impact on the American mind?

By August 1964, after finally emerging from a 'dark night of the soul', Bobby Kennedy announced his candidacy for the US Senate from New York. (Younger brother Ted was already representing their home state of Massachusetts in the US Senate, forcing Bobby to relocate.) Jimmy Hoffa, knowing Bobby would make a run for the White House, distributed a half-million pamphlets attacking Bobby's civil rights record, while other pamphlets painted Bobby as anti-Semitic, anti-Italian and anti-labor.

We can guess that Hoffa's concerns were shared by FBI director J. Edgar Hoover, but at least Hoover's job was safe: on 8 May 1964,

President Johnson signed an executive order exempting Hoover from compulsory retirement on account of age. From that day forward, only death could remove Hoover from the Bureau. Deke DeLoach said that Hoover had the declaration framed and hung on a wall in the conference room just outside Hoover's office.

The mob as a group also fared well under the new president. In July 1965, Johnson banned wiretapping. A ranking FBI agent said of the ban, 'When I received word of Johnson's executive order, I was flabbergasted. How could anyone put such a roadblock in the way of our efforts to track the mob? I could hardly believe it.'

Before the taps went dead, agents did pick up some interesting chatter. On 26 November 1963, just days after Kennedy's death, Buffalo don Stefano Magaddino was overheard talking to fellow mobsters inside his funeral home in Niagara Falls, New York. Incredibly, this old mafioso, who was born in Sicily and lived near the Canadian border, already knew far more about the recent tragedy than the American people. Magaddino said that Jack Kennedy was killed because Bobby 'pressed too many issues', and that Jack Ruby murdered Lee Harvey Oswald 'in order to cover up things'. Sounding more like the American diplomat and Soviet expert George Kennan, Magaddino also said that the government was now covering up the conspiracy to avoid being pushed into a war with the Russians. It would take years before the majority of the American public would draw these same conclusions. Magaddino then warned his men to be wary of informants since authorities must have been wondering what the mob knew about the crime. Only in this last regard was Magaddino wrong; by now, no one in the federal government wanted to hear what Magaddino had to say, or anyone else who might contradict the FBI's official conclusion that was drawn within hours of the assassination and confirmed by the Warren Commission.

In December, only one month after the assassination, a bug overheard Chicago mobsters Charles 'Chuckie English' Inglesia, Dominic 'Butch' Blasi and Sam Giancana talking about the expected shift in the FBI's policy toward the mob. 'I tell you something,' said English, 'in another two months from now, the FBI will be like it was five years ago. They won't be around no more. They say the FBI will get it [the investigation into President Kennedy's death]. They're gonna start running down Fair Play for Cuba . . . They call that more detrimental to the country than us guys.'

President Johnson also re-established White House relations with Jimmy Hoffa's mafia-infested Teamsters Union. On 18 October 1964, the *New York Times* quoted Hoffa who said he 'would urge members to support President Johnson' in the next election.

Approximately two weeks after the assassination, attorney Frank Ragano traveled to New Orleans to meet with Carlos Marcello, who, according to Ragano, 'had a smug look on his face . . . like the cat who ate the canary'. Marcello told Ragano, 'When you see Jimmy [Hoffa], you tell him he owes me and he owes me big!' Marcello was expecting several million dollars in loans from the Teamster pension fund and Ragano was convinced that carte blanche access to the fund was an incentive for Marcello and Trafficante to make Hoffa feel as if they had done him a personal favor by whacking Kennedy.

When Ragano met with Hoffa in December, Hoffa told Ragano, 'I told you they could do it. I'll never forget what Carlos and Santo did for me.' Ragano, who later regretted being a part of these conversations, admitted he had 'crossed the professional line . . . I had allowed Santo's friends to become my friends and his enemies, my enemies.'

After being elected to his second term as district attorney of New Orleans, Earling 'Jim' Garrison responded to a growing number of Americans who believed there was a conspiracy behind President Kennedy's death. Garrison began his investigation by reading the entire twenty-six volumes of the Warren report, which he concluded was a despicable cover-up. Garrison wondered why Guy Banister, the retired FBI agent who carried two sidearms, was all but ignored by the Warren Commission. Two days after the assassination, the same FBI agent who had questioned David Ferrie, had a quick telephone chat with Banister, never mentioning Lee Harvey Oswald, who had frequented Banister's office where Ferrie and Cuban militants dressed in olive-green fatigues were known to come and go.

Jim Garrison

Federal agents were a bit more assertive when Banister was found dead in June 1964; within an hour of his death, agents stormed into his office and carted away his file cabinets, which piqued Garrison's interest all the more. (Banister's wife, while sifting through his other belongings, found a stack of Oswald's Fair Play for Cuba pamphlets.) Garrison soon found out that Banister was 'heavily involved in anti-communist endeavors of all kinds', and that he and Ferrie were closely linked to the CIA.

One afternoon, Garrison took his fellow investigators to the street outside Banister's office so he and his team could observe the surrounding environment. Banister's office was inside a corner building, with entrances on Camp and Lafayette Streets. Across Lafayette was a US Post Office building which also housed the Secret Service, responsible for the curious last-minute change to the motorcade route, and the Office of Naval Intelligence (ONI), a super-secretive agency Banister had worked for during the Second World War, before beginning his twenty-year career with the FBI (assuming his employment with ONI had ceased). Note that the Marine Corps is a branch of the US Navy; if Oswald, as a marine, was part of military intelligence, as many suspect given the ease with which he returned to the States after defecting to the Soviet Union, then the department that ultimately controlled him was the Office of Naval Intelligence.

Several blocks away from Banister's office was the Masonic Temple building that housed the New Orleans CIA and FBI offices, as well as the immigration offices where Carlos Marcello was once ambushed before being dropped in Guatemala. 'By the late summer of 1963,' wrote Garrison, 'the parade in and out of Guy Banister's place would have been hard for these intelligence agencies to ignore.' Garrison went on to write that Banister would have 'known a good number of his intelligence community cousins and frequently would have been greeting them, if not stopping to chat'.

After assessing the lie of the land, Garrison sought out Jack Martin, 'a sometime private detective' and the man who had been pistol-whipped by Banister on the evening of the assassination after accusing Banister of being involved in the president's murder. Martin, who was left a 'bloody, battered mess', told Garrison, 'He nearly killed me,' and that Banister's office 'was like a circus' with Cubans coming and going. Martin, moreover, said that David Ferrie, who often wore green battle fatigues like his Cuban counterparts, 'practically lived there', as did Lee Harvey Oswald. One of Banister's secretaries, Mary

Brengel, remembered 'Rifles stacked all around his office up until the day of the assassination'.

Upon Ferrie's return from Texas, Garrison had been the first to question him on behalf of the New Orleans district attorney's office. Unhappy with Ferrie's answers, many of which were provably untrue, Garrison dutifully handed Ferrie over to the FBI, believing the Bureau would use him to crack open the case. Garrison was stunned to learn that the FBI released him with 'surprising swiftness'. Garrison now opened an investigation into Ferrie with intent to bring him before a grand jury.

In February 1967, Garrison's renewed interest in Ferrie was leaked to the press. When the story broke on the front page of the New Orleans *States-Item*, Ferrie made a telephone call to Lou Ivon, a police investigator assigned to Garrison's office. 'You know what this news does to me, don't you?' Ferrie said to Ivon. 'I'm a dead man. From here on, believe me, I'm a dead man.'

Postcard of the Fontainebleau Hotel in New Orleans

The next day, Ferrie called Ivon again, expressing his continuing fears and telling him the press had swarmed his apartment; he asked for 'physical protection against unnamed persons'. Ivon put Ferrie up in a suite at the Fontainebleau Hotel in New Orleans – which was built with Teamster pension funds and frequented by Santo Trafficante when visiting his fellow don, Carlos Marcello. Over the next four days, Ferrie was kept in protective custody as Garrison and his team pondered when to bring him before a grand jury. Before they reached a conclusion, Ivon received another telephone call, hung up the receiver and said to his colleagues, 'Dave Ferrie's dead. The coroner's already picked up the body at his place.'

In the two assassination books Garrison subsequently wrote, I could not find any specifics as to why Ferrie, who was supposed be under a twenty-four-hour guard, was free to leave the hotel without security. Garrison was a talented prosecutor, and in order to win cases, scattered facts must be presented to a jury in an orderly manner. Garrison shows off his prosecutorial talent in his convincing narrative about the assassination, yet in both of his books, when he arrives at the matter of Ferrie's exit from the hotel, he strangely departs from his usual lucidity and becomes uncharacteristically vague, omitting crucial pieces of the account, entirely inconsistent with his style of connecting dots. Furthermore, Garrison fails to tell us why Ferrie was not immediately dragged before a grand jury, or why his men were not guarding Ferrie's room around the clock or shadowing him when he left the hotel. The answers to these questions should have been easy to find but were not. What I eventually learned from other sources was that Lou Ivon was with Ferrie and, after a long day of questioning, Ivon had to go home to his family so he left his colleague, Lynn Loisel, to guard Ferrie. Mysteriously, however, Loisel ran out for cigarettes – which he should have done while Ivon was there – leaving Ferrie alone and, soon after, Ferrie took off. Why would Ferrie abandon a safe place? Or did Ferrie feel that it was not so safe and he had become nervous, wondering if Loisel had intentionally left him alone? It is strange that the notes Ivon made of his interviews with Ferrie in that hotel room disappeared from Garrison's files. The answer to the double disappearance of both Ferrie and the record of his interviews may lie in Garrison's allegiance to Carlos Marcello, whose connection to Ferrie was public knowledge.

Santo Trafficante's attorney, Frank Ragano, was surprised to hear of Garrison's New Orleans-based investigation into the president's death, aware that Marcello controlled the state machinery, including the district attorney's office, and would not want a thorough inquiry. Shortly after Garrison reopened the cold case, Ragano met with Marcello and asked him, 'Who is this fellow Jim Garrison?' to which Marcello replied, 'He's my man.'

'And his investigation of the assassination of Kennedy?' asked Ragano.

'It ain't goin' nowhere,' said Marcello, smugly. 'Nothin' to worry about.'

When Ragano later asked Garrison what he thought of Marcello, the New Orleans district attorney who was regularly seen dining with Marcello's brothers, replied, 'He's good people.'

Aaron Kohn, who headed the New Orleans Crime Commission, told investigative reporter Clark Mollenhoff that Garrison 'denies the existence in our city of provable organized crime. He and his staff have blocked our efforts to have grand juries probe the influence of the Cosa Nostra.'

If Garrison thought Marcello was 'good people', dined with his brothers and was known to run interference for the mob, why then was Garrison pursuing this particular investigation, and how was Marcello so sure it would not hurt him? Was Garrison's probe meant to throw the scent off Marcello? Garrison's timing certainly raised a few eyebrows in this regard. His investigation was launched just as an awakening nation began to consider a cover-up that involved organized crime. Did the ever-plotting Marcello decide it was best, if such allegations were to be explored, that his own explorer chart the course?

Bobby's one-time minion, Robert Blakey, who believed Marcello played an executive role in the assassination conspiracy, asked what appears to have been an obvious question: 'Why, with all the evidence that [Garrison] claimed implicated Ferrie in an assassination plot, did Garrison not suspect that Marcello himself was also involved?' Investigative reporter Peter Noyes wrote: 'In a series of interviews Garrison speculated about the possible forces behind the assassination, singling out such diverse groups as right-wing extremists, anti-Castro Cubans, Cubans in general, the FBI, the CIA, the "military-industrial complex", and "other" . . . Not once during the New Orleans investigation did Jim Garrison allude to Ferrie's ties to Marcello and the possibility that organized crime could have masterminded the assassination.'

The nude, hairless body of 49-year-old David Ferrie was found lying on his living-room couch, and although he had already been taken away by the coroner, Garrison told Lou Ivon to 'get five or six of your best policemen over to Ferrie's place' to sweep it before the feds arrived. Besides finding an apartment 'littered with newspaper clippings, magazine articles, and diagrams relating to the JFK assassination', there were two type-written suicide notes. Assuming they were authentic, neither provided any clues as to the murder of President Kennedy. The notes amounted to a morose farewell to a world he did not fit into.

Personal papers found in Ferrie's apartment revealed him to be the owner of an automotive service station that Marcello had purchased for him in early 1964. It is understandable that Marcello compensated

Ferrie for his legal services, but it is harder to explain why their business relationship continued after Marcello was acquitted at trial, and what such a large reward could have been for. After finding these business documents, Garrison remained oddly incurious as to why a tomato salesman would purchase a petrol station for a man who was, within twenty-four hours of the president's death, suspected of participating in the assassination.

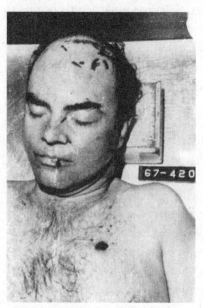

Eladio del Valle

The odd timing of Ferrie's death resulted in the press taking Garrison's investigation more seriously. As did the strange death of Eladio Ceferino del Valle, a once corrupt Cuban congressman who fled Castro and worked with Ferrie to coordinate aerial sabotage missions over Cuba. Since Ferrie and del Valle were known to work closely together, Garrison went looking for del Valle, who was quickly located at the Commercial Plaza Shopping Center in Miami – with his skull split open from an axe. He was also shot in the heart after being tortured. Del Valle was heavily involved in Santo Trafficante's drug smuggling and gambling rackets and the media believed that his death was linked to the assassination. Did Trafficante get rid of del Valle in Miami at the same time Marcello got rid of Ferrie in New Orleans?

As journalists eagerly awaited the coroner's report on Ferrie, they speculated about the cause of death and if there was foul play involved, while Bobby Kennedy and Lyndon Johnson were privately inquiring about his death. When the press learned that Ferrie had died from a ruptured blood vessel in the brain, they immediately quieted down – even though the coroner, Dr Nicholas Chetta, was later accused by an honorable FBI agent of being corrupt and producing 'dubious autopsy reports'. (Chetta was found dead a year later at the relatively young age of fifty. And we must wonder how Ferrie knew that his blood

vessel was about to rupture, prompting him to leave behind two suicide notes.)

Instead of calling it a day, Jim Garrison called a news conference
where he referred to Ferrie as 'one of history's most important individuals', admitting, 'we waited too long' to get him before a grand
jury. Garrison then steamed forward in another direction, targeting 54-year-old Clay LaVergne Shaw, a New Orleans businessman
and Second World War veteran who was an acquaintance of David
Ferrie. Garrison's case centered around two incidents: the first was
a telephone call Shaw allegedly made to one of Marcello's attorneys,
Dean Andrews, asking Andrews to represent Lee Harvey Oswald,
following Oswald's arrest in Dallas. The second incident occurred
at a party where Shaw was privy to a group conversation in which
a plan to assassinate the president was proposed by David Ferrie.
Garrison had Shaw arrested on 1 March 1967, charging him with
conspiracy to assassinate the president along with Ferrie and Oswald,
both of whom were dead, presenting Garrison with an insurmount-
able challenge unless he planned to bring a Ouija board into the
courtroom.

During an interview about the case, Garrison claimed that 'a
number of the men who killed the President were former employees
of the CIA involved in its anti-Castro underground activities in and
around New Orleans . . . We must assume that the plotters were acting
on their own rather than on CIA orders when they killed the President.
As far as we have been able to determine, they were not in the pay of
the CIA at the time of the assassination . . . The CIA could not face
up to the American people and admit that its former employees had
conspired to assassinate the President; so from the moment Kennedy's
heart stopped beating, the Agency attempted to sweep the whole conspiracy under the rug . . . In this respect, it has become an accessory
after the fact in the assassination.'

Garrison's shocking accusations and the arrest of Shaw sent CIA
director Richard Helms – who once hid the mafia–Castro plots from
then director, John McCone – into crisis mode. Helms instructed his
agents to 'do all we can to help Shaw', while at the same time the
government unleashed its media contacts on Garrison, whose close
connection to Carlos Marcello became the subject of a hit piece in
Look magazine. The article pointed out Garrison's weak to non-
existent prosecutorial record in Louisiana when it came to members of

organized crime. Garrison was also accused of purchasing an opulent home at a discount price from one of Marcello's favorite builders, Frank Occhipinti.*

The magazine's investigation into Garrison further revealed that he had received five thousand dollars in complimentary gambling credits at the mob-owned Sands Casino in Las Vegas, via Marcello's casino manager, Mario Marino, who also picked up Garrison's room and meals.

Life magazine followed up with a second hit piece on Garrison, pointing out the abundance of mafia cases he dismissed in New Orleans. The magazine reported that a member of Marcello's borgata had dropped dead in Garrison's house during a political strategy session.

The National Broadcasting Company (NBC) also dispatched a team to New Orleans to look into, not Garrison's case, but Garrison! Garrison viewed the multipronged attack on his character as proof that he was on to something big and deduced that he was being smeared by the same people who had covered up the conspiracy. He plodded on, undeterred.

Shaw's trial opened on 29 January 1969, amidst a packed courtroom and a media circus. With his nose arrogantly tilted upward, Shaw puffed on cigarettes, appearing as bored with the proceedings as England's luckless King Charles I, both of whom did not believe their accusers had any right to try them. Attorney Dean Andrews, who at first admitted to Garrison that he had received a telephone call from Shaw concerning Oswald's arrest, denied it when asked about it on the witness stand. As for the plan to assassinate the president that was talked about at a party, a 25-year-old partygoer and witness to the conversation, Perry Russo, testified that Shaw, Oswald and several Cuban militants listened to Ferrie explain how it would be easier to kill President Kennedy than it would be to kill Castro, which they had repeatedly tried to do but failed. Ferrie's plan was to assassinate Kennedy and blame it on Castro which, he believed, would lead to a US invasion of Cuba. (Recall that Jack Ruby had commented, while

---

* Marcello was alleged to have a partial ownership of at least two Holiday Inn hotels owned by brothers Frank and Roy Occhipinti. When it came to light, Holiday Inn executives were 'deeply concerned' and attempted to revoke the franchise charter but could not find any provable violations and were forced to allow the Occhipintis, and Marcello, to carry on until the hotels were eventually sold.

in police custody, that Cuba would now be invaded as a result of the president's murder.) Ferrie proposed a 'triangulation of crossfire' which would place Kennedy in the crosshairs of three separate snipers. Perry Russo's testimony was, in fact, perfectly consistent with a hand-drawn map police found in Oswald's room, following Oswald's arrest. Shortly after the assassination, the *Dallas Morning News* wrote: 'Oswald had placed marks at all major intersections along the motorcade route . . . There was also a line from the Texas School Book Depository building to Elm Street.' For some inexplicable reason, the original map is buried in the National Archives. Recall that Eugene Hale Brading, 'a man associated with the mafia and right-wing extremists', was inside the Dal-Tex building and was briefly taken into custody but mysteriously released. Moreover, most witnesses, some of whom were police and ex-military and therefore familiar with the sound of gunfire, believed that shots had been fired from the grassy knoll, and film footage shows people running up the incline moments after the shots rang out. Years later, Kenny O'Donnell, who was traveling in the motorcade, told Speaker of the House, Thomas 'Tip' O'Neill, that shots were fired from the grassy knoll. When O'Neill asked O'Donnell why he had told the Warren Commission they had come from behind the motorcade, O'Donnell said, 'I told the FBI what I had heard, but they said it couldn't have happened that way and that I must have been imagining things. So I testified the way they wanted me to.'

To prove that the president was the victim of a crossfire, Garrison was able to show the jury the Zapruder film, which clearly shows Kennedy's head being blown 'backward and to his left', consistent with a bullet fired from his front right. (The American public would not see the film until 1975.) Garrison accused Shaw of being a CIA asset, an accusation that was vehemently denied by Shaw's defense attorney – but later confirmed by a CIA senior official, Victor Marchetti, who also confirmed that Ferrie was a 'contract agent' for the CIA.

Garrison's dramatic prosecution convinced the jury that the president was indeed the victim of a conspiracy but the case against Shaw was weak and on Saturday, 1 March, he was acquitted. The national press, in lockstep with the government, treated Shaw's acquittal as a complete vindication of the Warren Commission's report.

Garrison ignored calls to resign and his life returned to normal until the morning of 30 June 1971, when federal agents launched an early morning raid at his home where he lived with his wife and children.

Garrison was marched out of his house and charged with protecting Marcello's rackets in New Orleans in exchange for thousands of dollars a month. Although Garrison candidly admitted that many of Louisiana's district attorneys were on the take, he insisted that his own integrity was beyond reproach. At trial, the government failed to convince the jury that Garrison had received at least $150,000 in bribes. He was acquitted, then indicted for tax evasion, and acquitted again.

After taking into consideration all of the available evidence, it is apparent that Jim Garrison had been in bed with Carlos Marcello for a long time, but the government's sudden interest in their cozy relationship was only brought about after Garrison had poked his nose where it did not belong. At one point, Garrison was foolish enough to issue a grand jury subpoena for Allen Dulles 'to testify about possible CIA connections with the assassination, Lee Harvey Oswald, and other curious events in New Orleans'. Needless to say, Dulles did not comply.

When Jim Garrison had first started snooping around in New Orleans, Bobby Kennedy was interested to know what he would turn up, so he asked Walter Sheridan, former chief of the Get Hoffa Squad, to quietly launch a probe of his own. Bobby wanted to confirm or deny his belief that Carlos Marcello had something to do with his brother's death. When Sheridan reported back to Bobby that Marcello had indeed played a crucial role in the conspiracy, Bobby cut Sheridan off before he could disclose the specifics of what he had learned. Sheridan felt that Bobby had become too emotionally distraught with the answer, knowing that his relentless pursuit of Marcello was a contributing factor in his brother's assassination. This self-condemnation would explain the numerous eyewitness accounts of Bobby's severe emotional collapse following the event.

Bobby Kennedy once said, 'I'd like to be remembered as the guy who broke up the mafia.' The mafia had instead broken Bobby, but his brief tenure as attorney general did mark a major turning point in the federal government's attitude toward the mob, and although it took the FBI a few more years to get started, they eventually threw themselves into the fight.

Bobby's crusade remains the most concentrated attack on organized crime to date, resulting in Congress passing anti-racketeering legislation and giving the federal government jurisdiction over a catalog of mafia-related crimes. An Organized Crime Task Force was formed in 1966, the Omnibus Crime Control and Safe Streets Act was passed in 1968, and the Organized Crime Control Act was passed in 1970, all of which provided law enforcement with massive funding to combat the mafia which Bobby nearly succeeded in destroying. But the question remains: did Bobby reach too far by making it personal, dispensing with civil liberties and corrupting an otherwise valiant mission? There is a childhood story from Bobby's life that may offer us insight. When Bobby was four years old, he was aboard a sailboat with his older brothers, Jack and Joe Jr. While at sea, Bobby repeatedly jumped overboard into the choppy waters of Nantucket Sound. Each time, his brothers fished him out of the water and warned him that he could have drowned. And each time, he jumped back in. Jack later looked back on that day and said that Bobby displayed 'either a lot of guts or no sense at all, depending on how you looked at it'. Can we not draw the same conclusion with regard to Bobby's fight against organized crime? It either took a lot of guts to attack sworn killers, undaunted by the dangers involved, or no sense at all. What can we make of Bobby's petty taunts, like telling Sam Giancana on public television that he giggled like a little girl; of Bobby's hypocrisy, like knowing Johnny Roselli was working with the CIA to assassinate a world leader while, at the same time, desperately trying to prosecute him; of Bobby's lawlessness, like breaking laws he was sworn to uphold by dropping Carlos Marcello in the middle of a hot jungle, then indicting him for having the audacity to return. Like Captain Ahab, Bobby's crazed obsession with Marcello gave the whale – in this case, a shrimp from Louisiana – the advantage, leaving us to sum up Bobby's work with the words of Molière:

Man's a strangely fashioned creature
Who seldom is content to follow Nature
But recklessly pursues his inclination
Beyond the narrow bands of moderation,
And often, by transgressing Reason's laws,
Perverts a lofty aim or noble cause.

Part Four

War

Chapter 24

Banana Split

After Joe Profaci's heir apparent, Joe Magliocco, was rejected by the Commission and called to account for planning a double hit on Carlo Gambino and Tommy Lucchese, he suffered a massive heart attack and died on 28 December 1963, leaving Joe Bonanno with no allies on the Commission.

When Bonanno was called before the Commission to respond to questions about his possible involvement in the planned double hit, Bonanno refused to appear and fled to Canada where he hid out with the Montreal faction of his borgata. Bonanno's defiance proved to be the first major dispute to test the authority of the Commission since the governing body was first created by Lucky Luciano thirty years earlier, in order to preserve peace and arbitrate matters of the highest order.

To be sure, the Commission's authority had been tested by Joe Profaci when he declared the sovereignty of his own borgata and refused to adhere to the Commission's wish that he step down. But the dispute had not been resolved due to Profaci's death. Bonanno now reawakened the debate when he, too, was told to step down, and adamantly refused. In an attempt to appear just, the Commission appointed a third party as an official mediator, Simone 'Sam the Plumber' DeCavalcante, 'whose biggest previous distinction had been in trying to develop a garbage disposal unit that would reduce a human body to a meatball'.

DeCavalcante was the boss of a small New Jersey borgata with thirty or so members whose rackets were intermingled with the larger New York families. Given DeCavalcante's New Jersey base of operations, his appointment was meant to convey the appearance of impartiality toward the New Yorkers, but his casual references to the Commission as 'The Supreme Court' and its members as 'Chief Justices' gave away his bias. It was quickly apparent to members of the Bonanno family that DeCavalcante's mission was not to mediate but to persuade its

*Simone 'Sam
the Plumber'
DeCavalcante*

soldiers to abandon their don or pressure him into bowing before the Commission's authority.

On a more personal level, DeCavalcante was thrilled with his appointment and told one of his capos, 'I'm trying to build a good relationship with everybody in the Commission. Our *borgata* is small but we could do things as good as anybody else.' The fact that DeCavalcante had unwittingly said this into an FBI microphone is overwhelming evidence to the contrary. Agents had planted a bug inside the main office of DeCavalcante's plumbing company, and although there is no indication that DeCavalcante had ever done any plumbing work himself, he did an excellent job of flushing out his windpipe. For several months, DeCavalcante endlessly talked to fellow mobsters in three different languages, Italian, Sicilian and English (four if we include Yiddish, whenever he called someone a *meshuggenah*).

When speaking inside his office with members of the Bonanno family, DeCavalcante would usually begin the conversation by sounding open-minded, then slowly come around to discrediting Bonanno as an out-of-touch don. Whenever he could not bring others around to his point of view, he would become aggravated.

When the Commission saw that DeCavalcante could not turn Bonanno's men against him, they set out to tarnish Bonanno's name by accusing him of poisoning Magliocco in order to prevent Magliocco from appearing as a witness against Bonanno at a Commission inquiry. Joe Bonanno's son, Bill, who was staying at Magliocco's estate, was said to have slipped a pill into Magliocco's food which did him in. But the accusation did not stick since everyone knew the overweight Magliocco, who *Life* magazine referred to as 'a fat hoodlum with high blood pressure', had consumed enough sausage and meatballs to end world hunger and his heart was further taxed by stress. (In 1969, the FBI, responding to rumors that Bonanno had poisoned Magliocco, exhumed his body and found no traces of poison.) Joe Bonanno deflected a number of other spurious accusations until he finally gave his enemies a legitimate gripe by appointing his inexperienced son Bill as the family consigliere.

Salvatore Bonanno was born on 5 November 1932. Since his youth, he was known as 'Bill', after the legendary frontiersman Wild Bill Hickok, a nickname he picked up at the Bonanno's vacation home in Arizona where Bill dressed like a cowboy, rode around on horses and worked at dude ranches. As a young man, Bill was briefly enrolled in Northern Arizona University; he had ambitions of becoming a lawyer before he was bitten by the mob bug and wanted his father to bring him into The Life.

In 1954, Bill was initiated into the borgata at the tender age of twenty-one. By 1959, he was promoted to a capo, heading a crew of much older, more experienced men. In 1964, when Joe Bonanno fled to Canada, he appointed Giovanni 'Johnny Burns' Morales, a fellow Sicilian immigrant from Castellammare del Golfo, as his acting boss. When the family consigliere, John Tartamella, became ill, the vacant position was expected to be filled by Gaspar DiGregorio, another old friend and relative of Joe Bonanno.

DiGregorio was the same age as the elder Bonanno, had been loyal to the borgata since the Castellammarese War, had served as best man at Joe Bonanno's wedding, was the christened godfather to Bill, and was also the brother-in-law of Joe Bonanno's uncle and fellow don, Stefano Magaddino of Buffalo. DiGregorio was well-liked by the soldiers and was, by all accounts, next in line for the job, but Joe Bonanno wanted to groom his son for the top spot and had passed over DiGregorio. To disguise the personal preference Joe Bonanno had for his own son, he told acting boss Johnny Burns to gather the capos and hold a vote between Bill and DiGregorio. The capos understood what the elder Bonanno wanted and acquiesced by electing Bill as their new consigliere, but many griped about the appointment in private, perfectly summed up by Bill's own wife, Rosalie, who said, 'Contrary to the wishes of some of the men in my husband's world, my husband had assumed the role of *consigliere* to his father. This was seen as nepotism and highly unusual because Bill was so young and because a *consigliere* traditionally is a kind of sounding board or counselor to the father of the "family". How could a son counsel a father, they reasoned.' We should recall that Santo Trafficante Sr had stepped down and become consigliere before appointing his son as acting boss so that he, the father, could advise him, the son. This was a brilliant move on the part of the Trafficantes, which headed off the criticism now endured by the Bonannos, as other New York families accused them of nepotism.

Don Stefano Magaddino gassed up his brother-in-law, DiGregorio, who expressed his displeasure at being bypassed then went into hiding, igniting a rift that split the Bonanno family in two. The Commission was thrilled by the break that weakened Joe Bonanno's hold over the borgata. They instructed DeCavalcante to talk up Bill's lack of experience while accusing him of being abusive toward his wife, Rosalie, who was a Profaci and, as such, considered mafia royalty. The attacks on Bill landed on open ears. One Bonanno soldier, Joe Bayonne, who had faithfully defended Joe Bonanno, did not feel the same loyalty toward Bill, telling DeCavalcante, '[Bill] is sick and I think he's a little crazy, between you and I. Or else he's immature . . . You can't take a kid out of a cradle and put him in a tuxedo and let him boss people in the gutter if he can't talk their language.' More and more men came around to the same conclusion and were unwilling to be ordered around by a fake cowboy from Arizona.

As Bill tried to find his footing in a pair of boots that were too big for his feet, Joe Bonanno applied for Canadian citizenship which was denied; he was briefly jailed then ejected from the country. He returned to New York where the United States attorney for the Southern District, Robert Morgenthau, had subpoenaed him before a grand jury. Between this new legal dilemma, his continuing beef with the Commission and a possible murder contract on his head derived from the recent rift in his borgata, Bonanno needed to pull a magic trick out of his hat.

When Joe Bonanno first arrived in America, he had ambitions of becoming a screen actor. While working a day job as a baker, he attended evening drama classes. His drama coach was fond of him but felt his imperfect English would hinder his dream of becoming a Hollywood sensation. Proving that none of our failed pursuits are for nought, Bonanno would now put his old drama classes to use. On 21 October 1964, one day before Bonanno was scheduled to appear before a grand jury, he went to dinner at a steakhouse in uptown Manhattan with his attorney, William Maloney. After dinner, Bonanno and Maloney got into a taxi together. When the cab stopped in front of Maloney's apartment building on Park Avenue, two men seized hold of Bonanno and spirited him into a waiting car. Maloney tried to intervene until the assailants fired a warning shot at the pavement in front of his feet.

With a mafia don having been kidnapped in public, the FBI

Joe Bonanno wanted poster

assigned dozens of field agents to question anyone who may have seen or heard anything, while surveillance agents listened to the bug planted inside DeCavalcante's office, hoping to glean clues as to who was behind the abduction. One moment, the ever-talkative DeCavalcante would express fears that Bonanno's disappearance could lead to an all-out war, the next moment he would wonder why Bonanno was only kidnapped and not killed on the spot. One of DeCavalcante's visitors wondered if Bonanno had staged the incident, but someone else in the room shot down the idea. Finally, DeCavalcante met with Carlo Gambino and Tommy Lucchese, who told him that Bonanno had choreographed the dramatic scene on a public street in order to duck his subpoena. DeCavalcante believed them while other mobsters wondered if Gambino and Lucchese were telling the truth, knowing how duplicitous they could be; perhaps they kidnapped and killed Bonanno and were trying to throw the scent off themselves.

In the same way the former nation of Yugoslavia had broken into pieces after Marshal Tito's death, the Bonanno family fractured into several warring factions once their patriarch was gone. Gambino wasted no time telling Joe Colombo to meet with the splinter groups and lure them over to DiGregorio's camp. As Colombo made the rounds across New York, Bill Bonanno and a few of his soldiers walked into a bar and happened upon DiGregorio. The soldiers reached for their guns, eager to snuff out the man at the center of the feud, but were stopped by Bill who physically stood in their way long enough for DiGregorio to escape the bar. Bill was ridiculed by his crew who voted to 'censure' him, which amounted to a free pass in a world where most errors were remedied by murder; he was obviously spared because of his father, adding to more charges of nepotism.

In January 1966, DiGregorio reached out to Bill and asked if they could meet to discuss the divided family. Bill and his men traveled to the meeting place on Troutman Street in Brooklyn, described at the time as 'a rundown neighborhood, edging its way into a slum'. As Bill and his crew waited inside of a house, they received word that DiGregorio was suddenly too ill to attend and needed to reschedule. Bill suspected that something was wrong, so he and his crew waited and watched the street outside through front windows. When they felt it was safe to leave, they made their way out – and were ambushed by DiGregorio's gunmen who were well hidden. Bill and his men crouched between parked cars and returned fire until they were able to escape the block. Some reports said that twenty shots were fired, others that over a hundred were fired without hitting anyone, attesting to the Bonanno family's lack of firearms training. The war was dubbed by the press as 'The Banana Split', and the don, who was portrayed as someone who had lost touch with reality, was dubbed 'Joe Bananas'.

After the botched ambush, DiGregorio's stock dropped as low as Bill's, but DiGregorio did not have a powerful daddy to save him so the Commission replaced DiGregorio with Paul Sciacca, a low-key businessman who was probably pushed into the post by Carlo Gambino, whose weekend retreat was near Sciacca's Long Island home. Sciacca was once the director of a bank and owned clothing manufacturers with a US government contract to produce military uniforms; he was the type of man who appealed to the business-minded Gambino.

In May, nineteen months after he had disappeared without a trace, Joe Bonanno reappeared in Manhattan, where he surrendered at the district attorney's office. The judge set bail at $500,000. Bonanno's lawyer argued it down to $150,000 and Bonanno was back on the street.

When confronted with questions about his alleged abduction, Bonanno insisted that he had been kidnapped, and despite numerous holes in his story, he somehow managed to convince a lot of people, including some historians who point to his 1983 memoir as proof. I have read the same memoir and have drawn the exact opposite conclusion. Besides the many contradictions in Bonanno's story, I noticed a dramatic change in his writing style when he relates the experience of his abduction. The prose of a snobbish mob boss who is quite full of himself suddenly shifts to a writer of cheap romance novels. I will paraphrase him in snippets so you, dear reader, can judge for yourself. Of his anonymous kidnappers, Bonanno writes: 'They had appeared suddenly out of the mist, like specters . . . familiar faces with strange, awkward and somber expressions.' Here's how he describes the long car ride in which he sat between these mysterious 'specters': 'I beheld a canopy of swooping and rising lights . . . our car drove through the rain, across the somnolent Hudson River . . . this phantasmagoric scene, I have never ceased to marvel at the dark magic of it, at the hocus-pocus circumstances . . . Through the wet windows the countryside appeared spectral, as if in a ghostly dream. We swooshed ahead . . . the steady hiss of the tires on the slick roads . . . A dreary mist that shrouded us during the night continued to swirl around us . . . Thick clouds smudged the feeble sun.'

Does this 'phantasmagoric scene' – whatever that is – sound like a hardened mobster abducted by violent goons, or a bored housewife fantasizing about being stolen away from her domestic chores by Timothée Chalamet? Bonanno went on to refer to the kidnapping as 'an enchanted affair' and eventually claimed that the culprit behind the ordeal was his cousin, Stefano Magaddino. When describing the end of his long captivity, Bonanno writes: 'Winter was approaching, and it was time to release me . . . We said goodbye with our eyes . . . We would never forget it for as long as we lived . . . Our silent stares expressed what we could not in words.' Note that Bonanno is not recounting a farewell to a beautiful goddess he fell passionately in love with on a Greek island but to an overweight 73-year-old geezer with hemorrhoids.

Later in his memoir, Bonanno admits to spending at least some of his time away, presumably after he was released from captivity, hiding out in a secret 6ft-by-6ft room in his Arizona house equipped with a bunk, a television and *books*! Ahh, he must have been cooped up in a hidden den with a few out-of-print bodice-rippers.

Rosalie Bonanno said that her father-in-law emerged from hiding 'fit and trim and tanned', while her husband, Bill, was pale and anxiety-ridden, as was Bill's mother who finally emerged from a New Jersey cellar where she had been hidden to avoid being served a subpoena by federal agents who were searching for her husband.

The Commission ordered Bonanno 'isolated' and refused to recognize him as the boss of his own borgata. They contemplated dissolving the entire Bonanno family and dispersing its members among the other New York families. Gambino and Lucchese were expected to make a grab for the top earners, while Magaddino complained, like Italy's Vittorio Orlando at Versailles, that he deserved a territorial reward for siding with the victors; he wanted the Bonanno family's outpost in Canada, which was just across the border from his home turf in Buffalo, New York.

As Joe Bonanno contemplated his next move, the cunning Gambino began to poke around inside of another don's borgata.

Chapter 25

Martin Luther King with a Pinky Ring

The extensive media coverage of the summit at Apalachin put cops across the country on the lookout for convoys of black Cadillacs that did not belong to a wedding or funeral procession. On the afternoon of 22 September 1966, New York police officers spotted a group of older Italian men entering La Stella restaurant in Forest Hills, Queens. Fairly sure they were not senior citizens out for the early bird special, the cops radioed for back-up. At 2:30 p.m., detectives entered the restaurant's private dining area where thirteen powerful mobsters sat around a long table with bottles of wine, baskets of semolina bread and plates of *antipasto*. The more notable characters were Carlo Gambino, his underboss Aniello 'Neil' Dellacroce and their consigliere, Joseph N. Gallo (no known relation to the Gallo brothers); acting Genovese family boss Tommaso 'Tommy Ryan' Eboli; Joe Colombo; Florida don Santo Trafficante and Louisiana don Carlos Marcello. According to the police who took them to the station house, they were dressed in expensive suits and carrying 'large amounts of cash'. One detective who, along with his colleagues, neglected to handcuff them, said, 'They acted like gentlemen, just like your grandfather.' None of the detainees answered any questions before they were charged with 'consorting with known criminals' – themselves. The men posted bail and walked. Marcello later told a journalist, 'What's the matter with some old friends gettin' together for lunch? Who would you expect me to have lunch with in New York, Nelson Rockefeller?'

In the course of the police investigation into what the press dubbed 'Little Apalachin', detectives learned that the luncheon was arranged to address an official protest made to the Commission by Louisiana mobster Anthony Carollo, who was also present at La Stella. Recall that Anthony Carollo was the son of Silvestro 'Silver Dollar Sam' Carollo and had challenged Marcello for the throne back in 1947. Carollo had since prospered under the stellar leadership of Marcello but was still discontented with his minor role in the borgata, so he threatened open rebellion unless Marcello appointed him underboss and heir apparent in place of Marcello's brother, Joseph, who was also present at La Stella. The Commission met for lunch to decide the dispute. The police investigation was unable to uncover anything more than what I have just related but there is much more to the story that has remained hidden – until now.

As you may recall, when Frank Costello wanted to distribute his slot machines across Louisiana, he enlisted the help of a young Marcello, who proved so efficient that Marcello was also invited into the casino business with Costello. Later on, after Vito Genovese pushed Costello aside and the borgata became the Genovese family, Genovese inherited the fruits of Costello's Louisiana alliance with Marcello. Once, when soldier Joe Valachi was traveling to Louisiana, he asked Genovese for a contact in New Orleans; Valachi was basically asking Genovese if he could call on an *amico nostro* for special treatment while he was in town. Genovese ordered Valachi to stay out of Louisiana altogether. Valachi – and historians – have misinterpreted Genovese's firm response to mean that Marcello was so powerful that even Genovese feared him. Marcello was indeed powerful but the 'feared' part was untrue; Genovese had no reason to fear Marcello, who he got along with. The truth is that Genovese did not want a chooch like Valachi bumbling around Louisiana where he could draw attention to Genovese's profitable business arrangements with Marcello. However, after the Kennedy assassination, Marcello was regularly in the news and reports of his booming empire raised eyebrows across the country, especially in New York where Gambino was in the habit of splitting up borgatas before replacing their bosses with puppets.

Marcello's long-term relationship with the Genovese family, which started with Costello, should have kept Gambino at bay, but, by 1966, Genovese was tucked away in Atlanta Penitentiary and, according to Valachi, crying into his pillow over memories of his beloved wife (and cousin), Anna. With Genovese in a steel cage, the covetous Gambino spotted an opportunity to exploit Genovese's weaker stand-in, Tommy Ryan, and viewed Anthony Carollo as a potential puppet. But, unlike Joe Colombo and Gaspar DiGregorio, Gambino's only interest in Carollo was to gas him up and use him to stir the pot so he could come to an acceptable arrangement with the Genovese family with regard to a partnership in the Louisiana rackets. With the powerful Gambino behind him, Carollo eagerly challenged Marcello, who had no choice but to appear before the Commission. Gambino, however, was prepared to withdraw his support for Carollo, which he did, after Gambino struck a side deal with Tommy Ryan that allowed him a share of the spoils. The slippery Gambino had used Carollo to get exactly what he wanted.*

Carlo Gambino's favorite ally on the Commission, Tommy Lucchese, was curiously missing from the La Stella line-up. That is because he was not feeling well; in July 1967, Lucchese succumbed to cancer, while surrounded by his immediate family at his home in Lido Beach, Long Island. One neighbor pointed out how much he liked Lucchese over the rest of his neighbors, saying, 'If he's a gangster, I wish all of them were.' The old-timer, who had once helped Lucky Luciano set up Salvatore Maranzano and had sold out Lepke Buchalter, replacing him in the garment industry, left behind a clothing empire worth a couple of hundred million dollars with factories across the tri-state area. Lucchese's grip on New York State politicians was second only to that of Frank Costello and he had easily gotten his son, who he kept away from the rackets, a highly coveted congressional appointment to the United States Military Academy at West Point. Lucchese was laid out in Massapequa, Long Island, and he was buried at Calvary Cemetery in Queens, not far from Detective Joe Petrosino's final resting place. Lucchese left the reins to Anthony 'Tony Ducks' Corallo, but Ducks was serving a brief stint in prison so Carmine Tramunti stood in for him until Ducks was released.

Also in 1967, Joe Bonanno, who had been weakened by a heart attack, begrudgingly accepted the Commission's installment of Paul Sciacca. Bonanno held a meeting with his capos and told them he was prepared to step down 'to avoid bloodshed', then retired to Arizona where he'd owned a ranch since the 1940s. His reign had lasted nearly four decades. Fate was not as generous to Sciacca, who soon dropped dead of a heart attack. Nine capos formed a committee to run the family until a vote could be held to elect a new boss.

*

---

* Future racketeering indictments reflect the partnership change that occurred in 1966. In 1991, for example, video poker was legalized in Louisiana. The Genovese *and* Gambino families partnered in supplying the New Orleans borgata with poker machines, a job once reserved for the Genovese family alone. By then, the head of their borgata was Anthony Carollo, who had patiently waited his turn.

Not long after the La Stella meeting, the disappointed revolutionary Larry Gallo was diagnosed with cancer. When Pete the Greek visited Larry at St Vincent Hospital in May 1968, Larry asked Greek to sneak him in a handgun so he could end his own life. 'It's costing too much keeping me here,' Larry said, concerned for his family who were buckling under the pressure of hospital bills. 'I'm not going to survive this fucking thing. I know it.' Greek told Larry he would sneak him in a gun but he could not bring himself to do it. Larry died that same month.

Joseph 'Joe Yak' Yacovelli

Since the truce Larry had negotiated with Joe Colombo had held firm, no one was prohibited from attending Larry's wake, which was held in a packed funeral home owned by Colombo, who also attended the services. Crazy Joe Gallo was still in prison and still grieving over the loss of his best friend, Ali Baba, when news of Larry's death hit him like a cinder block. In addition to his inconsolable grief, Joey feared that Colombo would put a contract on him in prison now that Larry was out of the picture. Joey's concern was warranted. Colombo's consigliere, Joseph 'Joe Yak' Yacovelli, had been pushing Colombo to put a hit on Joey even before Larry died. Since Crazy Joe was constantly getting into beefs with other inmates, Yak figured he could put a contract on him in prison and it would look like an ordinary prison fight had accidentally ended in death. But Colombo did not think Crazy Joe would be a problem, so he told Yak, 'Leave him be.'

Unaware that Colombo had spared him from death, Joey distanced himself from his fellow Italian convicts, unsure who he could trust. With a knowledge of Islam he had picked up from his Muslim crew members in Brooklyn, he got on well with Black Muslim inmates and gravitated toward them. This created a new problem for Joey as tougher prisons have strict racial divisions. When white barbers refused to trim the hair of Black convicts in Attica State Prison, Joey took the side of the Blacks and accused the white barbers of racism. He then ate with the Blacks in a segregated mess hall, which angered the whites who set his cell on fire, driving Joey even closer to the Blacks and resulting in rumors that he was the head of a Black prison gang. From then on, whenever recently released Black gangsters stuck up mob-connected businesses, or kidnapped a mobster for ransom, Joey was accused of directing them from prison. As a result, more mobsters called for Joey's head and pressured Colombo to okay the hit that Joe Yak had been pushing for. But Colombo was distracted by an issue that was much larger than Joey and it involved the civil rights of the entire Italian-American community in America.

In 1965, the US Mint changed the composition of dimes and quarters from mostly silver to mostly copper. Those who were tipped off beforehand stockpiled silver coins and melted them into ingots, breaking federal law which prohibits the destruction of US currency. Since numerous mobsters owned countless coin-operated vending machine businesses across the country, they were, yet again, in an excellent position to capitalize on the change in policy and accumulate tons of silver. By April 1970, Joe Colombo's son, Joe Jr, allegedly melted over a half-million dollars in coins. His arrest by the FBI enraged Joe Sr, who said, 'They ain't satisfied with going after me, they gotta go after my kids. They're fuckin' rotten.' On another occasion, he said, 'Next thing, they'll be coming after my daughter.'

That same month, Colombo ordered his men to picket the FBI building at 69th Street and 3rd Avenue in Manhattan. Colombo claimed the FBI was unfairly targeting *all* Italians. Since the Italian-American community had always felt discriminated against, the picket line swelled with men, women and children who showed up with handmade signs with phrases like: 'What Happened to American Italian Constitutional Rights?'; 'FBI Is Anti-Italian'; 'All Americans of Italian Descent Only Want a Fair Shake'; 'FBI, Think Twice. We Can Question Your Children and Picket Your Homes'.

The unexpected turnout emboldened Colombo, who suddenly found himself at the center of a movement. 'We're gonna set up an organization,' he said, 'an Italian civil rights organization – and we're gonna break the FBI's chops. I want it real legit, like the Jewish and Black groups.' Instead of finding a squeaky-clean Italian-American to front for the group, Colombo imagined himself as Martin Luther King with a pinky ring, and formed the Italian-American Civil Rights League.

The picketing continued into the summer as FBI agents took

photographs of everyone in the crowd. Colombo responded by having his men click photos of the agents walking in and out of the FBI building. He also told his men to photograph the picket line so they could analyze the pictures and identify undercover agents among the genuine protestors and know who to look out for when those same agents surveilled mafia hangouts. When the agents became hip to this, they disguised themselves better and began to use the building's basement entrance, accessible from a different street.

It was not long before prosecutors convened two federal grand juries to investigate the Colombo family, which should have alerted Joe Colombo to the dangers of publicity. But Colombo did not seem to care. On 28 June 1970, just two months since his first protest at FBI headquarters, Colombo held a rally in Manhattan's Columbus Circle, an appropriate venue as it was the site of a marble statue of Christopher Columbus which rests atop a seventy-six-foot column; the monument, erected in 1892, was paid for by the small donations of hard-working Italian-Americans who were appalled by the lynchings in New Orleans and wanted to raise a monument to one of their ancestors. Originally billed as the Italian Pride Rally, Colombo was hoping to draw a few hundred people and was shocked to see over 50,000 men, women and children flock to Columbus Circle. With so many supporters in attendance and not working, the city practically shut down. The waterfront was a ghost town without laborers, and even Chinese restaurants and laundromats closed for the occasion in a show of solidarity for their loyal Italian-American patrons. Politicians showed up, like the Irish-born Paul O'Dwyer, who stood on the stage and said, 'The Italians are damned well burnt up, and I think they're right. There are millions of Italians in the United States and just a dozen or two dozen or a hundred hoods, and yet these hoods have become symbolic of Italian Americans.' O'Dwyer's words were accurate but the irony was that the rally was organized by one of those hoods! 'What made Colombo's pitch so confusing,' said a former New York City police chief, 'is that he *was* absolutely right. Italians had every right to resent being lumped by the millions into a Mafia whose nationwide membership does not exceed nine thousand men. But however small the organization, Joe Colombo was part of it.' Journalist Nicholas Pileggi accurately wrote that Colombo had pulled off a 'Sicilian sleight of hand' by conflating genuine discrimination against Italians with lawful attacks on the mafia.

Before the large crowd, Colombo strutted up to the microphone and said, 'I was willing to suffer through the attacks made by authorities. I accepted it as a part of life. But when they framed my boy Joey, then I knew I had to do something . . . I decided that if the FBI and the Justice Department want to make me boss of a Mafia family, so that's what I'll be. I'll use my position, given so graciously by the authorities, to help people of Italian-American heritage.' The applause was so deafening that Colombo seemed startled by it. Before everyone went home, Colombo told the crowd, 'This day belongs to you, the people. You are organized, united, and nobody can take you apart anymore.'

Just two days after the rally, the law started to take apart Colombo. He was arrested for criminal contempt of court stemming from a grand jury appearance. 'If this isn't harassment,' Colombo told reporters after posting bail, 'then I don't know what to call it.' Colombo's attorney gave him sound advice, saying, 'You know, Joe, as long as you stay visible with the League, they will keep coming at you with these frivolous arrests.' Colombo brushed off the warning. He seemed to enjoy the limelight and viewed his league as a new racket with endless ways to skim, putting a number of mobsters on the books for $300 a week plus expenses. This was *pastina* compared to the big picture; the league signed up thousands of new members who all paid monthly dues. Colombo also held large fundraising events that raked in over a hundred grand a pop, including one in Madison Square Garden that netted the league over a half-million dollars. They also sold millions of dollars in merchandise. Frank Sinatra, who had been forgiven for the Kennedy debacle after it was rectified in Dealey Plaza, stood behind the movement and offered free performances, along with his pal and fellow Rat Packer, Sammy Davis Jr. New York governor Nelson Rockefeller was given an honorary league membership, as were other politicians who wanted the Italian-American vote.

With a powerful movement behind him, Colombo demanded that television advertisements that made Italians look like buffoons be taken off the air, starting with an Alka-Seltzer commercial in which a non-Italian actor was clearly made to look like an Italian slob who says to his plump, aproned wife, 'Mama Mia, datsa somma spicy meatball!' Next, Colombo went after a Ragú spaghetti sauce commercial that was guilty of portraying Italians in a similar light. The successful television series, *The Untouchables*, was told to dial down their depiction

of Italian-Americans as criminals, and when Hollywood began film-
ing *The Godfather* movie, Colombo demanded that any offensive
references toward Italian-Americans be omitted from the script. After
realizing that this would have resulted in the film being edited down to
the length of a promotional teaser, Colombo reached out to producer
Robert Evans of Paramount Pictures who told fellow producer, Al
Ruddy, 'You've got to get together with this guy Joe Colombo. He's
putting pressure on the studio about *The Godfather*. I told him you are
the producer – you meet with him.'

Ruddy agreed to meet with Colombo and tried to explain to him
that the movie was not only a jab at Italian-Americans but took a
'skeptical look at Irish cops and Jewish movie producers', as if collec-
tive discrimination was more admirable than a solitary assault on one
ethnic group. Ruddy invited Colombo to his office where he promised
to show him the 155-page screenplay. Colombo took Ruddy up on his
offer and was handed the script, but after flipping through a few pages
and fiddling with his reading glasses, he told one of his minions to
look it over. 'Soon they were passing the script around,' said Ruddy.
'None of them wanted to read a 155-page script.' Colombo finally said
to them, 'Hey, do we trust this guy or not?'

Luckily for Ruddy, Colombo and his crew only insisted on the words
'mafia' and 'La Cosa Nostra' being struck from the script and never
got to the part where Jack Woltz screams at Tom Hagen, referring to
Hagen's associates as 'dago guinea wop greaseball goombahs'.

Part of the motivation behind Ruddy and Paramount Pictures caving
to the demands of a violent godfather who was passing himself off as
Rosa Parks was not grounded in a desire to properly portray Italian-
Americans; nor was it, as many would surmise, the fear of violence.
The studio also had concerns which were summed up best by author
Harlan Lebo: 'What would happen to *The Godfather* production if
trucks stopped rolling, food quit arriving, union members started
striking? The quite legitimate concerns about the characterization of
Italians on-screen could have easily translated into production delays or
the forced cancellation of *The Godfather* project . . . As soon as Ruddy
reached a deal with Colombo, the production's problems evaporated.
Prospects of union troubles disappeared. Threats of picketing were
called off. Concerns about location shooting vanished.' Ruddy himself
later said, 'Without the Mafia's help, it would have been impossible to
make the picture. There would have been pickets, breakdowns, labor

problems . . . The picture simply could not have been made without their approval.'

Colombo had also insisted that some of his men be brought onto the set as consultants and technical advisors, 'Thus,' as one astute observer wrote, 'presenting the ludicrous spectacle of providing advice on subjects about which they kept telling police they knew nothing . . . the mafiosi were telling the movie people what the mafia was really like – while refusing to call it the mafia and insisting that the organization actually didn't exist.'

Under political pressure, US attorney general John Mitchell ordered his Justice Department to refrain from using the same labels – 'mafia' and 'La Cosa Nostra' – on official documents and at press conferences. Governor Rockefeller asked the same of the New York press, which obliged with only slight pushback from free speech advocates like the editors of the *Staten Island Advance*, who continued to print the word 'mafia'. In early 1971, one of their delivery trucks was burned and the deliverymen were beaten senseless, forcing police to protect the rest of their trucks with armed escorts. Politicians who did not sign on were burned at the polls. State senator John Marchi, who said that any public official who supported the league was 'incredibly naive', lost in a mayoral election to John Lindsay after the Italian-American voting bloc shifted its allegiance to Lindsay as a reward for his support.

Colombo's league, headquartered on Manhattan's Madison Avenue, quickly grew to fifty chapters across the country, with over 150,000 members. In January 1971, *New York* magazine listed Colombo as one of the top ten most powerful men in New York. By April, an irked FBI struck again, this time indicting Colombo for masterminding a $10 million-a-year gambling operation. Colombo voiced outrage over the charges and refused to back down. In May, he was interviewed by Walter Cronkite; it was the first time in history that a mafia don spoke so freely to the press, and the public ate it up. In July, Colombo made the cover of *Time* magazine. His league proclaimed him 'Man of the Year' and presented him with a solid-gold plaque (another way of skimming money from the coffers). He received a second plaque from the *Triboro Post*, the Italian community's favorite newspaper, which also named him 'Man of the Year'. Colombo was invited on television talk shows and happily obliged. On the *Dick Cavett Show*, Colombo pretended to be a businessman, saying he owned shares in a florist shop and a funeral home. The studio audience could not help

Joe Colombo, Man of the Year

but laugh at the connection between a mob boss and a funeral home. A different studio audience burst out laughing when Colombo was introduced as a real estate salesman. Instead of laughing along like a good sport, Colombo took offense at the laughter.

Colombo was not the only mob boss who was not laughing. Informants began to tell the FBI that Colombo was losing underworld support; the more attention he received from the media, the hotter the feds turned up the heat on the other bosses, and the more they wanted Colombo to pack up his dog and pony show. One federal agent said, 'Every time Joe Colombo's face appears on the front page of a newspaper or on the evening news, a lot of the old guys in the mafia hit the ceiling.' Colombo was unmoved by their displeasure, nor did he care about the negative return on his publicity: since he started the league, he had been indicted for a gambling ring, a million-dollar diamond heist and income tax evasion, with more indictments being prepared.

Because Carlo Gambino had installed Colombo as boss, it fell on Gambino to rein him in. As Colombo planned a second rally in Columbus Circle, Gambino sent for him. 'You can no longer be around this league,' Gambino told Colombo. 'This is a fight you can no longer win, Joseph. Why can't you see that? Can't you see how angry they are with you? All of these arrests . . . Let the rally happen without you.'

'Carl,' said Colombo, addressing Gambino by his American name, 'I cannot do that. They need to see me there.'

'Who needs to see you?' asked Gambino, sarcastically. 'The FBI? The media? They want to lock you up in prison for the rest of your life. Is that what you want? Then what happens to your league? What happens to your family? You're not making any sense, Joseph.'

'I have been preaching to everyone in that organization . . . not to be afraid and not to back down,' said Colombo. 'If I back down, what kind of message would I be sending them?'

Gambino's paternal patience now expired. 'You should have never given them that hope,' he said. 'You have commitments that are much more important.'

Gambino then told Colombo that the waterfront, which Gambino controlled, would not be closed for the second rally, sending a clear signal to the underworld and the overworld that Gambino had broken with Colombo and his league.*

Joe Cantalupo Sr, who owned the realty that 'employed' Colombo, pleaded with Colombo to listen to Gambino. 'Take Carl's advice,' said Cantalupo. 'Step down from the league. The old man asked you to step down . . . Jesus, Joey, do it.' Cantalupo recommended that Colombo cede his public post to a politician or an entertainer. 'Step away. Get out of the spotlight . . . You can do everything you're doing now, but do it from behind the scenes.'

'No!' said Colombo. 'This is *my* thing. I don't care what he says, what he thinks. This is *my thing*, and I'm gonna run it.'

As Colombo dangerously dismissed Gambino's wise advice, he was confronted with another threat – this time from Crazy Joe Gallo, who was finally released from prison.

---

* After Albert Anastasia was killed, Carlo Gambino allowed Anastasia's brother, Tony, to live. Tony was a capo in the Gambino family and ran the waterfront through his control of the 8,000-member International Longshoreman's Union. When Tony Anastasia died of natural causes, his vacancy was filled by his son-in-law, Anthony Scotto, who studied political science at Brooklyn College. The smart, well-educated hoodlum became Gambino's Trojan horse that regularly rolled into the governor's mansion and the White House. Scotto, while maintaining the rank of capo, became a major political donor and advised President Johnson on labor relations. He was named as a possible candidate for secretary of labor by President Jimmy Carter.

Chapter 26

Disunity Day

The moment Joe Yak heard that Crazy Joe Gallo was up for parole, he went to Joe Colombo and said, 'Larry's dead. If Larry was still around, maybe he could keep Joe under control. But he's gone, and Joe will never come in. We'll have a lot of trouble with him . . . The only thing to do is hit him as soon as he comes out.' Colombo again held off, assuring Yak that Albert 'Kid Blast' Gallo could 'bring Joey in', meaning Kid Blast, who Colombo was currently getting along with, could convince his brother, Joey, to submit to Colombo's authority.

When Crazy Joe went away in 1961, he was an energetic 32-year-old rebel-hero who took on the mafia's establishment. When he was released in April 1971, he was a worn-down 42-year-old flunky with no money. 'He looked like a different Joey Gallo altogether,' said Pete the Greek, who collected Joey from prison along with Kid Blast and Louie 'The Syrian' Hubela. 'I couldn't get over how bony his face had gotten.'

On the car ride home to Brooklyn, Joey asked Blast how he felt about Colombo's leadership. Blast told Joey that he and their crew had not won any sit-downs under Colombo but Blast downplayed the losses, not wanting to stir up his wild brother. It did not work. 'If we have to move on that fat cocksucker Mr. Joe Colombo,' said Joey, 'we'll move on him just like we did Profaci.'

Whether Colombo liked Joey or not, it is incumbent upon any godfather to welcome home a family member who had just served time. Colombo sent soldiers Rocco Miraglia and Nicky Bianco to greet Joey with an envelope. Joey opened it in front of them and counted out a thousand dollars, which amounted to a hundred bucks a year for the ten years he had just served in the pen. It was an insult. Joey told them, 'Who the fuck needs this money?' then told them to tell Colombo to 'stick it up his ass'. He demanded $100,000, plus four buttons for four of his crew members. Bianco said to Miraglia as they left, 'Can you believe the sense of entitlement of this guy? He really is *ubatz*.'

When Joe Yak heard about Joey's demands, he told Colombo, 'We never should have let him get out of the joint. We should have hit him while he was still inside.'

Even if Joey's attitude was warranted and his demands were justified, Colombo no longer had any other choice but to whack him. Joey had proven, while both in and out of prison, that he was a born troublemaker, unable to take orders from anyone. Colombo put Joey off, telling him he was busy with his league and they would eventually get around to discussing his future, while Joe Yak assembled a hit team who began stalking Joey. But his movements were hard to pin down. 'We heard Joe Gallo was all over town,' said Yak's driver and bodyguard, Joseph 'Joe Fish' Luparelli, 'but he never stood in one place long enough for us to get to him.'

As Joey ducked death on a daily basis, Colombo was busy prepping for his second Unity Day rally. As promised, Carlo Gambino kept the waterfront open while other mob-controlled unions, including the Teamsters, were also told to keep working. With four crime families signaling their withdrawal from the league, Colombo's closest associates again pleaded with him to call off the event. Just as Cornelia begged her husband, Pompey the Great, not to go ashore in Egypt, and Calpurnia warned her husband, Julius Caesar, to stay away from the Senate, Colombo's wife urged him not to attend the rally, fearing for his safety. Anthony Colombo also pleaded with his father, telling him, 'Stay home and I'll take care of it for you . . . We can always have another league, but I only have one father.'

When Crazy Joe Gallo noticed that Colombo was being set adrift by the other families, he ordered his crew to yank down Unity Day posters in storefront windows and to warn the store owners to keep their businesses open. The owners were confused. In the morning, a group of flat-nosed guys hung up posters; by evening, another group of cauliflower-eared guys pulled them down. Where was the unity?

Early on the morning of 28 June 1971, Colombo awoke in his modest Brooklyn home and ate a hearty breakfast with his family. The big day was upon him. After getting dressed in a white-collared polo shirt and dark pants, he put on reading glasses and made last-minute edits to the speech he planned to deliver at the rally. Carlo Gambino had told the politicians who were in his pocket to withdraw their names from the list of speakers, which they did, but others who were close with Colombo were scheduled to deliver speeches, including

Joe Colombo with Sammy Davis Jr, who stood firmly behind the Italian-American Civil Rights League

Congressman Mario Biaggi; New York City comptroller and future mayor Abraham 'Abe' Beame; and Manhattan borough president Percy Sutton. As for entertainment, Colombo lined up his pal, Sammy Davis Jr, along with Frankie Valli and the Four Seasons, Tom Jones and B.B. King.

At around 10:30 a.m., Rocco Miraglia picked up Colombo at his house and drove him to Columbus Circle. To highlight Colombo's contradictory role of mafia don turned activist, he carried a briefcase that contained his speech – and a fully loaded .38 caliber revolver. He arrived at Columbus Circle at around 11 a.m. and waved to the crowd of 65,000 people, which was thinner than the 200,000 he was hoping for, but the band was not scheduled to strike up until noon, marking the official start of the event; there was still time for people to arrive.

The towering Christopher Columbus obelisk was festooned with red, white and green flags that fluttered in the gentle breeze as a smiling Colombo made his way toward the elevated platform. Fifteen hundred uniformed police officers worked the crowd, which was also infiltrated by an elite undercover unit of detectives and FBI agents. Six private ambulances decorated with a mix of Italian and American flags were on call for sunstroke victims, but everyone knew the wagons were there in case of violence.

Of the dozens of press photographers who clicked away with their cameras, one in particular stood out to Colombo who nodded to one of his men and said, 'Watch him.' The young African-American photographer Colombo 'had eyes' on was approximately thirty feet away from him and seemed to be searching for the best camera angles to photograph Colombo. As Colombo smiled, shook hands, kissed and interacted with the excited crowd like a candidate for public office, the photographer in question moved closer to Colombo before he swapped his camera for a handgun, dropped into a tactical shooting stance, and fired three bullets at Colombo from several feet away. One bullet came to rest in Colombo's jaw, another in his neck, and a third tunneled four inches into his brain where it settled. With three rounds of lead in him, Colombo clumsily reached out a hand for a police barricade before collapsing to the ground with blood streaming from his mouth and ears.

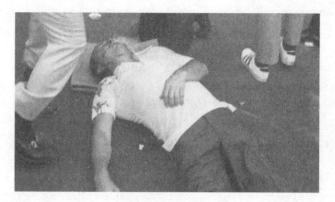

Colombo shot

After the sound of gunshots reverberated through Columbus Circle, there was an eerie silence and stillness before complete chaos broke out. Cops and civilians tackled the gunman to the ground and piled on top of him like a rugby scrum. One cop seized his wrist and smashed his hand against the ground to shake the gun loose while another pinned his other arm to the pavement. Suddenly, three more gunshots rang out, piercing the gunman's heart and lungs and instantly killing him; blood gurgled from his mouth. Fearing the gunman's body would be torn apart by the angry crowd, police loaded him into an ambulance instead of securing the crime scene, outlining his corpse and tagging evidence. Was the shooter silenced? And was the departure from police protocol intentional? Perhaps, since the second gunman has never been identified; nor do we know how he was able to fire three rounds then extricate himself from a tangled pile of human limbs and escape the scene with over 1,500 police officers present.

Colombo was taken to Roosevelt Hospital where he was given eight pints of blood, X-rayed and rushed into emergency surgery as his wife, Lucille 'Jo Jo' Colombo, and their four sons raced to the hospital. Surgeons removed the bullet in the middle of Colombo's brain and the slug in his neck, but decided it was best to leave the bullet in his jaw, at least for now. Colombo survived the five-hour surgery but had suffered a fate worse than death: his brain was dysfunctional; he would never walk or talk again.

Mobsters guarded the hospital's entrance and patrolled the hallways, unsure if someone would arrive to finish the job. 'Wherever I looked,' said Joe Cantalupo Jr, 'there were wiseguys.'

Sammy Davis Jr showed up at the hospital, as did another of Colombo's close friends, Rabbi Meir Kahane of the Jewish Defense League.*

By noon, when the band was scheduled to begin the event, radio broadcasts announced that mob boss Joe Colombo had been shot in Columbus Circle. Anthony Colombo called a press conference at the hospital where he sounded like J. Edgar Hoover, assuring everyone that his father had been shot by 'one maniac acting alone'. He blamed it on a 'deranged psychopath, the same kind that killed John Kennedy'. In response to speculation that Carlo Gambino was behind the hit, Anthony told everyone that Gambino was a 'very dear and close friend of my father's and is a real gentleman, and also the godfather of my six-year-old sister'.

In search of clues, Chief of Detectives Albert Seedman went to the hospital to view the dead gunman, who was lying on a cold steel rack, face down, with bullet holes in his back. Seedman was puzzled; it seemed as if someone had silenced the gunman just as Jack Ruby had silenced Lee Harvey Oswald. By 12:30 p.m., the Associated Press received a telephone call from someone who claimed responsibility for the shooting of Colombo on behalf of the Black Revolutionary Attack Team. Of the many Black revolutionary groups active at the time, the police had never heard of this one, which confused Seedman all the more. African-Americans were, moreover, fond of Colombo, had supported him, and had shown up in droves at both of his rallies.

Two months after Joe Colombo had been shot, he was discharged from the hospital and transported to Anthony Colombo's house in Brooklyn. The family boarded up the garage and converted it into a hospital room while they renovated their weekend home in upstate New York, where they planned to transport him once the proper accommodations were completed.

---

* Rabbi Kahane was an alleged bomb-maker and gun-runner who made Colombo look like a rabbi. Colombo once ordered his soldiers to march alongside Kahane's group, who were protesting the discrimination of Jews in Russia. 'What the hell have Russian Jews got to do with Cosa Nostra?' asked one capo, who was even more confused when Colombo pledged the borgata's support for Pakistani refugee relief. Kahane was assassinated nineteen years later while speaking at a rally in New York.

Consigliere Joe Yak assumed temporary control of the Colombo family which was no longer distracted by a civil rights campaign. Joe Yak was low-key to a fault. He dressed like a pauper and drove around in broken-down jalopies. Not surprisingly, he shunned the limelight and did not want to be boss, especially after Colombo had drawn so much attention to the position. 'This was a complete departure from his normal routine and way of operating,' said one investigator. The same could be said for the family's underboss, Charles 'Charlie Lemons' Mineo. Like an elderly man feeding pigeons to pass the afternoon, Mineo conducted most of his business from a park bench. He did not want to be boss, either.

As consigliere, it was Joe Yak's job to sound out the capos and choose a new boss who they would ultimately confirm by vote. Joe Yak would then run their choice by the Commission for final approval. But this was a strange affair since Gambino had put Colombo in place, and was also suspected of taking him out. Knowing Gambino would demand a say in who replaced Colombo, Joe Yak appointed 39-year-old businessman and capo, Vincent 'Vinny' Aloi, as acting boss. Vinny Aloi's father, Sebastian 'Buster' Aloi, was *compares* with Gambino for decades, and Gambino was also Vinny's christened godfather. 'He's smooth, lots of class,' one detective said of Vinny Aloi. 'A good family man with three children; goes to church on Sunday – the whole bit. That is why they gave him the family.' The capos were pleased, as was Gambino who quickly called for a Commission meeting where Aloi was unanimously approved and given a seat at the round table.

Since Colombo had been neglecting the borgata for months, Yak's next order of business was to demand an updated accounting of the family's rackets. His last order of business was to whack Crazy Joe Gallo, who Yak blamed for the attempted hit on Colombo, with no evidence to support his conclusion except that the shooter was Black and Joey was known to defend Black convicts in prison, and help them find jobs when they got out of jail. Joey also partnered with tough Black gangsters in African-American neighborhoods like East New York, Bedford-Stuyvesant and Brownsville. After being ostracized by the Colombo family, Joey vowed to start a 'sixth family' that would include Black mobsters. 'This is going to be an equal opportunity mob,' he said of his hybrid crew. In order for his crew members to get 'made' into his new family, Joey said he would 'dig up some Sicilian ancestors' that they could claim a relation to. No one took any of this seriously – until Colombo was gunned down by an African-American.

Although Joe Yak was quick to pin the shooting on Joey, the Gallo crew was shocked to learn that Colombo had been shot. Pete the Greek was half asleep at home when he heard a newsflash on television. 'A black guy shot him?' he asked his wife, confused. He ran down the hallway of their building and told Kid Blast, who was still in a bathrobe, yawning. 'Where?' asked Blast, before he contacted Joey and asked him if he had heard the news. Joey was just as surprised and confused as Greek and Blast. He told the crew to meet at Mondo the Midget's pool room, where Joey said, 'What a bum rap they're laying on us over here.' Greek felt the same way, saying, 'We still didn't know if Colombo was dead or what, but we knew that everyone would lay the shooting on us.'

Detective James O'Brien, who was surveilling President Street when Colombo was shot, said, 'I don't think Joey was responsible for the shooting – I don't buy that. I didn't see him there that day, but I could tell from the reaction of the guys. They weren't expecting it. I think they figured right away that they were going to be blamed for it anyway, so they'd better regroup, but I don't think they knew it was going to happen ahead of time.' Another investigator, who kept close tabs on the Colombo family, said, 'When the shooting took place, there weren't any indications Joey was involved.' With targets on their backs, the Gallo crew launched their own investigation as police identified the shooter by lifting his fingerprints at the morgue.

Jerome Addison Johnson was a 24-year-old drifter who was raised by his maternal grandmother in Waycross, Georgia. In 1965, he moved to New Brunswick, New Jersey, to live with his mother. After graduating high school, Johnson moved to Hollywood, California, to pursue his dream of becoming a movie star. He instead sold drugs, committed home burglaries and forged checks to get by. His long criminal history included violent crimes such as assault and rape, but he was hardly ever punished by the law. 'The most interesting thing about Johnson,' wrote Anthony Colombo, who eventually rethought his lone nut theory, 'was how he almost always managed to stay out of jail. While on probation, Johnson kept adding new and serious charges to his rap sheet. Who was coming to the aid of Johnson to make these charges go away?' It is now known that the FBI recruited Black informants to pose as photographers during the African-American civil rights movement. Although the Bureau adamantly denied having a file on Johnson, he had been issued an FBI number.

Johnson returned to New Jersey in 1969 and began to hang out on the campus of Rutgers University, where campus police arrested him on several occasions for illegal entry into girls' dormitories. It was the Age of Aquarius and Johnson, who called himself 'Pisces Man', mastered the subject of astrology, using it as a conversation starter. As a switch-hitter with a pretty good batting average, Johnson picked up men and women, sometimes passing himself off as a university professor, other times using phony business cards that said he was a Hollywood producer; he would offer people roles in his next film but was mostly 'interested in making pornographic movies'. In the spring of 1970, Johnson moved to Greenwich Village where he hung out in Washington Square Park and frequented gay bars and night-clubs owned or controlled by the Genovese and Gambino families. He survived by pimping and drug dealing, and crashed in seedy motels and rooming houses. While searching for evidence at his last known address in the Village, detectives found a steamer trunk and a terri-bly malnourished spider monkey. Cops cracked open the trunk but found nothing of interest: two Indian carvings, a box of incense, a few feathers, a book about astrology, and a stack of pornographic photographs, some depicting bestiality. The detectives found better clues inside the trousers Johnson was wearing when he was killed. In one pocket, there was an address book with sixty-six entries, mostly women he had dated. Cops also found blank checks with the name Bark Book Distributors, a wholesaler of pornographic books and magazines owned by Lucchese soldier Joseph Brocchini. Before the shooting of Colombo, the company's address was taken over by Club Orgy, a live adult entertainment center. Since Bark Books no longer existed, detectives never realized that Brocchini also owned Club Orgy. When the attorney on record for Bark Books was questioned by police, he simply said that the checks had been stolen.

The gun Johnson used to shoot Colombo was identified in police reports as a Menta Automatic handgun, which resembled a German Luger. Since the gun was manufactured in Germany during the First World War, the cops were unable to trace the weapon.

As for the murder of Johnson, several eyewitnesses reported that a police officer had shot him, or at least someone who was dressed like an officer. 'To get that close,' said New York City police chief Albert

Seedman, the assassin's killer 'must have burrowed into that pile-up like a human drill'. The revolver used to kill Johnson was discarded at the scene, and although it was traced to a police officer who reported it missing seven years earlier, the cops claimed it was untraceable. When, during a press conference, Chief Seedman was asked if a cop could have killed Johnson, Seedman said no. When asked how he could be so sure, Seedman said, 'Because we have the gun that killed Johnson; it's been tested by ballistics and it is not a police gun.' When asked who the last owner was, Seedman said, 'No comment on that question.'

Likely in an effort to lead the scent away from a police officer, the cops claimed that Colombo's bodyguard, Philip 'Chubby' Rossillo, removed a revolver from Colombo's briefcase, used it to kill Johnson, then escaped the scene. But Colombo's revolver was tested and proven not to have been fired, and no one bothered to explain how Chubby retrieved the revolver, penetrated the pile, shot Johnson, then master-fully extricated himself from this human pretzel and slipped past a screen of 1,500 cops, detectives and FBI agents who were all trained to subdue assailants as they had easily done with Johnson.

Bolex camera, inside which Addison is believed to have hidden his gun, if not in the camera's case

Detectives believed that Johnson had hidden his handgun inside his camera case, or inside the camera's empty magazine chamber. Unfortunately, the camera and its case disappeared on the day of the shooting. The missing camera was eventually dropped off at a police station by an ordinary citizen who had picked it up at the scene. He told police he did not hand it over to them at the time because he feared being mauled by the mob. He placed it in his automobile trunk and drove home. While drinking a beer in front of his television set, he and his brother-in-law checked the camera for film. He claimed that there was no film in it and decided to give the camera to the police, hoping they would owe him a favor.

The cops traced the empty camera to the Banner Camera Shop in Cambridge, Massachusetts. The next morning, Chief Seedman dispatched two detectives to visit the shop. The owner said that Johnson had rented the camera on Saturday after writing them a fraudulent check for $23.80. Seedman did not believe that a young drifter with no press credentials could stroll into a camera shop and write a bogus check for less than twenty-five bucks and walk out with a $1,200 Bolex camera. He called the story a 'bunch of crap' but mysteriously left it at that, never investigating the shop owner to see if he was somehow connected to Johnson, to organized crime, or to any other nefarious people.

Detectives also searched for a young African-American woman who had been seen with Johnson at the rally. She, too, was carrying a camera, believed to be a 35mm. It is quite possible she had been fooled into accompanying Johnson to the rally since detectives located a number of people, all women with the exception of one man, who Johnson had asked to assist him while he photographed the rally. By the time Johnson arrived at Columbus Circle, he had apparently found his assistant. After Johnson shot Colombo, witnesses saw this young woman hop over a police barricade. Two policemen stopped her, then let her go before she disappeared into the crowd. One cop described her as approximately five-foot-seven, wearing a mini-skirt and a sweater, while his partner said she was five-foot-two, wearing jeans. Actual photographs of her are believed to exist which makes sense given all the photographers inside Columbus Circle that day, but none have surfaced, adding yet another layer of mystery to this curious affair. Colombo capo Carmine 'The Snake' Persico was eventually able to get hold of a photo of her which he shared with his crew, hoping they could track her down and muscle her into telling them whatever she knew about Johnson. An FBI informant inside the Colombo family made a copy of the photo and shared it with his FBI handlers. Oddly, the Bureau buried the photo instead of searching for the woman or passing it on to the NYPD, who could have used it to break open the case.

With nothing to go on, detectives leaned toward Crazy Joe Gallo as the mastermind behind the entire ordeal, which is what Joe Yak wanted everyone to believe. Joey's association with Black prisoners and his reputation as an equal opportunity underworld employer cast him as the perfect suspect. Newspapers went so far as to portray Joey as the head of the Black mafia as detectives tried to discover a link between Joey and Johnson. They contacted the wardens at Greenhaven, Auburn and Attica state prisons, searching through their records to see if Joey had served time with any Black prisoners who might have introduced him to Johnson. The probe proved a big waste of time but detectives stuck with it anyhow, never stopping to consider what Joey's motive was when, in fact, Joey made no attempt at a power grab in the hours, days or weeks following the shooting of Colombo, a rather odd lack of initiative for someone who had supposedly masterminded a perfect coup without leaving behind a trace of evidence.

As the Gallo crew tried to make sense of the shooting, they put together a short list of suspects, beginning with FBI director J. Edgar Hoover, who Joey said, 'must be creaming his fucking pants' over the removal of a civil rights leader, however ludicrous Colombo may have been in this role. The crew did not think it beyond Hoover to have an African-American kill an Italian-American, hoping the Italians and Blacks would lunge at each other's throats while the rest of the country sat back and said, 'Let the animals kill each other.' The Gallo crew believed, if all went according to Hoover's plan, the Italian mafia would be at war with Black militants, two groups the government desperately wanted to destroy, while the Italian-American Civil Rights League would be leaderless. As it turned out, once Colombo was incapacitated the league did indeed fizzle out, its Madison Avenue headquarters were abandoned, and debts piled up.

Chief Seedman followed up on countless leads before lamenting, 'No crime in thirty years had left me so totally confused.' Of all the leads Seedman chased down, the most viable, in this author's opinion, came from a Black detective in Harlem who received a telephone call from one of his most reliable informants. The informant was afraid to meet in broad daylight so he asked if they could meet at night, inside Central Park. Under the cover of darkness, the informant told the detective that, a couple of weeks before Colombo was shot, he was contacted by a middle-aged heroin dealer named Harvey Turkman who owned a fabric store that was connected to the mob-controlled garment industry. Turkman also moved bales of imported heroin that were brought into the country by mafia drug traffickers via France, Corsica and Sicily; he, in turn, supplied Black drug lords who controlled the distribution networks in African-American neighborhoods. Turkman's wife and kids lived in Forest Hills, Queens, while Turkman spent most of his time in Manhattan. According to the informant, Turkman did not want to be seen with him in New York, so he paid for his cab fare from Harlem to Boston, Massachusetts, where they met inside of a bar. The informant said that Turkman, who was accompanied by an Italian man and a Black woman, told him that he wanted Colombo whacked at the upcoming Unity Day rally and would pay him $40,000 for the job, half up front and the other half after Colombo was dead. The street-savvy informant wanted to know why he would risk hitting Colombo at a public rally when the job could be done in a less dangerous setting. Turkman snapped at the question, telling him, 'Because we feel the effect will be best if we do it the way I just told you.' Whether the 'we' was Turkman and the two people he was sitting with, or a larger cabal, was unclear to the informant, who nodded along then asked how Turkman expected him to escape alive. The Black woman interjected, telling the informant that this was her responsibility and she would have plenty of Blacks planted in the crowd to cause a commotion and help him escape. Turkman insisted that the job was much easier than it sounded and offered the informant ten grand, spot cash, in good faith. The informant did not want to commit so he did not take the money and asked if he could sleep on it. He left the bar, knowing the job was a suicide mission despite promises to the contrary, but he was afraid to tell the trio no, feeling that he already knew too much for them to let him live. After sleeping on it, the informant decided it was safer to roll the dice on Turkman's wrath than get killed or arrested for murder in front of a hundred thousand people. The next evening, while packing a concealed handgun in case of trouble, he returned to the bar to decline Turkman's offer. To his great relief, he saw that Turkman had already moved on. It appeared that Turkman was having the same discussion with another young Black man who the informant knew to be Jerome Johnson. The informant returned home to Harlem, happy he was off the hook.

Note that the informant had no idea, when relating this story, that Jerome Johnson, a vagabond, had rented a $1,200 Bolex camera a short walking distance from where the informant had met with Turkman. Furthermore, detectives were able to account for most of Johnson's whereabouts in the weeks leading up to the shooting – except for forty-eight hours during which time the informant claimed to have seen Johnson in a Boston bar with Turkman.

Chief Seedman thought the informant's story was credible enough to do some digging and found out that the man seated beside Turkman was known as 'Butchie', an Italian-American mobster who lived in Boston's Black ghetto. In the months leading up to the shooting of Colombo, Butchie made an irregular number of telephone calls to Brooklyn and New Jersey, where Johnson lived. Seedman may have also figured out who directed Johnson to Turkman and Butchie. In the weeks leading up to the shooting, Johnson was often seen in the company of Michael Umbers, a hardened criminal with a record of arrests in New York and Boston. Umbers peddled pornographic material on the streets of Manhattan on behalf of the Gambino family and also frequented mob-owned gay bars; because he was trusted by both the gay community and the mob, he was nicknamed 'the fairy godfather'. Seedman questioned Umbers who was evasive.

With nothing else to go on, Seedman placed an authorized wiretap on Harvey Turkman's telephone. He took extraordinary measures to keep the tap a secret, yet a few days after it went live, Turkman shouted into the phone that he knew the cops were listening in on his calls. Who told Turkman that his telephone was tapped?

Two weeks before Colombo was shot at the rally, all five New York mob bosses were put under twenty-four-hour surveillance. Only days after the surveillance went up, Dennis Dillon, who worked for the Organized Crime Strike Force, told one of his minions, Michael Pollack, 'We are going to pull surveillance off of Joe Colombo.' Pollack thought this was crazy and inquired as to why but was only told, 'We're just not protecting Joe Colombo at this time.'

After Hollywood producer Al Ruddy had met with Colombo to discuss *The Godfather* movie script, he had been contacted by an FBI agent 'who gave me his information and told me to call him if I had any trouble with the League or Joe [Colombo]. He was just doing his job,' said Ruddy, 'offering protection in case someone tried to muscle me or anything. I never called him, but he would call me from time to time to check in. The night before the rally he called me and said, "Under no circumstances are you to be in Columbus Circle tomorrow!" The way he said it, it was like an order. I didn't know what it was about, he didn't explain it. He just hung up the phone.'

Daniel Hollman, chief of the Joint Strike Force to Combat Organized Crime, insisted it was not a mob hit. When questioned by reporters, Hollman insinuated that he was basing his conclusion on more than just a hunch, but he could not elaborate. 'I prefer to leave this now as my own observations,' he said. 'I don't want to get into my sources.'

The words of Dennis Dillon, Al Ruddy and Daniel Hollman pointed toward something more nefarious than an ordinary mob hit which can also be disproved by the utter and obvious lack of planning that went into filling the power vacuum left by Colombo's removal: Crazy Joe Gallo was still walking around with his thumb up his ass, Joe Yak and Charlie Lemons did not want the top spot, nor did Vinny Aloi, who was pushed into the promotion. Since Carlo Gambino had put Joe Colombo in place, and it therefore fell on Gambino to remove Colombo, could Gambino have been working with the FBI or the CIA?

In the early 1970s, FBI agent Anthony Villano handled top-secret assets for the Bureau's Top Hoodlum Intelligence Program. In Villano's memoir, he writes about a heroin trafficker named Moishe Kessler who moved skids of imported heroin for the Gambino family, as did Harvey Turkman. Once, when Kessler was arrested, he told the US attorney at his arraignment, 'You can't touch me, I'm CIA.' Agent Villano was shocked by the statement, and even more shocked when Kessler 'received a mysteriously light sentence for a heroin rap'. A puzzled Agent Villano tried to connect the dots and wrote, 'It has been gossiped that the Gambinos were the avenue of communication between the CIA and the underworld. It would be logical of the CIA not to deal with the hired help when they might go directly to the boss of bosses, Carlo Gambino.' Did Agent Villano unwittingly solve the Colombo case by connecting Gambino to the CIA? Was Harvey Turkman, who knew and dealt heroin with Moishe Kessler, another mafia-connected CIA asset? Was this how Turkman immediately knew that the NYPD was tapping his telephone? Was this why Jerome Johnson's killer was reported to be wearing a police uniform? And why that same killer was able to escape a twisted pile of men and a dragnet of 1,500 officers? Was this why the photo of Johnson's assistant never surfaced? Was there an elaborate plot to murder Colombo then immediately silence the man who killed him?

About ten months into the investigation, the homicide coordinator at Manhattan South, Captain McDermott, announced an abrupt end to the Colombo case. 'Why would the Police Department decide to abandon the Colombo investigation?' asked a confused Deputy Police Commissioner Robert Daley. 'And who gave the order?'

Closing the case was heavily criticized inside the NYPD, and since no one could figure out who issued the order, the consensus was that the feds had pulled the plug. When Daley and others inquired as to exactly who was responsible for closing a hot case, Captain McDermott only said that the call came from the very top. 'One day,' Daley later wrote in his memoir, 'I questioned Deputy Commissioner McCarthy, but he said he knew nothing about who had closed down the Colombo case.' Whoever was ultimately responsible, it was 'inconceivable' to Daley that a police commissioner would get involved in a homicide case, 'one way or the other'. The inference was that the commissioner was told to back off by someone more powerful.

Joe Cantalupo Jr, whose father employed Colombo at Cantalupo Realty, eventually became a confidential informant, and was asked by his FBI handler to see if the bedridden Colombo was truly broken beyond repair. 'The Feds weren't sure about Colombo,' said Cantalupo, 'they always had a lingering fear that he'd return and reorganize things and cause a whole lot of trouble again . . . so they pushed me, pressed me, to arrange to see for myself how he was.' When a legal folder of documents was being delivered to Colombo's upstate home by Cantalupo Sr, Cantalupo Jr asked if he could tag along. That day, he saw Colombo in his makeshift hospital bed, 'lying there like a lump with plugs in his head where he'd been shot'. Cantalupo later reported to his FBI handler that he had watched Colombo's wife spoon-feed him as the food dribbled over his lips and down his chin. The agent was thrilled to hear this and replied, 'You did good, Joe. We had to know.'

Chapter 27

Sticking His Head in the Noose

Whether Crazy Joe Gallo was innocent or guilty of being behind the attempted hit on Joe Colombo made no difference to Joe Yak, who ramped up his efforts to whack him, telling 'Joe Fish' Luparelli, while grinding his teeth, 'I want that bastard's head. I want to roll it down President Street like a bowling ball so everyone can see it . . . Watching him die, I'd actually come.' That same day, Yak called on the professional photographer who photographed many of the Colombo family weddings and other celebrations. Yak isolated photos of each Gallo crew member he wanted dead and circulated them among several hit teams. But the Gallo crew, all combat veterans of the Profaci war, were not so easy to ambush, especially on President Street where they knew every face that belonged on the block. As for Crazy Joe, he knew to stay away from anywhere he was invited and avoided Manhattan's mob-infested Little Italy for several weeks. But it was in his nature to dare people and his caution soon wore off. After being spotted at Luna's Italian restaurant on Mulberry Street, it got back to Joe Yak who said, 'This guy is sticking his head in the noose.' Yak told Fish to have a hit team stake out Luna's.

Joe Fish stationed snipers inside an apartment with a view of the restaurant, but the plan went awry when one of the snipers accidentally squeezed off a round that went through a wall and into the apartment of a Chinese family. No one was hurt but Yak called off the operation and again attempted to track Joey's movements, but his schedule was as schizophrenic as his mind; he constantly changed plans or forgot to show up at appointments. He would sometimes be on his way to a meeting, get a new thought in his head and make a U-turn, completely forgetting where he was originally headed. A combination of irresponsibility and vacuity was keeping him alive.

The press, which had been following the Colombo family since the first Gallo rebellion, was in awe of Joey and viewed him as a hero. In an age of hippies, Vietnam War demonstrators and the Black Panthers,

Joey, with his diverse ethnic crew that included a lion and a dwarf, was seen as the little man taking on the establishment. The media coverage gained Joey VIP status at trendy restaurants and popular places like the famous Elaine's, which opened in 1963 and catered to celebrities who all wanted to be around Joey.

Joey's forty-third birthday fell on 7 April 1972. Despite his underworld problems, he was in a festive mood and decided to celebrate with his second wife, Sina, and her ten-year-old daughter, Lisa; his sister, Carmella 'Cam' Fiorello; actor Jerry Orbach and his wife, Marta; Pete the Greek and his date, Edith Russo. The group started the evening at the Copacabana, where they emptied a few bottles of champagne while listening to comedian Don Rickles beat up on Blacks, Jews and Italians. Rickles knew Joey and directed some personal jokes at him, then said, 'Seriously, folks, Joey is turning forty-three today. Yeah, happy birthday, Joe. God bless ya. That's, what, a hundred fifteen in President Street years?' Following his act, Rickles visited Joey's table to pay his respects to the mafia's Che Guevara.

When the Copacabana closed, Joey was in the mood for a late-night meal and suggested Chinese food. Everyone piled into Pete the Greek's large black Cadillac and headed for Chinatown. On the way there, Joey changed his mind and suggested they eat at Luna's in Little Italy. After finding that Luna's was closed, the carpool drove around in search of an open restaurant and saw the lights on at Umberto's Clam House, a newly opened, cheaply decorated seafood restaurant with butcher-block tables and fishing nets strung between life preservers along the wall. The owner of Umberto's was Genovese capo Matthew 'Matty the Horse' Ianniello, who was standing on the sidewalk talking to 'Joe Fish' Luparelli when Pete the Greek's car pulled up. Fish later said, 'I turned my head so Gallo and the Greek couldn't get ahold of my face. They both knew me.'

After the car rolled to a stop, Joey asked Matty the Horse, 'How's the seafood, any good?'

Matty the Horse, knowing there was a contract on Joey's head, took a shot at dissuading the Gallo party from eating at his place by telling Joey he had not yet been approved for his liquor license and could not serve them alcohol. Joey said they were there to eat, not drink, and told Greek to park the car. The Gallo party entered the restaurant, sat down at a table in the back, and ordered pasta, shrimp, scungilli, mussels and calamari.

As they ate, Joe Fish ran over to King Wah, a Chinese restaurant on Mulberry Street owned by an Italian-American, Dickie Palatto, and his Chinese-American wife, Mona. Mobsters Carmine 'Sonny Pinto' DiBiase, Philip 'Fat Fungi' Gambino (no known relation to Carlo) and two brothers, Benjamin 'Benny' and Francisco 'Cisco' LoCicero (sons of the notorious Charles 'The Sidge' LoCicero, who was part of the delegation that visited President Street during the hostage crisis), were seated around a square table eating Late Night Combination Platter #1: beer and lo mein.

The dominant figure of this small crew was Sonny Pinto, who had a brain the size of a pinto bean but a sharp instinct for survival and a murderous streak that dated back twenty years. Back in 1951, Sonny Pinto was playing cards on Mulberry Street, less than two blocks from Umberto's Clam House, when he got into a heated argument with his longtime friend and partner in crime, Michael Errichiello. Pinto left the card game, returned with a gun and shot Errichiello three times in the head, then, when police arrived, pretended to be distraught over

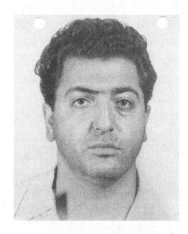

Errichiello's death while insisting that he had nothing to do with it. Through a combination of good acting and lousy police work, the cops let Pinto go then realized he was the killer. In the meantime, he took it on the lam. In 1959, he turned himself in, figuring, after eight years, the case was weak. But he was convicted and sentenced to die in the electric chair. He appealed the conviction and was acquitted after a second trial. Since then, Pinto was suspected of killing more people, including Joey's best friend, Ali Baba, who was shot after disembarking from a cruise ship.

Carmine 'Sonny Pinto' DiBiase

Joe Fish barged into King Wah and said to Pinto, 'Guess who's in the Clam House?'

'Who?' asked Pinto.

'Joe Gallo's in there with Pete the Greek.'

Pinto stared at Fish in disbelief then went to a public telephone to call Joe Yak for the green light. Yak only wanted to know what in hell

Pinto was waiting for. Pinto hung up the phone and said to his crew, 'We're going to load up, and we're going to hit him now. We'll whack him out right there.'

There was no time to steal cars, they would use their own. Joe Fish and Fat Fungi would park in a crash car, ready to block off the intersection or ram a patrol car, while Sonny Pinto, Benny and Cisco would drive up in another car and go in for the kill.

It was close to 5 a.m. when both cars parked outside of Umberto's, which was situated on a corner with windows on both sides. Its main entrance was on Hester Street with a side door on Mulberry Street. From Joe Fish's vantage point, he had a clear view of the restaurant and could see Sonny Pinto, dressed in a light tweed jacket, approach the side entrance and swing open the door. Pinto made brief eye contact with Pete the Greek before homing in on Joey like a laser. 'What the fuck is this?' Joey blurted before Pinto raised his gun and shouted, 'Die motherfucker!' Benny and Cisco followed him in and were firing over his shoulder as Matty the Horse, a decorated Second World War veteran, hit the floor face down with both hands over his head. Chef Salvatore LaMonica also dove for cover, as did a waiter and a half-dozen other patrons. Joey's wife, Sina, threw her fur coat over her ten-year-old daughter and told her to play dead as Joey overturned a table then sprinted the length of the narrow restaurant. Sonny Pinto 'blasted away at Gallo as if he were a duck in a shooting gallery', hitting him in the elbow, the buttocks, the spine, and cutting his carotid artery, stopping blood to the brain. Joey crashed through the front door and staggered into the street like a drunkard before he collapsed and rolled over onto his back.

With a big smile across his face, Sonny Pinto back-pedaled out of the side door followed by Cisco and Benny. They got into the getaway car and sped off. Pete the Greek ran outside and emptied his gun into the back of their car. He then raced back inside and threatened to kill Matty the Horse for setting them up. 'Jesus,' said Matty. 'In my own place? You gotta believe me.' Greek could see he was telling the truth. He rushed outside and kneeled beside Joey, whose blue pinstriped suit was soaked in blood; his green eyes stared at nothing. Carmella was already holding Joey's head in her lap as she wailed hysterically, 'It's my brother Joey Gallo!'

Officers Felice Agosta and Robert Barnes were in a squad car when they heard Carmella crying and screaming. As the officers cautiously approached the commotion, they saw Pete the Greek toss his empty gun under a car. Agosta retrieved the weapon then told his partner to call an ambulance. Greek insisted that they had no time to wait for an ambulance. 'Get him to the hospital!' Greek yelled at the cops as he picked up Joey and laid him across the back seat of their squad car. The cops sped off, sirens blaring, as Greek tried to resuscitate Joey in the back seat.

At Beekman Hospital, Joey was pronounced dead on arrival. Only then did Greek realize he had been shot in the hip and the hand; his adrenaline had masked the pain. No one else in the place had been hit despite the fact that Sonny Pinto and his pals had squeezed off over twenty rounds in less than ten seconds. All of the bullets inside Joey's body were from a .38 – Pinto's revolver.

Reporters sped to the crime scene at Umberto's Clam House and were disappointed to learn that Joey had already been taken away. Deputy Police Commissioner Robert Daley told them, '[Gallo] made a mistake . . . he should have gone to bed last night.' The residents of Mulberry Street peered down from windows, rooftops and fire escapes as crime scene tape was strewn between police barricades. Most of them clammed up when asked about the Clam House. An evidence team went to work inside the restaurant, dusting for fingerprints and digging deformed slugs out of the bar and paneling as detectives questioned Matty the Horse and Chef LaMonica, both of whom said they were staring down at the floor throughout the entire ordeal, which was true.

Almost incredibly, Sonny Pinto, Cisco and Benny returned to King Wah to finish their meals and order another round of drinks. When the men were satiated, 'Sonny lay down in the back seat [of my car],' said Joe Fish, 'and took a nap while I drove up to Nyack', where an anxious Joe Yak was waiting to greet them. Joe Yak gave Sonny Pinto a big wet kiss on the mouth then asked Joe Fish who else had been in the Clam House. To be sure, Joe Yak was not concerned about women and children, or any other innocent patrons; he wanted to know if there were any wiseguys from any other families so he could assess the political fallout. Fish told Yak that Matty the Horse was there. Yak knew that if Pinto admitted to knowingly shooting up Umberto's with the Horse present, the Genovese family could demand that Pinto be put down like a horse. Pinto prudently said, 'I didn't see nobody but Gallo. All I saw was that fuck's face and we were shooting at him.' Yak was satisfied with Pinto's excuse and told him to stick to it. He then asked Pinto, 'How do you know [Joey's] dead?'

'We musta hit him a few times,' said Pinto. 'And he went down. He must be dead.'

'What about Pete the Greek?' asked Yak. 'Is he dead?'

'I don't know,' said Pinto. 'I don't think so.'

'Why ain't he dead?' asked Yak, already dissatisfied.

'Maybe he is,' answered Pinto.

Yak turned on the radio and listened to round-the-clock news bulletins as Pinto lay down on a couch and dozed off. The first mention of the mayhem in Little Italy reported that 'Joe Gallo, head of Brooklyn's notorious Gallo gang, was reported shot', but the bulletin did not confirm that he was dead. 'If he's alive,' Yak said to Fish, 'we're gonna have to go in the hospital and kill him there. I don't give a fuck how many people are around.' By morning, a second newsflash confirmed that Gallo was dead. 'We all kissed Sonny Pinto on the mouth,' said Joe Fish, who experienced an extra sense of relief since he no longer had to cowboy it into a hospital, dressed as a doctor.

As the Gallo crew met at Mondo's club to mourn Joey's death and cry on each other's shoulders, Joe Yak was tying up loose ends from his safe house in Nyack. One of Pete the Greek's bullets pierced a back tire of Sonny Pinto's getaway car, leaving it flat. Just to be safe, Yak arranged for Pinto's car to be crushed. As for the unfortunate owners of King Wah, Dickie and Mona, Yak said, 'These people may have to go. They seen and heard too much.' And they went. Dickie Palatto died in mysterious circumstances; he drowned in three feet of water, which might not have been odd if he was only two feet tall. A week later, his wife Mona disappeared.

Crazy Joe Gallo was killed a mere ten months after Joe Colombo had been shot, an attempted hit that Gallo had been accused of but had nothing to do with. He was laid out in a funeral home in Brooklyn, dressed like a gangster in a dark blue pinstriped suit, similar to the threads he had once worn before the Rackets Committee, an appearance that pumped up his head and arguably got him into this mess.

Besides his big trip to appear before Congress, Joey Gallo's underworld claim to fame was the hit on Albert Anastasia, whose birth name was Umberto, also the name of the restaurant where Joey was murdered; we cannot help but think that this is how natural justice gives itself a chuckle to keep itself sane and point out to disbelievers that its hand is sometimes slow but always firm.

The Colombo and Gambino families were ordered to stay away from Joey's wake but the Gallo crew faithfully attended. To my non-Italian readers, I can tell you that, when I grew up, Italian funeral parlors were the poor man's opera house where the Italian drama was played out by the greatest of actors. My grandmother and her sisters would get a running start before throwing themselves onto a coffin, offering to exchange themselves for the dearly departed. At the Gallo wake, Joey's mother, Mary, did not disappoint. She threw herself onto the casket, screaming, 'Take me with you!' Joey's sisters joined in and heavily poured it on until a couple of uncles peeled them off the casket.

On the way to the cemetery, the long funeral procession passed Joey's headquarters on President Street, where construction workers paused and took off their hard hats like the respectful crane operators who bade farewell to Winston Churchill as his flag-draped casket was carried along the Thames. As Joey's casket was lowered into the ground next to Larry's, Joey's sister, Carmella, began screaming, 'The streets are going to run red with blood, Joey!' She was right. The first weekend after Joey was hit, 36-year-old Richard 'Rickie' Grossman was found in the trunk of a car that was abandoned in Sheepshead Bay. He was beaten before both eyes were shot out. After the weekend, on Monday, 10 April, Gennaro Ciprio's skull was blasted to pieces with buckshot as he left his own restaurant. The killer was perched on the roof above him.

The scarce remnants of the Gallo crew went back to the mattresses on President Street as the New York Times reported a resurgence of violence inside the Colombo family. Although the article said that both sides had an equal number of men, one side was far more invested in the fight: Joe Yak's army was made up of initiated soldiers and aspiring recruits while the Gallo crew, under the leadership of Kid Blast, was a hybrid band of ethnicities who could not advance through the ranks of the Italian underworld and were especially demoralized without Larry and Joey around to champion their cause. Within two months, over a dozen men were killed, knocking the Gallo crew out of the war. The Commission finally voted to break up the Gallo gang and scatter them among the five families. Kid Twist ended up with the Genovese family. Pete the Greek was given a pass for pointing a gun at Matty the Horse and, after serving ten months in prison for the bullets he fired at Sonny Pinto's getaway car, he left for Greece where dinner plates are smashed in celebration, not by bullets.

Throughout the war, Joe Yak, Joe Fish and Sonny Pinto stayed on the lam in their hideout in Nyack. Fish ordinarily drove Yak to secret meetings in one of two cars, both of which were registered to Fish's wife. One day, Yak told Fish to have his wife pick up both cars in Nyack. Fish wondered how his wife would get there since she did not have a car left at home to drive, and further wondered how she would drive both cars home. Fish began to question Yak's motives and remembered that Yak had once told Fish to murder his wife after she filed police charges against him over a domestic dispute. Although she quickly dropped the charges, Yak remained bitter toward her. Fish now concluded that Yak was planning to kill his wife when she arrived to pick up the cars. Yak was actually planning to kill Fish, but since he did not trust Fish's wife either, he decided to kill them both.

Joe Fish used creative excuses to put off calling his wife. When Fish figured out that Yak wanted him dead as well, he could not sleep a wink. One morning, Yak told Fish that a few Bonanno wiseguys were coming to visit them in Nyack. Once again, Yak told Fish to have his wife pick up the cars. Fish now wondered why Yak, who did not trust his wife to begin with, would want her around when even more wiseguys were present at a secret hideaway. Fish knew that hits were often a cooperative undertaking and concluded that Yak had asked the Bonanno mobsters to do him a favor and dispose of Fish and his wife. Appealing to Yak's obsessive penchant for caution, Fish told Yak he would run out and relay the message to his wife over a public telephone. He left the safe house and drove around for a while, wondering if he was delusional. He finally decided that he was not imagining any of this and made a telephone call, not to his wife, but to Yak.

'Where are you?' asked Yak.

'Just riding around,' said Fish. 'I gotta think.'

'Listen,' said Yak, 'before you do anything stupid, come back.'

'No, Joe, I'm not coming back. Why you turned against me, I don't know. I loved you like a brother, and you're doing this to me. Why? Because I love my wife and children? Because I didn't kill her? Have I ever dishonored anybody? Have I ever broke the code? I always done what you told me to do except that one time – and now you want my wife to come up there! Since when do you use a man's wife to come to a hideout and pick up cars? Joe, you think I don't know what you got in mind?'

'What are you gonna do?' asked Yak, never denying the accusation, and already considering the ramifications.

'I don't know,' answered Fish. 'I'm just taking off for a while.' A while, as in, the rest of his life. Fish drove to an airport in Philadelphia and boarded a flight for California where his sister lived with her family.

When Yak realized he had accidentally spooked Fish, he was beside himself with rage. He dispatched two goons to keep a close eye on Fish's wife with instructions to kill Fish on sight, along with his wife if they were seen together. The only reason Yak did not whack his wife straight away was because he did not have the bigger 'Fish' in the net, and killing his wife could drive Fish to snitch, which Yak was not yet certain he was doing.

On 18 April 1972, Joe Fish walked into an FBI office in Santa Ana, California, and said to the desk agent, 'My name is Joe Luparelli. I'm here for protection.'

'From what?' asked the agent. After listening to some of Joe Fish's story, the young California agent, unfamiliar with the New York mafia, assumed that a lunatic had walked in off the street. 'What's a consigliere?' he asked Joe Fish, baffled. The agent finally contacted the FBI's New York office and said, 'I think I've got a nut on my hands.'

'He's no nut,' said the New York agent. 'He's for real. Hang on to him.'

The New York office dispatched a team of agents to protect Fish's family and arranged to return Fish to New York under police protection.

Before Joe Fish had even entered the FBI office in Santa Ana, Joe Yak had abandoned his hideaway in Nyack and ordered a crew of grunts to dig up every murder victim Fish had helped the Colombo family kill and bury. In the dead of night, the stinking, decomposed bodies were relocated to new gravesites. One victim, however, was discovered by the law.

Joe 'Wagon Wheels' Viscovi was a two-bit hoodlum who preyed on gutter criminals like pushers, pimps and prostitutes. One day, Wagon Wheels and his rag-tag crew targeted the wrong guy – Joe Yak's brother. They robbed and beat him to within an inch of his life. When Yak found out about it, he ordered all hands on deck; the entire Colombo family went searching for Wagon Wheels with orders to bring him in alive so Yak could enjoy a slow revenge. Joe Fish found Wagon Wheels in a bar and told him he was looking to unload a bundle of stolen traveler's checks. Wagon Wheels assured Fish that he had approached the right man, which Joe Fish already knew. The next day, Fish picked up Wagon Wheels, who was dressed in a snakeskin jacket and alligator shoes. They drove to Little Italy where Fish led Wagon Wheels into an apartment on Elizabeth Street. Instead of a bundle of traveler's checks, Wagon Wheels was blindsided by Joe Yak, Sonny Pinto and others who slammed the door behind him and threw him to the floor. According to Fish, they strangled him with a wire as Yak repeatedly stabbed him with an ice pick that punctured organs until it got stuck in his cervical vertebrae. At some point, Sonny Pinto said in a low voice, 'Keep quiet. Somebody's knocking on the door.'

'For Christ's sake, Sonny,' said Yak, 'that's the guy's foot.' Wagon Wheels was kicking a shoe against the floor with his last ounce of life before he expired. Fish said, 'He was lying facedown on the floor with the ice pick handle sticking out of his back . . . They had to use the butt of a gun to knock it loose and get it out.'

After Joe Yak got his revenge, the killers went for drinks to wind down. Later that evening, Joe Fish wrapped up the stiff and buried him in the basement of a building, where the corpse remained interred until Fish went sour and Yak had it relocated to New Jersey. But although Yak's crew of gravediggers had severed the head and hands from the body and disposed of them in different places to avoid dental recognition and fingerprinting, they buried the legs and torso in its pimped-out, reptilian attire. When police discovered an incomplete corpse in New Jersey, dressed in a snakeskin jacket and one alligator shoe, they knew it was Joe 'Wagon Wheels' Viscovi, because of Joe Fish's detailed description of what he was wearing on the day he was killed.

Besides Wagon Wheels, Joe Fish admitted to 'five or six' other murders – he could not remember exactly how many because there were probably more – and detailed everything that happened on the night of the Gallo hit. As for Fish's wife, who had once called the police on Fish, when a detective told her that her husband had flipped, she said, 'I have the kids, one of them a boy in school. How am I going to explain to him about his father?'

'It was a good question,' said the detective. 'How *do* you explain to a wide-eyed kid that his father is a hood who helped murder another hood?'

'That's not what I mean,' answered Mrs Luparelli. 'I mean, how am I going to explain to my boy that his father is a squealer?'

In February 1974, after nearly three years on the run, Joe Yak surrendered to police, knowing the cases against him were old and too weak to stand up in court. He was quickly released. Sonny Pinto was eventually indicted by a Manhattan grand jury for the murder of Crazy Joe Gallo but, by then, he had gone on the lam and has never returned. (He is believed to have died naturally in 2011, while still at large.)

The Crazy Joe Gallo hit ranks up there with the greatest mob hits of all time, even though Joey was never a boss, and never even a capo. Unlike Joey's original boss, Joe Profaci, who left behind an estate estimated to be worth $100–200 million, Joey's estate, if we can call it that, was unable to cover his own funeral expenses. His fame rested solely on his wild personality and the Gallo rebellion that challenged the mafia's old regime during a volatile period in American history that saw civil rights marches, violent prison riots and anti-war protests. The press sympathized with the public's revolutionary spirit, and the Gallo rebellion checked off the mafia box in a long list of revolts that challenged authority on every level of society.

Like Virginia Hill's mansion which became an attraction for tourists after Benjamin Siegel was murdered there, Umberto's Clam House was pointed out by New York City tour guides as the place where Crazy Joe Gallo was whacked. (Matty the Horse benefitted from the uptick in patrons, who tried to furtively look around between bites of calamari.)

In 1976, Bob Dylan, an icon to the counter-culture movement, released an album titled *Desire*. One of Dylan's songs was 'Joey', in memory of Crazy Joe Gallo.

A homicide detective who tried to talk sense into Joey once said to him, 'One night we'll come out and the dead body will be yours.'

'You're right,' answered Joey, 'because I was never one of these guys who wants to live forever. I want to be a big winner or a big loser.'

One might argue that he was both. A newspaper headline following his death read: GALLO IS BURIED; HIS LEGACY LIVES ON.

Part Five

Reckonings

Chapter 28

The Return of Bobby and Hoffa

Following the assassination of President Kennedy, Teamster president Jimmy Hoffa no longer had Bobby Kennedy to worry about, but the prosecutions Bobby had set in motion eventually caught up with Hoffa who was convicted in two separate trials, one in Tennessee and the other in Chicago. By 1964, Hoffa received a combined sentence of thirteen years in prison.

Hoffa remained free on bail as his defense team filed appeals. At the same time, Carlos Marcello, whose real estate development projects received tens of millions of dollars in loans from the Teamster pension fund, set up a $2 million defense fund which was used, in part, to bribe witnesses into changing their previous testimony. The lead witness who had testified against Hoffa was Ed Partin, the union thug who had once passed a lie detector test after telling the feds that Hoffa had asked him to murder Bobby Kennedy. Marcello did not send his goons to talk with Partin; instead, he had his political contacts approach him. One of Marcello's messengers was an aide to Louisiana governor John J. McKeithen. When the aide was later questioned as to why he spent so much time with Marcello, he said, 'I go to the Town and Country [Motel] because there's always lots of politicians there.'

Another one of Marcello's messengers was pay-for-play influencer D'Alton Smith, whose brother was on the state board of education and whose sister was on the state insurance commission. Through Smith, Marcello recruited the help of the most decorated American war hero of all time, Audie Murphy, who asked Partin to reverse his testimony. When Partin would not budge, Marcello tried to get Walter Sheridan to help Hoffa stay out of prison. The former head of the Get Hoffa Squad, and the man Hoffa had once called 'a slimy, sleazy rat' on national television, was offered 'a million dollars in cash' if he would 'switch sides' and go to bat for Hoffa. Sheridan, who turned down the generous offer, said it was 'clear that money was no object if tape recordings or other information helpful to Hoffa could be produced'.

Before long, Justice Department officials launched a grand jury inquiry into Marcello's efforts to free Hoffa through bribery, but the Little Man's connections ran deep. Senator Russell Long of Louisianna swiftly 'threatened to get the officials indicted' if they did not desist. They backed off and Marcello was in the clear. Hoffa, however, was still heading to prison so in the summer of 1966 he changed the Teamsters' constitution so that he could remain the union's president and collect an annual salary of $100,000 while in prison, a grim reality that Hoffa was not coping with very well. 'The last couple of weeks before [Hoffa] went to jail were hellish,' said one Teamster who knew him intimately. 'He was on the verge of a nervous breakdown. He would lie on the floor and yell, "I'm not gonna go!"'

Early on the rainy morning of Tuesday, 7 March 1967, Hoffa climbed from a black Lincoln Continental and surrendered himself at the federal courthouse in Washington DC, where the media was waiting. He was handcuffed and placed in the back seat of a government sedan, wedged between two US marshals who accompanied him on the 200-mile drive to Lewisburg Penitentiary. Before departing, Hoffa spotted Clark Mollenhoff, the reporter who had once told Bobby Kennedy to target the Teamsters. Hoffa spat at Mollenhoff, his saliva splatting against the closed car window.

In mid-March 1968, as Hoffa sat in a prison cell, US senator from New York, Bobby Kennedy, entered the same ornate Senate Caucus Room where he had once worked as chief counsel to the Rackets Committee and announced his candidacy for president of the United States. Roger Mudd of CBS News, who described the style of the Caucus Room as a 'gilded German nightclub', noted that Senator Kennedy was making his bid for the presidency 'in the face of almost solid opposition from the Democratic party professionals and the state chairman of the Democratic party in this country . . . he's also making the announcement in the opposition of thousands of young Democrats who claim that Kennedy has become an opportunist'.

Richard Nixon watched the announcement on television in a hotel room with John Ehrlichman, who recorded the moment for posterity. 'When it was over and the hotel room TV was turned off,' wrote Ehrlichman, 'Nixon sat and looked at the blank screen for a long time, saying nothing. Finally, he shook his head slowly. "We've just seen some very terrible forces unleashed," he said. "Something bad is going to come of this." [Nixon] pointed at the screen, "God knows where this is going to lead.""

Hoffa and his mafia cronies felt the same way. Hoffa's fears that Bobby would restart their feud were confirmed when Bobby said to David Burke, who would later become president of CBS News, 'If I'm ever elected president of the United States, [Hoffa] has a darn slim chance of ever getting out of jail.' Others, who were involved in the assassination of Jack Kennedy, feared going to jail when Bobby said, on 3 June, 'I now fully realize that only the powers of the Presidency will reveal the secrets of my brother's death.'

During the Democratic primary, FBI associate director Clyde Tolson was presiding over an executive meeting when Bobby's name came up. 'I hope someone shoots and kills the son of a bitch,' said Tolson. A lot of people shared this sentiment and at least one man was prepared to act on it. After Bobby won the California primary on the evening of 4 June, he made a victory speech to his campaign supporters in the ballroom of a hotel shortly after midnight of the 5th. When Bobby left the podium, he walked through the hotel's kitchen on his way to a late-night news conference when multiple shots were fired at him by at least one assassin from the front – although county coroner Thomas Noguchi said that three bullets hit Bobby from the rear, with the fatal shot fired from 'less than one inch from Kennedy's head, behind his right ear'. After extensive neurosurgery, Bobby lingered in critical condition for another day then died. At the time of the incident, Eugene Hale Brading, who mysteriously appeared in Dealey Plaza on the day of Jack Kennedy's assassination, was only a block away from the scene when Bobby was shot.

On 8 June, Bobby's funeral service was held at New York's St Patrick's Cathedral and although J. Edgar Hoover was in the city that day and staying at the Waldorf-Astoria, which is a five-minute walk to the cathedral, he did not attend the service.

With Bobby out of the race, Hubert Humphrey secured the Democratic nomination but lost the general election to Republican Richard Nixon.

Ed Partin accused Nixon of receiving a suitcase stuffed with $500,000 in cash from none other than Carlos Marcello, who hoped Nixon would pardon Hoffa. Attorney and lobbyist Irving Davidson, as well as other Washington insiders, confirmed Partin's claim and, by 1968, it seemed that Hoffa, with Marcello's assistance, had helped the right president into the White House – while it became increas-ingly clear that Hoffa had put the wrong president inside the Marble Palace. The year before Hoffa went to prison, he called a meeting with his executive board to tell them that Frank Fitzsimmons would be in charge of the union while he was away.

Frank 'Fitz' Fitzsimmons was born near Pittsburgh, Pennsylvania, on 7 April 1908. The family left for Detroit while he was still a boy. As a young man, Fitz quit school and worked the loading dock for an auto parts company until he landed a job as a bus driver for the Detroit Motor Bus Company, then a long-distance hauler for the Teamsters. Hoffa took a shine to Fitz and welcomed him into his inner circle, where Fitz should have enjoyed a sense of prestige but instead became known around the Marble Palace as 'Hoffa's shoeshine boy', often used to fetch sandwiches and pour coffee. One Detroit journalist, who interviewed Fitz while the latter drank a glass of whiskey, called him 'unbelievably stupid'. But Fitz was much smarter than he let on; he not only collected a large salary with perks but used his proximity to Hoffa to cut quiet deals on the side. Because Hoffa was known to humiliate Fitz in the presence of others, Teamster executives were stunned when Hoffa chose him as their new leader. What was Hoffa thinking?

For a long time, Harold Gibbons was expected to take the helm if Hoffa was ever removed by death or criminal conviction, but Gibbons had made a crucial mistake following the assassination of President Kennedy. Hoffa, who was in a Miami restaurant when he heard the news from Dealey Plaza, 'got up on the table and cheered' while Harold Gibbons, who was in Washington DC, ordered the flags atop the Marble Palace flown at half-staff. When Hoffa was told about this, he called Washington and screamed at Gibbons, 'Why the hell did you do that for him? Who the hell was he?' Hoffa's reaction took Gibbons by surprise, and also took him out of the running for the Teamster leadership, since Hoffa distrusted anyone who expressed sympathy for the late president. Gibbons was also unacquainted with the key mobsters whose power was needed to run the union, the same reason Hoffa had to overlook another prime candidate, Bobby Holmes. The smart and tough Yorkshire native with a British accent had never dealt with the mob, and there is no crash course for navigating that rough terrain – unlike the corrupt Fitz who, as one lawman said, 'The Detroit mob had a high regard for'.

After assuming the Teamster leadership, Fitz did not immediately abandon his sycophantic ruse, telling Hoffa, 'When you get out, the keys will be right here . . . don't worry about a thing.' Although Hoffa was locked away in Lewisburg Penitentiary, his office inside the Marble Palace remained unchanged. Sure, Fitz enjoyed swiveling around in Hoffa's big executive chair and barking orders into the intercom, but Hoffa's framed awards and family photographs still adorned the desk and walls. But as the seat cushion began to take shape around the pudgy man's ass, his true character emerged and the office changed accordingly. Like executed Bolsheviks who were, one by one, air-brushed out of Stalin's party photographs, Hoffa's presence began to fade from the office, picture by picture, plaque by plaque, until any trace of him and his family had vanished. Fitz also booted Hoffa's loyalists, replacing them with his own men. If anyone complained about the changes, Fitz either got rid of them, too, or reminded them that he was only in charge because of the great Jimmy Hoffa, and bore no accountability to lesser men.

Like the Roman emperor, Claudius, who was presumed to be an idiot when he was placed on the throne and was later responsible for improving the empire, Fitz, who was thought of by many as 'unbelievably stupid', improved the Teamsters in many ways. Unlike Hoffa, who ran the union like a drill sergeant, Fitz encouraged a relaxed atmosphere and decentralized authority, giving vice presidents more autonomy over regional matters than they had ever enjoyed under Hoffa. He added over a half-million new members to the union, created a Health and Safety Department, and raised hourly wages. By 1972, the Teamsters were the largest and *only* major union to stand behind the re-election of President Nixon, who called Fitz 'my

Frank Fitzsimmons with Richard Nixon

kind of labor leader'. Nixon invited the former Detroit bus driver to White House galas, they flew together on Air Force One and teed off together at La Costa Fairways, a California country club built with a $27 million loan from the Teamster pension fund and known as the 'mecca for racketeers from all over the country'.*

With the exception of Carlos Marcello and Santo Trafficante, mob bosses across the nation were happier with Fitz than they had ever been with Hoffa. Sure, Hoffa knew how to keep the mob happy since they controlled enough union delegates to keep him in power, but if a loan application did not strike Hoffa as a sound investment for the Teamsters, Hoffa was not afraid to say no to any mafia don. Back in September 1963, the FBI recorded a conversation in which Sam Giancana complained that Hoffa had rejected a three-million-dollar loan request from the Chicago mob. One high-ranking Teamster said that Hoffa 'often said no [to the mob] and didn't give a reason why'. A Detroit capo was overheard telling his brother, 'Jimmy Hoffa is the type of a guy you can't bulldog.' This same capo referred to Fitz as 'the puppet', and the same Teamster, noted above, said, 'When Fitzsimmons became general president, the fucking door was open for everybody.' Fitz's open-door policy enraged Hoffa, as did Fitz's opulent lifestyle. Regardless of how high Hoffa had climbed, he was a proverbial working man who disliked luxuries. He wore white socks with dress suits because 'colored ones make my feet sweat', often telling people, 'I don't need to impress anybody.' While Hoffa was president, he took few vacations and would not even let a bell hop carry his luggage at a hotel, while Fitz seemed to be on one long vacation, surrounded by personal servants. Fitz played golf five times a week, dined at exclusive country clubs, had a chauffeur-driven limousine, chefs and a private jet, all paid for by the union. This decadent lifestyle for the representative of America's working men was too much for Hoffa to bear, but by the time Hoffa tried to get rid of Fitz, it was too late; the ex-shoeshine boy was too deeply entrenched for Hoffa to dislodge him by legal means. Hoffa therefore turned to Marcello and Trafficante, asking them to whack Fitz; however, this was not as acceptable as

* Eugene Hale Brading had the rare honor of becoming one of only 100 charter members of the La Costa Country Club – dubbed by the local police as 'Apalachin West' – indisputably placing the hardened convict and man of mystery in the company of the most powerful mafia dons, union leaders, A-list celebrities like Bing Crosby and Bob Hope, and the president of the United States.

killing President Kennedy who everyone in the mob wanted dead. La Cosa Nostra has strict rules and, in this particular case, the Chicago and Detroit borgatas had their claws deep into Fitz, as did the New Yorkers, especially the Genovese family whose chief liaison to Hoffa was capo Anthony Provenzano.

Anthony 'Tony Pro' Provenzano was born in 1917 on New York's Lower East Side. He was an amateur boxer before becoming a truck driver and protégé of Tony Bender, who made him a union organizer. With the backing of the Genovese family, Tony Pro became head of the 14,000-member Local 560 in Hoboken, New Jersey, then president of Joint Council 73, an association of locals stretching across the state. This gave Tony Pro immense power over the trucking companies in New Jersey as well as out-of-state trucks that drove cargo through New Jersey and had to pay a tax to Tony Pro for crossing his territory. One Teamster described Tony Pro's modus operandi as 'old school', saying, 'You get in his fuckin' local, you live by whatever contract they negotiate and there is no shit, he didn't want to hear it . . . and if an employer didn't sign the contract or didn't agree with him, he'd send a couple of his guys over there and they agreed.'

In 1957, Tony Pro used his power to help Hoffa clinch the Teamster presidency. Hoffa, in return, helped Tony Pro become one of the Teamsters' thirteen international vice presidents.

In 1962, before Tony Bender fell out of favor with Vito Genovese then disappeared without a trace, he was suspected of smuggling heroin through New Jersey's waterfront which was under the control of the Genovese family. Since Tony Pro was Tony Bender's hand-picked Teamster representative in New Jersey and trucks were used to move the heroin, Pro was suspected of conspiring with Bender and was put on notice. On 24 June 1962, he woke up at the bottom of an elevator shaft with six broken ribs. After being patched up at the hospital, Tony Pro claimed he had accidentally stepped into an empty shaft on the first floor and had fallen straight into the basement. Pro left out the part where he was beaten, kicked and thrown down the shaft. His attackers did not mean to kill him, just tune him up, since the twelve-foot drop is the recommended height for commanding someone's immediate attention on any given matter. Tony Pro got the message and returned to work where he remained until 1963, when, due to pressure from Bobby Kennedy, he was convicted of extortion and sent to prison for seven years.

In 1967, Tony Pro was serving time in Lewisburg when in walked Jimmy Hoffa. Pro was thrilled to see Hoffa, figuring they could catch up and make plans for the future, but by now Hoffa was embittered and beginning to rethink his costly relationship with the mob. He felt they had used him, and his most recent proof was how fast they had dumped him for Fitz. Since Hoffa was still the union's official president and was expected to retake the helm upon his release, Pro asked him if he could collect an early retirement settlement against his union pension, worth in the area of a million dollars. Long before Hoffa went to prison, a federal court-appointed board of monitors, established to clean up the Teamsters, ordered Hoffa to oust Tony Pro, but the stout union leader refused and never wavered in his support of the Genovese capo. But now that Hoffa was behind bars and the mob had cozied up to Fitz, he suddenly wanted to purge all mafia influence from his union. Knowing that Tony Pro was already collecting two salaries, one from Local 560 and another from Joint Council 73, Hoffa told him, 'No dice.' A fellow inmate who witnessed the exchange quoted Hoffa as saying, 'I dealt with you guys and it almost got me killed before and it's got me so I'm in here now and I don't like it in here. When you get out, you guys are going to have to be on your own.' The same inmate said that Tony Pro did not like Hoffa's response and flew into a rage until 'they were screaming and almost came to blows. Tony's cheeks were red and twitching, he was so mad.' Pro finally said to Hoffa, 'If you don't get out of my shit and back off of me, you'll end up like Castellito. They won't find so much as a fingernail of yours.' A prison employee confirmed the inmate's story.

Tony Pro's reference to Castellito made the threat all the more ominous. Anthony Castellito was the secretary-treasurer for Local 560, and for years he committed fraud and extortion in cahoots with Tony Pro. Castellito's mistake came in 1959 when he ran for re-election to secretary-treasurer, but not on the 'Vote Pro' ticket. Castellito's sudden break from Tony Pro made Pro wonder if Castellito was planning to run against him for local president. This turned out to be the case; in 1961, Castellito headed up an opposition ticket and declared his candidacy. Following a union hall meeting, Castellito went out for a cup of coffee and was never seen again. Tony Pro was responsible for his disappearance but he had a solid alibi; he was getting married that day. But Pro's buddy, Salvatore 'Sally Bugs' Briguglio, could not attend Pro's wedding – he was busy strangling Castellito to death with a piano wire and pushing his body through a woodchipper in upstate New York. One of Pro's campaign slogans was 'Grow and Grow with Tony Pro', an apt catchphrase after Castellito was turned into fertilizer. Needless to say, Tony Pro's threat of ending up like Castellito should not have been taken lightly by Hoffa, who sidled up to another inmate and high-ranking mobster for protection, Bonanno family consigliere Carmine 'Lilo' Galante.

Lilo and Tony Pro despised one another, probably because they had similar egos. When Lilo offered Hoffa protection from Tony Pro, Pro would have viewed Lilo as butting his nose where it did not belong, since Lilo did not have a claim on Hoffa nor any right to interfere in their beef. According to one inmate, Lilo and Tony Pro ended up having a big blow-out over Hoffa, but Tony Pro was hamstrung since, even if Lilo had no right to interfere, he was still a consigliere which ranks above a capo; this meant that Hoffa was safe for the moment.

Hoffa, however, had other problems. The energetic king of labor with a superhuman work ethic found the stillness of prison intolerable, calling it 'hell on earth, only hell couldn't be this bad'. Although the prison wardrobe may have been a step up in fashion from Hoffa's usual cheap suits with white socks, his 8ft-by-10ft cell, with steel bed and toilet, was equal to confining him to a straitjacket. His hair grayed, his cheeks became sunken, and he lost weight. Then there was the violence. Hoffa was a certified tough guy and Lilo was keeping Tony Pro at bay, but maximum-security prison is still a dangerous jungle where prison-made weapons and sneak attacks are rampant; the famous union leader felt he was a bright target and was concerned for his life. During his stay in Lewisburg, four inmates were murdered with knives. (As a Lewisburg alumnus, I can attest to the violence. On my very first day on the compound in August 1997, two inmates were viciously hacked to death with prison-made machetes.) Hoffa had the added stress of worrying about his wife, Josephine, known as Jo. Unlike typical mob wives who grow up in The Life and understand the risks involved, Jo was not taking any of this well. Lastly, as Hoffa was losing his grip over the Teamsters, he began to lose his mind, which was inextricably tied to the union making it no surprise that the two would deteriorate in tandem.

With President Nixon in office, Carlos Marcello restarted his drive to get Hoffa out of prison. Bobby Baker, the influence peddler who

Bobby Kennedy had once prosecuted in order to compromise Lyndon Johnson, said he had met with Marcello in a small restaurant in Louisiana where Marcello offered Baker a million dollars in cash for Hoffa's pardon. Baker told Marcello that White House counsel Chuck Colson was the man to see and that Colson had ultimately taken the cash and passed it on to Nixon.

With Hoffa's pardon paid for and likely to happen, Fitz had to appear in favor of his mentor's early release and outwardly lobbied on Hoffa's behalf while he secretly reached a compromise with the White House, in which Hoffa would be sprung from prison early while Fitz would remain in power. Fitz was blunt with Chuck Colson, telling him, 'I don't want him out unless the president has . . . the ability to bring him back in.' Colson, in turn, said to President Nixon, 'Fitz wants to get Hoffa out because that's the only way that he can keep control of the pro-Hoffa forces within the Teamsters . . . but he wants him out with strings.' To this end, a clause was added to the commutation document barring Hoffa from any involvement with the Teamsters, directly or indirectly, until March 1980. Desperate to get out of prison, Hoffa agreed to the terms, never intending to honor the deal. He figured, and was likely advised by his attorneys, that he could later have the clause stricken since it was unconstitutional.

While chairing a board meeting in June 1971, Fitz announced Hoffa's resignation then asked the board to vote him in as Hoffa's replacement, which they did on the spot. Minutes later, in a highly unusual move that was criticized by the *New York Times*, President Nixon walked into the meeting room and congratulated Fitz, whose coup was complete.

On 23 December, President Nixon signed an executive grant of clemency authorizing Hoffa's immediate release from prison, citing the failing health of Hoffa's wife as the main reason for Hoffa's release, leaving out the million-dollar bribe.*

---

* That same year, President Nixon also pardoned Genovese capo Angelo 'Gyp' DeCarlo who was caught on hours of surveillance tape discussing gangland murders. On one tape, DeCarlo, who was known to disembowel victims and use meat hooks to torture them, said, 'So we took the guy out in the woods and I said . . . "You got to go, why not let me hit you right in the heart and you won't feel a thing."' DeCarlo said the guy insisted he was innocent but understood that DeCarlo had no choice but to kill him. 'So I hit him in the heart and it went right through him.' An official with Nixon's Justice Department, stunned by DeCarlo's pardon, said, 'He is a very bad guy . . . Someone just had to give that thing a push.'

By 4 p.m., Hoffa exited Lewisburg Penitentiary. He had been locked up for a total of four years, nine and a half months. When accosted by reporters, Hoffa refused to comment as to why Nixon had pardoned him and said that he was just happy to be home for Christmas, adding, 'I have no intention of returning to the Teamsters.' It was a lie. Hoffa's plan was to reclaim the Teamster presidency after striking the clause that barred him from union activity.

Unwilling to wait until the clause was removed, Hoffa launched an aggressive campaign for his re-election. The press covered his vocal comeback which included an endless string of barbs directed at Fitz, whom Hoffa called a lazy golfer, adding that golf was a game for 'fat old men'. Fitz responded by firing Hoffa's wife, who was still collecting a Teamster salary of $48,000 a year for who knows what, and Hoffa's son, a highly competent attorney who was kept on an annual retainer of $30,000. Given that Hoffa had already lost his own $100,000-a-year salary, he was forced to withdraw $1.7 million from his Teamster pension.

Hoffa also criticized the government. For Chuck Colson's part in keeping Hoffa away from the reins by way of the clause, he was given a high-paying gig as general counsel to the Teamsters. Hoffa saw this for what it was, a blatant payoff, and said so on national television. His finger-pointing at Colson for the clause was extremely reckless since Colson had also taken a cash-stuffed suitcase in return for Hoffa's pardon.

As the battle between Hoffa and Fitz wore on, Fitz's glowing record of sweeping reforms that improved the union was overshadowed by Hoffa's star power. By 1974, a leading truckers' magazine, *Overdrive*, polled Teamsters across the country and found that 83 percent would cast a vote for Hoffa. The threat of a landslide victory worried Fitz and concerned his mafia partners who did not want him replaced by Hoffa. Hoffa only heightened the mob's concerns by telling anyone who would listen that, upon his re-election, he would purge the Teamsters of all mafia influence. Was this even possible? Back in 1958, when Bobby Kennedy was asked if the Teamsters could ever be purged of organized crime, Bobby replied, '[Hoffa] can't say, "You're out." He wouldn't live.' How, then, was Hoffa planning to conduct this purge? Rumor had it that Hoffa had agreed to become a federal informant if the government lifted the restriction on his commutation. Would Hoffa snitch? Some suspected that Hoffa had, years earlier, leaked tidbits of incriminating evidence about Teamster president Dave Beck which helped bring about Beck's downfall. 'Jimmy knew he was next in line to succeed Beck,' said one Teamster. 'It was just a matter of getting him out of the way.' Further evidence that Hoffa was prepared to snitch came from Walter Sheridan, formerly of the Get Hoffa Squad, who said that Hoffa had made overtures to the Justice Department, even before his release from Lewisburg. 'As Christmas drew near,' wrote Sheridan, 'a delegation of Teamsters visited the White House and promised Hoffa's cooperation before a grand jury in return for his release from prison.' Hoffa all but confirmed Sheridan's story when he appeared on a 30 November 1974 segment of *ABC News Close-Up* titled 'Hoffa'. The widely viewed television segment delved into the Teamsters' links to organized crime, and although Hoffa made no confessions and did not point fingers, his mere participation with the show concerned mobsters across the country who believed that Hoffa was the primary source of the news team's investigation.

On 13 June 1974, Hoffa was interviewed by a Detroit television station. When Fitz's name came up, Hoffa said, 'I understand from reliable sources that Fitzsimmons is seeing a psychiatrist twice a week,' adding that Fitz was an alcoholic. Hoffa seemed obsessed with destroying Fitz, exhibiting the same maniacal rants he had once spewed toward Bobby Kennedy. Fitz, in turn, called Hoffa 'a bum, a has-been . . . a liar and a stool pigeon'.

Next, Hoffa sat down to write his autobiography with author Oscar Fraley, who co-wrote *The Untouchables* with G-man Eliot Ness. Hoffa's story begins with a hypocritical tirade in which he accuses Fitz of everything he had previously done himself! 'I *charge* Frank Fitzsimmons with political influence peddling . . . I *charge* him with selling out to mobsters and letting known racketeers into the Teamsters . . . I *charge* him with making vast loans from the billion-dollar Teamster pension fund to known mobsters.'

Although the book was not yet published, the mob knew about it through others who had heard Hoffa communicating with Fraley over the telephone. 'I think the years he did in prison really mentally destroyed him a lot,' said a Teamster who once looked up to Hoffa. The same man also said, 'He got a lot of people nervous. A lot of people very nervous.'

It was apparent that if Hoffa could not rule the house, he was bent on burning it down, and with so many borgatas entangled in Teamster locals and the union's pension fund – which dished out half of its $1.2 billion in loans to mob-connected ventures between 1957 and the early 1970s – the mob felt threatened and had no choice but to keep Hoffa away from the Marble Palace – one way or another.

Chapter 29

Where's Hoffa?

Sylvia Pagano Paris was a secretary for a labor union where she met and married Kansas City mobster Sam Scaradino, who changed his name to Frank O'Brien. On 20 December 1933, the couple had a son named Charles Lenton O'Brien, better known as 'Chuckie'. After Frank O'Brien committed suicide, Sylvia and her seven-year-old son moved to Detroit where Sylvia dated Detroit mobster Frank Coppola, who introduced Sylvia to Jimmy Hoffa, beginning Hoffa's long relationship with the Detroit mob, as well as with Sylvia who he briefly dated. After the death of Sylvia's second husband, she moved into Hoffa's home with nine-year-old Chuckie, who Hoffa treated as his own son. The boy often called Hoffa 'Dad', while Hoffa referred to him as 'my other son'. Future Teamster boss Jackie Presser said, 'Hoffa loved Chuck as a true son and Chuck loved Hoffa as a father.'

Sylvia got along well with Hoffa's wife, Jo, and earned her keep while part of the Hoffa household, not by washing dishes and dusting furniture, but in her role as Hoffa's liaison to the Detroit mob, often acting as the conduit for Teamster pension fund loans to mob-connected projects. Hoffa had no trouble saying no to mob bosses, though he did have trouble saying no to Sylvia, who knew how to handle the battle-hardened labor leader. 'My mother had big balls,' said Chuckie. 'In those days, most women were intimidated. She wasn't – I don't care who it was. If she had to do something, if somebody asked her to do something . . . she'd get the job done.' In December 1970, when Hoffa was still in prison, 56-year-old Sylvia died of a heart attack and the only woman who could handle Jimmy Hoffa was gone.

To convey messages to Hoffa while he was still in prison, the mob turned to Sylvia's son, Chuckie O'Brien, who regularly visited Hoffa in Lewisburg and also carried messages between him and Fitz. O'Brien started out as a truck driver and became an agent for Detroit Local 299. When Hoffa ascended to the presidency, he elevated O'Brien to a general organizer and assistant to the president. As Frank Fitzsimmons slowly took over the union and Hoffa expressed his scathing discontent from prison, O'Brien felt stuck in the middle of their feud and had turned to another mentor for advice, a man Sylvia had always trusted to discipline her son when he was a boy: Tony Jack, who O'Brien referred to as Uncle Tony.

Anthony 'Tony Jack' Giacalone was born to Sicilian immigrant parents on the east side of Detroit on 19 January 1919. His father

Anthony 'Tony Jack' Giacalone

was a hard-working fruit and vegetable pushcart peddler, but the boy gravitated toward crime and got in with the Detroit mob. He was groomed by mob boss Joe Zerilli, 'an Italian immigrant who rose from the bootleg gangs of the 1920s to become the reputed czar of the Detroit mafia'. Zerilli grew to depend on Tony Jack and raised him to a capo. Wearing Brioni suits and large, tinted prescription eyeglasses, Tony Jack handed out business cards advertising himself as the president of an 'exterminating company', which was rather comical to FBI agents who said his 'propensity for violence is legendary in Detroit', and he was known to exterminate quite a few people.

By 1975, Tony Jack and Jimmy Hoffa had known each other for about thirty years and their relationship was reciprocal: Tony Jack's rise in the Detroit mob was, in large part, due to Hoffa's meteoric rise in the American labor movement, which depended on Tony Jack. Tony Jack was not only the designated contact between the Detroit mafia and the Teamster hierarchy but often acted as Hoffa's bridge to other borgatas across the country, especially the Chicago mob which controlled Teamster locals in the Midwest.

When Hoffa fell out with Fitz, and Chuckie went to Tony Jack for advice, Tony Jack told Chuckie to shift his allegiance to Fitz, making it clear where the mob stood. 'He's your fucking boss, nobody else,' said Tony Jack, who also told Chuckie to essentially act as a spy: 'Stay put, keep quiet, and listen.'

Upon Hoffa's release from prison, Tony Jack desperately tried to get him to accept the changes that had occurred in his absence, at one point promising Hoffa anything he wanted apart from the Teamsters; he said they would install him at the head of any company under their control, and even offered Hoffa ten million dollars to quietly fade away. Hoffa refused every offer; he only wanted *his* Teamsters and continued to make threats that would sink the mob if he did not get his way. At one of his many visits to Hoffa's lakefront house, Tony Jack told Hoffa, very calmly, 'You've got to stop what you're doing, Jim. You're not only hurting yourself, you're hurting everybody.' Chuckie said, 'Hoffa listened but never said nothing. He showed respect to Uncle Tony, but he just listened.' Chuckie also said, 'Uncle Tony . . . hated anybody that was a snitch. He told me to never . . . rat anybody out, because people like that, time will take care of them.' More often than not, time enlisted the help of Tony Jack, who displayed uncharacteristic patience in the face of Hoffa's threats and continued to plead with him. The reason for Tony Jack's restraint was not because he was a sympathetic man, but because Hoffa was a national hero to the labor movement and his murder would bring the mob untold heat.

While Tony Jack persisted in his failing diplomatic mission, violence plagued the Teamster union as men loyal to either Hoffa or Fitz took swipes at each other: homes were blown up, cars and boats were firebombed, and men were shot at. One victim who survived a shooting said, 'My eye actually came out of my head.' Finally, on 10 July 1975, Hoffa's men targeted Fitz's son, Richard, whose car was blown to smithereens in the parking lot of Nemo's, a tavern frequented by Teamsters from a nearby local. Richard, who was reported to be at the 'center of an internal struggle', was not in the car, and was 'hustled off the scene by other union officials' while parts of the car were found blocks away. Richard's near-death experience drove Fitz straight into the arms of his mafia guardians, namely Detroit capo Tony Jack and Genovese capo Anthony 'Tony Pro' Provenzano, who was now out of prison and concerned by Hoffa's threats to expose the mob. The two Tonys reluctantly decided that Hoffa had to go and went about getting approval from the Commission. Tony Pro's Genovese family easily got the Gambino and Lucchese families on board. Detroit don Joe Zerilli gave it the okay, as did the boss of rural Pennsylvania, Rosario 'Russell' Bufalino, who was heavily involved with the Teamsters. The Chicago mob, with its iron grip over Teamster locals in not only their own Windy City but Las Vegas, Los Angeles, Kansas City, Cleveland

and St Louis, also understood what had to be done. As for Carlos Marcello and Santo Trafficante, their hands were tied. Given Hoffa's threats to inform, they had no choice but to go along with his death sentence.

Once the hit was sanctioned by the Commission, Tony Jack, who was closest to Hoffa, was assigned the task of setting him up for the kill. To this end, he pushed Hoffa to air out his old prison grievances with Tony Pro, offering to arrange a meeting between them. Back when Hoffa and Pro were first released from prison, they met in Miami where both men had vacation homes. The meeting quickly descended into Part Two of their Lewisburg bout when, according to Hoffa, Pro 'threatened to pull my guts out or kidnap my children if I continue to attempt to return to the presidency of the Teamsters'. Lloyd Hicks of Miami's Local 390 – controlled by Santo Trafficante – made the mistake of bragging to friends that he had secretly tape-recorded the meeting, and thus the threat. Hicks was soon found dead with a dozen bullet holes and the tape has never surfaced. On another occasion, while Tony Pro was in Miami, he bumped into a former assistant to Hoffa, Joe Konowe, and told him, 'Tell Hoffa I'm gonna snatch his granddaughter and put her eyes out.' Given the above, Hoffa prudently declined Tony Jack's pleas to meet again with Tony Pro. But Hoffa knew, if he planned to run in 1976, regardless of how loud he barked about purging the union of mafia influence, he needed the delegates they controlled – a monkey could do the math. Detective Vincent Piersante, who *Life* magazine called 'one of the foremost authorities on organized crime in the Detroit-northern Ohio area', said, 'Because of the mob's tremendous influence in the Teamsters Union, [Hoffa] had no chance of returning to power unless the mob okayed it. That is a fact of life.' Hoffa therefore gave in and agreed to sit with Tony Pro, but only after a last-ditch attempt at enlisting the help of his old prison protector, Carmine 'Lilo' Galante, who was released from the penitentiary on 24 January 1974, after serving twelve years of his twenty-year sentence.

Given the forces aligned against Hoffa, Lilo would have immediately known he was powerless to alter events, but he was also aware of the hundreds of millions of dollars connected to the Teamster pension fund so he resorted to a common ploy in the mob: he made a phony claim on Hoffa based on their relationship in prison, hoping to get something out of it. A New Jersey bank under Tony Pro's control made a $25,000 'loan' to Lilo, and I would bet the farm that this was a payoff to have Lilo withdraw his beef, which he did.

With nowhere else to turn, Hoffa agreed to meet with Tony Pro. On the days leading up to the meeting, it was obvious to the people around Hoffa that he had developed a fatalistic outlook, telling his son-in-law, 'I've been fortunate. I was just a farm boy from Brazil, Indiana, and I became president of the world's greatest union. I've been able to smell the roses. How many other people can say that?' Hoffa talked to others about having lived a full life with no regrets as he inched closer to smelling the roses from the other side of the soil.

On the morning of 30 July 1975, Hoffa lounged around his house following a long, sleepless night. By 1 p.m., he told his wife he had a 2 p.m. appointment at the Machus Red Fox, a steak and seafood restaurant located in the suburb of Bloomfield, Michigan, approximately fifteen miles north of downtown Detroit. The busy area might have given Hoffa a sense of security.

At around 1:15 p.m., Hoffa left his Lake Orion house in his dark green Pontiac Grand Ville. On his way to the meeting, he stopped off at a limousine company run by his pal, Louis 'The Pope' Linteau, who was out to lunch. Hoffa and Linteau went back three or four decades together and, throughout Hoffa's most recent ordeal with the mob, Linteau sometimes served as a messenger between Hoffa and Tony Jack. Linteau's employees said that Hoffa was extremely upset that Linteau was not there, and felt that Linteau should have known to wait around. Was Linteau supposed to accompany Hoffa to the 2 p.m. meeting? If so, Linteau knew when to duck out, or was lured away so Hoffa would be alone. After some small talk with the employees during which 'Hoffa seemed kind of nervous about something', Hoffa left for the Machus Red Fox.

Hoffa arrived at the restaurant between 1:45 and 2 p.m. and parked his car in the parking lot. Neither Tony Pro nor Tony Jack, who was to accompany Tony Pro, was there. At around 2:30 p.m., Hoffa walked across the parking lot to a hardware store where he made two telephone calls from a public phone. The first call was to Linteau at his limousine service. Hoffa sounded aggravated when he told Linteau he had been stood up, a frustrating experience but he should have been so lucky. Hoffa's second call was to his wife, Jo. 'Giacalone didn't show up,' he said. 'Did he call? Where the hell is he?' Jo said that she had not heard from Tony Jack or anyone else. Hoffa told her that he would be home by 4 p.m. and hung up the phone. Following the phone calls, at approximately 2:45 p.m., witnesses saw Hoffa walking across the parking lot on his way back to his car when a maroon 1975 Mercury Marquis rolled up alongside him and stopped. There were three men in the car; two seated in the front and one in the back. The door opened and Hoffa climbed into the back seat. It was the last time anyone has ever seen Jimmy Hoffa.

Jo expected to see her husband by 4 p.m. When he did not show up at home or call to explain why he was running late, she became nervous and was too upset to eat dinner. By 10 p.m., she anxiously telephoned Hoffa's fellow Teamster and family friend, Joe Bane, who drove over to the Hoffa house. Before the evening was up, Hoffa's adult children, Jimmy and Barbara, were told that their father had not come home. As the overnight hours passed with dreadful uncertainty, the Hoffa family wondered when to report Hoffa missing, knowing he could still walk through the front door. As that prospect began to fade, they clung to the hope of a ransom demand which could mean he was still alive.

At around 10 p.m., Louis Linteau called Hoffa's home on the lake and learned from Jo that Hoffa had never returned home. Linteau then called Tony Jack who told him he had no meeting planned with Hoffa that day and did not even know what Linteau was talking about. Linteau, who knew this was a blatant lie, would have seen this as confirmation that Hoffa was gone for good. The next morning, Linteau drove to the Machus Red Fox and found Hoffa's car in the parking lot with the doors unlocked. By 6 p.m., just over twenty-four hours after Hoffa had last been seen, his family filed a missing persons report. James Hoffa Jr, who did not believe the mob would tolerate his father's return to the Teamsters, was pretty sure of what had happened though he had difficulty coming to terms with it.

The investigation into Jimmy Hoffa's disappearance started out slow and never picked up speed. After a long weekend of public pressure to enter the case, the FBI finally caved on the evening of Sunday, 3 August and assigned only two Detroit agents, which attested to the Bureau's lack of interest. Unhappy with the scant resources dedicated to the investigation, Hoffa's daughter, Barbara, who later became a judge, said, 'You used two thousand agents to put my father in jail, and you're only using two to find him.'

Hoffa's car was searched by authorities but revealed no traces of a crime. Inside Hoffa's house, Hoffa had written a memo to himself that read: 'T.J. – 2 p.m. – RED FOX.' Everyone knew that 'T.J.' was Tony Jack, who Hoffa was planning to meet that afternoon.

Of the six witnesses who saw Hoffa in the parking lot, one said that he had left in a car with three men and identified Chuckie O'Brien as the driver of that car, which was believed to have belonged to Tony Jack's son, Joseph 'Joey Jack' Giacalone. Although Chuckie may not have been in the car, he was in the know. When questioned the next day by James Hoffa Jr, Chuckie told 'conflicting stories' about his whereabouts on the day of Hoffa's disappearance. The reason was not necessarily because Chuckie was involved but because Chuckie was asked by Tony Jack to alibi him at one of his favorite haunts, the Southfield Athletic Club, where Tony Jack spent the afternoon coming into contact with as many people as possible. When the Hoffa children asked Chuckie to take a polygraph test, the man who was known as a 'pathological liar' declined, telling them he would need to consult with his attorney.

On the Friday after Hoffa disappeared, Tony Jack was scheduled to attend a wedding but decided to skip it and take his wife to dinner along with Chuckie O'Brien. When Tony Jack's wife left for the ladies' room, Tony Jack said to Chuckie, 'Life is very funny, Chuck. Very funny. Things happen and you don't have control over it.' Before parting ways for the evening, Tony Jack told Chuckie to visit Fitz at the Marble Palace and tell him to lie low and avoid television interviews.

Another witness, who had seen Hoffa climb into a car, identified a passenger as Salvatore 'Sally Bugs' Briguglio, the hitman Tony Pro had used to dispose of Anthony Castellito, who was pushed through a woodchipper in upstate New York. Bugs was on the books as a 'business agent' for Tony Pro's Local 560. Back in 1971, Sally Bugs, Stephen Angelo, Armand 'Cookie' Faugno and Tony Pro's brother, Sammy Pro, who also golfed with President Nixon, were indicted on federal counterfeiting charges. Since Sammy Pro was too important for Tony Pro to lose, a little arrangement was worked out in which Sally Bugs disposed of Cookie Faugno and Stephen Angelo then took the rap for Sammy Pro.

As for Tony Pro, telephone toll records revealed that he and Tony Jack had spoken with one another dozens of times from April until July, with the calls suddenly ceasing a few days before Hoffa disappeared; the calls never resumed. This pattern is typical in such circumstances, and is as close as we will ever get to physical evidence of their involvement. The two men were in contact while presumably planning the hit and apparently decided, as the big day neared, to distance themselves from one another, knowing that any post-hit telephone conversations could be recorded. Tony Pro was also seen in Detroit by the FBI in the days leading up to Hoffa's disappearance but was back home in New Jersey on the day it happened, more circumstantial evidence that points to his guilt. The following day, Tony Pro flew to Florida, the same place he had gone when Castellito disappeared. A team of reporters descended on his home in Miami. In a telling statement, Tony Pro told reporters, 'Jimmy was, or is, my friend.' Although Tony Pro could argue that the 'was' was applicable because they had since argued and their friendship had dissolved, it seemed more like a Freudian

Tony Pro questioned by reporters on his front lawn

slip: Pro knew Hoffa was dead. He went on to say, 'You're embarrassing me in front of everyone in the neighborhood. You guys . . . make me look like a mobster. I'm not. I'm just a truck driver.' Unlike most truck drivers, the suntanned, barechested 58-year-old was wearing swim trunks on his sprawling front lawn in the middle of the day.

Just three months after Hoffa went missing, the annual Frank Fitzsimmons Invitational Golf Tournament of 1975 was held at La Costa Country Club and had some interesting players teeing off together. The recently impeached president, Richard Nixon, shared a golf cart with Fitz, which must have made for interesting conversation being that Nixon said that Fitz 'can't string three words together'. The *New York Times* wrote: 'Among the participants were Anthony Provenzano . . . former ally of James R. Hoffa, the missing former teamster [*sic*] president.' The *Times* further reported, 'After he finished his round [of golf] Mr. Nixon spent about 45 minutes in a private meeting with a number of teamster officials and others linked to the union.'

Following Hoffa's demise, Chuckie O'Brien was seen wearing a 'FITZ 76' campaign button, clearing up any ambiguity as to where he stood in the Hoffa–Fitz feud. There was blood found in Joey Jack's car which Chuckie admitted to borrowing on the day in question. The blood was tested and said to be salmon blood. FBI tracking dogs 'detected Hoffa's scent in the right rear seat and trunk of the car' and a strand of hair found inside the car matched a strand plucked from Hoffa's hairbrush at his home. The FBI did not bring charges.

James Hoffa Jr made a public plea for help while outdated 'Free Hoffa' bumper stickers were covered with 'Where's Hoffa?' bumper stickers. Hoffa's children offered a $200,000 reward for information; Hoffa's alma mater, Detroit Local 299, put up another $25,000, and *Overdrive* magazine, which spoke for the rank-and-file Teamsters, put up $50,000, but there were no viable leads.

Responding to public pressure to solve the case, the feds stepped up the investigation. Since they could not find Hoffa's body, they went after the Teamster pension fund which Chuckie O'Brien called 'the whole ball of wax'. The FBI focused mainly on Fitz, whose Marble Palace was less than a mile away from the J. Edgar Hoover Building. Fitz was regularly questioned about his relationships with Hoffa and Tony Pro, and, before long, his involvement in a number of dirty loans came to light. He was forced to resign from the union and an outside management team was appointed to oversee the pension fund, delivering a blow to the mob that was equal to the end of Prohibition. Sure, they still had control of union locals across the country, but the pension fund party was over and done.

Within six months of Hoffa's disappearance, Tony Pro was indicted for a shady $2.3 million pension fund scam. Months after that arrest, he and Sally Bugs were picked up for the 1961 kidnapping and murder of Anthony Castellito. It was one year since Hoffa's disappearance and several years since Tony Pro had warned Hoffa that he would end up like Castellito, a promise he had apparently kept since we have not found 'so much as a fingernail' belonging to Jimmy Hoffa.

During Tony Pro's criminal trials, Sammy Pro held the fort at union headquarters in New Jersey, where he fit rather comfortably into his brother's shoes. One night, during a shop stewards meeting, Local 560 member Walter Glockner launched an insurrection, vowing to 'fight

Tony Pro until they put me in a pine box'. Glockner, who was also suspected of snitching, did not have to wait long for that to happen: the very next night, he was gunned down outside his home. Sammy Pro tried to appear sympathetic by ruling Glockner's death an accident so that his family could collect a death benefit. When reporters asked Tony Pro about his brother's broad application of the death benefit, he told them that Glockner was 'accident prone', which was true if we apply an equally broad definition of the word 'accident'; Glockner's latest and final accident was to challenge Tony Pro.

Toward the end of 1975, Chuckie O'Brien was living in South Florida where Tony Pro and Tony Jack also had winter homes. One afternoon, Tony Jack dialed Chuckie and told him to meet him at Tony Pro's house in an hour. Chuckie was a bit shaken by the sudden phone call but got his courage up and went. He greeted the men in Tony Pro's backyard where the wiseguys were sitting beside the pool. Tony Jack was dressed in pants and a shirt, while Tony Pro was in his work attire which he also donned for press conferences – swim trunks with no shirt and slippers. Tony Pro, fearing his house was under constant surveillance from across the Intracoastal Waterway, led Tony Jack and Chuckie a few steps away from the pool where they ducked behind a row of large bushes. Tony Pro told Chuckie, 'We just want to know that you're okay,' and went on to say, 'The little guy [Hoffa] had lost his fucking mind and was going to take everybody down.' Chuckie later described this tense situation to his astute stepson who accurately assessed the motive behind the confrontation, concluding that Tony Jack had vouched for Chuckie, who was in the know, but Tony Pro wanted to look Chuckie in the eyes and judge for himself. The mere fact that Chuckie arrived at Tony Pro's house after such a cold and spontaneous invitation, knowing he could be walking into an ambush, would have begun the process of easing Tony Pro's mind even before the men had spoken behind the bush. Later in life, Chuckie all but admitted the mob's guilt when he told his stepson, 'Whatever happened, I didn't have the power to change it.'

In 1977, Sally Bugs made a disastrous decision to sit for an interview with author Steven Brill, who was writing a book about the Teamsters. 'The ground rule,' said Brill, explaining how he got Bugs to talk, '[was] that I would not reveal our discussions ... which were conducted

Salvatore 'Sally Bugs' Briguglio

privately.' Bugs was still relatively tight-lipped; Brill wrote: 'He only passively confirmed with a nod of his head certain relatively minor aspects of the crime. He offered no elaboration and never revealed enough to implicate anyone except possibly himself.'

Why did Sally Bugs sit with Brill? Was he trying to discern how much the FBI knew about the crime, aware that investigative reporters regularly speak with members of law enforcement? Or was Bugs just plain nuts as the name implied? Whatever his reasoning, his indiscretion leaked and the Genovese family does not condone interviews. Hoffa was not the only man Bugs had disposed of, and Tony Pro was not the only mobster he had killed for. On 21 March 1978, Sally Bugs was swatted like a bug as he exited a restaurant in Manhattan's Little Italy: two hitmen shot him five times in the head and once in the chest then kept walking as Bugs collapsed to the pavement, dead.

In the summer of 1978, Tony Pro was convicted at both trials and sentenced to life in prison for the murder of Castellito. Ten years later, the 71-year-old capo died of a heart attack while handcuffed to a bed in a hospital near his California prison. He had outlived Fitz, who was whacked by Philip Morris – the heavy chain-smoker succumbed to lung cancer in May 1981. As for Tony Jack, he was jacked up on tax charges and hit with a ten-year bit. He was facing a new racketeering indictment when he dropped dead at eighty-two years old in 2001. Considering that Hoffa's disappearance ultimately led to the demise of Fitz, Tony Pro, Tony Jack and Sally Bugs, it can be said that Hoffa got his revenge from the grave. One might argue that the only real victims are the families of the deceased: Jo Hoffa went to her grave in 1980, asking till the end, 'Where's my Jimmy?'

What happened to Jimmy Hoffa on the day of his disappearance? And where is his body? Hoffa was murdered and a number of informants have pointed the finger at Sally Bugs and his brother, along with Thomas Andretta; all three were career criminals directly connected to the union and the Genovese family, specifically Tony Pro. Andretta was also one of the prime suspects in Sally Bugs's death, which meant that he did not particularly care for Sally Bugs's interview with author Steven Brill.

As for Hoffa's body, I am certain it was destroyed. Given Hoffa's notoriety and the expected manhunt that would follow in the wake of his disappearance, the mob had no choice but to dispose of him.

Over the years, false tips have sent investigators on wild goose chases. One informant said that Hoffa was in the concrete foundation of New Jersey's Giants Stadium; another said that he was in the concrete abutment of a bridge. Yet another claimed he was stuffed into a fifty-five-gallon drum and shipped to a New Jersey landfill. As recently as July 2022, a new search was conducted under a New Jersey bridge. I assure you, none of these leads are valid. I could have saved the FBI a lot of time and money by telling them to stop listening to chatterboxes who pretend to know what they are talking about. A hit team would never have risked the dangers involved in transporting a corpse hundreds of miles when there were a million places to dispose of Hoffa's body in Michigan.

Given the variety of leads that were considered at the time, I am absolutely convinced that Hoffa's last stop was the Central Sanitation Services in Hamtramck, Michigan, 'a shredder-compactor-incinerator facility' owned by Detroit borgata members Raffaele 'Jimmy Q' Quasarano and Peter 'Bozzi' Vitale. Vitale was a capo and Quasarano would rise to the rank of consigliere a few years after Hoffa disappeared. Their business was located less than twenty miles from the Machus Red Fox restaurant, about as long as anyone would want to travel with a body. Two confidential informants, both deemed credible by the FBI on account of their long history of providing reliable information, said that Hoffa was disposed of in this incinerator. An FBI memo, citing one of the informants, added that Quasarano and Vitale had gotten rid of 'at least ten murder victims' for the Detroit mafia in any one of their three garbage dumps. In the months leading up to Hoffa's disappearance, telephone toll records revealed a series of long-distance calls between Pennsylvania don Russell Bufalino, Vitale and Quasarano, who Hoffa had admitted to knowing 'for about ten years' while being grilled by Bobby Kennedy years earlier. Fitz was

Peter Vitale (left) and Jimmy Quasarano in later years

also friendly with Quasarano and Vitale and had visited them a few days before Hoffa disappeared. And Fitz's son, Donald (as opposed to Richard), had once worked for Quasarano's vending machine company.

The US Attorney's Office in New Jersey discovered that, in December 1974, when Tony Jack first began nudging Hoffa to meet with Tony Pro, Teamster funds were deposited into the Bank of Bloomfield, part of which formed a business loan of $85,000 to the Central Sanitation Services owned by Quasarano and Vitale. The 'loan', which was never repaid, was supposedly used to purchase a garbage disposal machine. Incinerating Hoffa would have settled the debt. When Quasarano and Vitale were questioned by the law, they were both noncompliant and one of their lawyers said in their defense, 'These men are not sophisticated individuals. They don't speak the English language fluently.' They both spoke perfect English. In 1978, author Steven Brill quoted an FBI affidavit that stated: 'Hoffa's body was destroyed . . . by means of a shredder, compactor and-or incinerator located on the premises,' and Brill pointed out that, 'No search warrant was ever requested, issued or executed by the FBI concerning the sanitation company.'

Given the typical formula for interfamily hits, it makes sense that the Genovese family supplied an out-of-town hit team while their Detroit counterparts disposed of the body.

What many people believe to be the most plausible account of Hoffa's death was published in the book *I Heard You Paint Houses*, by Frank Sheeran, later made into a movie, *The Irishman*. Based on the hype, I feel obligated to address Sheeran's deathbed confession in which he claimed to have killed Hoffa. To Sheeran's credit, there are a number of facts contained in his book that are indisputable. Sheeran was a legitimate mobster who answered directly to Russell Bufalino, and Bufalino was close with Tony Jack, and in contact with Quasarano and Vitale in the months leading up to Hoffa's disappearance. This evidence and more, albeit circumstantial, points to Bufalino's involvement in the conspiracy. The questions are: what part, if any, did Sheeran play in the conspiracy, and is his story solid?

In 2001, Sheeran first stated that Sally Bugs had killed Hoffa, a claim supported by reliable FBI informants. In 2003, Sheeran suddenly changed his story and said that he, himself, had killed Hoffa. Sheeran went on to tell so many blatant lies that documentaries, based on his story, were halted in mid-production when the producers could not, in good conscience, continue the projects. I have worked in television and can only imagine the level of mendacity that would prompt producers to stop a production in lieu of covering their ears. One of Sheeran's outlandish lies is his claim to have personally committed the hit on Crazy Joe Gallo at Umberto's Clam House, which we have thoroughly covered in Chapter 27. Everyone in the mob knows that Sonny Pinto killed Gallo. Not only did Joe Fish Luparelli *watch* Sonny Pinto kill Gallo from across the street then report the details to the FBI, but Pete the Greek unloaded his gun into Pinto's car as Pinto made his escape. Sonny Pinto also went on the lam and never returned and, as of the late 1990s, the Colombo family was still sending him a monthly stipend allotted to him for the sacrifice he had made for the borgata when whacking Gallo. Why in the world would Sheeran claim responsibility for the hit on Gallo, knowing it was Sonny Pinto, and the hit on Hoffa, knowing it was Sally Bugs? Sheeran's book sold incredibly well and Netflix dished out somewhere in the area of $200 million to make the movie, giving him 200 million reasons to lie.

A highly suspicious fire in March 1976 incinerated the incinerator at Central Sanitation Services when it burned to the ground in what is believed to have been an act of arson. Federal prosecutor Keith Corbett, who worked on the Hoffa investigation, recalled the fire during his retirement, saying, 'Betting odds would dictate, the fact that the place mysteriously burnt to the ground shortly thereafter wasn't a coincidence.' Corbett also said, 'The best intelligence we received regarding how Hoffa's body was done away with was the Central Sanitation angle. We were being told a lot of bodies were . . . incinerated there in the 1970s. Vitale and Quasarano were running out of there at that point in time and both those two fellas were pegged pretty early on as being involved in this murder.' Keith Corbett finally nailed Quasarano and Vitale on unrelated racketeering charges and they both died of natural causes in ripe old age, taking the secret of Hoffa's disappearance to their graves.

Chapter 30

Convenient Corpses

In the years since the Warren Commission report was published, quite a few men *who actually sat on the Warren Commission* became its chief skeptics. Judge Bert Griffin, for example, said, 'We accepted the answers we got, even though they were inadequate and didn't carry the battle any further. To do so, we'd have had to challenge the integrity of the FBI. Back in 1964, that was something we didn't do.' This universal reluctance to challenge the Bureau began to erode on the evening of 2 May 1972, when 77-year-old J. Edgar Hoover, who had been FBI director for over forty years, let out his two terriers for a poop in his backyard then dropped dead inside his home. President Nixon, who was still in office, publicly said of the all-powerful director's passing, 'His death only heightens the respect and admiration felt for him across this land and in every land where men cherish freedom,' while privately Nixon said, 'That old cocksucker . . . He's got files on everybody.'

In the hours after Hoover's death, his personal secretary, Ms Helen Gandy, destroyed most of his secret files in the basement of his home with the exception of twelve cardboard boxes which she gave to Deputy Associate Director Mark Felt (later revealed to be the infamous Deep Throat who secretly helped journalist Bob Woodward break open the Watergate scandal that led to Nixon's resignation. Felt would also be charged with authorizing burglaries). Of the undestroyed files, three folders disappeared, one of which bore the name of a top FBI official who was alleged to have deep connections to organized crime; the others were considered 'very sensitive and explosive files, containing political information . . . on key figures in the country'.

Hoover's passing heralded a major climate change in Washington DC, where Senator Frank Church of Idaho assembled the Church Committee to probe into, among other things, the relationship between the mafia and the CIA. The committee wanted to question a long list of people including CIA director Richard Helms, who admitted that his agency worked with the mob. The committee also targeted Johnny Roselli, who, over the years, had never lost contact with America's 007, Wild Bill Harvey.

When the committee subpoenaed Roselli, he was worn down by legal battles that had begun in 1954 when his citizenship was questioned by the Immigration and Naturalization Service. At that time, Roselli lawyered up and used delaying tactics until 1961 when Bobby Kennedy launched a new and aggressive probe into Roselli with intent to lock him up, then deport him upon his release from prison. This second probe also petered out after President Kennedy was killed and Bobby left the Justice Department. By then, Roselli had other problems. After his name surfaced in the Giancana–Rowan bugging affair, Hoover wanted to know what Roselli was doing with the agency and, in the course of his investigation, he uncovered Roselli's true identity.

On the afternoon of 5 May 1966, two FBI agents approached Roselli on a sidewalk in Beverly Hills, telling him they wanted to talk. Roselli politely told them to contact his attorney. As Roselli was walking away, one agent held an old photograph in front of his face. Roselli was stopped in his tracks, visibly shaken by the photo of a little boy with his mother. 'Filippo Sacco,' said the agent, rattling Roselli. 'We know where you were born and when you entered the United States.' The cute, innocent four-year-old boy in the photo bore little resemblance to the crafty, dangerous adult who oversaw Hollywood and Las Vegas for the Chicago mob.

How the FBI had discovered that Roselli was not a Renaissance painter began with mobster Sal Piscopo. At least once a year, Roselli had Piscopo travel to Boston carrying a bag filled with cash for Roselli's elderly mother, Maria Sacco, who Roselli had not seen in over thirty years. One day, FBI agents followed Piscopo to the airport where he met with another man, who took the cash and passed it on to Roselli's brother, Al Sacco, who finally delivered it to Roselli's mom. After the agents looked into Al Sacco, they pieced together the rest of the puzzle and caught up with Roselli in Beverly Hills, showing him the photo and telling him he could avoid deportation if he agreed to become a confidential informant. Roselli again told the agents to contact his attorney, then shuffled away.

The day after Roselli was approached by FBI agents, he booked a flight to Washington where he visited his retired CIA handler, Sheffield Edwards, asking him to get the FBI off his back. Edwards knew Roselli had the agency 'in an unusually vulnerable position' given its past relationship with the mob but said there was nothing he could do to call off the implacable Hoover. Roselli then reached out to Wild Bill Harvey who had even less pull than Edwards and had already been warned by the FBI to stay away from Roselli. Harvey ignored the warning, telling another agent, 'I don't turn my back on my friends. And Johnny is my friend.' With the threat of deportation hanging over his head, Roselli finally called on his Washington-based attorney, Edward Morgan, and explained to him all he had done for the CIA, adding, 'It's the one thing in my life that I'm really proud of.' Whatever we may think of Johnny Roselli, his patriotic love of country – attested to by multiple CIA agents – placed him in Hoover's crosshairs, and his eternal love for his mother, who he supported for decades, broke open the investigation. It is a curious trend in human affairs that our hearts often do us in.

After conferring with his attorney, Roselli fired a warning shot across the government's bow by leaking tidbits of information to the press. Journalist Drew Pearson and his assistant, Jack Anderson, both known for uncovering political scandals, broke the story which was framed as a political hit piece, accusing Bobby Kennedy (who was alive at the time) of directing the CIA's secret plot to eliminate Fidel Castro. Although Bobby denied being the maestro, he was admittedly distressed by the article and wasted no time arranging lunch with CIA director Richard Helms to assess the fallout and bury any files that might bear out his culpability. Roselli's bold gambit, though consistent with his daring nature, was an extremely dangerous move. He was threatening an all-powerful government, as well as the mafia; Sam Giancana and Santo Trafficante did not want their CIA secrets aired out in the press and were displeased with Roselli, whose waning strength in the underworld was revealed when he asked for a contract on Sal Piscopo, who had betrayed him and his family when interrogated by the FBI. That the contract was approved but never carried out means that Roselli was no longer worth avenging. The mob was, moreover, beginning to wonder if it made more sense to kill Roselli.

The government did not back down and Roselli was charged with a gambling indictment and a fraud case, accompanied by an increased effort to deport him. With no other cards to play, Roselli continued to leak damaging information to his attorney, telling him, in a moment of extraordinary indiscretion, that certain members of the same cabal who had tried to kill Fidel Castro had taken out President Kennedy who was shot by several Cuban snipers who were sent to Dallas by Santo Trafficante.

In May 1968, Roselli was convicted, and again in February 1969. At sentencing, Roselli's attorney made an impassioned plea for leniency based on Roselli's patriotic duty, which he was never paid for. The judge was unmoved. 'I don't think Mr. Roselli is entitled to brownie points,' he said. 'I am not going to concede that a court should give credit to a person who attempts the assassination of anybody.' The judge then sentenced Roselli to a nickel, which feels like a dime at age sixty-four. In February 1971, Roselli was sent to prison on McNeil Island in Washington State.

Over the course of his lifetime, Roselli had been arrested over a dozen times but had never served hard time, until now. He did not adjust to prison life and was still anxious about being deported when, in a moment of desperation, he broke weak and agreed to testify before a federal grand jury looking into the mob's control of Las Vegas. Even though federal prosecutors promised to keep his appearance secret, and although Roselli gave them hardly anything of value while testifying, the government now had him by the balls; if they ever wanted him dead, they need only leak choice bits of his testimony.

In early October 1973, the 68-year-old Roselli was released from prison early. Frightened of being deported, he again contacted journalist Jack Anderson and fed him more information about the government's dirty deeds, also confirming that the mob had ordered Jack Ruby to silence Lee Harvey Oswald. Roselli then flew to Plantation, Florida, where he moved into a guest room at the home of his sister, Edith Daigle, and her husband, Joe. Roselli lived the quiet life of a Florida retiree: mornings by the pool, afternoons on the golf course, and lazy evenings watching television. He complained about having no money, which was probably true. There is no doubt that millions of dollars had passed through Roselli's hands, but he lived high on the hog and had nothing to show for it, the reason he was crashing at his sister's house.

In February 1974, Roselli was subpoenaed by Special Prosecutor Leon Jaworski, who was investigating the Watergate scandal that toppled President Nixon and wanted to know if there was any connection between the Watergate burglars and the Bay of Pigs invasion since Cubans and CIA agents were involved in both incidents. Jaworski's theory was that President Nixon had ordered the burglary to seize and destroy documents that connected him to the CIA and the mafia. Roselli's attorney, who was present when Roselli was questioned, said the theory 'was so convoluted, you really had to be John le Carré to follow it'. Whether or not the theory was valid, Roselli denied any knowledge of it and returned to his sister's home in Florida. But the government knew, after Roselli had testified twice, they had a talker on their hands, which returns us to the Church Committee which subpoenaed Roselli in June 1975.

As expected, Roselli appeared, yet again. He entered the building in a hand-tailored sport jacket with a leather attaché case, looking

more like a Washington lobbyist than a mobster (if there is any difference between the two). Like everything else about Roselli, his testimony was a carefully balanced mix of truth and lies. As he exited the hearing room, the press was waiting for him with cameras flashing. One reporter asked him if he had any reason to fear for his life. Roselli shrugged and replied, 'Who'd want to kill an old man like me?' Santo Trafficante for starters, but the list was growing by the hour.

Johnny Roselli talking too much

The Church Committee had also subpoenaed Trafficante, but, unlike Roselli, Trafficante knew how to dodge a subpoena; he fled to his vacation home in Costa Rica and ducked the summons. Sam Giancana was also called before the committee, and it is necessary to retrace his steps leading up to this moment as we have done with Roselli.

The relentless pressure Bobby Kennedy had put on Carlos Marcello, Santo Trafficante and Sam Giancana had eased up after the assassination of President Kennedy. By 1970, Aaron Kohn said that Marcello's borgata still had 'corrupt collusion of public officials at every critical level – including police, sheriffs, justices of the peace, prosecutors, mayors, governors, state legislators, and at least one member of Congress', although there were more. In April, *Life* magazine ran an article headlined: Louisiana Still Jumps for Mobster Marcello. Inside the article, *Life* reported that the sixty-year-old Marcello 'controlled the State of Louisiana . . . with little interference from local public officials or police, and indeed often with their help'. As for Trafficante, he resumed command over the state of Florida while living in a modest bungalow and driving around in an old sun-bleached car, with rolls of coins in his pockets so he could conduct his business from public pay phones. At night, Trafficante sat in his living room and read books across from his longtime wife who did the same.

In contrast to the two smarter dons noted above, Giancana never abandoned his glitzy lifestyle and continued to attract attention from both the media and the FBI, which placed him under suffocating surveillance, called him before grand juries, and put the squeeze on everyone around him, including Murray 'The Camel' Humphreys, who dropped dead from the pressure. In an unprecedented move for a mob boss, Giancana sued the government, claiming that the FBI's constant surveillance was a violation of his civil rights. A judge thought the complaint had legal merit but Giancana's real judge, Anthony 'Joe Batters' Accardo, saw Giancana's legal whining as a violation of *omertà*. An FBI memo indicated that Giancana was in an 'extremely tenuous situation because of publicity' and 'may be replaced'.

As early as 1964, Accardo decided to come out of retirement but held off on killing Giancana, figuring Giancana's legal problems would soon carry him off to prison and spare the Chicago mob a final round of publicity that would undoubtedly stem from his murder or disappearance. In early 1965, Giancana was called before two grand juries and he took the Fifth both times. The third time he was called, he was granted immunity, which meant that he had to start answering questions or risk a perjury charge for contempt of court, which could land him in jail for up to eighteen months. One FBI agent commented, 'If he lied, we could get him for perjury. If he told the truth, his associates would get him.' Giancana kept his mouth shut, and on 1 June, he appeared before Judge William Campbell, who told him, 'You have the key to your own cell,' then sent him to jail. With Giancana locked away, Accardo revoked his lease on the throne and replaced him with a changing cast of characters that included confidants Paul 'The Waiter' Ricca, Salvatore 'Sam' Battaglia and Giuseppe 'Joey Doves' Aiuppa.

After a year in prison, Giancana was set free. He hit the streets on Memorial Day, 1966. If he was expecting a welcoming party, he was gravely disappointed. Within days of his release, he was called in by Accardo who told him that he was finished as boss. Accardo then broke him down to a soldier in order to extinguish any lingering aspirations of a triumphant return. Rather than endure the humiliations of a demoted mobster while facing more grand juries, Giancana retired to Mexico City, where he temporarily took up residence in a fully staffed, multi-room hotel suite before he moved on to a private estate.

From his new home base in Mexico City, Giancana traveled the world, opening casinos in exotic places and operating gambling ships that roamed international waters. Once again, he began dating glamorous women, the real pleasure of his life. While Johnny Roselli was discussing Giancana with another mobster, Roselli said Giancana was 'having a ball. He's been to Europe, the Middle East, thinking of getting an apartment in Beirut, one in Paris, and planning a trip to Africa.' Giancana told Roselli, 'I'm enjoying this new life. Let the cocksuckers back there knock each other off all they want, who cares?'

The president of Mexico began to care when US prosecutors decided to call Giancana before more grand juries and pressured the Mexican president to deport him. In late July 1974, Mexican authorities took Giancana into custody and ejected him from the country. From the US–Mexican border, he was put on a plane and flown to Chicago's O'Hare International Airport where FBI agents were awaiting his return. One agent, who had tailed Giancana for years, said of the 66-year-old once dapper don who now wore cube-heeled boots, bell-bottom pants, and a salt and pepper goatee, 'He was undoubtedly the wealthiest person on that plane, but he looked like some Italian immigrant landing at Ellis Island, destitute and frail.' The agent called him a 'shadow of the great godfather'. The real Chicago godfather, Anthony Accardo, did not view Giancana as a shadow but saw him as a real threat who was, once again, creating a new wave of real publicity.

Unlike the old days in Chicago, Giancana no longer had his own social club and now conducted his street business from his Oak Park home or on the move, usually inside luncheonettes and restaurants. After seeing that Giancana was back in the swing of things, Accardo demanded a full accounting of Giancana's overseas income and assets. Giancana balked; he felt that everything he had created outside the country belonged to him, alone. This defiance would have been enough for Accardo to whack Giancana, but what really melted the last layer of thin ice under Giancana's platform boots was his scheduled appearance before the Church Committee, which wanted to question him about the Kennedy assassination.

On the evening of 19 June 1975, Giancana invited guests to his house for dinner. The dinner party included his youngest daughter, Francine, son-in-law Jerome 'Jerry' DePalma, and mobsters Charles 'Chuckie English' Inglesia and Dominic 'Butch' Blasi. The party arrived at 7 p.m. and broke up before 10 p.m., at which time a police unit surveilling the house watched Chuckie English and Butch Blasi leave together. Not long afterward, the same cops saw Butch Blasi return to the house, park his car in the driveway and walk inside. The cops reasoned that Blasi had returned to discuss mob business that could not have been talked about in the presence of Giancana's daughter. They left their stake-out position and took a spin past Anthony Accardo's house to see what the big tuna was up to.

Around midnight, Giancana lit up the stovetop and started to cook a meal considered an Italian favorite: sausage, escarole, garlic and beans. He was frying it up in a pan when Blasi crept up behind him and raised a .22 caliber pistol with silencer to the back of his head. The first bullet cut a path through Giancana's brain, sending him to the kitchen floor. Blasi leaned down and squeezed off six more rounds under Giancana's chin. (The *pistola* had a ten-shot clip; it is likely that Blasi had saved three bullets in case someone got in his way as he made his exit.) Blasi searched Giancana's wallet for any clues relating to his grand jury testimony or his rackets abroad. He then threw the wallet a few feet away from Giancana's body, not even bothering to take the wad of $1,429 in cash. While driving away from the house, Blasi tossed the murder weapon which was found nearby. Later on, Blasi, described by Giancana's daughter, Antoinette, as 'a man my father trusted more than anyone else', bragged to associates that he had whacked Giancana – on Accardo's orders – but he was never charged with the crime even though a police unit had watched him return to the house, alone, and there was reported to be a twenty-four-hour federal surveillance unit watching him as well. Antoinette said that the home's caretaker saw both cars leave at the same time, adding, 'I believe they were ordered off the property.'

Johnny Roselli was a guest at the Watergate Hotel when his attorney, Leslie Scherr, told him that Giancana had been murdered. 'He wasn't shocked,' said Scherr. Likely because Roselli had already heard about it, or anticipated it – probably both.

Church Committee staff investigator David Bushong, who had just lost one of his two mafia witnesses, said, 'It was clear to me that [Roselli] was the only live witness. I wanted him on record, and I wanted him quick.' Bushong scheduled Roselli to appear on 24 June, the first Tuesday after Giancana's death. Senators Frank Church, Barry Goldwater, Walter Mondale and others were aware of the target on Roselli's back when they asked Capitol Police to escort him into the Capitol Building through a back door. The closed session was held in a windowless chamber where Roselli enthralled his audience with a 'fully detailed description' of the CIA–mafia plots to kill Castro. Senator Goldwater was amazed at Roselli's recollection of facts that meshed with the testimony of FBI and CIA agents who regularly referred to notes in lieu of memory. Goldwater asked Roselli if he kept a written record, to which Roselli replied, 'Senator, in my business, we don't take notes.'

When Senator Schweiker from Pennsylvania delved into the Kennedy assassination, Roselli was careful, denying any insider knowledge. When questioned about Trafficante, he only revealed the Florida don's role as a Spanish interpreter for the CIA's mission to assassinate Castro.

In September, Roselli appeared before the committee again, and was again asked about the Kennedy assassination. He denied knowing anything more than '200 million' other Americans who held 'different views' as to what happened in Dealey Plaza. When asked, Roselli also denied having any knowledge of why Giancana was murdered. After the hearings were concluded, Roselli returned to his sister's home in Plantation, Florida, and resumed his quiet life. But the man whose business card simply read 'Strategist' had committed an abysmal failure in strategic thinking. Trafficante was disturbed by Roselli's appearances, and Roselli was well within Trafficante's reach in Florida.

In conversations with Los Angeles mobster Jimmy 'The Weasel' Fratianno, who considered Roselli an early mentor, Roselli expressed regret that he, Giancana and Trafficante had blown the hit on Castro and called into question Trafficante's loyalty to the plot, saying, 'He was probably reporting everything to Castro's agents, and Miami's full of them.' Roselli also ridiculed the bosses in Chicago, admitting that his relationship with Accardo was 'piss poor' while blaming it on a jealous rivalry that dated back to the Capone days. Fratianno asked Roselli if he was concerned about the articles that outed him as a leaker. 'Did Joe Batters ever mention the column?' asked Fratianno.

'Not a word.'

'Christ,' said Fratianno, 'that's a relief. Maybe he don't know about it.'

'Oh, don't worry, he goddamn well knows. What can he do about it? Sam and Santo were involved. I was just following orders.'

In a moment of bitter resignation, Roselli told Fratianno, 'There's nothing you can do when bosses turn on you. That's the trouble with this thing of ours . . . I'll retire. I've made my contribution, the least they can do is let me live the remaining years in peace . . . So that's why I'm down here in Miami.' (Plantation was just north of Miami where Roselli often met with Fratianno.)

Unable to make amends with the bosses on earth, Roselli wanted to make peace with the Big Boss above. In the summer of 1976, he visited his friend, Father Joseph Clark, and made confession, a sacrament which, if honest and forthright, should have taken Roselli weeks to complete and ended with Clark receiving treatment for PTSD.

On the morning of 28 July 1976, Roselli slept in then lounged by the pool while reading the newspaper. His sister, Edith, made him brunch before he showered and dressed in a pink silk shirt and blue pants. Just before 1 p.m., the suntanned, silver-haired wiseguy drove away from the house in his sister's 1975 silver Chevy Impala with his golf clubs in the trunk. His first stop was a marina where he met with two fellow mobsters who invited him on a leisurely yacht ride on the calm waters of the Intracoastal. As the yacht pushed off, Roselli was sipping a cocktail on the aft deck.

Later that evening, his sister, Edith, became concerned when she did not hear from him. Her husband, Joe, recalled Roselli once saying, 'If I'm ever missing, check the airports, because that's where they usually leave the car.' On Saturday morning, Joe Daigle drove to Miami International Airport and cruised around the parking garage until he spotted the silver Impala and wondered if Roselli was in the trunk. The aeronautical engineer, who must have felt like he had been thrust into a gangster movie, opened the trunk with trepidation but found only golf clubs.

On the morning of 7 August 1976, three fishermen in their early twenties decided to try their luck in Miami's Dumfoundling Bay. As one young man cast his line into the water, he noticed a 55-gallon steel drum bobbing along the water's edge; thick chains encircled the drum as though Harry Houdini had used it for an escape act. The curious young man walked along the embankment until he was standing directly above the floating drum and could see crudely made gashes in its steel. He leaned down to look inside one of the holes and noticed a pink shirt before he was blasted with the stench of death. He recoiled in horror then yelled to his buddies who ran off and called the police.

A short while later, a police helicopter was circling above the bay as a police team hoisted the drum out of the water and placed it onto a flatbed truck. Police scuba divers dropped into the water to have a look around and confirmed that the bay's only regurgitated meal was already on its way to the Dade County medical examiner, who removed the wet corpse for a closer inspection. The legs had been sawed off at the thighs and placed alongside the torso. A washcloth was stuffed into the mouth before adhesive tape was wrapped tightly around the head holding the gag in place. A rope was knotted around the neck and the bloated face was grotesquely twisted into a frozen grin. The coroner believed the cause of death to be asphyxiation, but the victim was also stabbed and shot before his torso was sliced open from neck to naval. Between the opened chest cavity, the heavy chains that encircled the drum and the crude gashes in its steel, it was presumed that the victim's killers wanted him to sink to the bottom of the bay and remain there forever. But the gases trapped inside his decomposing body launched him to the surface like a cork. The medical examiner believed that this was because the victim suffered from emphysema, which forms pockets of air in the upper body and carried the corpse to the surface. In time, had the young fisherman not found him, the gases would have been expelled from the body and the drum would have returned to the bottom.

Detectives checked a list of missing persons while the corpse's soggy thumb was fingerprinted, which confirmed that the victim was 71-year-old Johnny Roselli. After the gruesome discovery of Roselli's mutilated body was reported in the news, there was a clamor of accusations that the CIA had killed Roselli to shut him up, forcing CIA director William Colby to issue a public denial, saying, 'I can guarantee you that the CIA had nothing to do with his death.'*

FBI director Clarence Kelley said he could not investigate Roselli's

---

* William Colby later became a CIA apologist. In a single year, he testified thirty-two times before congressional committees, telling the press, 'I think the best way was to get rid of the past and transition into a future of intelligence under the constitution.' He died in mysterious circumstances.

murder for lack of federal jurisdiction. The *Washington Post* pointed out that the FBI could have easily found cause to step in, hinting that the Bureau was quite satisfied with the permanent gag in Roselli's mouth. The Church Committee had already been disbanded but senators on the Select Committee on Intelligence prodded US attorney general Edward Levi to pursue an investigation into Roselli's death in order to protect the integrity of congressional witnesses. Levi initially resisted then succumbed to political pressure and directed the FBI to investigate, which they did with indifference.

Although no one was ever arrested for Roselli's murder, a mafia informant told the FBI that the frail retiree was sipping a drink when a garrote was slipped around his neck from behind; as he gasped for air, a rag was stuffed into his open mouth. The informant said that the older mobster, suffering from emphysema, barely struggled. Since Roselli's frail frame could have easily been folded into the drum, the sawing off of his legs meant that he had been left lying around for a while and become stiff as rigor mortis set in; his legs were sawed off before he was placed in the drum for the same reason we break raw spaghetti, so it fits in the pot.

Several underworld informants pointed to Trafficante as the man responsible for the hit on Roselli. One of Trafficante's soldiers, Sam Cagnina, bragged about killing Roselli, which confirmed the reports. Since Roselli belonged to the Chicago mob, Trafficante would have had to clear it with acting boss Joey Doves Aiuppa, who was overheard saying, 'Trafficante had the job, and he messed it up,' meaning Roselli's body was discovered when it was meant to disappear forever.

Jack Anderson, whose column likely contributed to the hit on Roselli, wrote after he was killed, 'Roselli may have taken the secret of the John F. Kennedy assassination with him to his death.' It would now depend on the House Select Committee on Assassinations to see if that was true.

In 1976, the House of Representatives voted to establish the House Select Committee on Assassinations to investigate the deaths of President John F. Kennedy and Reverend Dr Martin Luther King Jr, who was also murdered in mysterious circumstances in April 1968. Interestingly, Bill and Rosalie Bonanno were traveling from New York to California when they heard a radio news report of the Reverend Dr King's assassination. Bill immediately turned to his wife and said,

'You see? He was getting too powerful and the government had to cut him down.' Bill's immediate response to the tragedy is now widely believed by most Americans.

The committee's first chief counsel was Richard Sprague, a Philadelphia prosecutor who directed much of his investigative resources toward the CIA, which spooked a few people in Washington so Congress replaced him with the more reliable G. Robert Blakey, a 41-year-old Cornell law professor who had once worked in Bobby Kennedy's Organized Crime Section. Blakey, like Jim Garrison before him, believed that President Kennedy was the victim of a conspiracy and that more than one shooter was involved, but Blakey differed with Garrison as to who the conspirators were. Blakey was inclined to lean more toward the mafia and thought that Garrison had conducted a sham investigation, designed to throw the scent off Carlos Marcello.

The House Select Committee subpoenaed Marcello to appear before a secret executive session. Under a grant of immunity, the 68-year-old mob boss denied any involvement in the assassination of President Kennedy, but admitted to working closely with David Ferrie on his 1963 trial defense. When questioned about a large sum of money he had given to Ferrie following the assassination, Marcello claimed that it was recompense for Ferrie's trial services. Marcello was *not* asked about Lee Harvey Oswald, a strange omission given that Oswald lived with, and worked for, Marcello's bookmaker Charles 'Dutz' Murret, and that a number of witnesses had seen Oswald in the company of Ferrie, placing Marcello one person removed from the president's alleged assassin.

During one telling exchange, Blakey noted how angry Marcello became when questioned about his illegal deportation to Guatemala at the hands of Bobby Kennedy. 'Generally, his answers were in curt monosyllables,' Blakey later wrote. 'But when the subject of his deportation came up, the atmosphere in the hearing room turned tense. Marcello showed fire in his eyes and resentment in the tone of his voice.'

Almost incredibly, FBI agent Regis Kennedy, whose turf was New Orleans, testified that he still believed Marcello was a tomato salesman.

The committee did an excellent job of tracing Jack Ruby's extensive mafia connections, something the Warren Commission had neglected to do. They subpoenaed Dallas underboss Joe Campisi, who had dined with Ruby on the night before the assassination, and had visited Ruby in jail after Ruby killed Oswald. When questioned, Campisi openly admitted to knowing Ruby as well as Joe Civello and Carlos Marcello, but he stopped there, denying any knowledge of a conspiracy to kill the president.

Santo Trafficante was called before the committee; this time, he did not take off for Costa Rica. When the servers showed up with a subpoena at Trafficante's house in Miami, the Florida don 'appeared at the screen door' and said, 'Shove it under the door.' Trafficante was ordered to bring all documents relating to the attempts on Fidel Castro's life, and the assassination of President Kennedy. Needless to say, Trafficante brought nothing with him and invoked his Fifth Amendment right to remain silent after he insisted on having an open hearing as opposed to a closed session; he did not want anyone in the underworld wondering what he might have said behind closed doors. He was called back under a grant of immunity, forcing him to testify or go to jail. Trafficante bobbed and weaved under questioning; he admitted to working with Roselli and the CIA in a plot to assassinate Castro, which was arguably patriotic, but denied any involvement in a conspiracy to assassinate the president. Trafficante's attorney, Frank Ragano, described his testimony as a 'recital of evasive answers'.

José Aleman appeared before the committee in a closed session where he reaffirmed his September 1962 report to the FBI in which he stated that Trafficante had expressed foreknowledge of the president's assassination, which shocked Aleman after it came to pass. When Aleman was called back before a public session, his story changed. Although Aleman reiterated Trafficante's comment that the president was 'going to be hit', he now altered his understanding of it, claiming that Trafficante had only meant that Kennedy would be hit by a 'lot of votes from the Republican party' in the upcoming election. The committee was stunned by his revised interpretation of the event. Later, in private, Aleman confessed to the committee's incredulous staff that he was terrified of Trafficante and feared for his life.

Aleman left the hearing room certain that he was a marked man. But Trafficante let him live, choosing to ostracize him instead. At the behest of Trafficante, none of Aleman's Floridian business associates, both Cuban and Italian, dealt with him or his family. Completely isolated, the once wealthy son of Cuba's former education minister quickly sank into financial ruin. After his fortune was removed by Trafficante's invisible hand, he suffered a nervous breakdown and moved into a tiny bungalow with members of his extended family. On the morning of 1 August 1983, Aleman woke up 'penniless, depressed and convinced the mafia was out to kill him', when he shot to death his elderly aunt, injured three cousins including a six-year-old child, exchanged gunfire with a SWAT team, then placed the muzzle of his gun to his temple and blew his brains out. One of Aleman's surviving relatives told the press that Aleman 'believed he and his family were on a mafia hit list'. The cunning, ever-plodding Trafficante had somehow managed to have Aleman fulfill a contract on himself.

After interviewing approximately five thousand people and deposing three hundred witnesses, G. Robert Blakey concluded that 'organized crime had a hand in the assassination of President Kennedy'. The committee believed that Marcello was the driving force behind the president's assassination while Trafficante and Jimmy Hoffa were his main accomplices. Blakey also said that the 'murder of Oswald by Jack Ruby had all the earmarks of an organized crime hit, an action to silence the assassin, so he could not reveal the conspiracy'. 'We also concluded,' wrote Blakey, 'that Ruby had been in contact with organized crime figures before and after the assassination, and we discovered evidence that organized crime figures were present during at least part of his trial for the murder.'

Blakey reluctantly admitted that 'rogue elements of the CIA, acting either on their own or in concert with members of organized crime, might have been involved'. He drew the same conclusion with regard to members of the Cuban exile community. The FBI was cleared of having any active role in the conspiracy, but the Bureau's blatant negligence leading up to the assassination was called into question. Blakey criticized the Secret Service for not doing all they could to protect the president but gave them a pass, as well. This conflicted with Dallas police chief Jesse Curry, who wrote a book in which he directed much of the blame at the Secret Service, specifically Winston Lawson who arrived in Dallas on 12 November, ten days before the assassination. Chief Curry said, 'The Dallas Police Department carefully carried out the security plans which were laid out by Mr. Lawson, the Secret Service representative from Washington, D.C.' who was 'the central figure and primary planner of all the security arrangements'. Chief Curry further said that 'Mr. Lawson was in command' and had 'directed the security arrangements in every detail'. What were those details?

To start with, '[Winston] Lawson told his men to leave the top off', meaning Secret Service agents were ordered to remove the protective bubbletop from the presidential limousine. Agents Clint Hill and Jack Ready were told not to stand on the limousine's rear riding steps. Hill's large frame would have obstructed a clean shot from either the School Book Depository, where Lee Harvey Oswald worked, or the Dal-Tex building, where Eugene Hale Brading was taken into custody. Furthermore, Chief Curry said that Winston Lawson 'laid out the planned number of vehicles in the parade and their relative order', adding that 'Mr. Lawson felt that eight motorcycles around the president's vehicle were too many. Instead, he stated that he thought two motorcycles on either side would be sufficient, and that they should be about even with the rear fender of the President's car,' as opposed to riding alongside the car which could have interfered with a shot from the grassy knoll. The other four motorcycles that would normally encircle the limousine were sent to the rear of the motorcade, far away from the action. The press vehicle, which was loaded with professional photographers who knew how to snap pictures, was supposed to be two cars behind the presidential limousine but was bumped to the rear without an explanation.

Dallas police were told to stand with their backs to the crowd, making it impossible to spot suspicious persons, and the police crowd detail was deliberately ended one block short of the kill zone on Elm Street. The ninety-degree turn onto Elm Street was a last-minute change made by the Secret Service that slowed the presidential limousine to a crawl, making Kennedy an easy target with a canyon of high buildings all around him. Chief Curry wrote that the 'Security was comparatively light along the short stretch of Elm Street where the President was shot . . . it seems a freak of history that this short stretch of Elm Street would be the assassination site, and that the Texas Book Depository Building was virtually ignored in the security plans for the motorcade'. It is apparent what Curry is telling us, that whoever ordered these strange changes was either involved in the conspiracy, or controlled by men who were involved.

In all fairness to Winston Lawson, it seems he was following orders from a higher power; he told the Warren Commission that to have the motorcade ride through the more dangerous downtown area was 'wanted back in Washington, D.C.' The president's longtime secretary, Evelyn Lincoln, wrote, 'Our own advance man urged that the motorcade not take the route through the underpass and past the

Book depository but he was overruled.' By whom? Who exactly was Lawson and Lincoln referring to? Perhaps it was Secret Service Agent in Charge Gerald Behn, who had been the head of the presidential detail since Kennedy's inauguration. In the three years since Kennedy was elected, Behn had never left the president's side, traveling everywhere with him and, during motorcades, always sitting in the front passenger seat, directly in front of Kennedy. However, when the shots rang out at Dealey Plaza, Behn was sitting at his desk in the East Wing of the White House. Behn supposedly took a vacation, excusing himself from the trip to Texas, then, on second thought, decided to go to work at his office in Washington, calling the shots throughout the trip. Without the many puzzling changes that resulted in a lack of security around the president, the perfect hit could never have happened. For example, when agent Ron Pontius could not believe that his fellow agents were prohibited from riding on the back steps of the presidential limousine, he called Behn in Washington and asked if it were true. Behn answered, 'That's right.' Then added, 'Tell the agents not to be too overzealous in crowding the president.' When Pontius hung up the phone, another agent, Bert DeFreese, who was listening in on the conversation, commented, 'I thought Behn was on vacation.'

After the president was assassinated, Behn was not sacked or asked to resign but became Special Agent in Charge of President Johnson's detail. And Lawson was rewarded for the many inexcusable failures on his watch with a cushy, high-paying job at the Department of Defense. After losing a president, neither man should have been trusted to walk someone's dog. Lawson himself said, 'I'm the only agent in the history of the Secret Service . . . that had the President of the United States killed.' And Urbanus Edmund Baughman, a longtime Secret Service chief who retired in 1961, called Behn's actions into question, stopping just shy of accusing him of complicity.

After President Kennedy was dead, the Secret Service wrested his body away from the Dallas County medical examiner, Dr Earl Rose, who had every lawful right to perform the autopsy. Kenny O'Donnell, who was present with Secret Service agents, described a tense stand-off with foul language and 'fists doubled [when] Dr. Rose . . . did not get out of our way'. A judge was called to mediate the dispute and said that Kennedy's body must remain in Dallas, stating 'as far as I'm concerned, it's just another homicide case'. O'Donnell said, 'We shoved Dr. Rose aside' before the Secret Service stole off with the corpse. 'I was sure that the medical examiner and the police would follow us to the airport and try to stop us from putting the casket on the plane,' said O'Donnell. 'I kept looking back to see if any police cars were coming, and telling the others to hurry.' The stolen corpse was taken to the Bethesda Naval Hospital in Maryland, where many believe an autopsy was performed in order to hide the real results and thus the true direction of the bullet that ended Kennedy's life.

The bloodied presidential limousine with brain tissue on the seats and floorboards was also treated strangely. *Time* magazine reporter Hugh Sidey said, 'A guard was set up around the Lincoln as Secret Service men got a pail of water and tried to wash the blood from the car.' This rolling piece of physical evidence that should never have been tampered with was then driven back to Love Field, placed on a cargo plane and flown to Washington, where it was quickly and inexplicably repaired and reupholstered, destroying any remaining evidence.

It is quite apparent to anyone without blinders on that whatever the mob was able to contribute to the death of President Kennedy, they could not have succeeded or gotten away with it without an elite government cabal making the decisions noted above. Even the murder of Lee Harvey Oswald, confirmed to be a mob hit by G. Robert Blakey, needed assistance from this same cabal. Chief Curry had originally planned to transfer Oswald to the local jail at night and in secret but, according to Dallas detective Don Archer, 'outside political pressures coming from as far as Washington insisted that Oswald be shown' to the public.

The contrasting conclusions reached by G. Robert Blakey and Jim Garrison seem to have been guided by the parties each man was out to protect. Garrison pointed the finger at the CIA while pretending La Cosa Nostra was the name of an Italian restaurant, and Blakey laid the blame on the mafia while carefully tiptoeing around the federal government. Judging from their most conspicuous omissions, it becomes quite apparent that the natural inquisitiveness that should have guided each of their investigations was curtailed by invisible hands that *guided each investigator*. The truth, it seems, does not lie in one conclusion or the other, but in the overlap. If the mob and the government worked together in a plot to kill Fidel Castro, why then should it shock us that they worked together to take out who they believed was another mutual enemy?

Epilogue

When Joe Valachi became a snitch and went before Congress, his testimony did not lead to any major takedowns across the country but
the underworld still wanted him dead, concerned that his betrayal of
La Cosa Nostra could spark a trend resulting in a flood of informants.
Fortunately for the mob, their fears were unfounded and snitching
would not become trendy until, after a curious lapse of thirty years, a
Gambino family underboss went sour in 1991, prompting other mobsters to follow in his footsteps. In the interim, there were a few excep-
tions, like New England mobster Vincent 'Fat Vinnie' Teresa, who
became a snitch in December 1969. Teresa ended up in the 'rat suite' at
La Tuna Penitentiary in Texas where he met inmate Joe Valachi, who
was living out the remainder of his life in fear. 'Joe wouldn't even come
near me or talk to me,' said Teresa. 'He was scared stiff . . . and he was
convinced I was there to kill him.' After Teresa told Valachi that he,
too, was an informant and had no interest in killing him, the two men
hit it off and became fast friends. But Valachi's paranoia never ceased.
Once, while the two inmates were sunning themselves in the prison
yard and a small airplane flew overhead, Teresa said that Valachi
'was convinced that that plane carried a hitman who was going to
shoot us'.

Teresa, who was not only an efficient killer but also a big earner,
may have unwittingly revealed the root of Valachi's bitterness toward
Vito Genovese which never waned, even years later. According to
Teresa, whenever they reminisced about the old days, Valachi only
talked about murders he had committed. When Teresa asked Valachi
to stop talking about contracts and to 'talk about making money',
Valachi replied, 'How can I talk about making money, Vinnie? . . . I
never made any.' Valachi's reply makes it apparent that Genovese had
only used Valachi to kill people, and Valachi blamed his own lack of
earning power on his boss.

'Valachi was bitter about other things,' said Teresa. 'He kept saying
over and over that Bobby Kennedy had promised him he would get out

of jail, but it was all a snow job.' Valachi died a lonely, miserable death inside prison in April 1971, outliving Bobby whose crusade against the mafia was stopped by Carlos Marcello.

In the years following the Kennedy assassination, many of Carlos Marcello's suspected co-conspirators either turned up murdered or were found dead under mysterious circumstances. In 1980, the Louisiana don, who was still riding high and had 'never been convicted of a major crime' in five decades, became the target of an FBI sting. Agents broke into Marcello's private office, still at the nondescript Town and Country Motel, and planted a microphone in the ceiling above his desk. They then posed as insurance salesmen, offering Marcello generous bribes in return for state contracts.

By 1981, the 71-year-old Marcello was indicted. On the tapes that were entered into evidence, the mafia don who doubled as a power broker, openly admitted his grasp over blocs of voters, public officials, politicians and union leaders. According to the *Des Moines Tribune*, the recordings 'cut through the shroud of secrecy surrounding Marcello, one of the most secretive crime bosses in the United States'. The article referred to Marcello's mafia empire as 'one of the most powerful, most entrenched in the country', and went on to say, 'If the tapes are to be believed, Marcello's influence on state government is pervasive. He is a man with clout, publicly shunned but privately courted by campaign fundraisers and businessmen in search of public work.'

'For years, political candidates have sought Marcello's support,' said one attorney involved in the case which also netted such characters as the Louisiana commissioner of administration, as well as a former top aide to the Louisiana governor, and the high-powered Washington lobbyist, Irving Davidson, whose clientele included the CIA. A follow-up indictment stemming from the same sting charged the speaker of the Texas House of Representatives with similar pay-for-play crimes. As in the Kennedy assassination plot, it seems that Marcello felt immune from prosecution when partnering with people in the highest circles of government, unaware that the feds had undergone a monumental change in attitude and were not averse, at least in some cases, to taking down state officials and their mafia cronies.

The indictment, which cast Marcello as the mastermind of the conspiracy, came as a shock to the old don, who received support from pillars of the community who were quick to attest to the 'good character and charity' of the loving father of four children who doted on his ten grandchildren.

During the 'laborious process of choosing a jury', prospective jurors were asked what came to mind when they heard the name Marcello. Over and over, the replies were 'the mafia' and 'the godfather'. The Chinese-American sheriff of Jefferson Parish said of Marcello, 'he doesn't look much like Marlon Brando', referring to the actor who played Don Corleone in *The Godfather* which was released a decade after President Kennedy's assassination. But even if Marcello's 'short, pudgy' build and grandfatherly features did not resemble Marlon Brando, Marcello's raspy voice on the tapes sounded very much like that of Don Corleone as Marcello revealed his unlimited reach into the darkest and dirtiest rooms of Louisiana politics.

When a jury was finally chosen and the trial began, United States attorney John Volz told the courtroom that Marcello was a 'corrupting influence on the affairs of government'. Marcello was convicted on only one count of the twelve-count indictment and sentenced to seven years in prison. He received another seven years from a subsequent indictment, but one of the convictions was thrown out by a federal appellate court, so Marcello only served a total of six and a half years in prison. In that time, Marcello's health deteriorated and he suffered a series of minor strokes. Another inmate, who was an informant, told the government that the ailing and aging mob boss, while cooped up for the first time in his long reign, was becoming rather chatty. The inmate was wired up, and although most of what Marcello said on tape about the Kennedy assassination remains locked away in the National Archives, a heavily redacted FBI memo slipped out in 2006, over twenty years after it was recorded. It reads as follows:

> On December 15, 1985, he [inmate Jack Ronald Vanlaningham who was secretly recording Marcello] was in the company of CARLOS MARCELLO and another inmate at the FEDERAL CORRECTIONAL INSTITUTE (FCI), Texarkana, Texas, in the court yard engaged in conversation. CARLOS MARCELLO discussed his intense dislike of former President JOHN KENNEDY as he often did. Unlike other such tirades against KENNEDY, however, on this occasion CARLOS MARCELLO said, referring to President KENNEDY, 'Yeah, I had the son of a bitch killed. I'm glad I did. I'm sorry I couldn't have done it myself.'

In March 1987, two years after Marcello admitted to committing the crime of the century, his fellow don, Santo Trafficante, was nearing death's door. Following a triple bypass operation that complicated other health problems, Trafficante said to his trusted attorney, Frank Ragano, 'I think Carlos fucked up in getting rid of Giovanni [the Italian translation of John] – maybe it should have been Bobby.' That same year, Trafficante died of heart failure at the Texas Heart Institute in Houston, not far from where JFK was assassinated. With the exception of the time he had served in Cuba's Triscornia Detention Camp, Trafficante had never spent a night in jail.

Marcello's exit from this world came on 2 March 1993, just over three and a half years after his release from prison. The 83-year-old don who entered the United States in his mother's arms eighty-two years earlier went to sleep and never awakened, a quiet, painless death widely believed by the world's religions and spiritual believers to be reserved for the purer of heart. Rather ironically, Trafficante and Marcello died of natural causes in ripe old age while the Kennedy brothers each bought it with a bullet to the head.

In his *A Study of History*, Arnold Toynbee examined the rise and fall of various civilizations throughout the course of human history and concluded that a small minority of creative individuals were responsible for each civilization's response to challenges that would have otherwise doomed it prematurely. Although the mafia is not a civilization, Marcello and Trafficante meet the definition of Toynbee's 'creative minority' when they masterfully rid the mafia of its nearly unstoppable Savonarola, Bobby Kennedy, saving it from a premature death and allowing us to move on to the concluding volume of our history, *Autumn of Empire*.

For a glimpse of what lies ahead, let us turn to Sir Arthur Helps, who wrote in his four-volume masterpiece, *The Spanish Conquest in America*, an anecdote that can just as readily apply to the Italian-American mafia's conquest of America, and its subsequent decline in our upcoming volume: 'When the wild beasts of a forest have hunted down their prey, there comes the difficulty of tearing it into equal or rather into satisfying shares, which mostly ends in renewed bloodshed.' We are about to encounter the wild beasts of the underworld who will viciously fight like savages over the rancid carcass of empire.

Acknowledgments

As in Volume One, I must thank the late Lord George Weidenfeld for asking me to write this history, along with Lady Annabelle Weidenfeld, who contributed to that fateful day. I also thank Bruce and Madeline Ramer, Danny Passman, Reggie Glosson, Alan Samson, Jenny Lord, Lily McIlwain, Jo Roberts-Miller, Lorraine Jerram, Claiborne Hancock, Jessica Case, and Julia Romero.

SOURCE NOTES

Introduction

1   'What is your . . .': St Augustine, *The City of God*. Translated by Henry Bettenson (London: Penguin, 2003), 139.

1   'History is nothing . . .': *The Oxford Dictionary of Quotations*, Elizabeth Knowles, Editor (Oxford: Oxford University Press, 1999), 797. Original in the French by Voltaire, *L'Ingénu, Histoire Véritable, Tirée de Manuscrits du Père Quesnel* (London, 1767), 107.

2   'This town ain't . . .': From the film, *The Western Code*, written by Milton Krims, produced by Samuel J. Briskin and directed by John P. McCarthy, Columbia Pictures, 1932.

2   'This world isn't . . .': From the film, *The Virginian*, written by Owen Wister, Kirke La Shelle and Grover Jones, directed and produced by Victor Fleming, Paramount Pictures, 1929.

3   'deep in crime . . .': T. Adolphus Trollope, *A Decade of Italian Women*, Volume I (London: Chapman and Hall, 1859), 103.

4   'was restrained by . . .': Leopold Ranke, *The Popes of Rome: Their Ecclesiastical and Political History During the Sixteenth and Seventeenth Centuries*. Translated from the German by Sarah Austin. Fourth Edition, Volume 1 (London: John Murray, 1866), 31.

4   'temporary intrigues in . . .': *ibid.*

5   'add sacrilege to . . .': Janey Penrose Trevelyan, *A Short History of the Italian People: From the Barbarian Invasions to the Attainment of Unity* (New York & London: G.P. Putnam's Sons, 1920), 255.

5   'God would see him': Janet Ross, *Lives of the Early Medici: As Told in Their Correspondence* (London: Chatto & Windus, 1910), 189.

5   'who were familiar . . .': Jean Charles Léonard de Sismondi, as quoted in Jacob Burckhardt, *The Civilisation of the Renaissance in Italy: An Essay*. Translated by S.G.C. Middlemore (London: Folio Society, 2004), 48.

6   the 'Irish mafia': Saul Pett, 'Fun, Zip Gone for Kennedy's "Irish Mafia"', *Des Moines Register* (9 February 1964), 5.

6   'Going to church . . .': Kenneth P. O'Donnell and David F. Powers, with Joe McCarthy, *"Johnny, We Hardly Knew Ye": Memories of John Fitzgerald Kennedy* (Boston, MA: Little, Brown & Co., 1972), 20.

7   'Don't worry, man . . .': John H. Davis, *Mafia Kingfish: Carlos Marcello and the Assassination of John F. Kennedy* (New York: McGraw-Hill, 1989), 114.

7   'What good dat . . .': *ibid.*

Chapter 1: Father and Sons

11   'an almost uncanny . . .': David Nasaw, *The Patriarch: The Remarkable Life and Turbulent Times of Joseph P. Kennedy* (New York: Penguin Press, 2012), 168.

11   'better than any . . .': Ronald Kessler, *The Sins of the Father: Joseph P. Kennedy and the Dynasty He Founded* (New York: Warner Books, 1996), 2.

11   'partners': Denny Walsh, 'The Secret Story of Frank Costello That Was Almost Written', *New York Times* (27 February 1973), 78.

11   'The way [Costello] talked . . .': *ibid*, 36.

11   'the father belonged . . .': Gore Vidal, *Palimpsest: A Memoir* (New York: Penguin Books, 1996), 348.

12   'Owney and Joe Kennedy . . .': Seymour M. Hersh, *The Dark Side of Camelot* (Boston, MA: Little, Brown & Co., 1997), 50.

12   'Kennedy was no . . .': Bill Bonanno and Gary B. Abromovitz, *The Last Testament of Bill Bonanno: The Final Secrets of a Life in the Mafia* (New York: Harper, 2011), 46.

12   'heavy with her . . .': *ibid*, 43.

12   'had associates in . . .': Hersh, *The Dark Side of Camelot*, 47, 48.

12   'In scores of . . .': *ibid*, 47.

12   'Kennedy was bootlegging . . .': *ibid*, 50.

13   'I had been involved . . .': Joseph P. Kennedy memorandum, as quoted in Joseph P. Kennedy, *Hostage to Fortune: The Letters of Joseph P. Kennedy*, edited by Amanda Smith (New York: Viking, 2001), 138.

13   'It takes a thief . . .': Hersh, *The Dark Side of Camelot*, 45.

14   'At a time when . . .': Harold L. Ickes, *The Secret Diary of Harold L. Ickes. Volume II: The Inside Struggle, 1936–1939* (New York: Simon & Schuster, 1954), 370.

14   'a very foul specimen . . .': Associated Press, 'Secret Papers Disclose: British Mistrusted US in Early WWII Years', *Boston Globe* (1 January 1971), 1.

14   'four-flusher and . . .': Jeanne Humphreys, as quoted in Hersh, *The Dark Side of Camelot*, 143.

14   'Using his name . . .': Philip Whitehead interview with Harvey Klemmer, as quoted in Hersh, *ibid*, 66.

14   'an economic collaboration': Breckinridge Long, *The War Diary of Breckinridge Long: Selections from the Years 1939–1944*, selected and edited by Fred L. Israel (Lincoln, NE: University of Nebraska Press, 1966), 147.

14   'not believe in . . .': *ibid*, 148.

15   'Democracy is all . . .': Louis M. Lyons, 'Kennedy Says Democracy All Done in Britain, Maybe Here', *Boston Sunday Globe* (10 November 1940), 1, 21.

15   'very nice and polite . . .': Letter from Joseph P. Kennedy Jr to Joseph

P. Kennedy, 23 April 1934, as quoted in Joseph P. Kennedy, *Hostage to Fortune*, 130.

15 'well-founded': *ibid*, 131.

15 'a great thing . . .': *ibid.*

15 'very pleased and gratified': Letter from Joseph P. Kennedy to Joseph P. Kennedy Jr, 4 May 1934, as quoted in Joseph P. Kennedy, *Hostage to Fortune*, 133.

15 'conclusions are very sound': *ibid.*

15 'went to bed . . .': Winston S. Churchill, *The Second World War. Volume III: The Grand Alliance* (Boston, MA: Houghton Mifflin Co., 1950), 608.

16 'exhausted and dispirited': Robert J. Donovan, *PT 109: John F. Kennedy in World War II* (New York: McGraw-Hill, 1961), 140.

16 'I can't go any further': *ibid.*

17 'For a guy from . . .': *ibid.*

17 'Bearded, gaunt, unwashed . . .': *ibid*, 187.

17 'Come and have . . .': *ibid*, 189.

17 'It was like being . . .': Bob Considine, 'John Kennedy Wanted to Be a Writer', *Omaha World-Herald* (1 December 1963), 10.

17 'I got Jack into . . .': Eleanor Harris, 'The Senator is in a Hurry', *McCall's* magazine (August 1957), 123.

Chapter 2: The Runt of the Litter

18 'We don't want . . .': Rose Fitzgerald Kennedy, *Times to Remember* (New York: Doubleday & Co., 1974), 143.

18 'wanted them to . . .': Seymour M. Hersh, *The Dark Side of Camelot* (Boston, MA: Little, Brown & Co., 1997), 17.

18 'We soon learned . . .': 'Democrats: Man Out Front', *Time* magazine, Vol. LXX, No. 23 (2 December 1957).

18 'the runt of a . . .': Penn Kimball, 'The New Kennedy Identity, and How He Uses Power', *Life* magazine, Vol. 61, No. 21 (18 November 1966), 132.

18 'He was the . . .': Nick Thimmesch and William Johnson, *Robert Kennedy at 40* (New York: W.W. Norton & Co., 1965), 28.

18 'very sensitive': Eunice Kennedy Shriver, in recorded interview by Roberta Greene, 29 April 1971, 41–42, 44, RFK Oral History Program.

18 'got hurt easily': *ibid.*

18 'We don't want . . .': Rose Fitzgerald Kennedy, *Times to Remember*, 144.

18 'a fistfight with . . .': Victor Lasky, *Robert F. Kennedy: The Myth and the Man* (New York: Trident Press, 1968), 60.

19 'I didn't go to . . .': *The Kennedy Circle*, edited by Lester Tanzer (Washington, DC: Luce, 1961), 195.

19 'didn't pay much . . .': Lasky, *Robert F. Kennedy*, 62.

19 'liked to play . . .': *ibid.*

19 'I just didn't . . .': Robert E. Thompson and Hortense Myers, *Robert F.*

Kennedy: The Brother Within (New York: The Macmillan Co., 1962), 46.

19   'had [Bobby] lived . . .': Igor Cassini, with Jeanne Molli, *I'd Do It All Over Again* (New York: G.P. Putnam's Sons, 1977), 218.

19   'dull': Thompson and Myers, *Robert F. Kennedy*, 113.

20   'The pressure comes . . .': 'Labor Probe is Pressured', *Omaha World-Herald* (29 November 1953), 1.

20   'political suicide': C. David Heymann, *RFK: A Candid Biography* (London: William Heinemann, 1998), 121.

20   'The old man saw . . .': Peter Collier and David Horowitz, *The Kennedys: An American Drama* (New York: Summit Books, 1984), 220.

20   'furious argument': Jean Kennedy Smith interview, 15 September 1975, with Arthur M. Schlesinger Jr, as quoted in *Robert Kennedy and His Times*, Volume I (Boston, MA: Houghton Mifflin Co., 1978), 149.

20   'edged out': W.H. Lawrence, 'Kefauver Nominated for Vice President; Beats Kennedy, 755 1/2 – 589, On Second Ballot; Stevenson Vows Drive for a "New America"', *New York Times* (18 August 1956), 1.

20   'did his investigations . . .': Clark Mollenhoff interview, in Collier and Horowitz, *The Kennedys*, 219.

20   'that one Kennedy . . .': Robert F. Kennedy, *The Enemy Within* (New York: Harper & Brothers, 1960), 24.

20   'grand-standing little runt': Sam Houston Johnson, *My Brother Lyndon*, edited by Enrique Hank Lopez (New York: Cowles Book Co., 1970), 252.

21   'known to everybody . . .': Jim Row interview, in Ralph G. Martin, *Seeds of Destruction: Joe Kennedy and His Sons* (New York: G.P. Putnam's Sons, 1995), 223.

21   'completely dominated by . . .': James Clay, *Hoffa! Ten Angels Swearing: An Authorized Biography* (Beaverdam, VA: Beaverdam Books, 1965), 107.

Chapter 3: The Brother Act Versus the Brotherhood

22   'staunch Baptist mean . . .': Jack Goldsmith, *In Hoffa's Shadow: A Stepfather, a Disappearance in Detroit, and My Search for the Truth* (New York: Farrar, Straus and Giroux, 2019), 48.

22   'She worked damned . . .': James R. Hoffa, as told to Oscar Fraley, *Hoffa: The Real Story* (New York: Stein and Day, 1975), 29.

23   'Strawberry Boys': Steve Babson, *Working Detroit: The Making of a Union Town* (New York: Adama Books, 1984), 65.

23   'This little guy . . .': Woodrow Sylvester, as quoted in James Clay, *Hoffa! Ten Angels Swearing: An Authorized Biography* (Beaverdam, VA: Beaverdam Books, 1965), 67.

23   'Every time you . . .': James Clay, *Hoffa! Ten Angels Swearing: An Authorized Biography* (Beaverdam, VA: Beaverdam Books, 1965), 60.

23   'We had a number . . .': Hoffa, as told to Oscar Fraley, *Hoffa*, 35.

23 'professional hoodlums and gangsters': 'Police Fear Armed War by Unions', *Detroit Free Press* (13 September 1941), 10.
23 'Jimmy dealt with . . .': Dan E. Moldea, *The Hoffa Wars: Teamsters, Rebels, Politicians, and the Mob* (New York: Paddington Press Ltd, 1978), 38.
24 'young gorilla who . . .': 'Dewey Will Tell How Thugs Escape', *New York Times* (8 October 1937), 10.
24 'threatened to cut . . .': 'Knifing Threat in Racket Bared', *New York Times* (6 June 1937), 36.
24 'Dio Locals': A.H. Raskin, 'More Dio Locals Join Teamsters', *New York Times* (13 March 1957), 22.
25 'as long as . . .': 'Man to Contend With: Mr. Jimmy Hoffa', *Life* magazine, Vol. 50, No. 15 (9 April 1956), 54.
25 'The most powerful . . .': Robert F. Kennedy, *The Enemy Within* (New York: Harper & Brothers, 1960), 161.
25 'evolved into the . . .': Kenneth O'Donnell, as quoted in Ovid Demaris, *The Director: An Oral Biography of J. Edgar Hoover* (New York: Harper's Magazine Press, 1975), 173.
26 'I would like . . .': Testimony of John Dioguardi, 8 August 1957. Investigation of Improper Activities in the Labor or Management Field. Hearings Before the Select Committee on Improper Activities in the Labor or Management Field. Eighty-Fifth Congress, First Session. Part 11 (Washington, DC: United States Government Printing Office [USGPO], 1957), 4169.
26 'lurking presence': Robert F. Kennedy, *The Enemy Within*, 158.
26 'I recognize my . . .': Testimony of Jimmy/James Hoffa, 23 August 1957. Investigation of Improper Activities in the Labor or Management Field. Hearings Before the Select Committee on Improper Activities in the Labor or Management Field. Eighty-Fifth Congress, First Session. Part 13 (Washington, DC: USGPO, 1957), 5252.
26 'knew that organized . . .': Moldea, *The Hoffa Wars*, 125–6.
26 'brought 40 men into . . .': Interim Report of the Select Committee on Improper Activities in the Labor or Management Field. United States Senate. Eighty-Fifth Congress, Second Session. Report No. 1417, 24 March 1958 (Washington, DC: USGPO, 1958), 167.
27 'I thought only little . . .': Testimony of Sam Giancana, 9 June 1959. Investigation of Improper Activities in the Labor or Management Field. Hearings Before the Select Committee on Improper Activities in the Labor or Management Field. Eighty-Sixth Congress, First Session. Part 53 (Washington, DC: USGPO, 1959), 18681.
27 'To be womanly . . .': Nancy Gager Clinch, *The Kennedy Neurosis: A Psychological Portrait of an American Dynasty* (New York: Grosset & Dunlap, 1973), 289.
27 'It makes me boil . . .': 'Young Man with Tough Questions', *Life* magazine, Vol. 43, No. 1 (1 July 1957), 81.

27   'sometimes lost his . . .': Clark R. Mollenhoff, *Tentacles of Power: The Story of Jimmy Hoffa* (Cleveland & New York: The World Pub. Co., 1965), 129.

28   'Without quite realizing . . .': Evan Thomas, *Robert Kennedy: His Life* (New York: Simon & Schuster, 2000), 70.

28   '[Bobby] hates the same . . .': 'What Makes Kennedy Family Tick?', *Boston Daily Globe* (20 March 1957), 33.

28   'I'm like Bobby . . .': Oleg Cassini interview, 15 June 1994, in Ronald Kessler, *The Sins of the Father: Joseph P. Kennedy and the Dynasty He Founded* (New York: Warner Books, 1996), 306.

28   'For him the world . . .': Nick Thimmesch and William Johnson, *Robert Kennedy at 40* (New York: W.W. Norton & Co., 1965), 22.

28   'driven by a conviction . . .': Arthur M. Schlesinger Jr, *Robert Kennedy and His Times*, Volume I (Boston, MA: Houghton Mifflin Co., 1978), 197.

28   'a sadistic little monster': Dan Wakefield, 'Bobby & Teddy', *Esquire*, Vol. LVII, No. 4 (April 1962), 122.

28   'We had guilt by . . .': Statement by Sidney Zagri, 18 August 1965. Free Press and Fair Trial. Hearings Before the Subcommittee on Constitutional Rights and the Subcommittee on Improvements in Judicial Machinery of the Committee on the Judiciary, United States Senate. Eighty-Ninth Congress, First Session. Part 1 (Washington, DC: USGPO, 1966), 172.

28   'blood feud': Pierre Salinger, *P.S.: A Memoir* (New York: St Martin's Press, 1995), 61.

28   'Bobby wasn't too . . .': Victor Lasky, *Robert F. Kennedy: The Myth and the Man* (New York: Trident Press, 1968), 168.

29   'a spoiled young millionaire . . .': *Triumph and Tragedy: The Story of the Kennedys*. Writers, Photographers and Editors of the Associated Press (Associated Press, 1968), 138.

29   'Why do you reporters . . .': Mollenhoff, *Tentacles of Power*, 149.

29   'unhappy, angry young man': Schlesinger, *Robert Kennedy and His Times*, Volume I, 113.

29   'not a simple man . . .': Kenneth P. O'Donnell and David F. Powers, with Joe McCarthy, *"Johnny, We Hardly Knew Ye": Memories of John Fitzgerald Kennedy* (Boston, MA: Little, Brown & Co., 1972), 319.

29   'irritating little man': Jim Bishop, 'Wonders If Jack Can Afford Brother Robert', *Franklin News-Herald* (26 October 1960), 4.

29   'serfs on some . . .': *ibid.*

29   'mean, little asshole': Barry M. Goldwater interview, in Richard D. Mahoney, *Sons & Brothers: The Days of Jack and Bobby Kennedy* (New York: Arcade Pub., 1999), 26.

29   'a son of a bitch': Schlesinger, *Robert Kennedy and His Times*, Volume I, 223.

29   'nasty little man': Nelson Thompson, *The Dark Side of Camelot* (Chicago, IL: Playboy Press, 1976), 77.

29   'snot-nosed little . . .': Jeff Shesol, *Mutual Contempt: Lyndon Johnson, Robert Kennedy, and the Feud That Defined a Decade* (New York: W.W. Norton & Co., 1997), 66.
29   'little fart': Bobby Baker, with Larry L. King, *Wheeling and Dealing: Confessions of a Capitol Hill Operator* (New York: W.W. Norton & Co., 1978), 138.
29   'little shitass': *ibid*, 130.

Chapter 4: A Paranoid Schizophrenic with Homicidal Tendencies
30   'defiant, uncooperative and . . .': Donald Goddard, *Joey* (New York: Harper & Row, 1974), 14.
30   'emotionally immature, egocentric . . .': Raymond V. Martin, *Revolt in the Mafia* (New York: Duell, Sloan and Pearce, 1963), 118.
30   'insane': *ibid.*
31   'I'm a paranoid schizophrenic . . .': Goddard, *Joey*, 31.
31   'barbershop quintet': Nicholas Gage, 'The Mafia at War, Part II', *New York* magazine (17 July 1972), 27.
32   'These Americans are . . .': Joseph Bonanno with Sergio Lalli, *A Man of Honor: The Autobiography of Joseph Bonanno* (New York: Simon & Schuster, 1983), 168.
32   'They want to . . .': Peter Diapoulos and Steven Linakis, *The Sixth Family* (New York: E.P. Dutton & Co., 1976), 111.
32   '[Crazy Joe] strode into . . .': Robert F. Kennedy, *The Enemy Within* (New York: Harper & Brothers, 1960), 249.
32   'could determine her . . .': *ibid.*
32   'So you're Joe . . .': Paul O'Neil, 'The No. 2 Man in Washington', *Life* magazine, Vol. 52, No. 4 (26 January 1962), 78.
33   'No one is going . . .': Robert F. Kennedy, *The Enemy Within*, 249.
33   'They split my . . .': Testimony of Milton Green, 11 February 1959. Investigation of Improper Activities in the Labor or Management Field. Hearings Before the Select Committee on Improper Activities in the Labor or Management Field. United States Senate. Eighty-Sixth Congress, First Session. Part 46 (Washington, DC: USGPO, 1959), 16664.
33   'My nose was completely . . .': Testimony of Sidney Saul, 17 February 1959. Investigation of Improper Activities in the Labor or Management Field. Hearings Before the Select Committee on Improper Activities in the Labor or Management Field. United States Senate. Eighty-Sixth Congress, First Session. Part 46 (Washington, DC: USGPO, 1959), 16831.
33   'excellent actor': *ibid*, 16829.
33   'I'll line up . . .': Robert F. Kennedy, *The Enemy Within*, 252.
33   'The biggest favor . . .': *ibid.*
33   'went merrily on . . .': *ibid.*
33   'one of the most . . .': *ibid*, 249.
33   'A national strike by . . .': Pierre Salinger, *With Kennedy* (Garden City, NY: Doubleday & Co., 1966), 14.

33   'such power constitutes . . .': John L. McClellan, 'These Labor Abuses Must Be Curbed', *Reader's Digest* (December 1962), 98.

34   'If you did not . . .': Executive Session Testimony of Lloyd Speidell, 13 August 1959. Investigation of Improper Activities in the Labor or Management Field. Hearings Before the Select Committee on Improper Activities in the Labor or Management Field. Eighty-Sixth Congress, First Session. Part 58 (Washington, DC: USGPO, 1960), 20095.

34   'Robert Kennedy has ignored . . .': 'Labor Rackets – A Senate Feud?', *Newsweek*, Vol. 50, No. 4 (22 July 1957), 21.

34   'a too searching inquiry . . .': 'Forgotten Man', *Chicago Tribune* (20 July 1960), 12.

34   'a clear pattern . . .': 'Republicans Size Up Reuther's Union – And Democrats Reply', *U.S. News & World Report*, Vol. 48, No. 9 (29 February 1960), 96.

34   'professional hoodlums': *ibid.*

34   'terroristic tactics': *ibid.*

34   'Fortunately, Jack Kennedy . . .': Victor Lasky, *Robert F. Kennedy: The Myth and the Man* (New York: Trident Press, 1968), 115.

34   'You take any industry . . .': John Bartlow Martin interview with Jimmy Hoffa, as quoted in Arthur M. Schlesinger Jr, *Robert Kennedy and His Times*, Volume I (Boston, MA: Houghton Mifflin Co., 1978), 168.

34   'Twenty years ago . . .': Roy Rowan, 'What Hoffa's Up To, as Jimmy Himself Tells It', *Life* magazine, Vol. 46, No. 21 (25 May 1959), 113.

35   'Booby': Frank Ragano and Selwyn Raab, *Mob Lawyer* (New York: Charles Scribner's Sons, 1994), 104.

35   'Bobby Boy': 'Hoffa Hits Out in All Directions', *Detroit Free Press* (25 November 1962), 1.

35   'by the front . . .': James R. Hoffa, as told to Oscar Fraley, *Hoffa: The Real Story* (New York: Stein and Day, 1975), 93–4.

35   'Unless something is . . .': Robert F. Kennedy, on *The Tonight Show Starring Jack Paar*, Season 2, Episode 229, 22 July 1959, as quoted in James Neff, *Vendetta: Bobby Kennedy Versus Jimmy Hoffa* (New York: Little, Brown & Co., 2015), 177.

36   'I am extremely . . .': 'Kennedy Shuns Longshoremen Union, Hoffa', Oregon *Statesman Journal* (7 August 1960), 8.

Chapter 5: Atypical Ambassadors

37   I AM VERY . . .: telegram in the files of the narcotics bureau in New York, as quoted in Ed Reid and Ovid Demaris, *The Green Felt Jungle* (New York: Pocket Books, 1964), 75.

38   'Nobody wanted to . . .': Peter Evans and Ava Gardner, *Ava Gardner: The Secret Conversations* (London: Simon & Schuster, 2013), 237.

38   'When Christ died . . .': Authors' interview with Patricia Breen, Las Vegas, May 1989, in Charles Rappleye and Ed Becker, *All American Mafioso: The Johnny Roselli Story* (New York: Doubleday, 1991), 38.

38 'did a lot of . . .': Authors' interview with Jimmy Fratianno, in Rappleye and Becker, *All American Mafioso*, 48.
38 'The Hollywood Kid': *ibid*, 78.
39 'casting couch': 'Radio Ed Mixes Bureau, Couch; Chi Faces Red', *Variety*, Vol. 128, No. 11 (24 November 1937), 1.
39 'Who the fuck would . . .': James Bacon, *Made in Hollywood* (Chicago, IL: Contemporary Books, 1977), 4.
39 '[Sinatra] got it . . .': Authors' interview with Ed Seide, in Rappleye and Becker, *All American Mafioso*, 133.
40 'I'm the only . . .': Dean Martin at The Sands, as quoted in Peter Wyden, 'How Wicked is Vegas?', *Saturday Evening Post*, Vol. 234, Issue 45 (11 November 1961), 18.
40 'visited by many gangsters': From a personal memo from Hoover to Attorney General Robert Kennedy, 16 August 1962, as quoted in Kitty Kelley, *His Way: The Unauthorized Biography of Frank Sinatra* (New York: Bantam Books, 1986), 279.
40 'I think that you can . . .': Tina Sinatra, as quoted in Seymour M. Hersh, *The Dark Side of Camelot* (Boston, MA: Little, Brown & Co., 1997), 138.
40 'Dad felt that . . .': *ibid*, 139.
41 'big ideas . . . about being . . .': FBI transcript, 21 December 1961, as quoted in Antoinette Giancana and Thomas C. Renner, *Mafia Princess: Growing Up in Sam Giancana's Family* (New York: Avon, 1985), 311.
41 'He hated having . . .': Jeanne Humphreys, as quoted in Hersh, *The Dark Side of Camelot*, 143.
41 'I didn't know . . .': *ibid*, 144.
42 'one of the most . . .': 'Election Corruption', *York Daily News-Times* (27 May 1960), 4.
42 'We were fairly . . .': Allen L. Otten, as quoted in Hersh, *The Dark Side of Camelot*, 92.
42 'were spreading it . . .': Curtis B. Trent, as quoted in Hersh, *ibid*, 98.
42 'in a shoe box . . .': Rein Vander Zee, as quoted in Hersh, *ibid*, 99.
43 'All I had to . . .': Victor Gabriel, as quoted in Hersh, *ibid*, 98.
43 'I know they . . .': Evelyn Lincoln interview, as quoted in Hersh, *ibid*, 95.
43 'shocked': Robert F. Kennedy, *The Enemy Within* (New York: Harper & Brothers, 1960), 187.
43 'I take my . . .': *ibid*.
43 'just killed': Barry M. Goldwater interview, in Richard D. Mahoney, *Sons & Brothers: The Days of Jack and Bobby Kennedy* (New York: Arcade Publishing, 1999), xv.
43 'The reason being . . .': C. David Heymann, *RFK: A Candid Biography* (London: William Heinemann, 1998), 216*n*.
43 'They won't ask . . .': Victor Lasky, *J.F.K.: The Man and the Myth* (New York: Macmillan, 1963), 45.

Chapter 6: Faustian Bargains

45   'I began dating . . .': Judith Exner, as told to Ovid Demaris, *My Story* (New York: Grove Press, 1977), 61.

46   'Show girls from . . .': Los Angeles Airtel to Director Hoover, Frank Sinatra File, Federal Bureau of Investigation, # LA 100-41413 (1 April 1960).

46   'Jack was mesmerized . . .': Kitty Kelley, 'The Dark Side of Camelot', *People Weekly* (29 February 1988), 106–14.

46   'girl-passing': G. Robert Blakey and Richard N. Billings, *Fatal Hour: The Assassination of President Kennedy by Organized Crime* (New York: Berkley Books, 1992), 410.

46   'presents a very real . . .': James R. Hoffa, 'Message from the General President: Kennedy Vendetta Continues', *The International Teamster*, Vol. 57, Issue 9 (September 1960), 3.

46   'There wasn't a . . .': Mickey Cohen, *In My Own Words: The Underworld Autobiography of Michael Mickey Cohen as told to John Peer Nugent* (Englewood Cliffs, NJ: Prentice-Hall, 1975), 233.

46   'There were strong . . .': Jeremiah O'Leary, 'Haig Probe: Did Nixon Get Cash from Asia?', *Washington Star* (5 December 1976).

47   'They weren't dealing . . .': Robert L. Rose, 'JFK Friend's Mafia Link Puzzles Ex-Mate', *Minneapolis Star* (20 December 1975), 1.

47   'Giancana rules the . . .': Sandy Smith, 'The Fix', *Life* magazine (1 September 1967), 42B.

47   'No one who . . .': William F. Roemer Jr, *Accardo: The Genuine Godfather* (New York: Donald I. Fine, 1995), 130.

47   'collected vast sums . . .': Daley FBI Files, Correlation Summary, as quoted in Adam Cohen and Elizabeth Taylor, *American Pharaoh: Mayor Richard J. Daley: His Battle for Chicago and the Nation* (Boston, MA: Little, Brown & Co., 2000), 191.

48   'This mayor has . . .': William F. Roemer Jr, *Roemer: Man Against the Mob* (New York: Donald I. Fine, 1989), 112.

48   'with a little bit . . .': Benjamin C. Bradlee, *Conversations with Kennedy* (New York: W.W. Norton & Co., 1975), 33.

48   'If it wasn't . . .': Exner, as told to Ovid Demaris, *My Story*, 194.

48   'something deeply shocking . . .': Fulton Lewis Jr, as quoted in Victor Lasky, *J.F.K.: The Man and the Myth* (New York: Macmillan, 1963), 12.

48   'devoted ten exhausting . . .': Nicholas Gage, editor, *Mafia, U.S.A.* (Chicago, IL: Playboy Press, 1972), 310.

49   '[Bobby] never had . . .': George Smathers, as quoted in Seymour M. Hersh, *The Dark Side of Camelot* (Boston, MA: Little, Brown & Co., 1997), 153.

49   'too young, too . . .': Nicholas deB. Katzenbach, *Some of It Was Fun: Working with RFK and LBJ* (New York: W.W. Norton & Co., 2008), 22.

49   'Do you know . . .': 'Transcript of News Parleys on 2 Cabinet Choices', *New York Times* (17 December 1960), 14.

49   'No, we are . . .': *ibid.*

49   'travesty of justice': *Newsweek*, as quoted in James Neff, *Vendetta: Bobby Kennedy Versus Jimmy Hoffa* (New York: Little, Brown & Co., 2015), 209.

49   'the greatest example . . .': *The Nation*, as quoted in Neff, *ibid.*

49   'held hearings for . . .': Alexander M. Bickel, 'Robert F. Kennedy: The Case Against Him for Attorney General', *New Republic* (9 January 1961).

49   'It's not as if . . .': Gore Vidal, 'The Best Man', *Esquire* magazine, Vol. LIX, No. 3 (March 1963), 61.

49   'could use his . . .': 'Kennedy's Cabinet', *Chicago Tribune* (17 December 1960), 14.

49   'I was in the room . . .': Igor Cassini, with Jeanne Molli, *I'd Do It All Over Again* (New York: G.P. Putnam's Sons, 1977), 218.

49   'Well, maybe you'd . . .': Ronald Goldfarb, *Perfect Villains, Imperfect Heroes: Robert F. Kennedy's War Against Organized Crime* (New York: Random House, 1995), 7.

50   'Bobby is going . . .': Clark Clifford, with Richard Holbrooke, *Counsel to the President: A Memoir* (New York: Random House, 1991), 337.

50   'very serious reservations': Clark Clifford interview by Larry J. Hackman, 16 December 1974. JFK Oral History Program: https://www.jfklibrary.org/asset-viewer/archives/jfkoh-cmc-01

50   'The big hope is . . .': Charles Bartlett, 'Scramble is on to Sink Kennedy', *Richmond Times-Dispatch* (29 May 1960), 17.

50   'We were happy . . .': Robert E. Thompson and Hortense Myers, *Robert F. Kennedy: The Brother Within* (New York: Macmillan, 1962), 12.

50   'gross and palpable fraud': 'Once an Election is Stolen', *Chicago Tribune* (11 December 1960), 28.

50   'exquisite narrowness': 'Ambiguous Answer', *The Economist*, Vol. 197, Issue 6116 (12 November 1960), 653.

50   'enough votes were . . .': G. Robert Blakey, as quoted in Hersh, *The Dark Side of Camelot*, 140.

51   'sore loser': Richard Nixon, *The Memoirs of Richard Nixon* (New York: Grosset & Dunlap, 1978), 224.

51   'any possibility of . . .': *ibid.*

51   'I can't see that it's . . .': John F. Kennedy remarks to Alfalfa Club, in Washington DC, 21 January 1961, as quoted in William Manchester, *Portrait of a President: John F. Kennedy in Profile*. Revised edition, with a new Introduction and Epilogue (Boston, MA: Little, Brown & Co., 1967), 160.

51   'Well, since the old . . .': Bobby Baker, with Larry L. King, *Wheeling and Dealing: Confessions of a Capitol Hill Operator* (New York: W.W. Norton & Co., 1978), 138.

51   'Mr. Kennedy, who is . . .': Anthony Lewis, 'Robert Kennedy Wins Approval of Senate Panel', *New York Times* (14 January 1961), 1.

51   'You have, as I . . .': Senate Judiciary Committee, Robert F. Kennedy: Attorney-General-Designate Hearing, 13 January 1961. Eighty-Seventh Congress, First Session (Washington, DC: Government Printing Office, 1961), 30.

51   'I doubt if I . . .': *ibid.*

52   'we found substantial . . .': Neff, *Vendetta*, 278.

52   'A few months after . . .': Hersh, *The Dark Side of Camelot*, 4.

Chapter 7: The Chairman and Leader

53   'big men': Robert B. Asprey, *Frederick the Great: The Magnificent Enigma* (New York: History Book Club, 1999), 10.

53   'an obsession that would . . .': *ibid.*

53   'The most beautiful . . .': Ernest Lavisse, *La Jeunesse du Grand Frédéric* (Paris: Librairie Hachette, 1894), 71–2.

53   'Weight–height rules . . .': 'A New G-Man Shakes the FBI', *Life* magazine, Vol. 13, No. 15 (13 October 1972), 48.

53   'bald-headed men . . .': William C. Sullivan, with Bill Brown, *The Bureau: My Thirty Years in Hoover's FBI* (New York: W.W. Norton & Co., 1979), 80.

53   'Though a bald-headed . . .': *ibid.*

53   'Don't shake Mr. Hoover's . . .': Robert M. Morgenthau interview by Victor S. Navasky, Victor S. Navasky Personal Papers, Box 22, John F. Kennedy Library, as quoted in James Neff, *Vendetta: Bobby Kennedy Versus Jimmy Hoffa* (New York: Little, Brown & Co., 2015), 235.

54   'I'm sure he . . .': Richard Harwood, 'FBI Chief Hoover "Knows" Everybody but Few Know Him', *Omaha World-Herald* (25 February 1968), 17.

54   'The greatest deposit . . .': Westbrook Pegler, as quoted in Fred J. Cook, 'The FBI', *The Nation* (18 October 1958), 240.

54   'I get a migraine . . .': Seymour M. Hersh, *The Dark Side of Camelot* (Boston, MA: Little, Brown & Co., 1997), 389.

54   'There is just . . .': Victor Lasky, *J.F.K.: The Man and the Myth* (New York: Macmillan, 1963), 10.

54   'get Allen Dulles . . .': *ibid.*

54   'godfather': Benjamin C. Bradlee, *Conversations with Kennedy* (New York: W.W. Norton & Co., 1975), 33.

54   'that he felt he . . .': Sullivan, with Bill Brown, *The Bureau*, 49.

55   'thumb his nose': *ibid*, 38.

55   'Should I get . . .': William G. Hundley Oral History Interview by James A. Oesterle, John F. Kennedy Library (9 December 1970).

55   'with a red face . . .': Ovid Demaris, *The Director: An Oral Biography of J. Edgar Hoover* (New York: Harper's Magazine Press, 1975), 143.

55   'reputation was that . . .': Harris Wofford, *Of Kennedys and Kings: Making Sense of the Sixties* (Pittsburgh, PA: University of Pittsburgh Press, 1980), 32.

55   'It is ridiculous . . .': William Sullivan, quoted in Arthur M. Schlesinger
     Jr, *Robert Kennedy and His Times*, Volume I (Boston, MA: Houghton
     Mifflin Co., 1978), 268.

56   'large and ill-tempered . . .': Schlesinger, *ibid*, 250.

56   'invisible government': *New York Herald Tribune*, as quoted in *Inves-
     tigating the FBI*, edited by Pat Watters and Stephen Gillers (New York:
     Ballantine Books, 1973), 149. Quote is also found in 'Paper Says Apala-
     chin "Hoods" Keep in Touch by Phone Calls', *Scranton Tribune* (7 May
     1958), 3.

56   'some newspaper clippings': *Robert Kennedy, In His Own Words: The
     Unpublished Recollections of the Kennedy Years*. Edited by Edwin O.
     Guthman and Jeffrey Shulman (New York: Bantam Books, 1988), 120.

56   'hit the FBI like . . .': Sullivan, with Bill Brown, *The Bureau*, 118.

56   'Incredible as it may . . .': Cartha D. 'Deke' DeLoach, *Hoover's FBI: The
     Inside Story by Hoover's Trusted Lieutenant* (Washington, DC: Regnery
     Pub. Co., 1995), 298.

56   'baloney': Schlesinger, *Robert Kennedy and His Times*, Volume I, 275.

57   'Hoover was very . . .': Richard B. Ogilvie, as quoted in Harry Singer
     and Gerald Duncan, 'Cancer of Crime – Time for a Showdown with the
     Mob', *New York Mirror* (3 April 1961).

57   'fully half . . . earmarked . . .': Milton R. Wessel, as told to Stanley Frank,
     'How We Bagged the Mafia: Callers on a "Sick Friend"', *Saturday Eve-
     ning Post*, Vol. 233, Issue 4 (23 July 1960), 72.

57   'Nothing could be . . .': 'The Path of Democratic Justice' Address by
     Director J. Edgar Hoover before the Annual Conference of the Interna-
     tional Association of Chiefs of Police in Washington, DC, on 3 October
     1960, as quoted in *FBI Law Enforcement Bulletin*, Vol. 29, No. 11 (No-
     vember 1960), 3.

57   'The eye sees . . .': William Shakespeare, *Julius Caesar*, edited by Richard
     Grant White (Boston, MA: Houghton Mifflin Co. The Riverside Press,
     1894), 12.

57   'read over two . . .': Sullivan, with Bill Brown, *The Bureau*, 120.

57   'the *New York Times* . . .': *ibid*.

57   'black bag jobs': FBI Memorandum from William Sullivan to Cartha
     DeLoach, 19 July 1966, Exhibit 6, as quoted in Hearings Before the
     Select Committee to Study Governmental Operations with Respect to
     Intelligence Activities, United States Senate, Ninety-Fourth Congress,
     First Session, Volume 6, Federal Bureau of Investigation. (Washington,
     DC: USGPO, 1976), 358.

58   'develop particularly qualified . . .': FBI memo, 'Criminal Informants-
     Criminal Intelligence Program'. SAC Letter No. 61–34 (21 June 1961).

59   'Organized crime has . . .': Robert F. Kennedy, Law Day Address, Univer-
     sity of Georgia Law School (Athens, Georgia, 6 May 1961).

59   'hit list': Victor S. Navasky, *Kennedy Justice* (New York: Atheneum,
     1971), 62.

59   'centralized control of . . .': Ronald Goldfarb, *Perfect Villains, Imperfect Heroes: Robert F. Kennedy's War Against Organized Crime* (New York: Random House, 1995), 42.

59   'multi-agency drive': William Beecher, 'Crime Crackdown: Robert Kennedy Plans Multi-Agency Drive Against Top Racketeer', *Wall Street Journal* (23 January 1961), 1.

59   'his own mini . . .': Nicholas deB. Katzenbach, *Some of It Was Fun: Working with RFK and LBJ* (New York: W.W. Norton & Co., 2008), 25.

59   'in the soup': James R. Hoffa, as told to Oscar Fraley, *Hoffa: The Real Story* (New York: Stein and Day, 1975), 150.

59   'I'll have to hire . . .': Jack Anderson, 'The Washington Merry-Go-Round' (16 November 1960): https://dra.american.edu/islandora/object/pearson%3A34389#page/1/mode/1up

60   'One of the things . . .': Mortimer Caplin interview by Shelley L. Davis and Kecia L. McDonald, 18, 19, 25 November 1991: https://www.taxnotes.com/research/federal/other-documents/other-irs-documents/irs-releases-oral-history-interview-of-former-commissioner-caplin/13rxp

60   'As part of the . . .': Victor Lasky, *Robert F. Kennedy: The Myth and the Man* (New York: Trident Press, 1968), 169.

60   'The purpose of . . .': Navasky, *Kennedy Justice*, 58.

60   'What you're basically . . .': *ibid.*

60   'to collect taxes . . .': Courtney Evans Oral History Interview by James A. Oesterle, John F. Kennedy Presidential Library (10 December 1970).

60   'perhaps $500-million': Alden Whitman, 'Kennedy, Financier and Diplomat, Built Fortune to Gain Real Goal, Fame for Sons', *New York Times* (19 November 1969), 50.

60   'Joe spent his . . .': Hersh, *The Dark Side of Camelot*, 44.

60   'the Vatican, in turn . . .': Ronald Kessler, *The Sins of the Father: Joseph P. Kennedy and the Dynasty He Founded* (New York: Warner Books, 1996), 135.

60   'pizza squad': Navasky, *Kennedy Justice*, 51.

61   'Although the Fifth . . .': Robert F. Kennedy, *The Enemy Within* (New York: Harper & Brothers, 1960), 317.

61   'make organized crime . . .': Katzenbach, *Some of It Was Fun*, 26.

61   'Can't we just . . .': Goldfarb, *Perfect Villains, Imperfect Heroes*, 64.

61   'squirmed at his suggestion . . .': *ibid.*

61   'Under Robert Kennedy . . .': Lasky, *Robert F. Kennedy*, 174–5.

61   'The great Mafia . . .': Luigi Barzini, *The Italians* (New York: Atheneum, 1985), 199.

61   'The thing that's . . .': Paul Meskil, *Don Carlo: Boss of Bosses* (New York: Popular Library, 1973), 22.

61   'revolutionary priest': *American Journey: The Times of Robert Kennedy*, interviews by Jean Stein. Edited by George Plimpton (New York: Harcourt Brace Jovanovich, 1970), 193.

62   'zeal to break up . . .': William V. Shannon, *The Heir Apparent: Robert*

Kennedy and the Struggle for Power (New York: Macmillan, 1967), 66.
62 'drew up genealogical . . .': Barzini, *The Italians*, 199.
62 'almost incestuous atmosphere': C. David Heymann, *A Woman Named Jackie* (New York: A Lyle Book, 1989), 148.
62 'preyed off each . . .': *ibid.*
62 'When he was . . .': *ibid*, 149.

Chapter 8: The Big Little Man
66 'ruled the delta . . .': 'Crime: The King Meets a Christian', *Time* magazine, Vol. LVII, No. 8 (19 February 1951), 21.
66 'The Little Man': Bill Crider, 'Tomato Salesman Carlos Marcello Becomes Investor', *Town Talk* (25 June 1980), 12.
66 'the big little man': Bill Rose, 'Crime Empire's "Big Little Man"', *Des Moines Tribune* (11 July 1981), 11.
66 'tomato salesman': Testimony of Carlos Marcello, 1 June 1972, Hearings Before the Select Committee on Crime, House of Representatives, Ninety-Second Congress, Second Session. Part 1 (Washington, DC: Government Printing Office, 1973), 970.
67 'an old hand at . . .': Bill Rose, 'Crime Empire's "Big Little Man"', *Des Moines Tribune* (11 July 1981), 11.
67 'virtually the entire . . .': Michael Dorman, *Payoff: The Role of Organized Crime in American Politics* (New York: David McKay Co., 1972), 101.
67 'I don't come from . . .': *ibid*, 106.
67 'Sure, I've got . . .': *ibid*, 110–11.
68 'When Carlos and . . .': *ibid*, 111–12.
68 'We didn't ask for . . .': *ibid*, 112.
69 THREE CAN KEEP . . .: John H. Davis, *Mafia Kingfish: Carlos Marcello and the Assassination of John F. Kennedy* (New York: McGraw-Hill, 1989), 65.

Chapter 9: The Jungles of Central America
70 'crime czar': 'Gretna Hoodlum Called Crime Czar', *New Orleans Item* (12 October 1950), 1.
70 'I wouldn't know': Testimony of Carlos Marcello, 24 March 1959. Investigation of Improper Activities in the Labor or Management Field. Hearings Before the Select Committee on Improper Activities in the Labor or Management Field. Eighty-Sixth Congress, First Session. Part 48 (Washington, DC: USGPO, 1959), 17265.
71 'General Swing is . . .': FBI memo: Marcello file, Belmont to Parsons, 3/2/61, as quoted in Burton Hersh, *Bobby and J. Edgar: The Historic Face-Off Between the Kennedys and J. Edgar Hoover that Transformed America* (New York: Carroll & Graf, 2007), 255.
72 'My view is . . .': Heraldo Munoz, *The Dictator's Shadow: Life Under Augusto Pinochet* (New York: Basic Books, 2008), 16.

73   'I didn't have . . .': John H. Davis, *Mafia Kingfish: Carlos Marcello and the Assassination of John F. Kennedy* (New York: McGraw-Hill, 1989), 95.

73   'very happy Carlos . . .': 'Birch Society Mocked by Attorney General', *Baltimore Sun* (7 April 1961), 1.

73   'in strict accordance . . .': Susan Wagner, 'Lawyer Raps U.S. Eviction of Marcello', *Alexandria Daily Town Talk* (6 April 1961), 1.

74   In light of . . .: Davis, *Mafia Kingfish*, 92.

74   'persecution, revenge and . . .': *New Orleans Times-Picayune*, 8 June 1961, as quoted in Mark North, *Betrayal in Dallas: LBJ, the Pearl Street Mafia, and the Murder of President Kennedy* (New York: A Herman Graf Book, 2011), 22.

74   'bureaucratic tyranny': *ibid.*

74   'darkest and foulest . . .': *New Orleans Times-Picayune*, 25 October 1961, as quoted in North, *Betrayal in Dallas*, 25.

74   'dumped off the . . .': *ibid*, 98.

74   'If I don't make . . .': *ibid.*

75   'purchasing the necessities . . .': *New Orleans Times-Picayune*, 14 April 1961, as quoted in North, *Betrayal in Dallas*, 21.

75   'the boss': Pierre V. DeGruy, 'Brilab Trial Peeling Shroud of Secrecy from Around Reputed Mafia Boss', *Daily Oklahoman* (22 May 1981), 18.

75   'Uncle Snookums': *ibid.*

76   'controlled things in Louisiana': Davis, *Mafia Kingfish*, 416.

76   'best-connected man . . .': *ibid.*

76   'high-ranking U.S. government . . .': *ibid*, 100.

76   'Trujillo was wounded . . .': Tim Mansel, 'I Shot the Cruellest Dictator in the Americas', *BBC News* (28 May 2011): https://www.bbc.com/news/world-latin-america-13560512

76   'The Kennedy White . . .': Arthur M. Schlesinger Jr, *Robert Kennedy and His Times*. Volume I (Boston, MA: Houghton Mifflin Co., 1978), 511–12.

Chapter 10: A Strategic Alliance

78   'first and only time . . .': Stephen Kinzer, *Overthrow: America's Century of Regime Change from Hawaii to Iraq* (New York: Times Books, 2006), 122.

79   'Castro would be . . .': Lucien S. Vanden Broucke, 'The "Confessions" of Allen M. Dulles: New Evidence on the Bay of Pigs', *Diplomatic History*, Vol. 8, No. 4 (Fall 1984), 374.

79   'There is a plot . . .': Ralph G. Martin, *Seeds of Destruction: Joe Kennedy and His Sons* (New York: G.P. Putnam's Sons, 1995), 327.

79   'Someone was supposed . . .': Michael R. Beschloss, *The Crisis Years: Kennedy and Khrushchev, 1960–1963* (New York: Edward Burlingame Books, 1991), 139.

80   'had no desire to . . .': Richard M. Bissell Jr, with Jonathan E. Lewis and

Frances T. Pudlo, *Reflections of a Cold Warrior: From Yalta to the Bay of Pigs* (New Haven, CT & London: Yale University Press, 1996), 157.

80   'delicate or clandestine matters': Robert Maheu and Richard Hack, *Next to Hughes: Behind the Power and Tragic Downfall of Howard Hughes by His Closest Advisor* (New York: HarperCollins, 1992), 41.

80   'seemed like a . . .': *ibid*, 109.

80   'and every other . . .': *ibid.*

81   'told me to sit . . .': *ibid.*

81   'I'll be wearing . . .': *ibid.*

81   'rolled out the . . .': *ibid.*

81   'a beautiful bungalow . . .': *ibid.*

81   'just shooting the breeze . . .': Dan E. Moldea, *The Hoffa Wars: Teamsters, Rebels, Politicians, and the Mob* (New York: Paddington Press Ltd, 1978), 127.

81   'key to the city': Maheu and Hack, *Next to Hughes*, 159.

81   'the ultimate mob . . .': *ibid.*

81   'big Maine-style clambakes': *ibid*, 113.

81   'took to calling . . .': *ibid*, 111.

81   'So that night . . .': Lee Server, *Handsome Johnny: The Life and Death of Johnny Roselli: Gentleman Gangster, Hollywood Producer, CIA Assassin* (New York: St Martin's Press, 2018), 102.

82   'big business organizations . . .': Central Intelligence Agency Memorandum for the Record, Prepared by Sheffield Edwards, CIA Director of Security. Sent to Attorney General Kennedy (14 May 1962): https://history.state.gov/historicaldocuments/frus1961-63v10/d337

82   'Me? . . . You want *me* . . .': Maheu and Hack, *Next to Hughes*, 115.

82   'That son of a . . .': Antoinette Giancana and Thomas C. Renner, *Mafia Princess: Growing Up in Sam Giancana's Family* (New York: Avon, 1985), 15.

82   'thought he was going . . .': *ibid.*

82   'That rotten bastard . . .': Michael J. Cain, *The Tangled Web: The Life and Death of Richard Cain* (New York: Skyhorse, 2007), 71.

83   'the Borgia of . . .': Fabián Escalante, *The Cuba Project: CIA Covert Operations, 1959–62*, translated by Maxine Shaw (Australia: Ocean Press, 2004), 51.

83   'a strong but never . . .': H.P. Albarelli Jr, *A Terrible Mistake: The Murder of Frank Olson and the CIA's Cold War Experiments* (Walterville, OR: Trine Day, 2009), 51.

84   'mentally handicapped children . . .': Stephen Kinzer, *Poisoner in Chief: Sidney Gottlieb and the CIA Search for Mind Control* (New York: Henry Holt & Co., 2019), 131.

84   'sing like birds': Albarelli, *A Terrible Mistake*, 128.

84   'it was fashionable among . . .': Ray Cline, as quoted in John Marks, *The Search for the 'Manchurian Candidate': The CIA and Mind Control* (New York: Times Books, 1979), 56.

84 'Health Alterations Committee': Alleged Assassination Plots Involving Foreign Leaders. An Interim Report of the Select Committee to Study Governmental Operations with Respect to Intelligence Activities. United States Senate, Ninety-Fourth Congress, First Session, Report No. 94-165 (Washington, DC: USGPO, 20 November 1975), 181.

84 'everything from mind-control . . .': Joseph J. Trento, *The Secret History of the CIA* (New York: MJF Books, 2001), 194.

84 '1951, a team of CIA . . .': Gordon Thomas, *Secrets & Lies: A History of CIA Mind Control & Germ Warfare* (London: JR Books, 2008), 66.

84 '1952, Dulles brought Dr. Gottlieb . . .': *ibid*, 66–7.

85 'What Gottlieb and his . . .': Sidney Gottlieb obituary, London *Times* (12 March 1999), 25.

85 'You know, my . . .': Kinzer, *Poisoner in Chief*, 201.

Chapter 11: The Bay of Betrayal

86 'peasants and fishermen . . .': Haynes Johnson, et al., *The Bay of Pigs: The Leaders' Story of Brigade 2506* (New York: W.W. Norton & Co., 1964), 98.

86 'from sixteen to sixty-one': *ibid*.

86 'hulking old cargo vessels': *ibid*, 78.

87 'don't know how . . .': Evan Thomas, *The Very Best Men: Four Who Dared: The Early Years of the CIA* (New York: Touchstone/Simon & Schuster, 1995), 242.

87 'To a Cuban . . .': Justin Gleichauf, as quoted in Gus Russo, *Live by the Sword: The Secret War Against Castro and the Death of JFK* (Baltimore, MD: Bancroft Press, 1998), 143.

87 'dangerous and hair-brained project': 'Editorial: Are We Training Cuban Guerillas?', *The Nation*, Vol. 191, No. 17 (19 November 1960), 378.

87 'I can't believe what . . .': Pierre Salinger, *With Kennedy* (Garden City, NY: Doubleday & Co., 1966), 146.

87 'We knew who . . .': Tad Szulc, *Fidel: A Critical Portrait* (New York: William Morrow & Co., 1986), 543.

87 'an open secret': *ibid*.

87 'Little Havana': *ibid*.

87 'operation was conducted with . . .': Karl E. Meyer and Tad Szulc, *The Cuban Invasion: The Chronicle of a Disaster* (New York: Frederick A. Praeger, 1962), 95.

88 'The extremely vigilant and . . .': From the Foreign Broadcast Information Service Report, 10 April 1961, as quoted in Russo, *Live by the Sword*, 17.

88 'If we decided . . .': Kenneth P. O'Donnell and David F. Powers, with Joe McCarthy, *"Johnny, We Hardly Knew Ye": Memories of John Fitzgerald Kennedy* (Boston, MA: Little, Brown & Co., 1972), 306.

88 'Cuban Invasion Authority': William V. Shannon, 'CIA Kept Its Secret

– Even From the Rebels', *Congressional Record: Proceedings and Debates of the U.S. Congress – Appendix*, Vol. 107, Part 22 (27 April 1961), A2932.

88   'If you fail . . .': Johnson, et al., *The Bay of Pigs*, 68.

89   'There will not . . .': President John F. Kennedy, News Conference 9, John F. Kennedy Presidential Library & Museum (12 April 1961): https:// www.jfklibrary.org/archives/other-resources/john-f-kennedy-press-conferences/news-conference- 9#:~:text=THE%20PRESIDENT%3A% 20Well%2C%20first%20I,involved%20in%20any%20actions%20 inside

89   'told that ten to fifteen . . .': Arthur M. Schlesinger Jr, *A Thousand Days: John F. Kennedy in the White House* (Boston, MA: Houghton Mifflin Co./Riverside Press, 1965), 281.

90   'Fifteen hundred men's . . .': Russo, *Live by the Sword*, 20.

90   'absolutely reprehensible, almost criminal': *ibid.*

90   'Cabell drove through . . .': David Wise and Thomas B. Ross, *The Invisible Government* (New York: Random House, 1964), 22.

90   'Do you people . . .': Telegram from the Commander of Special Task Group 81.8 (John E. Clark) to the Commander in Chief, Atlantic (Robert Dennison) (18 April 1961). Naval Historical Center, Area Files, Bumpy Road Materials. Top Secret: https://history.state.gov/ historicaldocuments/frus1961-63v10/d135

90   'This is Cuba . . .': 'Cuba: The Massacre', *Time* magazine, Vol. LXXVII, No. 18 (28 April 1961), 21.

91   'Shoot us, but . . .': Johnson, et al., *The Bay of Pigs*, 183.

91   'Cuba's Pearl Harbor': 'U.S. Blamed for Raids', *Orlando Sentinel* (17 April 1961), 1.

91   'Welcome to the Site . . .': Max Holland, 'After Thirty Years: Making Sense of the Assassination', *Reviews in American History*, Vol. 22, No. 2 (June 1994), 195.

91   'to the wall': 'Cuba: Castro's Triumph', *Time* magazine, Vol. LXXVII, No. 19 (5 May 1961), 32.

92   'Yellow, yellow, yellow': Johnson, et al., *The Bay of Pigs*, 217.

92   'I hated the United . . .': *ibid*, 213–14.

92   'I've got to do . . .': Richard Reeves, *President Kennedy: Profile of Power* (New York: Touchstone/Simon & Schuster, 1993), 103.

92   'splinter the C.I.A. . . .': Tom Wicker, John W. Finney, Max Frankel, E.W. Kenworthy, 'C.I.A.: Maker of Policy, or Tool?', *New York Times* (25 April 1996), 20.

92   'They were sure . . .': O'Donnell and Powers, with Joe McCarthy, *"Johnny, We Hardly Knew Ye"*, 310.

93   'No matter how . . .': L. Frank Baum, *The Wonderful Wizard of Oz* (Chicago/New York: George M. Hill Co., 1900), 44–5.

94   'The enemy of my . . .': *The New Yale Book of Quotations*, edited by Fred R. Shapiro (New Haven, CT: Yale University Press, 2021), 655.

From the Yale book: 'Often attributed to the *Arthasastra*, a pre-fourth century B.C. Sanskrit text by Kautilya.'

Chapter 12: James Bond, Three Stooges and a Comedian

95   'When Castro smokes . . .': Jimmy Breslin, 'Money-Hungry Men Continue to Bug CIA', *Fort Lauderdale Sun-Sentinel* (14 January 1987).

95   'How soon does . . .': *ibid.*

95   'This doesn't kill . . .': *ibid.*

95   'I thought we were . . .': *ibid.*

95   'death ray': Evan Thomas, *The Very Best Men: Four Who Dared: The Early Years of the CIA* (New York: Touchstone/Simon & Schuster, 1995), 212.

95   'was fascinated by all . . .': Taylor Branch and George Crile III, 'The Kennedy Vendetta: How the CIA Waged a Silent War Against Cuba', *Harper's Magazine* (August 1975), 60.

96   'weird ideas – exploding . . .': Sam Halpern, as quoted in Gus Russo, *Live by the Sword: The Secret War Against Castro and the Death of JFK* (Baltimore, MD: Bancroft Press, 1998), 83.

96   'The president wants this': Thomas, *The Very Best Men*, 295.

96   'America's James Bond': David C. Martin, 'The CIA's Loaded Gun: The Life and Hard Times of "America's James Bond", William King Harvey', *Washington Post* (10 October 1976), C1.

96   'If you ever know . . .': *ibid*, C2.

97   'Harvey's hole': David C. Martin, *Wilderness of Mirrors* (New York: Harper & Row, 1980), 89.

97   'one of the most valuable . . .': Allen Dulles, *The Craft of Intelligence* (New York: Signet/New American Library, 1965), 193.

97   'My husband always . . .': C.G. Harvey, interview with Scott and Andy Alderton, 1999: https://jfkfacts.org/cia-widow-denounced-jfk-jackie-and-rfk-then-she-expressed-love-for-a-gangster/

97   'integrity as far . . .': Testimony of William K. Harvey, 25 June 1975. Report of Proceedings. Hearing Held before the Senate Select Committee to Study Governmental Operations with Respect to Intelligence Activities. Afternoon Session. (Washington, DC: Ward & Paul, 1975), 91: https://www.maryferrell.org/showDoc.html?docId=33930#relPageId=33

97   'secret, martini-fueled rendezvous': David Talbot, *The Devil's Chessboard: Allen Dulles, the CIA, and the Rise of America's Secret Government* (London: William Collins, 2015), 471.

97   'hated Bobby Kennedy's guts . . .': David C. Martin, 'The CIA's Loaded Gun: The Life and Hard Times of "America's James Bond", William King Harvey', *Washington Post* (10 October 1976).

97   'little fucker': Joseph J. Trento, *The Secret History of the CIA* (New York: MJF Books, 2001), 212.

97   'rich boys who were . . .': Talbot, *The Devil's Chessboard*, 472.

97   'enjoyed his work . . .': Trento, *The Secret History of the CIA*, 195.

98   'took orders from Trafficante': *ibid*, 200.

98   'kingpin of narcotics . . .': William Scott Malone, 'The Secret Life of Jack Ruby', *New Times*, Vol. 10, No. 7 (23 January 1978), 48.

98   'kept Santo Trafficante . . .': Federal Bureau of Narcotics memo, 21 July 1961, as cited in George Crile, 'The Mafia, the CIA, and Castro', *Washington Post* (16 May 1976).

99   'flushed them down . . .': Frank Ragano and Selwyn Raab, *Mob Lawyer* (New York: Charles Scribner's Sons, 1994), 209.

99   'His wife had . . .': Jack Hawn, 'McGuire Sisters: No Sad Song Second Time Around', *Los Angeles Times*, Part VI (25 April 1986), 4.

99   'Since it wouldn't . . .': Robert Maheu and Richard Hack, *Next to Hughes: Behind the Power and Tragic Downfall of Howard Hughes by His Closest Advisor* (New York: HarperCollins, 1992), 121.

99   'What the hell were . . .': Dan E. Moldea, *The Hoffa Wars: Teamsters, Rebels, Politicians, and the Mob* (New York: Paddington Press Ltd, 1978), 132.

100   'in the bottom of . . .': Thomas Maier, *Mafia Spies: The Inside Story of the CIA, Gangsters, JFK, and Castro* (New York: Skyhorse, 2019), 87.

100   'Hoover wanted to debrief . . .': Maheu and Hack, *Next to Hughes*, 37.

100   'turned [Hoover] down flat': *ibid*.

100   'Hoover was jealous . . .': William C. Sullivan, with Bill Brown, *The Bureau: My Thirty Years in Hoover's FBI* (New York: W.W. Norton & Co., 1979), 62.

101   'You sure get your . . .': William F. Roemer Jr, *Roemer: Man Against the Mob* (New York: Donald I. Fine, 1989), 184.

101   'Monroe on all . . .': Gus Russo, *The Outfit: The Role of Chicago's Underworld in the Shaping of Modern America* (New York: Bloomsbury, 2001), 432.

101   'disgusting': *ibid*.

101   'I thought you would be . . .': Memorandum from J. Edgar Hoover to Kenneth O'Donnell, 27 February 1962, No. 92-3267-125, as cited in Richard D. Mahoney, *Sons & Brothers: The Days of Jack and Bobby Kennedy* (New York: Arcade Pub., 1999), 156.

101   'Here I am, helping . . .': Michael Hellerman, with Thomas C. Renner, *Wall Street Swindler: An Insider's Story of Mob Operations in the Stock Market* (New York: Doubleday, 1977), 86.

101   'pushed to get Giancana . . .': Nicholas Gage, '2 Mafiosi Linked to C.I.A. Treated Leniently by U.S.', *New York Times* (13 April 1976), 22.

101   'That rat bastard . . .': Ragano and Raab, *Mob Lawyer*, 218.

102   'Many people have . . .': Maheu and Hack, *Next to Hughes*, 116.

102   'I trust that if . . .': Inspector General of the CIA, 'Assassination plots to Report on Plots to Assassinate Fidel Castro' (23 May 1967), 62a: https://www.archives.gov/files/research/jfk/releases/104-10213-10101.pdf

Chapter 13: A King's Ransom

107 'Olive Oil King': 'Quiz 3 Hoodlums in Anastasia Murder Case', *Boston Globe* (22 November 1957), 5.

108 'was a hand-carved . . .': Rosalie Bonanno, with Beverly Donofrio, *Mafia Marriage: My Story* (New York: William Morrow & Co., 1990), 30.

108 'his only predictable . . .': Raymond V. Martin, *Revolt in the Mafia* (New York: Duell, Sloan and Pearce, 1963), 89.

108 'I want one . . .': Anthony Villano, with Gerald Astor, *Brick Agent: Inside the Mafia for the FBI* (New York: Ballantine Books, 1977), 121.

108 'I have to meet somebody . . .': Harold Phelan and I. Kaufman, 'Shrine Theft Linked to "Ride": Girl Reveals Call to Fatal Rendezvous', *Brooklyn Daily Eagle* (4 June 1952), 1.

108 'bullet-pierced body': *ibid.*

108 'weed-grown sidewalk': *ibid.*

110 'Who are they?': Martin, *Revolt in the Mafia*, 52.

110 'When you want somebody . . .': Ralph Salerno and John S. Tompkins, *The Crime Confederation: Cosa Nostra and Allied Operations in Organized Crime* (Garden City, NY: Doubleday & Co., 1969), 135.

110 'threw it on . . .': Peter Diapoulos and Steven Linakis, *The Sixth Family* (New York: E.P. Dutton & Co., 1976), 50.

112 'Our fathers were not . . .': Rosalie Bonanno, with Beverly Donofrio, *Mafia Marriage*, 29.

114 'Settle it yourselves': *ibid*, 110.

114 'whimpering': Diapoulos and Linakis, *The Sixth Family*, 20.

114 'whining': *ibid.*

114 '[Colombo] was the coolest . . .': *ibid.*

Chapter 14: Sleeping with the Fish

115 'Whatsa matter, Larry? . . .': Harvey Aronson, *The Killing of Joey Gallo* (New York: Signet/New American Library, 1974), 35.

116 'the smartest hood . . .': *ibid*, 36.

118 'Some of the boys . . .': Donald Goddard, *Joey* (New York: Harper & Row, 1974), 79.

118 'How are things?': William Federici, Edwin Ross and Sidney Kline, 'Mob's Eraser Still Poised for Rubout of Gallo Boys', *New York Daily News* (22 August 1961), 6.

118 'Is that something . . .': Raymond V. Martin, *Revolt in the Mafia* (New York: Duell, Sloan and Pearce, 1963), 147.

119 Cop Halts 'Rub Out' . . .: 'Cop Halts "Rub Out" of Gallo, Gets Shot', *New York Newsday* (21 August 1961), 4.

119 'still slated for murder . . .': William Federici, Edwin Ross and Sidney Kline, 'Mob's Eraser Still Poised for Rubout of Gallo Boys', *New York Daily News* (22 August 1961), 2.

119 'Still alive, as . . .': Joseph Kiernan, Edwin Ross and Sidney Kline,

'Gunned Cop's Finger Points – "That's Him"', *New York Daily News* (23 August 1961), 2.

119 'It looks like . . .': Ralph Salerno and John S. Tompkins, *The Crime Confederation: Cosa Nostra and Allied Operations in Organized Crime* (New York: Doubleday & Co., 1969), 162.

120 'They're going to settle . . .': William Federici, Edwin Ross and Sidney Kline, 'Mob's Eraser Still Poised for Rubout of Gallo Boys', *New York Daily News* (22 August 1961), 2.

120 'Even the members . . .': *ibid*, 6.

120 'How can I be . . .': Martin, *Revolt in the Mafia*, 161.

121 'If I were in his . . .': Goddard, *Joey*, 82.

121 'You should have . . .': Salerno and Tompkins, *The Crime Confederation*, 138.

121 'I believe in curfews . . .': Frank DiMatteo and Michael Benson, *Carmine the Snake: Carmine Persico and His Murderous Mafia Family* (New York: Citadel Press, 2018), 12.

123 'My God, that's . . .': Nathan Kanter and Sidney Kline, 'Gallo Mob War Cuts Down Mug in Street', *New York Daily News* (5 October 1961), 3.

123 'Walter, someday I'm . . .': Joseph Kiernan and Sidney Kline, 'Cops Raid Gallo Ratholes, Arrest 13 & Seize Arsenal', *New York Daily News* (11 October 1961), 3.

123 'I saw his belt . . .': Frank DiMatteo, *The President Street Boys: Growing Up Mafia* (New York: Kensington Pub., 2016), 34.

123 'Sure, take time! . . .': Martin, *Revolt in the Mafia*, 204.

124 'You better put on your . . .': Nathan Kanter, 'Hood Tony Bender Missing Since Sunday, Wife Reports', *New York Daily News* (13 April 1962), 5.

124 'I'm sure something . . .': *ibid*.

124 'attractive brunette sports . . .': William Federici and Henry Lee, 'Tony's Mistress Missing; Cops: Both May Be Dead', *New York Daily News* (17 April 1962), 2.

Chapter 15: Mistaken Identity?

127 'weasel-faced postal thief': 'Valachi Victim Got "Start" Here', *Pittsburgh Press* (28 September 1963), 1.

128 'They're both ugly . . .': *ibid*.

128 'I told the warden . . .': *ibid*.

128 'Bobby Kennedy called . . .': Dan E. Moldea, *The Hoffa Wars: Teamsters, Rebels, Politicians, and the Mob* (New York: Paddington Press Ltd, 1978), 138.

129 'made it sound . . .': Joseph Bonanno with Sergio Lalli, *A Man of Honor: The Autobiography of Joseph Bonanno* (New York: Simon & Schuster, 1983), 227.

131 'He was part . . .': Donald Goddard, *Joey* (New York: Harper & Row, 1974), 210.

131 'They loved each . . .': Peter Diapoulos and Steven Linakis, *The Sixth Family* (New York: E.P. Dutton & Co., 1976), 38.

Chapter 16: He is Going to be Hit

133 'He sold out his . . .': Paul Meskil, *Don Carlo: Boss of Bosses* (New York: Popular Library, 1973), 200.

134 'spread the bread': Ralph Salerno and John S. Tompkins, *The Crime Confederation: Cosa Nostra and Allied Operations in Organized Crime* (New York: Doubleday & Co., 1969), 142.

134 'Indictments secured [against mobsters] rose . . .': Ronald Goldfarb, *Perfect Villains, Imperfect Heroes: Robert F. Kennedy's War Against Organized Crime* (New York: Random House, 1995), 43.

134 'very idea of retirement . . .': Cartha 'Deke' DeLoach, *Hoover's FBI: The Inside Story by Hoover's Trusted Lieutenant* (Washington, DC: Regnery, 1995), 109.

134 'It was not his . . .': *ibid*, 97.

135 'Bob Kennedy won't stop . . .': Investigation of the Assassination of President John F. Kennedy. Appendix to Hearings Before the Select Committee on Assassinations of the U.S. House of Representatives, Ninety-Fifth Congress, Second Session. Volume IX: Staff and Consultant's Reports on Organized Crime, March 1979 (Washington, DC: USGPO, 1979), 41.

135 'I'd like to hit . . .': John H. Davis, *Mafia Kingfish: Carlos Marcello and the Assassination of John F. Kennedy* (New York: McGraw-Hill, 1989), 285.

135 'With Kennedy, a guy . . .': Final Report of the Select Committee on Assassinations U.S. House of Representatives, Ninety-Fifth Congress, Second Session. Summary of Findings and Recommendations, 2 January 1979 (Washington, DC: USGPO, 1979), 165.

135 Maggio: [President Kennedy] wants . . .: JFK Exhibit F-620. Investigation of the Assassination of President John F. Kennedy. Hearings Before the Select Committee on Assassinations of the U.S. House of Representatives, Ninety-Fifth Congress, Second Session. Volume V (Washington, DC: USGPO, 1979), 445.

135 'fucking cocksucker': C. David Heymann, *RFK: A Candid Biography* (London: William Heinemann, 1998), 215.

135 'squat to pee': Richard D. Mahoney, *Sons & Brothers: The Days of Jack and Bobby Kennedy* (New York: Arcade Pub., 1999), 98.

135 'rapid rise would . . .': Curt Gentry, *J. Edgar Hoover: The Man and the Secrets* (New York: W.W. Norton & Co., 1991), 190.

135 'J. Edna': Mahoney, *Sons & Brothers*, 98.

136 'We tried to prove . . .': Burton Hersh, *Bobby and J. Edgar: The Historic Face-Off Between the Kennedys and J. Edgar Hoover that Transformed America* (New York: Carroll & Graf, 2007), 302.

136 'Bobby mentioned . . .': Ovid Demaris, *The Director: An Oral Biography of J. Edgar Hoover* (New York: Harper's Magazine Press, 1975), 147.

136 'Don't worry, man . . .': Ed Reid, *The Grim Reapers: The Anatomy of Organized Crime in America* (New York: Bantam Books, 1970), 162.

136 'the dog will keep . . .': Investigation of the Assassination of President John F. Kennedy. Appendix to Hearings Before the Select Committee on Assassinations of the U.S. House of Representatives, Ninety-Fifth Congress, Second Session. Volume IX: Staff and Consultant's Reports on Organized Crime, March 1979 (Washington, DC: USGPO, 1979), 83.

136 'already thought of . . .': *ibid.*

137 'He's driving my . . .': Davis, *Mafia Kingfish*, 107.

137 'an incomparably corrupt': Tad Szulc, *Fidel: A Critical Portrait* (New York: William Morrow & Co., 1986), 155.

137 'in suitcases': Carlos Prío Socarrás, as quoted in Warren Hinckle and William W. Turner, *The Fish is Red: The Story of the Secret War Against Castro* (New York: Harper & Row, 1981), 8.

137 'already been cleared . . .': George Crile III, 'The Mafia, the CIA, and Castro', *Washington Post* (16 May 1976).

137 'spoke almost poetically': *ibid.*

137 'Mark my words . . .': *ibid.*

137 'No, José . . .': *ibid.*

138 'instigated by Robert Kennedy': Investigation of the Assassination of President John F. Kennedy. Appendix to Hearings Before the Select Committee on Assassinations of the U.S. House of Representatives, Ninety-Fifth Congress, Second Session. Volume IX, Staff and Consultant's Reports on Organized Crime, March 1979 (Washington, DC: USGPO, 1979), 39.

138 'murdering the Italian name': *ibid.*

138 'I've got to do . . .': Walter Sheridan, *The Fall and Rise of Jimmy Hoffa* (New York: Saturday Review Press, 1972), 217.

138 'drives alone in a . . .': Edward G. Partin, 'An Insider's Chilling Story of Hoffa's Savage Kingdom', *Life* magazine, Vol. 56, No. 20 (15 May 1964), 45.

138 'so many enemies . . .': *ibid.*

138 'the ambassador between . . .': Bill Woodfield, as quoted in Seymour M. Hersh, *The Dark Side of Camelot* (Boston, MA: Little, Brown & Co., 1997), 142.

139 'There were moments . . .': Ronald Kessler, *The Sins of the Father: Joseph P. Kennedy and the Dynasty He Founded* (New York: Warner Books, 1996), 400.

139 'The tragedy was Joe . . .': David Talbot, *Brothers: The Hidden History of the Kennedy Years* (London: Pocket Books, 2008), 84.

139 'was very strong . . .': Hersh, *The Dark Side of Camelot*, 16.

139 'was in an instant . . .': David Nasaw, *The Patriarch: The Remarkable Life and Turbulent Times of Joseph P. Kennedy* (New York: Penguin Press, 2012), 777.

Chapter 17: Missiles and Whistles

144   'crushed into powder': Nikita Khrushchev, *Khrushchev Remembers: The Glasnost Tapes*. Translated and edited by Jerrold L. Schecter with Vyacheslav V. Luchkov (Boston, MA: Little, Brown & Co., 1990), 183.

144   'For all of his . . .': Thomas Maier, *Mafia Spies: The Inside Story of the CIA, Gangsters, JFK, and Castro* (New York: Skyhorse, 2019), 175.

144   'done with it': Alistair Horne, *Harold Macmillan, Volume II: 1957–1986* (New York: Viking, 1989), 365.

144   'I'm in favor . . .': The Presidential Recordings: John F. Kennedy, Volume III, p. 72, as quoted in Robert A. Caro, *The Years of Lyndon Johnson: The Passage of Power* (New York: Alfred A. Knopf, 2012), 216.

144   'with a vehemence . . .': Kenneth P. O'Donnell and David F. Powers, with Joe McCarthy, *"Johnny, We Hardly Knew Ye": Memories of John Fitzgerald Kennedy* (Boston, MA: Little, Brown & Co., 1972), 359.

144   'blacken the name . . .': Theodore C. Sorensen, *Kennedy* (New York: Harper & Row, 1965), 684.

145   'destroy New York, Chicago . . .': Nikita Khrushchev, *Khrushchev Remembers*. Translated and edited by Strobe Talbott (Boston, MA: Little, Brown & Co., 1970), 496.

145   'that the United States . . .': Khrushchev, *Khrushchev Remembers: The Glasnost Tapes*, 180.

145   'It would be foolish . . .': Khrushchev, *Khrushchev Remembers*, 494.

145   'missed the big bus': Robert Hurwich, in recorded interview by John Plank, JFK Oral History Program (24 April 1964) p. 151.

146   'terminated CIA financial support': Arthur M. Schlesinger Jr, *Robert Kennedy and His Times*, Volume II (Boston, MA: Houghton Mifflin Co., 1978), 565.

146   'only . . . one development': William Manchester, *The Death of a President: November 20–November 25, 1963* (New York: Harper & Row, 1967), 46.

146   'if an inspired . . .': *ibid*.

146   'Someday, I'm going to be . . .': Anna Itz, as quoted in 'LBJ is More Than a President to the People of Stonewall', *Mexia Daily News* (6 December 1963), 1.

146   'I won't need . . .': From 'This is LBJ's Country', *U.S. News & World Report*, 23 December 1963, as quoted in Robert A. Caro, *The Years of Lyndon Johnson: The Path to Power* (New York: Alfred A. Knopf, 1982), 100.

146   'He stole that election': Caro, *ibid*, 262.

146   'that damn Johnson . . .': *ibid*, 336.

146   'The first time the . . .': *ibid*, 337.

146   'Manipulative, a schemer . . .': Robert A. Caro, *The Years of Lyndon Johnson: Means of Ascent* (New York: Vintage Books, 1990), 400.

147   'if the District Attorney . . .': J. Evetts Haley, *A Texan Looks at Lyndon: A Study in Illegitimate Power* (Canyon, TX: Palo Duro Press, 1964), 53.

147 'You Johnson people . . .': Bobby Baker, with Larry L. King, *Wheeling and Dealing: Confessions of a Capitol Hill Operator* (New York: W.W. Norton & Co., 1978), 118.

147 'leaning forward, clenching . . .': *ibid.*

147 'Obviously, it was . . .': 'Kennedy's Choice', *St Louis Post-Dispatch* (15 July 1960), 18.

147 'will help keep the . . .': 'Part of the Way with LBJ', *Newsweek*, Vol. LVI, No. 7 (15 August 1960), 20.

147 'Lyndon was in the . . .': Jessie Hatcher Oral History Interview by Paul Bolton, LBJ Presidential Library (28 March 1968), 12.

147 'if he couldn't . . .': Ben Crider Oral History Interview by Paul Bolton, LBJ Presidential Library (1 August 1968), 13.

147 'Master of the Senate': Ronnie Dugger, *The Politician: The Life and Times of Lyndon Johnson: The Drive for Power, from the Frontier to Master of the Senate* (New York: W.W. Norton & Co., 1982).

147 'worth an estimated . . .': Vera Glaser, 'Millionaire H.L. Hunt Talks Politics', Chicago *News* (27 August 1964).

147 'I began to advance . . .': *ibid.*

148 'Few men in . . .': *Miami Herald*, 17 March 1963, as quoted in Caro, *The Years of Lyndon Johnson: The Passage of Power*, 226.

148 'sending him fewer . . .': Evelyn Lincoln, *Kennedy and Johnson* (New York: Holt, Rinehart & Winston, 1968), 188.

148 '[Johnson] had the feeling . . .': Schlesinger, *Robert Kennedy and His Times*, Volume I, 548.

148 'They're supposed to . . .': Baker, with Larry L. King, *Wheeling and Dealing*, 119.

148 'Can you tell the Vice . . .': Louis Martin Oral History Interview by David G. McComb, LBJ Presidential Library (14 May 1969), 10.

148 'Didn't I tell . . .': *ibid*, 10–11.

148 'losers' table': Evan Thomas, *Robert Kennedy: His Life* (New York: Simon & Schuster, 2000), 290.

148 'literally couldn't look . . .': Caro, *The Years of Lyndon Johnson: The Passage of Power*, 227.

148 'Johnson found himself . . .': *ibid.*

148 'Bobby saw LBJ's . . .': Nicholas deB. Katzenbach, *Some of It Was Fun: Working with RFK and LBJ* (New York: W.W. Norton & Co., 2008), 146.

149 'I think we just . . .': Ron Linton, as quoted in Jeff Shesol, *Mutual Contempt: Lyndon Johnson, Robert Kennedy, and the Feud that Defined a Decade* (New York: W.W. Norton & Co., 1997), 105.

149 'Fuck 'im': *ibid.*

149 'Johnson blamed his . . .': O'Donnell and Powers, with Joe McCarthy, *"Johnny, We Hardly Knew Ye"*, 4.

149 'real bastard': Transcript, from a sound recording of a telephone call between President John F. Kennedy and Attorney General Robert F.

Kennedy. Dictation Belt 9A.6. Digital Identifier: JFKPOF-TPH-09A-6 (4 March 1963), 4: https://static.jfklibrary.org/yb764g2q2ge6qmx58w g75iwooyojt8ky.pdf?odc=20231115174914-0500

149 'half-assed': *Robert Kennedy, In His Own Words: The Unpublished Recollections of the Kennedy Years*. Edited by Edwin O. Guthman and Jeffrey Shulman. (New York: Bantam Books, 1988), 379.

150 'screaming match': Tim Weiner, *Legacy of Ashes: The History of the CIA* (New York: Doubleday, 2007), 207.

150 'liars and sons-of-bitches': Gus Russo, *Live by the Sword: The Secret War Against Castro and the Death of JFK* (Baltimore, MD: Bancroft Press, 1998), 81.

150 'If you fuckers . . .': Bayard Stockton, *Flawed Patriot: The Rise and Fall of CIA Legend Bill Harvey* (Washington, DC: Potomac Books, 2006), 141.

150 'destroyed himself': David C. Martin, *Wilderness of Mirrors* (New York, Harper & Row, 1980), 144.

151 'have been very bad . . .': Testimony of Joseph Valachi, 27 September 1963, Organized Crime and Illicit Traffic in Narcotics, Hearings before the Permanent Subcommittee on Investigations of the Committee on Government Operations, United States Senate, Eighty-Eighth Congress, First Session, Part 1 (Washington, DC: USGPO, 1963), 119.

151 'I would be dead . . .': Bob Greene, 'Valachi Recounts Prison Terror', *New York Newsday* (28 September 1963), 3.

152 'La Cosa Nostra, the . . .': J. Edgar Hoover, 'The Inside Story of Organized Crime and How You Can Help Smash It', *Parade* magazine (15 September 1963).

Chapter 18: Master of Intrigue

153 'erratic personal behavior': Robert Sam Anson, *"They've Killed the President!": The Search for the Murderers of John F. Kennedy* (New York: Bantam Books, 1975), 105.

153 'There is nothing . . .': Richard H. Popkin, 'Garrison's Case', *New York Review* (14 September 1967), 28.

154 'master of intrigue': Fensterwald, Bernard Jr, *Assassination of JFK: By Coincidence or Conspiracy?* Produced by the Committee to Investigate Assassinations, compiled by Michael Ewing (New York: Zebra, 1977), 295.

154 'delighted in weaving . . .': John H. Davis, *Mafia Kingfish: Carlos Marcello and the Assassination of John F. Kennedy* (New York: McGraw-Hill, 1989), 156.

154 'ought to be shot': Special Agents Ernest C. Wall Jr and Theodore R. Viater interview with David Ferrie. File # NO-89-59. New Orleans, Louisiana (27 November 1963).

154 'wanted to express . . .': Eastern Airlines legal memorandum, 2 May 1963, 'Personal and Confidential, Re: Captain Ferrie', as quoted in Fensterwald, *Assassination of JFK*, 305.

155 'Cuban refugees were . . .': Gus Russo, *Live by the Sword: The Secret War Against Castro and the Death of JFK* (Baltimore, MD: Bancroft Press, 1998), 136.
155 'substantial donation': Appendix to Hearings Before the Select Committee on Assassinations of the U.S. House of Representatives. Investigation of the Assassination of President John F. Kennedy. Ninety-Fifth Congress, Second Session. Volume X: Anti-Castro Activities and Organizations, Lee Harvey Oswald in New Orleans, CIA Plots Against Castro, Rose Cheramie, March 1979 (Washington, DC: USGPO, 1979), 112.
156 'to establish a democratic . . .': *ibid*, 141.
156 'one of the more . . .': Fensterwald, *Assassination of JFK*, 496.
156 'had just shown . . .': Russo, *Live by the Sword*, 145.
156 'For all the business . . .': *ibid*, 137.
156 'I got 2,000 empty . . .': William Dalzell interview, as quoted in Russo, *ibid*, 137.
157 'The Louisiana Intelligence Digest': William W. Turner, 'The Garrison Commission', *Ramparts* (January 1968), 47.
157 'militantly conservative publication . . .': Russo, *Live by the Sword*, 140.
158 'the biggest and most . . .': Appendix to Hearings Before the Select Committee on Assassinations of the U.S. House of Representatives. Investigation of the Assassination of President John F. Kennedy. Ninety-Fifth Congress, Second Session. Volume IX: Staff and Consultant's Reports on Organized Crime, March 1979 (Washington, DC: USGPO, 1979), 97.
160 'This would be a nice . . .': John H. Davis, *The Kennedys: Dynasty and Disaster 1848–1983* (New York: McGraw-Hill, 1984), 494.
160 'He's with us': Earl Golz, 'Did Oswald Act Alone', *D* magazine (November 1983).
161 'crated for shipment . . .': Harold Weisberg, *Oswald in New Orleans* (New York: Canyon Books, 1967), 374.
162 'Grand Central Station': Warren Hinckle and William W. Turner, *The Fish is Red: The Story of the Secret War Against Castro* (New York: Harper & Row, 1981), 204.

Chapter 19: Sparky from Chicago
163 'What about Hoffa?': Joseph Nolan interviewed by Francis J. Hunt DeRosa, as quoted in Arthur M. Schlesinger Jr, *Robert Kennedy and His Times*, Volume II (Boston, MA: Houghton Mifflin Co., 1978), 562.
163 'despite 1500 witnesses . . .': Peter Collier and David Horowitz, *The Kennedys: An American Drama* (New York: Summit Books, 1984), 227.
163 'the game isn't over': Robert A. Caro, *The Years of Lyndon Johnson: The Passage of Power* (New York: Alfred A. Knopf, 2012), 242.
163 'Get Hoffa Squad': David Halvorsen, 'Court Fails to Find More Hoffa Jurors', *Chicago Tribune* (6 May 1964), Section C1, 5.

163 'rather odd, you know . . .': Victor Lasky, *Robert F. Kennedy: The Myth and the Man* (New York: Trident Press, 1968), 168.

163 'so-called legitimate . . .': Walter Sheridan memo to Herbert J. Miller Jr, 19 April 1961, as quoted in James Neff, *Vendetta: Bobby Kennedy Versus Jimmy Hoffa* (New York: Little, Brown & Co., 2015), 222.

163 'Bobby just wasn't . . .': Lasky, *Robert F. Kennedy*, 168.

163 'Sure we had a vendetta . . .': Steven Brill, *The Teamsters* (New York: Simon & Schuster, 1978), 40.

164 'I'd hate to see . . .': *ibid.*

164 'They go to school . . .': 'Nation: Freedom of Speech', *Time* magazine, Vol. LXXXI, No. 1 (4 January 1963).

164 'I want information from . . .': Joseph Franco, with Richard Hammer, *Hoffa's Man: The Rise and Fall of Jimmy Hoffa as Witnessed by His Strongest Arm* (New York: Prentice Hall, 1987), 231–2.

164 'We need some help . . .': Dan E, Moldea, *The Hoffa Wars: Teamsters, Rebels, Politicians, and the Mob* (New York: Paddington Press Ltd, 1978), 183.

165 'If Jack Kennedy is elected . . .': Neff, *Vendetta*, 151.

165 'Lawyers who take . . .': Neil Hickey, 'For the Defense', *The American Weekly* (17 July 1960), as quoted in 'Complaint on Kennedy: Bar Panel Scored on Inaction', *The International Teamster*, Vol. 57, Issue 9 (September 1960), 3.

165 'Somebody is going . . .': Frank Ragano and Selwyn Raab, *Mob Lawyer* (New York: Charles Scribner's Sons, 1994), 135.

165 'Something has to be . . .': *ibid*, 144.

165 '[Hoffa] wants you . . .': *ibid*, 145.

165 'I had blindly . . .': *ibid.*

166 'Next to New Orleans . . .': John H. Davis, *The Kennedy Contract: The Mafia Plot to Assassinate the President* (New York: Harper Paperbacks, 1993), 47.

167 'anonymous officer . . .': 'Apalachin's Mob is In and Its Secret is Out', *Life* magazine, Vol. 48, No. 3 (25 January 1960), 24.

167 'had no trouble . . .': John H. Davis, *Mafia Kingfish: Carlos Marcello and the Assassination of John F. Kennedy* (New York: McGraw-Hill, 1989), 140.

167 'No evidence of . . .': Investigation of the Assassination of President John F. Kennedy. Appendix to Hearings Before the Select Committee on Assassinations of the U.S. House of Representatives, Ninety-Fifth Congress, Second Session. Volume IX: Staff and Consultant's Reports on Organized Crime, March 1979 (Washington, DC: USGPO, 1979), 60.

167 'a full-scale investigation . . .': 'Gambling Inquiry Stalls When Two Refuse to Talk', *Wichita Falls Times* (2 October 1963), 10B.

168 'Dago Town': Earl Ruby Warren Commission Testimony, 3 June 1964. Investigation of the Assassination of President John F. Kennedy. Hearings Before the President's Commission on the Assassination of President

Kennedy. Volume XIV (Washington, DC: USGPO, 1964), 367.

168 'recommended that he . . .': G. Robert Blakey and Richard N. Billings, *The Plot to Kill the President* (New York: Times Books, 1981), 283.

168 'had been run . . .': Investigation of the Assassination of President John F. Kennedy. Appendix to Hearings Before the Select Committee on Assassinations of the U.S. House of Representatives, Ninety-Fifth Congress, Second Session. Volume IX: Staff and Consultant's Reports on Organized Crime, March 1979 (Washington, DC: USGPO, 1979), 427.

168 'Sparky from Chicago': *ibid*, 163.

169 'he beat with . . .': Blakey and Billings, *The Plot to Kill the President*, 292.

169 'Jack had seven . . .': Garry Wills and Ovid Demaris, *Jack Ruby* (New York: New American Library, 1968), 13.

Chapter 20: The Hit Heard Round the World

171 'They should kill . . .': JFK Exhibit F-630, Investigation of the Assassination of President John F. Kennedy. Hearings Before the Select Committee on Assassinations of the U.S. House of Representatives, Ninety-Fifth Congress, Second Session. Volume V (Washington, DC: USGPO, 1979), 448.

172 'as if the President . . .': Kenneth P. O'Donnell and David F. Powers, with Joe McCarthy, *"Johnny, We Hardly Knew Ye": Memories of John Fitzgerald Kennedy* (Boston, MA: Little, Brown & Co., 1972), 42.

172 'He's the one who . . .': *ibid*, 43.

172 'rightwing para-military fanatics': Edwin Black, 'The Plot to Kill JFK in Chicago November 2, 1963', *Chicago Independent* (November 1975), 5.

172 'disaffiliated member of . . .': 'Quiz North Sider on Weapons Count', *Chicago Daily News* (3 December 1963).

172 'suddenly felt compelled . . .': John H. Davis, *Mafia Kingfish: Carlos Marcello and the Assassination of John F. Kennedy* (New York: McGraw-Hill, 1989), 164.

172 'the mob's favored . . .': Seth Kantor, *The Ruby Cover-Up* (New York: Zebra Books, 1978), 72.

172 'underworld's major financial . . .': *Washington Post* (6 April 1978), as quoted in Investigation of the Assassination of President John F. Kennedy. Appendix to Hearings Before the Select Committee on Assassinations of the U.S. House of Representatives, Ninety-Fifth Congress, Second Session, March 1979. Volume IX (Washington, DC: USGPO, 1978), 1040.

173 'Marcello mobster': David Chandler, 'The Little Man is Bigger Than Ever', *Life* magazine (10 April 1970), 33.

173 'Ambassador of Violence': Robert F. Kennedy, *The Enemy Within* (New York: Harper & Brothers, 1960), 60.

175 'feel better if . . .': William Manchester, *The Death of a President: November 20–November 25, 1963* (New York: Harper & Row, 1967), 34.

175 'I sure wish to . . .': Stanley Marcus, as quoted in Merle Miller, *Lyndon: An Oral Biography* (New York: G.P. Putnam's Sons, 1980), 310.

175 'Dallas is a very . . .': Manchester, *The Death of a President*, 39.

175 Somerset: I think Kennedy . . .: Transcript of conversation between William Somerset and Joseph Milteer (9 November 1963): https://www.maryferrell.org/pages/Transcript_of_Milteer-Somersett_Tape.html

176 'aggressive homosexual with . . .': G. Robert Blakey and Richard N. Billings, *The Plot to Kill the President* (New York: Times Books, 1981), 168.

176 'didn't have no . . .': Davis, *Mafia Kingfish*, 95.

177 'This is one of . . .': Thurston Clarke, *JFK's Last Hundred Days* (New York: Penguin Press, 2013), 288.

178 'one of our boys': Jack Anderson, from a transcript, on *The David Susskind Show* (24 October 1977): https://history-matters.com/archive/jfk/cia/russholmes/pdf/104-10400-10010.pdf

178 'pick up some money . . .': Appendix to Hearings Before the Select Committee on Assassinations of the U.S. House of Representatives. Investigation of the Assassination of President John F. Kennedy. Ninety-Fifth Congress, Second Session. Volume X: Anti-Castro Activities and Organizations, Lee Harvey Oswald in New Orleans, CIA Plots Against Castro, Rose Cheramie, March 1979 (Washington, DC: USGPO, 1979), 201.

179 'It will not . . .': Evelyn Lincoln, *Kennedy and Johnson* (New York: Holt, Rinehart & Winston, 1968), 205.

179 'I didn't take . . .': Mark Collom and Glen Sample, *The Men on the Sixth Floor* (Garden Grove, CA: Sample Graphics, 1997), 120.

180 'Little Lyndon Johnson': Bobby Baker, with Larry L. King, *Wheeling and Dealing: Confessions of a Capitol Hill Operator* (New York: W.W. Norton & Co., 1978), 118.

180 'Baker knew as much . . .': Doris Kearns, *Lyndon Johnson and the American Dream* (New York: New American Library, 1977), 124.

180 'right arm . . . the last person . . .': 'Investigations: The Silent Witness', *Time* magazine (6 March 1964).

180 'LBJ's ties to Marcello . . .': Richard D. Mahoney, *Sons & Brothers: The Days of Jack and Bobby Kennedy* (New York: Arcade Pub., 1999), 384.

180 'as an effort on Bobby's . . .': Nicholas deB. Katzenbach, *Some of It Was Fun: Working with RFK and LBJ* (New York: W.W. Norton & Co., 2008), 147.

180 'Of course there was . . .': Miller, *Lyndon*, 298.

180 'snot-nosed brother's . . .': Baker, with Larry L. King, *Wheeling and Dealing*, 117.

181 Capital Buzzes Over . . .: 'Capital Buzzes Over Stories of Misconduct in High Places. The Bobby Baker Bomb Shell', *Life* magazine, Vol. 55, No. 19 (8 November 1963).

181 'millionaire': Robert A. Caro, *The Years of Lyndon Johnson: The Passage of Power* (New York: Alfred A. Knopf, 2012), 298.

181 'looks like a bandit . . .': *ibid.*
181 'had used public . . .': *ibid.*
181 'many senators would . . .': Baker, with Larry L. King, *Wheeling and Dealing*, 271.
182 'Those guys were bombed': Christopher Evans, 'Remembering the Cellar', *Fort Worth Star-Telegram* (25 May 1984), 14.
183 'We're in nut . . .': O'Donnell and Powers, with Joe McCarthy, *"Johnny, We Hardly Knew Ye"*, 26.
183 'It would not be . . .': Vincent Bugliosi, *Reclaiming History: The Assassination of President John F. Kennedy* (New York: W.W. Norton & Co., 2007), 21.
183 'often talked about . . .': O'Donnell and Powers, with Joe McCarthy, *"Johnny, We Hardly Knew Ye"*, 19.
183 'If somebody wants somebody . . .': *ibid*, 26.
183 'locked eyes with . . .': Jim Marrs, *Crossfire: The Plot that Killed Kennedy* (New York: Carroll & Graf, 1989), 18.
184 'bigger and bigger': William Lambert, as quoted in Caro, *The Years of Lyndon Johnson: The Passage of Power*, 308.
184 'Lyndon Johnson's Money': *ibid*, 309.
184 'This trip is turning . . .': O'Donnell and Powers, with Joe McCarthy, *"Johnny, We Hardly Knew Ye"*, 27.
185 'There's certainly nothing . . .': *ibid*, 28.
185 'Mr President, you . . .': Mrs Nellie Connally, Warren Commission Testimony, 21 April 1964. Investigation of the Assassination of President John F. Kennedy. Hearings Before the President's Commission on the Assassination of President Kennedy. Volume IV (Washington, DC: USGPO, 1964), 147.
185 'eyes met mine . . .': Nellie Connally and Mickey Herskowitz, *From Love Field: Our Final Hours with President John F. Kennedy* (New York: Rugged Land, 2003), 7.
185 'My God, they . . .': Mrs Nellie Connally, Warren Commission Testimony, 21 April 1964. Investigation of the Assassination of President John F. Kennedy. Hearings Before the President's Commission on the Assassination of President Kennedy. Volume IV (Washington, DC: USGPO, 1964), 147.
186 'We saw pieces . . .': O'Donnell and Powers, with Joe McCarthy, *"Johnny, We Hardly Knew Ye"*, 29.
186 'a red sheet of blood . . .': Jesse E. Curry, *Retired Dallas Police Chief Jesse Curry Reveals His Personal JFK Assassination File* (Dallas, TX: American Poster & Printing Co., 1969), 30.
186 'I have my husband's brains . . .': Mrs Nellie Connally, Warren Commission Testimony, 21 April 1964. Investigation of the Assassination of President John F. Kennedy. Hearings Before the President's Commission on the Assassination of President Kennedy. Volume IV (Washington, DC: USGPO, 1964), 144.

186 'very slowly, with . . .': Affidavit of Ralph W. Yarborough, 10 July 1964, Investigation of the Assassination of President John F. Kennedy. Hearings Before the President's Commission on the Assassination of President Kennedy. Volume VII (Washington, DC: USGPO, 1964), 440.

186 'look of shock . . .': Davis, *Mafia Kingfish*, 180.

187 'I have news . . .': Arthur M. Schlesinger Jr, *Robert Kennedy and His Times*, Volume II (Boston, MA: Houghton Mifflin Co., 1978), 635.

187 'Jack's been shot . . .': *ibid.*

187 'shock and horror': Bill Davidson, 'A Profile in Family Courage', *Saturday Evening Post* (14 December 1963), 32b.

187 'The President's dead': Manchester, *The Death of a President*, 257.

187 'Not quite as . . .': *ibid.*

187 'I think Hoover . . .': Katzenbach, *Some of It Was Fun*, 130.

187 'Hoover's cold-blooded attitude . . .': William C. Sullivan, with Bill Brown, *The Bureau: My Thirty Years in Hoover's FBI* (New York: W.W. Norton & Co., 1979), 50.

187 'Let's call it . . .': Leonard Mosley, *Dulles: A Biography of Eleanor, Allen, and John Foster Dulles and Their Family Network* (New York: The Dial Press, 1978), 477.

187 'Did you kill . . .': Curt Gentry, *J. Edgar Hoover: The Man and the Myth* (New York: W.W. Norton & Co., 1991), 557.

188 'There was a fairly . . .': William K. Harvey Testimony, 25 June 1975. Report of Proceedings. Hearing Held before Senate Select Committee to Study Governmental Operations with Respect to Intelligence Activities (Washington, DC: Ward & Paul, 1975), 66.

188 'I thought they . . .': Edwin Guthman, *We Band of Brothers* (New York: Harper & Row, 1971), 244.

188 'too old for . . .': O'Donnell and Powers, with Joe McCarthy, *"Johnny, We Hardly Knew Ye"*, 8.

188 'You won't need those': Clark R. Mollenhoff, *Despoilers of Democracy: The Real Story of What Washington Propagandists, Arrogant Bureaucrats, Mismanagers, Influence Peddlers, and Outright Corrupters are Doing to Our Federal Government* (Garden City, NY: Doubleday & Co., 1965), 299.

188 'It was going to blow . . .': James Wagenvoord, as quoted in Peter Janney, *Mary's Mosaic: The CIA Conspiracy to Murder John F. Kennedy, Mary Pinchot Meyer, and Their Vision for World Peace* (New York: Skyhorse, 2013), 307.

189 'About forty of us . . .': Victor S. Navasky, *Kennedy Justice* (New York: Atheneum, 1971), 51.

189 'He never mentioned . . .': Evan Thomas, *Robert Kennedy: His Life* (New York: Simon & Schuster, 2000), 283.

189 'Every reasonable presumption . . .': Ronald Goldfarb, *Perfect Villains, Imperfect Heroes: Robert F. Kennedy's War Against Organized Crime* (New York: Random House, 1995), 245.

189 'Everyone knew it . . .': John H. Davis, *The Kennedy Contract: The Mafia Plot to Assassinate the President* (New York: Harper Paperbacks, 1993), 176.

189 'It was a quiet . . .': *American Journey: The Times of Robert Kennedy*, interviews by Jean Stein. Edited by George Plimpton (New York: Harcourt Brace Jovanovich, 1970), 78.

189 'Suddenly, it occurred . . .': Goldfarb, *Perfect Villains, Imperfect Heroes*, 256.

189 'After the President's . . .': Blakey and Billings, *The Plot to Kill the President*, 199.

189 'The minute that . . .': Anthony Summers, *Official and Confidential: The Secret Life of J. Edgar Hoover* (New York: G.P. Putnam's Sons, 1993), 332.

189 'We need you . . .': Walter Sheridan Oral History Interview by Roberta W. Greene. RFK#5, JFK Library (1 May 1970).

190 'He didn't know . . .': Davis, *Mafia Kingfish*, 276.

190 'looked like the . . .': Katzenbach, *Some of It Was Fun*, 134.

190 'he could not focus . . .': *ibid*, 133.

190 'he was withdrawn . . .': *ibid*, 135.

190 'He was the most . . .': Pierre E. G. Salinger Oral History Interview by Larry J. Hackman. RFK#1, JFK Library (26 May 1969).

190 'Bobby was destroyed': John Davis interview with Gus Russo, 20 November 1993, as quoted in Gus Russo, *Live by the Sword: The Secret War Against Castro and the Death of JFK* (Baltimore, MD: Bancroft Press, 1998), 382.

190 'It was as though . . .': Lester David and Irene David, *Bobby Kennedy: The Making of a Folk Hero* (New York: Dodd, Mead & Co., 1986), 217.

190 'He was a walking zombie': G. Robert Blakey, as quoted in Goldfarb, *Perfect Villains, Imperfect Heroes*, 302.

190 'I never saw anyone . . .': William vanden Heuvel interview with Gus Russo, 7 August 1993, as quoted in Russo, *Live by the Sword*, 382.

190 'could not bring . . .': Katzenbach, *Some of It Was Fun*, 146.

190 'I think he lost . . .': Murray Kempton Oral History Interview by Jean Stein. RFK#1, JFK Library (28 March 1970).

190 'I'm tired of . . .': James Reston, 'Tired of Chasing People – Robert Kennedy', *New York Times* (6 May 1964), 46.

190 'The son-of-a-bitch . . .': Frank Ragano and Selwyn Raab, *Mob Lawyer* (New York: Charles Scribner's Sons, 1994), 147.

190 'For a hundred years . . .': *ibid*, 148.

190 'Have you heard . . .': Davis, *The Kennedy Contract*, 98.

191 'Bobby Kennedy is just . . .': Walter Sheridan, *The Fall and Rise of Jimmy Hoffa* (New York: Saturday Review Press, 1972), 300.

191 'Within a month . . .': Fred P. Graham, 'Setback is Noted in Fight on Crime', *New York Times* (18 July 1965), 26.

191 'until President Kennedy ...': Sullivan, with Bill Brown, *The Bureau*, 122.

191 'Starting at 1:10 on ...': Davis, *Mafia Kingfish*, 297.

Chapter 21: Silenced

192 'something urgent on ...': John H. Davis, *Mafia Kingfish: Carlos Marcello and the Assassination of John F. Kennedy* (New York: McGraw-Hill, 1989), 181.

192 'calmly sipping a ...': John H. Davis, *The Kennedy Contract: The Mafia Plot to Assassinate the President* (New York: Harper Paperbacks, 1993), 93.

193 'Ruby seemed to ...': *ibid*, 102.

194 'Ruby simply could not ...': Seth Kantor, *Who Was Jack Ruby?* (New York: Everest House, 1978), 11.

195 'The Fair Play ...': Henry Wade, Warren Commission Testimony, 8 June 1964. Investigation of the Assassination of President John F. Kennedy. Hearings Before the President's Commission on the Assassination of President Kennedy. Volume V (Washington, DC: USGPO, 1964), 223.

195 'It is most rewarding ...': Letter from Lyndon B. Johnson to Henry Wade, 22 June 1960, as quoted in Mark North, *Betrayal in Dallas: LBJ, the Pearl Street Mafia, and the Murder of President Kennedy* (New York: A Herman Graf Book, 2011), 214.

195 'known Ruby on ...': 'Ruby Trial Might be Moved', *Casper Morning Star* (30 November 1963), 2.

195 'I am a pretty good ...': Kenneth Lawry Dowe, Warren Commission Testimony, 25 July 1964. Investigation of the Assassination of President John F. Kennedy. Hearings Before the President's Commission on the Assassination of President Kennedy. Volume XV (Washington, DC: USGPO, 1964), 434.

195 'We have reason to ...': From *Dallas Morning News* (1 November 1963), as quoted in North, *Betrayal in Dallas*, 65.

195 'I don't think there's ...': From *Dallas Morning News*, as quoted in G. Robert Blakey and Richard N. Billings, *The Plot to Kill the President* (New York: Times Books, 1981), 328.

195 'What are you going ...': Appendix to Hearings Before the Select Committee on Assassinations of the U.S. House of Representatives. Investigation of the Assassination of President John F. Kennedy. Ninety-Fifth Congress, Second Session. Volume X: Anti-Castro Activities and Organizations, Lee Harvey Oswald in New Orleans, CIA Plots Against Castro, Rose Cheramie, March 1979 (Washington, DC: USGPO, 1979), 130.

196 'a longtime colleague ...': Blakey and Billings, *The Plot to Kill the President*, 166.

196 'a black leather ...': Josiah Thompson, *Six Seconds in Dallas: A*

Micro-Study of the Kennedy Assassination (New York: Bernard Geis Associates, 1967), 139.

196 'was in building . . .': Decker Exhibit No. 5323, C.L. Lewis' Supplement Investigation Report. Investigation of the Assassination of President John F. Kennedy. Hearings Before the President's Commission on the Assassination of President Kennedy. Volume XIX (Washington, DC: USGPO, 1964), 527.

197 'a real Chicago thug': Jerry Fink, 'Q & A Breck Wall', *Las Vegas Sun* (30 November 2005): https://lasvegassun.com/news/2005/nov/30/q-a-breck-wall/

197 'to stay with . . .': *ibid.*

198 'had no trouble with . . .': Davis, *Mafia Kingfish*, 140.

198 'You have to suspect . . .': Seth Kantor, *The Ruby Cover-Up* (New York: Zebra Books, 1978), 295.

199 'As Capt. Fritz was . . .': Jesse E. Curry, *Retired Dallas Police Chief Jesse Curry Reveals His Personal JFK Assassination File* (Dallas, TX: American Poster & Printing Co., 1969), 127.

199 'Here he comes!': Warren Commission Exhibit 2326. Investigation of the Assassination of President John F. Kennedy. Hearings Before the President's Commission on the Assassination of President Kennedy. Exhibits 2190 to 2651. Warren Commission Hearings, Volume XXV (Washington, DC: USGPO, 1964), 287.

199 'Man, it was a . . .': Ed Reid and Ovid Demaris, *The Green Felt Jungle* (New York: Pocket Books, 1964), 157.

199 'If anyone had wanted . . .': London *Daily Telegraph* quoted in the *Congressional Record*, 29 November 1963, Proceedings and Debates of the Eighty-Eighth Congress, First Session, Volume 109, Part 17 (Washington, DC: USGPO, 1963), 22950.

199 'You son of . . .': Warren Commission Exhibit 2326. Investigation of the Assassination of President John F. Kennedy. Hearings Before the President's Commission on the Assassination of President Kennedy. Exhibits 2190 to 2651. Warren Commission Hearings, Volume XXV (Washington, DC: USGPO, 1964), 287.

200 'Hey, you all . . .': Warren Commission Exhibit 2409. Investigation of the Assassination of President John F. Kennedy. Hearings Before the President's Commission on the Assassination of President Kennedy. Exhibits 2190 to 2651. Warren Commission Hearings, Volume XXV (Washington, DC: USGPO, 1964), 411.

200 'It's a plot': William Manchester, *The Death of a President: November 20–November 25, 1963* (New York: Harper & Row, 1967), 528.

200 'Of course': *ibid.*

200 'suppress something': *ibid*, 5.

201 'been working on . . .': David Ferrie, FBI interview, New Orleans, Louisiana. Interview conducted by SA Ernest C. Wall Jr and SA L.M. Shearer Jr. Warren Commission Document 75 (25 November 1963), 287.

201 'a farm owned by Carlos . . .': *ibid.*

201 'it was not until an attorney . . .': Fensterwald, Bernard Jr, *Assassination of JFK: By Coincidence or Conspiracy?* Produced by the Committee to Investigate Assassinations, compiled by Michael Ewing (New York: Zebra, 1977), 301.

201 'a real bad guy': Peter Noyes, *Legacy of Doubt: Did the Mafia Kill JFK?* (Orlando, FL: P & G Publications, 2010), 28.

Chapter 22: The Exhaustive Report

203 'in the category of . . .': J. Edgar Hoover Memorandum to Clyde Tolson, et al., FBI Document No. 62-109060-57 (22 November 1963).

203 'The thing I am . . .': Memorandum to the Files by Walter Jenkins, 24 November 1963. Investigation of the Assassination of President John F. Kennedy. Appendix Hearings Before the Select Committee on Assassinations of the U.S. House of Representatives, Ninety-Fifth Congress, Second Session. Volume XI: The Warren Commission, CIA Support to the Warren Commission, The Motorcade, Military Investigation of the Assassination. March 1979 (Washington, DC: USGPO, 1979), 3.

203 'to set out the . . .': FBI Memorandum from Alan Belmont to Clyde Tolson, 24 November 1963, JFK Exhibit F-463. Investigation of the Assassination of President John F. Kennedy. Hearings Before the Select Committee on Assassinations of the U.S. House of Representatives, Ninety-Fifth Congress, Second Session. 18, 19, 20 and 21 September 1978. Volume III (Washington, DC: USGPO, 1979), 666.

203 'The public must be . . .': FBI Memorandum from Nicholas deB. Katzenbach to Bill Moyers. FBI Document No. 62-109060, JFK HQ File, Section 18 (25 November 1963).

204 'Parkland Hospital doctors . . .': *JFK: What the Doctors Saw.* Documentary directed by Barbara Shearer. Paramount Pictures, 2023.

204 'there was an entrance . . .': UPI, 'Wound Described, Doctor Reports', *Spokane Daily Chronicle* (22 November 1963), 13.

204 'a single shot through . . .': *Dallas Morning News*, Early Edition (23 November 1963).

204 'witness . . . explained the . . .': Mark North, *Betrayal in Dallas: LBJ, the Pearl Street Mafia, and the Murder of President Kennedy* (New York: A Herman Graf Book, 2011), 71.

204 'could be seen to . . .': Dan Rather, account for CBS News (25 November 1963): www.youtube.com/watch?v=kiSoxFHyjGY

205 'wasn't interested': Appendix to Hearings Before the Select Committee on Assassinations of the U.S. House of Representatives. Investigation of the Assassination of President John F. Kennedy. Ninety-Fifth Congress, Second Session. Volume X: Anti-Castro Activities and Organizations, Lee Harvey Oswald in New Orleans, CIA Plots Against Castro, Rose Cheramie, March 1979 (Washington, DC: USGPO, 1979), 202.

205 'I wouldn't want to . . .': George Crile III, 'The Mafia, the CIA and Castro', *Washington Post* (16 May 1976).
205 '[There is] a price . . .': John H. Davis, *The Kennedy Contract: The Mafia Plot to Assassinate the President* (New York: Harper Paperbacks, 1993), 119.
205 'You take care of . . .': Lyndon B. Johnson, *Taking Charge: The Johnson White House Tapes, 1963–1964*. Edited and with Commentary by Michael R. Beschloss (New York: Simon & Schuster, 1997), 62.
206 'lobbied hard for . . .': Joseph J. Trento, *The Secret History of the CIA* (New York: MJF Books, 2001), 269.
206 'duplicitous man . . . not . . .': Tim Weiner, *Legacy of Ashes: The History of the CIA* (New York: Doubleday, 2007), 24.
206 'I don't think Allen . . .': Earl Warren Oral History Interview by Joe B. Frantz, LBJ Presidential Library (21 September 1971), 13.
206 'look after FBI . . .': William C. Sullivan, with Bill Brown, *The Bureau: My Thirty Years in Hoover's FBI* (New York: W.W. Norton & Co., 1979), 53.
206 'our man, our . . .': *ibid.*
207 'derogatory dossiers': Fensterwald, Bernard Jr, *Assassination of JFK: By Coincidence or Conspiracy?* Produced by the Committee to Investigate Assassinations, compiled by Michael Ewing (New York: Zebra, 1977), 263.
207 'would discover important . . .': Investigation of the Assassination of President John F. Kennedy. Hearings Before the Select Committee on Assassinations of the U.S. House of Representatives, Ninety-Fifth Congress, Second Session. 18, 19, 20 and 21 September 1978. Volume III (Washington, DC: USGPO, 1979), 489.
208 'knowledge of the . . .': J. Edgar Hoover letter to J. Lee Rankin, 9 June 1964. The Harold Weisberg Archive, Hood College, Frederick, MD.
208 'Lee Oswald of . . .': Jim Marrs, *Crossfire: The Plot that Killed Kennedy* (New York: Carroll & Graf, 1989), 405.
208 'Witnesses to the shooting . . .': Jesse Curry, *Retired Dallas Police Chief Jesse Curry Reveals His Personal JFK Assassination File, Limited Collectors Edition* (Dallas, TX: American Poster & Printing Co., 1969), 133.
209 'there is a possibility . . .': J. Edgar Hoover Memo, 3 June 1960, as quoted in Ben A. Franklin, 'Data on Oswald Apparently Withheld from Key Warren Investigation Aides', *New York Times* (23 February 1975), 32.
209 'The Central Intelligence Agency . . .': Memorandum from J. Edgar Hoover to James J. Rowley, 22 November 1963. Final Report of the Select Committee on Assassinations, U.S. House of Representatives, Ninety-Fifth Congress, Second Session. Summary of Findings and Recommendations (Washington, DC: USGPO, 1979), 249–50.
209 'We have up here . . .': Johnson, *Taking Charge*, 23.

210 'he would keep . . .': Nikita Khrushchev, *Khrushchev Remembers*. Translated and edited by Strobe Talbott (Boston, MA: Little, Brown & Co., 1970), 505.

210 'appeared to be . . .': From an FBI report of an interview of Victor Robertson by Special Agent Vincent E. Drain, 9 June 1964. Investigation of the Assassination of President John F. Kennedy. Hearings Before the President's Commission on the Assassination of President Kennedy. Exhibits Paine to Yarborough, Volume XXI (Washington, DC: USGPO, 1964), 311.

211 'a one-eyed, chain-smoking . . .': North, *Betrayal in Dallas*, 94.

211 'for about ten years': FBI interview with Joe Civello on 14 January 1964, as quoted in G. Robert Blakey and Richard N. Billings, *The Plot to Kill the President* (New York: Times Books, 1981), 314.

212 'Joe, you should . . .': 'A Note from Jack Ruby', *Newsweek* (27 March 1967), 21.

212 'story of trying . . .': Melvin Belli, with Maurice C. Carroll, *Dallas Justice: The Real Story of Jack Ruby and His Trial* (New York: David McKay, 1964), 41.

212 'It's strange that . . .': Jack Ruby Warren Commission Testimony, 18 July 1964. Investigation of the Assassination of President John F. Kennedy. Hearings Before the President's Commission on the Assassination of President Kennedy. Volume XIV (Washington, DC: USGPO, 1964), 564–5.

212 'Sy, one of our . . .': Blakey and Billings, *The Plot to Kill the President*, 325.

213 'Santo was visited . . .': U.S. State Department Cable (28 November 1963): https://www.archives.gov/files/research/jfk/releases/2018/104-10048-10063.pdf.

213 'psychopath': *ibid.*

213 'Ruby was hooked . . .': William Scott Malone, 'The Secret Life of Jack Ruby', *New Times* magazine, Vol. 10, No. 7 (23 January 1978), 50.

213 'An exhaustive FBI report . . .': JFK Exhibit F-459. Investigation of the Assassination of President John F. Kennedy. Hearings Before the Select Committee on Assassinations of the U.S. House of Representatives, Ninety-Fifth Congress, Second Session. 18, 19, 20 and 21 September 1978. Volume III (Washington, DC: USGPO, 1979), 459.

213 'exhaustive report': John H. Davis, *Mafia Kingfish: Carlos Marcello and the Assassination of John F. Kennedy* (New York: McGraw-Hill, 1989), 253.

214 'I want to tell you . . .': Jack Ruby Warren Commission Testimony, 7 June 1964. Investigation of the Assassination of President John F. Kennedy. Hearings Before the President's Commission on the Assassination of President Kennedy. Volume V (Washington, DC: USGPO, 1964), 194.

214 'Is there any way to get . . .': *ibid*, 190.

215 'to look for more . . .': Robert A. Caro, *The Years of Lyndon Johnson: The Path to Power*, 303.

215 'thousands of letters . . .': Douglas Brinkley, *Cronkite* (New York: Harper, 2012), 282.

215 'Oh no, oh my . . .': John Connally, Warren Commission Testimony, 21 April 1964. Investigation of the Assassination of President John F. Kennedy. Hearings Before the President's Commission on the Assassination of President Kennedy. Volume IV (Washington, DC: USGPO, 1964), 133.

215 'My God, what are . . .': William Manchester, *The Death of a President: November 20–November 25, 1963* (New York: Harper & Row, 1967), 160.

215 'caked with blood': Audio Diary and Annotated Transcript, Lady Bird Johnson, Lady Bird Johnson's White House Diary Collection, LBJ Presidential Library (22 November 1963).

215 'No. Let *them* see . . .': Manchester, *The Death of a President*, 348.

215 'Daddy, *they* just . . .': Earl Warren, *The Memoirs of Earl Warren* (Garden City, NY: Doubleday & Co., 1977), 353.

215 'But Daddy . . .': *ibid.*

216 'To me, it's just . . .': John Connally, *48 Hours: JFK*, CBS News (5 February 1992): https://www.youtube.com/watch?v=m4QRd2LviQo

216 'I heard Governor Connally . . .': John Cooper, *The Assassination of President Kennedy, Part I*, Documentary (1978): https://texasarchive.org/2013_01482

216 'disgusted by the . . .': Cato, 'From Washington Straight', *National Review* (21 April 1964), 311.

216 'I think someone . . .': Don Oberdorfer, 'Russell Says He Never Believed Oswald Alone Planned Killing', *Washington Post* (19 January 1970), A3.

217 'doubt that [Oswald] . . .': *ibid.*

217 'They are trying to . . .': Lyndon Johnson telephone call with Richard Russell, 18 September 1964, as quoted in Johnson, *Taking Charge*, 559–60.

217 'I don't either': *ibid.*

217 'I never believed . . .': Leo Janos, 'The Last Days of the President', *Atlantic Monthly* (July 1973), 39.

217 'Everybody who has . . .': Judge Burt W. Griffin Testimony, 28 September 1978. Investigation of the Assassination of President John F. Kennedy. Hearings Before the Select Committee on Assassinations of the U.S. House of Representatives, Ninety-Fifth Congress, Second Session. Volume V: (Washington, DC: USGPO, 1979), 494.

217 'I had and continue . . .': Burt Griffin to Seth Kantor, 12 July 1976, as quoted in Seth Kantor, *The Ruby Cover-Up* (New York: Zebra Books, 1978), 273.

217 'I know of no credible . . .': Robert F. Kennedy letter to Chief Justice Earl Warren, 4 August 1964. Commission Exhibit 3025. Investigation of the Assassination of President John F. Kennedy. Hearings Before the

President's Commission on the Assassination of President Kennedy. Volume XXVI (Washington, DC: USGPO, 1964), 573.

217 'My own feeling . . .': David Talbot, *Brothers: The Hidden History of the Kennedy Years* (London: Pocket Books, 2008), 277.

218 'Bobby Kennedy understood . . .': Seymour M. Hersh, *The Dark Side of Camelot* (Boston, MA: Little, Brown & Co., 1997), 2.

218 'There was no . . .': Harris Wofford, *Of Kennedys and Kings: Making Sense of the Sixties* (Pittsburgh, PA: University of Pittsburgh Press, 1980), 415.

218 'If anyone was . . .': Talbot, *Brothers*, 305.

218 'We know the CIA . . .': *ibid*, 303.

218 'He didn't read very . . .': Victor Lasky, *Robert F. Kennedy: The Myth and the Man* (New York: Trident Press, 1968), 46.

218 'All arrogance will . . .': Edith Hamilton, *The Greek Way* (New York: The Modern Library, 1942), 177.

218 'Hush now, a Kennedy . . .': Warren Rogers, *When I Think of Bobby: A Personal Memoir of the Kennedy Years* (New York: HarperCollins, 1993), 16.

219 'Why, God, why?': Charles Spalding Oral History Interview with Larry J. Hackman. John F. Kennedy Presidential Library (22 March 1964).

219 'those Cuban cunts': C. David Heymann, *RFK: A Candid Biography* (London: William Heinemann, 1998), 360.

219 'guy from New Orleans': Evan Thomas, *Robert Kennedy: His Life* (New York: Simon & Schuster, 2000), 337.

219 'have insulated themselves . . .': Robert F. Kennedy, 25 September 1963. Organized Crime and Illicit Traffic in Narcotics. Hearings Before the Permanent Subcommittee on Investigations of the Committee on Government Operations, United States Senate, Eighty-Eighth Congress, First Session, Part 1 (Washington, DC: USGPO, 1963), 23.

Chapter 23: It Ain't Goin' Nowhere

220 'Whatever you do . . .': Frank Ragano and Selwyn Raab, *Mob Lawyer* (New York: Charles Scribner's Sons, 1994), 242.

220 'The same people . . .': 'Jack Ruby Says He's Sorry He Shot Down Oswald, But', *Dallas Times Herald* (21 November 1966), as quoted in Mark North, *Betrayal in Dallas: LBJ, the Pearl Street Mafia, and the Murder of President Kennedy* (New York: A Herman Graf Book, 2011), 132.

220 'Your Buddy, Jack Ruby': Earl Golz, 'Ex-Officer Fears "Setup"', *Dallas Morning News* (25 March 1979), 35.

221 'Agent 008': Andrew Lycett, *Ian Fleming* (London: Weidenfeld & Nicolson, 1995), 418.

221 'President Kennedy and I . . .': Allen W. Dulles Oral History Interview with Thomas Braden. John F. Kennedy Presidential Library (5–6 December 1964), 16.

221 'I kept in constant ...': Allen Dulles, 'The Spy Boss Who Loves Bond', *For Bond Lovers Only*. Compiled and edited by Sheldon Lane (New York: Dell, 1965), 153, 155–6.

221 'Lee watched that ...': Robert L. Oswald, with Myrick and Barbara Land, *Lee: A Portrait of Lee Harvey Oswald by His Brother* (New York: Coward-McCann, 1967), 47.

221 'microphone-equipped wristwatch ...': Jim Garrison, *On the Trail of the Assassins* (New York: Warner Books, 1991), 254.

221 'dark night of ...': Nancy Gager Clinch, *The Kennedy Neurosis: A Psychological Portrait of an American Dynasty* (New York: Grosset & Dunlap, 1973), 294. The phrase is originally from a poem written by sixteenth-century Spanish mystic and poet, St John of the Cross.

222 'When I received ...': William F. Roemer Jr, *Roemer: Man Against the Mob* (New York: Donald I. Fine, 1989), 227.

222 'pressed too many issues': Investigation of the Assassination of President John F. Kennedy. Appendix to Hearings Before the Select Committee on Assassinations of the U.S. House of Representatives, Ninety-Fifth Congress, Second Session. Volume IX: Staff and Consultant's Reports on Organized Crime, March 1979 (Washington, DC: USGPO, 1979), 43.

222 'in order to ...': G. Robert Blakey and Richard N. Billings, *The Plot to Kill the President* (New York: Times Books, 1981), 256.

222 'I tell you something ...': Investigation of the Assassination of President John F. Kennedy. Appendix to Hearings Before the Select Committee on Assassinations of the U.S. House of Representatives, Ninety-Fifth Congress, Second Session. Volume IX: Staff and Consultant's Reports on Organized Crime, March 1979 (Washington, DC: USGPO, 1979), 43.

223 'would urge members ...': Emanuel Perlmutter, 'Hoffa Asks Union to Back Johnson', *New York Times* (18 October 1964), 73.

223 'had a smug ...': John H. Davis, *The Kennedy Contract: The Mafia Plot to Assassinate the President* (New York: Harper Paperbacks, 1993), 6.

223 'like the cat ...': Ragano and Raab, *Mob Lawyer*, 360.

223 'When you see Jimmy ...': *ibid*, 151.

223 'I told you they ...': *ibid*, 150.

223 'crossed the professional ...': *ibid*, 149.

224 'heavily involved in ...': Garrison, *On the Trail of the Assassins*, 27.

224 'By the late summer ...': *ibid*, 46.

224 'known a good ...': *ibid*.

224 'a sometime private detective': *ibid*, 3.

224 'bloody, battered mess': *ibid*.

224 'He nearly killed me': *ibid*, 33.

224 'was like a circus': *ibid*, 34.

224 'practically lived there': *ibid*, 35.

225 'Rifles stacked all ...': Mary Brengel interview with Gus Russo, 6 June 1993, as quoted in Gus Russo, *Live by the Sword: The Secret War*

Against Castro and the Death of JFK (Baltimore, MD: Bancroft Press, 1998), 153.

225 'surprising swiftness': Garrison, *On the Trail of the Assassins*, 10.

225 'You know what . . .': *ibid*, 160.

225 'physical protection against . . .': Peter Noyes, *Legacy of Doubt: Did the Mafia Kill JFK?* (Orlando, FL: P & G Publications, 2010), 113.

225 'Dave Ferrie's dead . . .': Garrison, *On the Trail of the Assassins*, 162.

226 'Who is this . . .': Davis, *The Kennedy Contract*, 177.

226 'He's good people': *ibid*, 183.

226 'denies the existence . . .': Aaron M. Kohn, 13 August 1970. Federal Effort Against Organized Crime: Role of the Private Sector. Hearings Before a Subcommittee on Government Operations House of Representatives. Ninety-First Congress, Second Session (Washington, DC: USGPO, 1970), 11.

227 'Why, with all . . .': Blakey and Billings, *The Plot to Kill the President*, 50.

227 'In a series of . . .': Noyes, *Legacy of Doubt*, 105, 106.

227 'get five or six . . .': Garrison, *On the Trail of the Assassins*, 163.

227 'littered with newspaper . . .': Noyes, *Legacy of Doubt*, 109.

228 'dubious autopsy reports': John H. Davis, *Mafia Kingfish: Carlos Marcello and the Assassination of John F. Kennedy* (New York: McGraw-Hill, 1989), 333.

228 'one of history's . . .': 'Important Figure in Assassination Case is Found Dead', Hazelton *Standard-Speaker* (23 February 1967), 1.

228 'we waited too long': *ibid*.

228 'a number of the men . . .': Eric Norden, 'Playboy Interview: Jim Garrison: A Candid Conversation with the Embattled District Attorney of New Orleans', *Playboy* (October 1967), 68, 70.

228 'do all we can . . .': Fensterwald, Bernard Jr, *Assassination of JFK: By Coincidence or Conspiracy?* Produced by the Committee to Investigate Assassinations, compiled by Michael Ewing (New York: Zebra, 1977), 299.

230 'deeply concerned': *Congressional Record: Proceedings and Debates of the 91st Congress, First Session*. Vol. 115, Part 17 (12 August 1969), 23570.

231 'triangulation of crossfire': 'Shaw Lawyer to Question Perry Russo', *Shreveport Journal* (15 March 1967), 1.

231 'Oswald had placed . . .': Carl Freund and Lewis Harris, 'Oswald's Room Yields Map of Bullets' Path', *Dallas Morning News* (25 November 1963), Section 4, 1.

231 'a man associated with . . .': Noyes, *Legacy of Doubt*, 38.

231 'I told the FBI . . .': Tip O'Neill, with William Novak, *Man of the House: The Life and Political Memoirs of Speaker Tip O'Neill* (New York: Random House, 1987), 178.

231 'backward and to . . .': Jim Garrison, *A Heritage of Stone* (New York: G.P. Putnam's Sons, 1970), 45.

231 'contract agent': *True* magazine, 1975, as quoted in Garrison, *On the Trail of the Assassins*, 274.

232 'to testify about possible . . .': Steven J. Burton, 'Garrison Subpoenas Ex-CIA Head', *Los Angeles Free Press* (1 March 1968).

232 'I'd like to be . . .': Stan Opotowsky, *The Kennedy Government* (London: George G. Harrap & Co., 1961), 74.

233 'either a lot of . . .': Robert E. Thompson and Hortense Myers, *Robert F. Kennedy: The Brother Within* (New York: The Macmillan Co., 1962), 43.

233 Man's a strangely . . .: From *Tartuffe*, Act One, in *Molière: The Complete Richard Wilbur Translations*, Volume 2 (New York: Library of America, 2021).

Chapter 24: Banana Split

237 'whose biggest previous . . .': 'How Joe Bonanno Schemed to Kill – and Lost', *Life* magazine, Vol. 63, No. 9 (1 September 1967), 18.

237 'The Supreme Court': Henry A. Zeiger, *Sam the Plumber: One Year in the Life of a Cosa Nostra Boss* (New York: Signet, 1970), 73.

237 'Chief Justices': *ibid*, 47.

238 'I'm trying to build . . .': *ibid*, 20.

238 'a fat hoodlum with . . .': 'How Joe Bonanno Schemed to Kill – and Lost', *Life* magazine, Vol. 63, No. 9 (1 September 1967), 18.

239 'Contrary to the wishes . . .': Rosalie Bonanno, with Beverly Donofrio, *Mafia Marriage: My Story* (New York: William Morrow & Co., 1990), 123.

239 'This was seen as . . .': *ibid*.

240 '[Bill] is sick and . . .': Zeiger, *Sam the Plumber*, 148.

242 'a rundown neighborhood . . .': Ralph Salerno and John S. Tompkins, *The Crime Confederation: Cosa Nostra and Allied Operations in Organized Crime* (Garden City, NY: Doubleday & Co., 1969), 146.

242 'The Banana Split': Nicholas Gage, 'The Mafia at War, Part II', *New York* magazine (17 July 1972), 32.

242 'Joe Bananas': 'Joe Bananas' Rich Partner Dead in Trunk', *New York Daily News* (5 January 1960), 36.

242 'They had appeared . . .': Joseph Bonanno with Sergio Lalli, *A Man of Honor: The Autobiography of Joseph Bonanno* (New York: Simon & Schuster, 1983), 260–1.

243 'I beheld a canopy . . .': *ibid*, 261–2.

243 'an enchanted affair': *ibid*, 271.

243 'Winter was approaching . . .': *ibid*.

243 'fit and trim and tanned': Rosalie Bonanno, with Beverly Donofrio, *Mafia Marriage*, 123.

Chapter 25: Martin Luther King with a Pinky Ring

245 'large amounts of cash': '13 Seized in Queens in "Little Apalachin"', *New York Times* (23 September 1966), 24.

245 'They acted like . . .': *ibid.*

245 'consorting with known criminals': *ibid.*

245 'What's the matter . . .': Michael Dorman, *Payoff: The Role of Organized Crime in American Politics* (New York: David McKay Co., 1972), 108.

245 'Little Apalachin': '13 Seized in Queens in "Little Apalachin"', *New York Times* (23 September 1966), 1.

247 'If he's a gangster . . .': Ralph Salerno and John S. Tompkins, *The Crime Confederation: Cosa Nostra and Allied Operations in Organized Crime* (Garden City, NY: Doubleday & Co., 1969), 199.

247 'to avoid bloodshed': United States, Federal Bureau of Investigation, *The F.B.I. Transcripts on Exhibit in U.S.A. V De Cavalcante, Vastola, and Annunziata: U.S. District Court, District of New Jersey; Index Number: Criminal 111-68, Volume 2* (New York: Lemma Pub., 1970), 270.

248 'It's costing too much . . .': Peter Diapoulos and Steven Linakis, *The Sixth Family* (New York: E.P. Dutton & Co., 1976), 132.

248 'Leave him be': Paul S. Meskil, *The Luparelli Tapes* (Chicago, IL: Playboy Press, 1977), 181.

249 'They ain't satisfied . . .': Joseph Cantalupo and Thomas C. Renner, *Body Mike: An Unsparing Exposé by the Mafia Insider Who Turned on the Mob* (New York: Villard Books, 1990), 96.

249 'Next thing, they'll . . .': Craig R. Whitney, 'Italians Picket F.B.I. Office Here', *New York Times* (2 May 1970), 35.

249 'All Americans of Italian . . .': Dorman, *Payoff*, 303.

249 'We're gonna set up . . .': Cantalupo and Renner, *Body Mike*, 99.

250 'The Italians are damned . . .': Harlan Lebo, *The Godfather Legacy* (New York: Fireside, 1997), 41.

250 'What made Colombo's . . .': Albert A. Seedman and Peter Hellman, *Chief!* (New York: Arthur Fields Books, 1974), 354.

250 'Sicilian sleight of hand': *New York* magazine, as quoted in David E. Scheim, *Contract on America: The Mafia Murder of President John F. Kennedy* (New York: Shapolsky, 1988), 397.

251 'I was willing . . .': Meskil, *The Luparelli Tapes*, 153.

251 'This day belongs . . .': Cantalupo and Renner, *Body Mike*, 107.

251 'If this isn't harassment . . .': William Federici, 'Joe Colombo, 23 Indicted by L.I. Jury', *New York Daily News* (1 July 1970), 3.

251 'You know, Joe . . .': Don Capria and Anthony Colombo, *Colombo: The Unsolved Murder* (San Diego, CA: Unity Press, 2013), 173.

251 'Mama Mia, datsa . . .': 'Commercial Wins Award', *New York Times* (24 March 1971), 40.

252 'You've got to . . .': Lebo, *The Godfather Legacy*, 90.

252 'skeptical look at . . .': *ibid*, 91.

252 'Soon they were . . .': *ibid.*

252 'Hey, do we . . .': *ibid.*

252 'dago guinea wop . . .': *The Godfather*, Screenplay by Mario Puzo and Francis Ford Coppola, 1971.

252 'What would happen . . .': Lebo, *The Godfather Legacy*, 44.

252 'Without the Mafia's . . .': *ibid*, 97.

253 'Thus presenting the . . .': Dorman, *Payoff*, 307.

253 'incredibly naïve': Douglas Robinson, 'Mafia Believed Behind the Italian-American Protests Over "Harassment"', *New York Times* (19 July 1970), 57.

254 'Every time Joe . . .': Dorman, *Payoff*, 309.

254 'You can no longer . . .': Capria and Colombo, *Colombo*, 313.

254 'Carl, I cannot . . .': *ibid.*

255 'You should have . . .': *ibid.*

255 'Take Carl's advice . . .': Cantalupo and Renner, *Body Mike*, 113.

255 'Step away. Get . . .': *ibid.*

255 'No! This is *my* . . .': *ibid.*

Chapter 26: Disunity Day

256 'Larry's dead. If . . .': Paul S. Meskil, *The Luparelli Tapes* (Chicago, IL: Playboy Press, 1977), 181.

256 'He looked like a . . .': Peter Diapoulos and Steven Linakis, *The Sixth Family* (New York: E.P. Dutton & Co., 1976), 5.

256 'I couldn't get over . . .': *ibid.*

256 'If we have to . . .': *ibid*, 6.

256 'who the fuck . . .': *ibid*, 13.

256 'stick it up . . .': Meskil, *The Luparelli Tapes*, 182.

256 'Can you believe . . .': Don Capria and Anthony Colombo, *Colombo: The Unsolved Murder* (San Diego, CA: Unity Press, 2013), 287.

257 'We never should . . .': Meskil, *The Luparelli Tapes*, 182.

257 'We heard Joe Gallo . . .': *ibid*, 237.

257 'Stay home and I'll . . .': Capria and Colombo, *Colombo*, 311.

258 'Watch him': Albert A. Seedman and Peter Hellman, *Chief!* (New York: Arthur Fields Books, 1974), 362.

259 'had eyes': *ibid.*

259 'Wherever I looked . . .': Joseph Cantalupo and Thomas C. Renner, *Body Mike: An Unsparing Exposé by the Mafia Insider Who Turned on the Mob* (New York: Villard Books, 1990), 113.

260 'What the hell have . . .': Paul Meskil, *Don Carlo: Boss of Bosses* (New York: Popular Library, 1973), 207.

260 'one maniac acting alone': Seedman and Hellman, *Chief!*, 365.

260 'deranged psychopath, the . . .': Robert Daley, *Target Blue: An Insider's View of the N.Y.P.D.* (New York: Delacorte Press, 1971), 220.

260 'very dear and close . . .': *ibid.*

261 'This was a complete . . .': Nicholas Gage, editor, *Mafia, U.S.A.* (Chicago, IL: Playboy Press, 1972), 380.

261 'He's smooth, lots . . .': *ibid*, 381.
261 'sixth family': Meskil, *The Luparelli Tapes*, 183.
261 'This is going . . .': *ibid*.
261 'made': *ibid*.
261 'dig up some . . .': *ibid*.
262 'A black guy . . .': Diapoulos and Linakis, *The Sixth Family*, 45.
262 'Where?': *ibid*.
262 'What a bum rap . . .': *ibid*, 46.
262 'We still didn't know . . .': *ibid*.
262 'I don't think Joey . . .': Donald Goddard, *Joey: A Biography* (New York: Harper & Row, 1974), 353–4.
262 'When the shooting . . .': Gage, *Mafia, U.S.A.*, 380.
262 'The most interesting . . .': Capria and Colombo, *Colombo*, 339.
263 'Pisces Man': 'Jerome A. Johnson is Depicted by the People Who Knew Him', *New York Times* (30 June 1971), 27.
263 'interested in making . . .': Meskil, *Don Carlo*, 212.
263 'To get that close . . .': Seedman and Hellman, *Chief!*, 364.
264 'Because we have . . .': Capria and Colombo, *Colombo*, 352.
264 'No comment on . . .': *ibid*, 352–3.
265 'bunch of crap': Seedman and Hellman, *Chief!*, 377.
266 'must be creaming . . .': Diapoulos and Linakis, *The Sixth Family*, 46.
266 'No crime in . . .': Seedman and Hellman, *Chief!*, 360.
267 'Because we feel . . .': *ibid*, 386.
268 'the fairy godfather': Meskil, *Don Carlo*, 212.
268 'We are going . . .': Capria and Colombo, *Colombo*, 309.
268 'We're just not . . .': *ibid*.
268 'who gave me his . . .': *ibid*, 316.
268 'I prefer to leave . . .': *ibid*, 349.
269 'You can't touch . . .': Anthony Villano with Gerald Astor, *Brick Agent: Inside the Mafia for the FBI* (New York: Ballantine Books, 1978), 134.
269 'received a mysteriously . . .': *ibid*.
269 'It has been gossiped . . .': *ibid*.
269 'Why would the Police Department . . .': Daley, *Target Blue*, 515.
270 'One day, I . . .': *ibid*.
270 'inconceivable': *ibid*.
270 'one way or . . .': *ibid*.
270 'The feds weren't sure . . .': Cantalupo and Renner, *Body Mike*, 118.
270 'lying there like . . .': *ibid*, 119.
270 'You did good . . .': *ibid*, 120.

Chapter 27: Sticking His Head in the Noose
271 'I want that bastard's . . .': Frank DiMatteo and Michael Benson, *Mafia Hit Man: Carmine DiBiase, the Wiseguy Who Really Killed Joey Gallo* (New York: Citadel Press, 2021), 106.

271 'This guy is sticking . . .': Paul S. Meskil, *The Luparelli Tapes* (Chicago, IL: Playboy Press, 1977), 227.

272 'Seriously, folks, Joey . . .': DiMatteo and Benson, *Mafia Hit Man*, 26.

272 'I turned my head . . .': Meskil, *The Luparelli Tapes*, 242.

272 'How's the seafood . . .': Paul Meskil, 'Gallo a Swaggering Target But Hard to Nail', *New York Daily News* (26 November 1974), 21.

273 'Guess who's in . . .': *ibid.*

273 'Who?': Meskil, *The Luparelli Tapes*, 242.

273 'Joe Gallo's in . . .': *ibid.*

274 'We're going to . . .': *ibid.*

274 'What the fuck . . .': DiMatteo and Benson, *Mafia Hit Man*, 162.

274 'Die, motherfucker': *ibid*, 167.

274 'blasted away at . . .': Albert A. Seedman and Peter Hellman, *Chief!* (New York: Arthur Fields Books, 1974), 400.

274 'Jesus. In my . . .': Donald Goddard, *Joey* (New York: Harper & Row, 1974), 10.

274 'It's my brother . . .': Peter Diapoulos and Steven Linakis, *The Sixth Family* (New York: E.P. Dutton & Co., 1976), 128.

275 'Get him to . . .': *ibid.*

275 '[Gallo] made a mistake . . .': Eric Pace, 'Joe Gallo is Shot to Death in Little Italy Restaurant', *New York Times* (8 April 1972), 1.

275 'Sonny lay down . . .': Meskil, *The Luparelli Tapes*, 245.

275 'I didn't see nobody . . .': *ibid*, 246.

276 'How do you . . .': *ibid.*

276 'Joe Gallo, head of . . .': *ibid*, 247.

276 'If he's alive . . .': *ibid.*

276 'We all kissed . . .': Paul Meskil, 'Gallo a Swaggering Target But Hard to Nail', *New York Daily News* (26 November 1974), 21.

276 'These people may . . .': Meskil, *The Luparelli Tapes*, 253.

277 'Take me with you!': Diapoulos and Linakis, *The Sixth Family*, 143.

277 'The streets are going . . .': William Federici and Harry Stathos, 'Cops Hold Gallo Finger Man', *New York Daily News* (3 May 1972), 5.

278 'Where are you?': Meskil, *The Luparelli Tapes*, 277.

279 'What are you . . .': *ibid.*

279 'I don't know . . .': *ibid.*

279 'My name is Joe . . .': Paul Meskil, 'Luparelli, Fleeing Death, Heads for Coast and the FBI', *New York Daily News* (28 November 1974), 5.

279 'From what?': Meskil, *The Luparelli Tapes*, 279.

279 'What's a consigliere?': *ibid*, 280.

279 'I think I've . . .': Paul Meskil, 'A Mobster Talks: Luparelli, Fleeing Death, Heads for Coast and the FBI', *New York Daily News* (28 November 1974), 5.

280 'Keep quiet. Somebody's . . .': Meskil, *The Luparelli Tapes*, 174.

280 'He was lying facedown . . .': *ibid.*
280 'five or six': Paul Meskil, 'A Mobster Talks: They're Out to Kill Me', *New York Daily News* (24 November 1974), 82.
280 'I have the kids . . .': Seedman and Hellman, *Chief!*, 412.
280 'It was a good . . .': *ibid.*
281 'That's not what . . .': *ibid.*
281 'One night we'll . . .': Harvey Aronson, *The Killing of Joey Gallo* (New York: Signet/New American Library, 1974), 177.
281 'You're right . . .': *ibid.*
281 GALLO IS BURIED . . .: 'Gallo is Buried; His Legacy Lives On', *New York Daily News* (11 April 1972).

Chapter 28: The Return of Bobby and Hoffa
285 'I go to the Town . . .': Sandy Smith, 'The Fix', *Life* magazine, Vol. 63, No. 9 (1 September 1967), 22.
285 'a slimy, sleazy rat': *ABC News Close-Up: Hoffa*, ABC Network (30 November 1974).
285 'a million dollars . . .': Jack Anderson, 'Big Effort Made to Free Jimmy Hoffa', *Bismarck Tribune* (10 January 1973), 4.
285 'switch sides': *ibid.*
285 'clear that money . . .': Walter Sheridan, *The Fall and Rise of Jimmy Hoffa* (New York: Saturday Review Press, 1972), 389.
286 'threatened to get the . . .': Jack Anderson, 'Big Effort Made to Free Jimmy Hoffa', *Bismarck Tribune* (10 January 1973), 4.
286 'The last couple of . . .': Arthur A. Sloane, *Hoffa* (Cambridge, MA: The MIT Press, 1991), 329.
286 'gilded German nightclub': CBS News Special Report with Roger Mudd: Senator Robert F. Kennedy Presidential Campaign Announcement (16 March 1968): https://www.youtube.com/watch?v=c9Wc9ArvpBo
286 'in the face of almost . . .': *ibid.*
286 'When it was over . . .': John Ehrlichman, *Witness to Power: The Nixon Years* (New York: Simon & Schuster, 1982), 40.
287 'If I'm ever elected . . .': David W. Burke Oral History Interview with Larry J. Hackman, Robert F. Kennedy Oral History Program, John F. Kennedy Presidential Library (7 December 1971).
287 'I now fully . . .': Warren Hinckle and William W. Turner, *The Fish is Red: The Story of the Secret War Against Castro* (New York: Harper & Row, 1981), 198.
287 'I hope someone . . .': William C. Sullivan, with Bill Brown, *The Bureau: My Thirty Years in Hoover's FBI* (New York: W.W. Norton & Co., 1979), 56.
287 'less than one inch . . .': Michael Taylor, '40 Years After RFK's Death, Questions Linger', *San Francisco Chronicle* (3 June 2008): https://www.sfgate.com/crime/article/40-years-after-rfk-s-death-questions-linger-3281692.php

288 'Hoffa's shoeshine boy': Dan E. Moldea, *The Hoffa Wars: Teamsters, Rebels, Politicians, and the Mob* (New York: Paddington Press Ltd, 1978), 8.

288 'unbelievably stupid': Sloane, *Hoffa*, 317.

288 'got up on the . . .': Walter Sheridan Oral History Interview with Roberta W. Greene, Robert F. Kennedy Oral History Program, John F. Kennedy Presidential Library (1 May 1970).

288 'Why the hell . . .': Moldea, *The Hoffa Wars*, 161.

288 'The Detroit mob . . .': *ibid*, 181.

289 'When you get . . .': *ibid*, 185.

289 'my kind of . . .': A.H. Raskin, 'What the "Little Fellow" Says to the Teamsters is What Counts', *New York Times* (30 May 1970), 12.

290 'mecca for racketeers . . .': Sheridan, *The Fall and Rise of Jimmy Hoffa*, 528.

290 'Apalachin West': Peter Noyes, *Legacy of Doubt: Did the Mafia Kill JFK?* (Orlando, FL: P & G Publications, 2010), 34.

290 'often said no . . .': Jack Goldsmith, *In Hoffa's Shadow: A Stepfather, a Disappearance in Detroit, and My Search for the Truth* (New York: Farrar, Straus and Giroux, 2019), 90.

290 'Jimmy Hoffa is the . . .': 'Earlier Plan to Kidnap Hoffa Reported', *New York Times* (3 August 1976), 12.

290 'the puppet': Goldsmith, *In Hoffa's Shadow*, 155.

290 'When Fitzsimmons became . . .': *ibid*, 158.

290 'colored ones make . . .': 'Labor: The Engine Inside the Hood', *Time* magazine (9 September 1957).

290 'I don't need . . .': Paul Jacobs, 'The World of Jimmy Hoffa – II', *The Reporter*, Vol. 16, No. 2 (7 February 1957), 11.

291 'old school': Goldsmith, *In Hoffa's Shadow*, 87.

292 'No dice': James R. Hoffa, as told to Oscar Fraley, *Hoffa: The Real Story* (New York: Stein and Day, 1975), 22.

292 'I dealt with you . . .': Steven Brill, *The Teamsters* (New York: Simon & Schuster, 1978), 48.

292 'they were screaming . . .': *ibid*.

292 'If you don't get . . .': *ibid*.

293 'Grow and Grow . . .': *ibid*, 141.

293 'hell on earth . . .': Hoffa, as told to Oscar Fraley, *Hoffa*, 187.

294 'I don't want him out . . .: Goldsmith, *In Hoffa's Shadow*, 167.

294 'Fitz wants to . . .': Richard Nixon and Charles Colson, Conversation 016-053 (8 December 1971). White House Tapes: Sound Recordings of Meetings and Telephone Conversations of the Nixon Administration, 1971–1973, Richard Nixon Presidential Library and Museum: https://www.nixonlibrary.gov/white-house-tapes/016/conversation-016-053

294 'So we took . . .': Commission Hearings, Volume 2. National Commission for the Review of Federal and State Laws Relating to Wiretapping and Electronic Surveillance. (Washington, DC: 1976), 1604.

294 'He is a very . . .': Russell Sackett, 'Clemency Irks Justice Dept.', *Courier-News* (2 April 1973), A-4.

295 'I have no intention . . .': 'Union Office is Forbidden', *Detroit Free Press* (24 December 1971), 1.

295 'fat old men': Sloane, *Hoffa*, 362.

295 '[Hoffa] can't say . . .': Tom Nicholson with Tom Joyce, 'The Teamsters and the Mob', *Newsweek*, Vol. LXXXVI, No. 7 (18 August 1975), 17.

296 'Jimmy knew he . . .': Moldea, *The Hoffa Wars*, 71.

296 'As Christmas drew . . .': Sheridan, *The Fall and Rise of Jimmy Hoffa*, 468.

296 'I understand from . . .': Ralph Orr, 'Hoffa Hits Back at Fitz on TV', *Detroit Free Press* (14 June 1974), 2-B.

296 'a bum, a has-been': 'Teamsters Chief Backs President', *Wilmington News Journal* (3 March 1975), 8.

296 'I *charge* Frank Fitzsimmons . . .': Hoffa, as told to Oscar Fraley, *Hoffa*, 15.

296 'I think the years . . .': Goldsmith, *In Hoffa's Shadow*, 197.

Chapter 29: Where's Hoffa?

298 'Dad': Arthur A. Sloane, *Hoffa* (Cambridge, MA: The MIT Press, 1991), 59.

298 'my other son': James R. Hoffa, as told to Donald I. Rogers, *The Trials of Jimmy Hoffa: An Autobiography* (Chicago, IL: Henry Regnery, 1970), 114.

298 'Hoffa loved Chuck . . .': FBI interview with Jackie Presser, 7 August 1975, as quoted in Jack Goldsmith, *In Hoffa's Shadow: A Stepfather, a Disappearance in Detroit, and My Search for the Truth* (New York: Farrar, Straus and Giroux, 2019), 82.

298 'My mother had . . .': *ibid*, 47–8.

299 'an Italian immigrant who . . .': Kathy Warbelow, 'Mafia Czar Zerilli Dies at Age 79', *Detroit Free Press* (31 October 1977), 1.

299 'exterminating company': Lester Velie, *Desperate Bargain* (New York: Reader's Digest Press, 1977), 32.

299 'propensity for violence . . .': Unsigned, undated FBI Memorandum, in Wayne State University, Archives of Labor and Urban Affairs, Jimmy Hoffa FBI Files, as quoted in Goldsmith, *In Hoffa's Shadow*, 20–21.

299 'He's your fucking . . .': *ibid*, 171.

299 'Stay put, keep . . .': *ibid*, 196.

300 'You've got to . . .': *ibid*, 211.

300 'Hoffa listened but . . .': *ibid*.

300 'Uncle Tony . . . hated . . .': *ibid*, 62.

300 'My eye actually . . .': Dan E. Moldea, *The Hoffa Wars: Teamsters, Rebels, Politicians, and the Mob* (New York: Paddington Press Ltd, 1978), 304.

300 'center of an . . .': Susan Brown, 'Bomb Wrecks Parked Car; Top Teamster's Son Unhurt', *Detroit Free Press* (11 July 1975), 1.

300 'hustled off the . . .': *ibid.*

301 'threatened to pull . . .': John Camp and James Savage, 'Tony Pro: I'm Not Hiding, I'd Like to Help Jimmy', *Miami Herald* (6 August 1975), 1.

301 'Tell Hoffa I'm . . .': Sloane, *Hoffa*, 364.

301 'one of the foremost . . .': Denny Walsh, 'Leniency for a Hoodlum, Slush-Fund Income', *Life* magazine, Vol. 66, No. 17 (2 May 1969), 31.

301 'Because of the mob's . . .': Moldea, *The Hoffa Wars*, 364.

302 'I've been fortunate . . .': Sloane, *Hoffa*, 366.

302 'Hoffa seemed kind . . .': Moldea, *The Hoffa Wars*, 388.

303 'Giacalone didn't show . . .': James R. Hoffa, as told to Oscar Fraley, *Hoffa: The Real Story* (New York: Stein and Day, 1975), 237.

304 'You used two . . .': *ibid*, 240.

304 'T.J. – 2 p.m. – RED FOX': *ibid*, 238.

304 'conflicting stories': 'Hoffa Family Puzzled Over Adopted Son's Whereabouts', *Michigan Daily* (6 August 1975), 1.

304 'pathological liar': FBI Memorandum, Hoffex Conference, FBI Headquarters. Document is widely known as the Hoffex Memorandum (27–28 January 1976), 31: https://web.archive.org/web/20170301154608/http://www.uncharted.ca/images/stories/articles/labour/hoffex0616.pdf

304 'Life is very funny . . .': Goldsmith, *In Hoffa's Shadow*, 224.

305 'Jimmy was, or . . .': William K. Stevens, 'Hoffa's Foster Son Turns Up in Detroit and Is Questioned', *New York Times* (7 August 1975), 18.

305 'You're embarrassing me . . .': 'Investigations: Hoffa Search: Looks Bad Right Now', *Time* magazine, Vol. 106, No. 7 (18 August 1975), 17.

305 'can't string three . . .': Richard Nixon, Conversation 541-002 (21 July 1971). White House Tapes: Sound Recordings of Meetings and Telephone Conversations of the Nixon Administration, 1971–1973, Richard Nixon Presidential Library and Museum, as quoted in Goldsmith, *In Hoffa's Shadow*, 160.

305 'Among the participants . . .': Robert Lindsey, 'Nixon Plays Golf with Fitzsimmons at Resort Built with Teamster Loans', *New York Times* (10 October 1975), 11.

306 'detected Hoffa's scent . . .': 'FBI Checking Tip Hoffa Disappeared at Raleigh House', *Detroit Free Press* (3 October 1975), 12.

306 'the whole ball . . .': Goldsmith, *In Hoffa's Shadow*, 89.

306 'so much as . . .': Steven Brill, *The Teamsters* (New York: Simon & Schuster, 1978), 48.

306 'fight Tony Pro . . .': *ibid*, 134.

307 'accident prone': Maggie Bartel and Sidney Kline, 'For the Victim's Two Kids: Tony Pro Scholarships', *New York Daily News* (30 May 1963), 5.

307 'We just want . . .': Goldsmith, *In Hoffa's Shadow*, 241.

307 'The little guy . . .': *ibid*, 241.

307 'Whatever happened, I . . .': *ibid*, 212.

307 'The ground rule . . .': Brill, *The Teamsters*, 69.

308 'Where's my Jimmy?': Goldsmith, *In Hoffa's Shadow*, 292.

309 'a shredder-compactor-incinerator facility': Bernie Shellum and Lori Montgomery, 'Mob Has History in Area Trash Contracts', *Detroit Free Press* (6 July 1993), 3.

309 'at least ten . . .': Brill, *The Teamsters*, 56.

309 'for about ten years': Moldea, *The Hoffa Wars*, 90.

310 'These men are not . . .': 'Reputed Mafia Figures Appear Before Hoffa Grand Jury', *Ironwood Daily Globe* (23 October 1975), 7.

310 'Hoffa's body was . . .': 'Was Hoffa's Body Shredded? FBI Calls Theory Speculative', *Petoskey News-Review* (11 September 1978), 4.

310 'No search warrant . . .': *Ibid.*

311 'The best intelligence we . . .': Scott Burnstein interview with Keith Corbett, 'Jimmy Hoffa's Corpse Most Likely Cremated at Detroit Mob's Central Sanitation', Gangsterreport.com (28 July 2015).

Chapter 30: Convenient Corpses

313 'We accepted the . . .': Robert Blair Kaiser, 'The JFK Assassination: Why Congress Should Reopen the Investigation', *Rolling Stone* (24 April 1975), 27.

313 'His death only . . .': Eulogy Delivered by President Richard Nixon at Funeral Services for J. Edgar Hoover (4 May 1972): https://www.presidency.ucsb.edu/documents/eulogy-delivered-funeral-services-for-j-edgar-hoover

313 'That old cocksucker': Confidential source as quoted in Curt Gentry, *J. Edgar Hoover: The Man and the Secrets* (New York: W.W. Norton & Co., 1991), 28.

313 'He's got files . . .': Transcript of a Recording of a Meeting Between President Nixon and John Dean (28 February 1973): https://nsarchive2.gwu.edu/NSAEBB/NSAEBB156/865-14.pdf

313 'very sensitive and explosive . . .': William Sullivan, as quoted in David Wise, *The American Police State: The Government Against the People* (New York: Random House, 1976), 282.

314 'Filippo Sacco . . .': Thomas Maier, *Mafia Spies: The Inside Story of the CIA, Gangsters, JFK, and Castro* (New York: Skyhorse, 2019), 272. Original is a memo, not a quote, found in an FBI report, dated 12 May 1966.

315 'in an unusually . . .': Memorandum for Mr William Sullivan from W.R. Wannall, 'CIA's Intention to Send Hoodlums to Cuba to Assassinate Castro' (6 March 1967). FBI Vault.

315 'I don't turn . . .': Maier, *Mafia Spies*, 285. Actual quote is from Howard Osborn Luncheon Meeting with William K. Harvey, NARA Record Number: 1993.07.01.10:05:48:530800, p.3.

315 'It's the one . . .': Ovid Demaris, *The Last Mafioso: The Treacherous World of Jimmy Fratianno* (New York: Times Books, 1981), 196.

316 'I don't think Mr. Roselli . . .': John Kobler, 'The (Million-Dollar) Sting at the Friars Club', *New York* magazine (21 July 1975), 34.

316 'I am not going . . .': Maier, *Mafia Spies*, 289.
317 'was so convoluted . . .': Charles Rappleye and Ed Becker, *All American Mafioso: The Johnny Roselli Story* (New York: Doubleday, 1991), 307.
317 'Who'd want to . . .': Nicholas Gage, 'Mafia Said to Have Slain Rosselli Because of His Senate Testimony', *New York Times* (25 February 1977), 1.
317 'corrupt collusion of public . . .': Statement of Aaron M. Kohn, 11 June 1970. House Judiciary Committee Subcommittee No. 5, 11 June 1970, as quoted in Investigation of the Assassination of President John F. Kennedy. Appendix to Hearings Before the Select Committee on Assassinations of the U.S. House of Representatives, Ninety-Fifth Congress, Second Session. Volume IX: Staff and Consultant's Reports on Organized Crime, March 1979 (Washington, DC: USGPO, 1979), 63.
318 Louisiana Still Jumps . . .: David Chandler and *Life*'s Investigative Reporting Team, 'Louisiana Still Jumps for Mobster Marcello. The "Little Man" is Bigger than Ever', *Life* magazine (10 April 1970), 31.
318 'controlled the State . . .': *ibid.*
318 'extremely tenuous situation . . .': FBI report, 8 August 1963, as quoted in Antoinette Giancana and Thomas C. Renner, *Mafia Princess: Growing Up in Sam Giancana's Family* (New York: Avon, 1985), 286.
318 'may be replaced': *ibid.*
318 'If he lied . . .': William F. Roemer Jr, *The Enforcer: Spilotro: The Chicago Mob's Man Over Las Vegas* (New York: Donald I. Fine, 1994), 93.
318 'You have the . . .': 'Refusal to Talk Jails Giancana', *San Antonio Express* (2 June 1965), 11-C.
319 'having a ball . . .': Demaris, *The Last Mafioso*, 220.
319 'I'm enjoying this . . .': *ibid.*
319 'He was undoubtedly . . .': William F. Roemer Jr, *Roemer: Man Against the Mob* (New York: Donald I. Fine, 1989), 352.
319 'shadow of the . . .': *ibid.*
320 'a man my father . . .': Giancana and Renner, *Mafia Princess*, 324.
320 'I believe they . . .': Antoinette Giancana, John R. Hughes and Thomas H. Jobe, *JFK and Sam: The Connection Between the Giancana and Kennedy* Assassinations (Nashville, TN: Cumberland House, 2005), 69.
320 'He wasn't shocked': Rappleye and Becker, *All American Mafioso*, 310.
321 'It was clear to me . . .': *ibid*, 311.
321 'fully detailed description': *ibid*, 312.
321 'Senator, in my . . .': *ibid*, 313.
321 '200 million': Testimony of John Roselli, 23 April 1976, U.S. Senate Select Committee to Study Governmental Operations with Respect to Intelligence Activities, 6. NARA: 157-10014-10000: https://www.maryferrell.org/showDoc.html?docId=1445#relPageId=3&search=200%20million
321 'different views': *ibid.*
321 'piss poor': Demaris, *The Last Mafioso*, 266.

321 'Did Joe Batters . . .': *ibid*, 267.

322 'There's nothing you . . .': *ibid*, 266–7.

322 'If I'm ever missing . . .': Joe Daigle statement, as quoted in Rappleye and Becker, *All American Mafioso*, 321.

323 'I can guarantee you . . .': William Tucker, 'Killers Gave Roselli Drink, Shot Him in Belly', *Miami News* (10 August 1976), 4.

324 'I think the best . . .': *The Man Nobody Knew: In Search of My Father, CIA Spymaster William Colby*, Documentary. Produced by Act 4 Entertainment, 2011.

324 'Trafficante had the . . .': Rappleye and Becker, *All American Mafioso*, 8.

324 'Roselli may have . . .': Jack Anderson with Les Whitten, 'Washington Merry-Go-Round', *Anniston Star* (7 September 1976), 14.

325 'You see? He was . . .': Rosalie Bonanno, with Beverly Donofrio, *Mafia Marriage: My Story* (New York: William Morrow & Co., 1990), 136–7.

325 'Generally, his . . .': G. Robert Blakey and Richard N. Billings, *The Plot to Kill the President* (New York: Times Books, 1981), 244.

326 'appeared at the . . .': Jack Anderson and Les Whitten, 'Did Castro Hire Mob to Kill JFK', *The Press Democrat* (24 March 1977), 4.

326 'recital of evasive answers': Frank Ragano and Selwyn Raab, *Mob Lawyer* (New York: Charles Scribner's Sons, 1994), 326.

326 'going to be hit': George Crile III, 'The Mafia, the CIA, and Castro', *Washington Post* (16 May 1976).

326 'a lot of votes . . .': Testimony of Jose Aleman, 27 September 1978. Investigation of the Assassination of President John F. Kennedy. Hearings Before the Select Committee on Assassinations of the U.S. House of Representatives, Ninety-Fifth Congress, Second Session. Volume V (Washington, DC: USGPO, 1979), 306.

327 'penniless, depressed and convinced . . .': Helga Silva, 'Autopsy: Aleman Killed Self', *Miami Herald* (2 August 1983), 16.

327 'believed he and his . . .': *ibid*.

327 'organized crime had . . .': G. Robert Blakey and Richard N. Billings, *Fatal Hour: The Assassination of President Kennedy by Organized Crime* (New York: Berkley Books, 1992), 179.

327 'murder of Oswald . . .': *ibid*, 339.

327 'We also concluded . . .': *ibid*, 312.

327 'rogue elements of the . . .': John H. Davis, *The Kennedy Contract: The Mafia Plot to Assassinate the President* (New York: Harper Paperbacks, 1993), 191–2.

327 'The Dallas Police Department . . .': Jesse E. Curry, *Retired Dallas Police Chief Jesse Curry Reveals His Personal JFK Assassination File* (Dallas, TX: American Poster & Printing Co., 1969), 21.

327 'the central figure . . .': *ibid*, 10.

327 'Mr. Lawson was . . .': *ibid*, 24.

327 'directed the security . . .': *ibid*, 15.

327 '[Winston] Lawson told . . .': Jim Bishop, *The Day Kennedy was Shot* (New York: Funk & Wagnalls, 1968), 69.

328 'laid out the planned . . .': *ibid*, 11.

328 'Mr. Lawson felt that . . .': *ibid*, 16.

328 'Security was comparatively . . .': *ibid*, 21.

328 'wanted back in . . .': Winston Lawson Warren Commission Testimony, 23 April 1964. Investigation of the Assassination of President John F. Kennedy. Hearings Before the President's Commission on the Assassination of President Kennedy. Volume V (Washington, DC: USGPO, 1964), 326.

328 'Our own advance man . . .': Evelyn Lincoln, *Kennedy and Johnson* (New York: Holt, Rinehart & Winston, 1968), 199.

329 'That's right': Gerald Blaine with Lisa McCubbin, *The Kennedy Detail: JFK's Secret Service Agents Break Their Silence* (New York: Gallery Books, 2010), 162.

329 'Tell the agents . . . ': *ibid*, 163.

329 'I thought Behn . . . ': *ibid*.

329 'I'm the only agent . . .': Greg McQuade, 'Secret Service Agent Still Haunted by JFK's Assassination' (20 November 2013): https://www.wtvr.com/2013/11/20/jfk-winston-lawson-secret-service-kennedy-assassination

329 'fists doubled when . . .': Kenneth P. O'Donnell and David F. Powers, with Joe McCarthy, *"Johnny, We Hardly Knew Ye": Memories of John Fitzgerald Kennedy* (Boston, MA: Little, Brown & Co., 1972), 36.

329 'as far as I'm . . .': *ibid*.

329 'We shoved Dr. . . .': *ibid*.

329 'I was sure that . . .': *ibid*, 37.

330 'A guard was set up . . .': Hugh Sidey, 'Nation: The Assassination', *Time* magazine (29 November 1963), 24.

330 'outside political pressures . . .': Dallas police officer Don Archer, in Part Five: 'The Witness', *The Men Who Killed Kennedy*. Documentary, Nigel Turner Productions/History Channel (1991). Time stamp: 3:54:14.

Epilogue

331 'Joe wouldn't even . . .': Vincent Teresa with Thomas C. Renner, *My Life in the Mafia* (Garden City, NY: Doubleday & Co., 1973), 320.

331 'was convinced that . . .': *ibid*, 321.

331 'talk about making money': *ibid*.

331 'How can I talk . . .': *ibid*.

331 'Valachi was bitter . . .': *ibid*, 322.

332 'never been convicted . . .': 'BRILAB Jury Convicts Carlos Marcello and Former Louisiana Official', *New York Times* (4 August 1981), 13.

332 'cut through the . . .': Bill Rose, 'Crime Empire's "Big Little Man"', *Des Moines Tribune* (11 July 1981), 11.

332 'one of the most . . .': *ibid*.

332 'If the tapes are . . .': *ibid.*

332 'For years, political . . .': *ibid.*

332 'good character and charity': *ibid.*

333 'laborious process of . . .': 'Jury Selection in Racketeering Trial Enters Third Week', *New York Times* (13 April 1981), B9.

333 'the mafia': *ibid.*

333 'the godfather': *ibid.*

333 'he doesn't look . . .': Bill Crider, 'Tomato Salesman Carlos Marcello Becomes Investor', *Town Talk* (25 June 1980), A-12.

333 'short, pudgy': Organized Crime Control. Hearings Before Subcommittee No. 5 of the Committee on the Judiciary House of Representatives Ninety-First Congress, Second Session, Serial No. 27 (Washington, DC: USGPO, 1970), 419.

333 'corrupting influence on . . .': 'Alleged Underworld Leader is Assailed at Bribery Trial', *New York Times* (22 April 1981), 17.

333 On December 15, 1985 . . .: FBI Confidential Source Report (6 March 1986): https://anthonysummersandrobbynswan.wordpress.com/wp-content/uploads/2013/11/confidential-source-report.pdf

334 'I think Carlos . . .': Frank Ragano and Selwyn Raab, *Mob Lawyer* (New York: Charles Scribner's Sons, 1994), 348.

334 'creative minority': Arnold J. Toynbee, *A Study of History.* Abridgement of Volumes I–VI by D.C. Somervell (New York: Oxford University Press, 1987), 50.

334 'When the wild beasts . . .': Arthur Helps, *The Spanish Conquest of America: And Its Relation to the History of Slavery and to the Government of Colonies*, Fourth Volume (London: Parker Son and Bourn, 1861), 5.

BIBLIOGRAPHY

Books

Albarelli, H.P. Jr. *A Terrible Mistake: The Murder of Frank Olson and the CIA's Cold War Experiments.* Walterville, OR: Trine Day, 2009.

American Journey: The Times of Robert Kennedy. Interviews by Jean Stein. Edited by George Plimpton. New York: Harcourt Brace Jovanovich, 1970.

Anson, Robert Sam. *"They've Killed the President!": The Search for the Murderers of John F. Kennedy.* New York: Bantam Books, 1975.

Aronson, Harvey. *The Killing of Joey Gallo.* New York: A Signet Book/ New American Library, 1974.

Asprey, Robert B. *Frederick the Great: The Magnificent Enigma.* New York: History Book Club, 1999.

Babson, Steve. *Working Detroit: The Making of a Union Town.* New York: Adama Books, 1984.

Bacon, James. *Made in Hollywood.* Chicago, IL: Contemporary Books, 1977.

Baker, Bobby, and Larry L. King. *Wheeling and Dealing: Confessions of a Capitol Hill Operator.* New York: W.W. Norton & Co., 1978.

Baker, Judyth Vary. *David Ferrie: Mafia Pilot, Participant in Anti-Castro Bioweapon Plot, Friend of Lee Harvey Oswald and the Key to the JFK Assassination.* Walterville, OR: Trine Day, 2014.

Barzini, Luigi. *The Italians.* New York: Atheneum, 1985.

Baum, Frank L. *The Wonderful Wizard of Oz.* Chicago/New York: George M. Hill Co., 1900.

Belli, Melvin, with Maurice C. Carroll. *Dallas Justice: The Real Story of Jack Ruby and His Trial.* New York: David McKay, 1964.

Beschloss, Michael R. *The Crisis Years: Kennedy and Khrushchev 1960–1963.* New York: Edward Burlingame Books, 1991.

Bishop, Jim. *The Day Kennedy was Shot.* New York: Funk & Wagnalls, 1968.

Bissell, Richard M. Jr, with Jonathan E. Lewis and Frances T. Pudlo. *Reflections of a Cold Warrior: From Yalta to the Bay of Pigs.* New Haven, CT & London: Yale University Press, 1996.

Blaine, Gerald, with Lisa McCubbin. *The Kennedy Detail: JFK's Secret Service Agents Break Their Silence.* New York: Gallery Books, 2010.

Blakey, G. Robert, and Richard N. Billings. *Fatal Hour: The Assassination of President Kennedy by Organized Crime*. New York: Berkley Books, 1992.

———. *The Plot to Kill the President*. New York: Times Books, 1981.

Bonanno, Bill, and Gary B. Abromovitz. *The Last Testament of Bill Bonanno: The Final Secrets of a Life in the Mafia*. New York: Harper, 2011.

Bonanno, Joseph, with Sergio Lalli. *A Man of Honor: The Autobiography of Joseph Bonanno*. New York: Simon & Schuster, 1983.

Bonanno, Rosalie, with Beverly Donofrio. *Mafia Marriage: My Story*. New York: William Morrow & Co., 1990.

Bradlee, Benjamin C. *Conversations with Kennedy*. New York: W.W. Norton & Co., 1975.

Brandt, Charles. *I Heard You Paint Houses: Frank "The Irishman" Sheeran and the Inside Story of the Mafia, the Teamsters, and the Last Ride of Jimmy Hoffa*. Hanover, NH: Steerforth Press, 2005.

Breslin, Jimmy. *The Good Rat: A True Story*. New York: Harper Perennial, 2009.

Brill, Steven. *The Teamsters*. New York: Simon & Schuster, 1978.

Brinkley, Douglas. *Cronkite*. New York: Harper, 2012.

Bugliosi, Vincent. *Reclaiming History: The Assassination of President John F. Kennedy* (New York: W.W. Norton & Co., 2007.

Burckhardt, Jacob. *The Civilisation of the Renaissance in Italy: An Essay*. Translated by S.G.C. Middlemore. London: Folio Society, 2004.

Cain, Michael J. *The Tangled Web: The Life and Death of Richard Cain*. New York: Skyhorse, 2007.

Cantalupo, Joseph, and Thomas C. Renner. *Body Mike: An Unsparing Exposé by the Mafia Insider Who Turned on the Mob*. New York: Villard Books, 1990.

Capria, Don, and Anthony Colombo. *Colombo: The Unsolved Murder*. San Diego, CA: Unity Press, 2013.

Caro, Robert A. *The Years of Lyndon Johnson: Master of the Senate*. New York: Aldred A. Knopf, 2002.

———. *The Years of Lyndon Johnson: Means of Ascent*. New York: Vintage Books, 1990.

———. *The Years of Lyndon Johnson: The Passage of Power*. New York: Alfred A. Knopf, 2012.

———. *The Years of Lyndon Johnson: The Path to Power*. New York: Alfred A. Knopf, 1982.

Cassini, Igor, with Jeanne Molli. *I'd Do It All Over Again*. New York: G.P. Putnam's Sons, 1977.

Churchill, Winston S. *The Second World War. Volume III: The Grand Alliance*. Boston, MA: Houghton Mifflin Co., 1950.

Clarke, Thurston. *JFK's Last Hundred Days*. New York: Penguin Press, 2013.
Clay, James. *Hoffa! Ten Angels Swearing: An Authorized Biography*. Beaverdam, VA: Beaverdam Books, 1965.
Clifford, Clark, with Richard Holbrooke. *Counsel to the President: A Memoir*. New York: Random House, 1991.
Clinch, Nancy Gager. *The Kennedy Neurosis: A Psychological Portrait of an American Dynasty*. New York: Grosset & Dunlap, 1973.
Cohen, Adam, and Elizabeth Taylor. *American Pharaoh: Mayor Richard J. Daley: His Battle for Chicago and the Nation*. Boston, MA: Little, Brown & Co., 2000.
Cohen, Mickey. *In My Own Words: The Underworld Autobiography of Michael Mickey Cohen as told to John Peer Nugent*. Englewood Cliffs, NJ: Prentice-Hall, 1975.
Collier, Peter, and David Horowitz. *The Kennedys: An American Drama*. New York: Summit Books, 1984.
Collom, Mark, and Glen Sample, *The Men on the Sixth Floor*. Garden Grove, CA: Sample Graphics, 1997.
Connally, Nellie, and Mickey Herskowitz. *From Love Field: Our Final Hours with President John F. Kennedy*. New York: Rugged Land, 2003.
Curry, Jesse E. *Retired Dallas Police Chief Jesse Curry Reveals His Personal JFK Assassination File*. Limited Collectors Edition. Dallas, TX: American Poster, 1969.
Daley, Robert. *Target Blue: An Insider's View of the N.Y.P.D*. New York: Delacorte Press, 1971.
Davis, John H. *The Kennedy Contract: The Mafia Plot to Assassinate the President*. New York: Harper Paperbacks, 1993.
———. *The Kennedys: Dynasty and Disaster 1848–1983*. New York: McGraw-Hill, 1984.
———. *Mafia Kingfish: Carlos Marcello and the Assassination of John F. Kennedy*. New York: McGraw-Hill, 1989.
DeLoach, Cartha D. 'Deke'. *Hoover's FBI: The Inside Story by Hoover's Trusted Lieutenant*. Washington, DC: Regnery Pub. Co., 1995.
Demaris, Ovid. *The Director: An Oral Biography of J. Edgar Hoover*. New York: Harper's Magazine Press, 1975.
———. *The Last Mafioso: The Treacherous World of Jimmy Fratianno*. New York: Times Books, 1981.
Diapoulos, Peter, and Steven Linakis. *The Sixth Family*. New York: E.P. Dutton, 1976.
DiMatteo, Frank. *The President Street Boys: Growing Up Mafia*. New York: Kensington Books, 2016.
DiMatteo, Frank, and Michael Benson. *Carmine the Snake: Carmine Persico and His Murderous Mafia Family*. New York: Citadel Press, 2018.

————. *Mafia Hit Man: Carmine DiBiase, the Wiseguy Who Really Killed Joey Gallo*. New York: Citadel Press, 2021.

Donovan, Robert J. *PT 109: John F. Kennedy in World War II*. New York: McGraw-Hill, 1961.

Dorman, Michael. *Payoff: The Role of Organized Crime in American Politics*. New York: David McKay Co., 1972.

Dugger, Ronnie. *The Politician: The Life and Times of Lyndon Johnson: The Drive for Power, from the Frontier to Master of the Senate*. New York: W.W. Norton & Co., 1982.

Dulles, Allen. *The Craft of Intelligence*. New York: Signet/New American Library, 1965.

Ehrlichman, John. *Witness to Power: The Nixon Years*. New York: Simon & Schuster, 1982.

Ergang, Robert. *The Potsdam Fuhrer: Frederick William I, Father of Prussian Militarism*. New York: Columbia University Press, 1941.

Escalante, Fabián. *The Cuba Project: CIA Covert Operations, 1959–62*. Translated by Maxine Shaw. Australia: Ocean Press, 2004.

Evans, Peter, and Ava Gardner. *Ava Gardner: The Secret Conversations*. London: Simon & Schuster, 2013.

Exner, Judith, as told to Ovid Demaris. *My Story*. New York: Grove Press, 1977.

Farrell, Joseph P. *LBJ and the Conspiracy to Kill Kennedy: A Coalescence of Interests*. Kempton, IL: Adventures Unlimited Press, 2011.

Fensterwald, Bernard Jr. *Assassination of JFK: By Coincidence or Conspiracy?* Produced by the Committee to Investigate Assassinations, compiled by Michael Ewing. New York: Zebra, 1977.

Fetzer, James H. (ed.). *Murder in Dealey Plaza: What We Know Now that We Didn't Know Then About the Death of JFK*. Chicago, IL: Catfeet Press, 2000.

Folsom, Tom. *The Mad Ones: Crazy Joe Gallo and the Revolution at the Edge of the Underworld*. New York: Weinstein Books, 2010.

Franco, Joseph, with Richard Hammer. *Hoffa's Man: The Rise and Fall of Jimmy Hoffa as Witnessed by His Strongest Arm*. New York: Prentice Hall, 1987.

Gage, Nicholas (ed.). *Mafia, U.S.A.* Chicago, IL: Playboy Press, 1972.

Garrison, Jim. *A Heritage of Stone*. New York: G.P. Putnam's Sons, 1970.

————. *On the Trail of the Assassins*. New York: Warner Books, 1991.

Gentry, Curt. *J. Edgar Hoover: The Man and the Secrets*. New York: W.W. Norton & Co., 1991.

Giancana, Antoinette, John R. Hughes and Thomas H. Jobe. *JFK and Sam: The Connection Between the Giancana and Kennedy Assassinations*. Nashville, TN: Cumberland House, 2005.

Giancana, Antoinette, and Thomas C. Renner. *Mafia Princess: Growing Up in Sam Giancana's Family.* New York: Avon Books, 1985.

Giancana, Sam, and Scott M. Burnstein. *Family Affair: Greed, Treachery, and Betrayal in the Chicago Mafia.* New York: Berkley Books, 2010.

Giancana, Sam, and Chuck Giancana. *Double Cross: The Explosive, Inside Story of the Mobster Who Controlled America.* New York: Warner Books, 1992.

Gibbons, S.R. *The Cold War.* Harlow, Essex, UK: Longman, 1986.

Goddard, Donald. *Joey: A Biography.* New York: Harper & Row, 1974.

Goldfarb, Ronald. *Perfect Villains, Imperfect Heroes: Robert F. Kennedy's War Against Organized Crime.* New York: Random House, 1995.

Goldsmith, Jack. *In Hoffa's Shadow: A Stepfather, a Disappearance in Detroit, and My Search for the Truth.* New York: Farrar, Straus and Giroux, 2019.

Groden, Robert J. *The Killing of a President: The Complete Photographic Record of the JFK Assassination, the Conspiracy, and the Cover-Up.* New York: Viking Studio Books, 1993.

———. *The Search for Lee Harvey Oswald: A Comprehensive Photographic Record.* New York: Penguin Studio, 1995.

Grose, Peter. *Gentleman Spy: The Life of Allen Dulles.* Boston, MA: Houghton Mifflin Company, 1994.

Guthman, Edwin. *We Band of Brothers.* New York: Harper & Row, 1971.

Haley, J. Evetts. *A Texan Looks at Lyndon: A Study in Illegitimate Power.* Canyon, TX: Palo Duro Press, 1964.

Hamilton, Edith. *The Greek Way.* New York: The Modern Library, 1942.

Hellerman, Michael, with Thomas C. Renner. *Wall Street Swindler: An Insider's Story of Mob Operations in the Stock Market.* New York: Doubleday, 1977.

Hersh, Burton. *Bobby and J. Edgar: The Historic Face-Off Between the Kennedys and J. Edgar Hoover that Transformed America.* New York: Carroll & Graf, 2007.

Hersh, Seymour M. *The Dark Side of Camelot.* Boston, MA: Little, Brown & Co., 1997.

Heymann, C. David. *RFK: A Candid Biography.* London: William Heinemann, 1998.

———. *A Woman Named Jackie.* New York: A Lyle Stuart Book, 1989.

Hibbert, Christopher. *The House of Medici: Its Rise and Fall.* New York: Morrow Quill Paperbacks, 1980.

Hinckle, Warren, and William Turner. *Deadly Secrets: The CIA–MAFIA*

War Against Castro and the Assassination of J.F.K. New York: Thunder's Mouth Press, 1992.

———. *The Fish is Red: The Story of the Secret War Against Castro.* New York: Harper & Row, 1981.

Hoffa, James R., as told to Oscar Fraley. *Hoffa: The Real Story.* New York: Stein and Day, 1975.

Hoffa, James R., as told to Donald I. Rogers. *The Trials of Jimmy Hoffa: An Autobiography.* Chicago, IL: Henry Regnery, 1970.

Horne, Alistair. *Harold Macmillan, Volume II: 1957–1986.* New York: Viking, 1989.

Ickes, Harold L. *The Secret Diary of Harold L. Ickes. Volume II: The Inside Struggle, 1936–1939.* New York: Simon & Schuster, 1954.

Janney, Peter. *Mary's Mosaic: The CIA Conspiracy to Murder John F. Kennedy, Mary Pinchot Meyer, and Their Vision for World Peace.* New York: Skyhorse, 2013.

Joey, with David Fisher. *Killer: Autobiography of a Hit Man for the Mafia.* Chicago, IL: Playboy Press, 1973.

Johnson, Haynes, et al. *The Bay of Pigs: The Leaders' Story of Brigade 2506.* New York: W.W. Norton & Co., 1964.

Johnson, Lyndon B. *Taking Charge: The Johnson White House Tapes, 1963–1964.* Edited and with Commentary by Michael R. Beschloss. New York: Simon & Schuster, 1997.

Johnson, Sam Houston. *My Brother Lyndon.* Edited by Enrique Hank Lopez. New York: Cowles Book Co., 1970.

Kantor, Seth. *The Ruby Cover-Up.* New York: Zebra Books, 1992.

———. *Who was Jack Ruby?* New York: Everest House, 1978.

Katzenbach, Nicholas deB. *Some of It Was Fun: Working with RFK and LBJ.* New York: W.W. Norton & Co., 2008.

Kearns, Doris. *Lyndon Johnson and the American Dream.* New York: New American Library, 1977.

Kelley, Kitty. *His Way: The Unauthorized Biography of Frank Sinatra.* New York: Bantam Books, 1986.

Kennan, George F. *Memoirs 1925–1950.* Boston, MA: Little, Brown & Company, 1967.

Kennedy, Joseph P. *Hostage to Fortune: The Letters of Joseph P. Kennedy.* Edited by Amanda Smith. New York: Viking, 2001.

Kennedy, Robert F. *The Enemy Within.* New York: Harper & Brothers, 1960.

———. *In His Own Words: The Unpublished Recollections of the Kennedy Years.* Edited by Edwin O. Guthman and Jeffrey Shulman. New York: Bantam Books, 1988.

———. *The Pursuit of Justice.* Edited by Theodore J. Lowi. New York: Harper & Row, 1964.

Kennedy, Rose Fitzgerald. *Times to Remember*. New York: Doubleday & Co., 1974.

Kessler, Ronald. *Inside the CIA: Revealing the Secrets of the World's Most Powerful Spy Agency*. New York: Pocket Books, 1994.

——. *The Sins of the Father: Joseph P. Kennedy and the Dynasty He Founded*. New York: Warner Books, 1996.

Khrushchev, Nikita. *The Glasnost Tapes*. Translated and edited by Jerrold L. Schecter with Vyacheslav V. Luchkov. Boston, MA: Little, Brown & Co., 1990.

——. *Khrushchev Remembers*. Translated and edited by Strobe Talbott. Boston, MA: Little, Brown & Co., 1970.

Kinzer, Stephen. *Overthrow: America's Century of Regime Change from Hawaii to Iraq*. New York: Times Books, 2006.

——. *Poisoner in Chief: Sidney Gottlieb and the CIA Search for Mind Control*. New York: Henry Holt & Co., 2019.

Klagsbrun, Francine, and David C. Whitney (eds.). *Assassination: Robert F. Kennedy, 1925–1968*. By the editors of United Press International and Cowles. New York: Cowles, 1968.

Knowles, Elizabeth (ed.). *The Oxford Dictionary of Quotations*. Oxford: Oxford University Press, 1999.

Lamothe, Lee, and Adrian Humphreys. *The Sixth Family: The Collapse of the New York Mafia and the Rise of Vito Rizzuto*. Ontario, Canada: John Wiley & Sons, 2006.

Lane, Mark. *Plausible Denial: Was the CIA Involved in the Assassination of JFK?* NY: Thunder's Mouth Press, 1991.

Lane, Sheldon (ed.). *For Bond Lovers Only*. New York: Dell, 1965.

Langton, Jerry. *Cold War: How Organized Crime Works in Canada and Why It's About to Get More Violent*. Toronto, Canada: HarperCollins Ltd, 2016.

Lasky, Victor. *It Didn't Start with Watergate*. New York: The Dial Press, 1977.

Lasky, Victor. *J.F.K.: The Man and the Myth*. New York: Macmillan, 1963.

——. *Robert F. Kennedy: The Myth and the Man*. New York: Trident Press, 1968.

Lebo, Harlan. *The Godfather Legacy*. New York: Fireside, 1997.

Leonetti, Philip, with Scott Burnstein and Christopher Graziano. *Mafia Prince: Inside America's Most Violent Crime Family and the Bloody Fall of La Costa Nostra*. Philadelphia, PA: Running Press, 2012.

Lester, David, and Irene David. *Bobby Kennedy: The Making of a Folk Hero*. New York: Dodd, Mead & Co., 1986.

Lewy, Guenter. *The Catholic Church and Nazi Germany*. Boulder, CO: Da Capo Press, 2000.

Lincoln, Evelyn. *Kennedy and Johnson*. New York: Holt, Rinehart & Winston, 1968.

Long, Breckinridge. *The War Diary of Breckinridge Long: Selections from the Years 1939–1944*. Selected and edited by Fred L. Israel. Lincoln, NE: University of Nebraska Press, 1966.

Longrigg, Clare. *No Questions Asked: The Secret Life of Women in the Mob*. New York: Miramax Books/Hyperion, 2004.

Longworth, Alice Roosevelt. *Crowded Hours: Reminiscences of Alice Roosevelt Longworth*. NY: Charles Scribner's Sons, 1933.

Lycett, Andrew. *Ian Fleming*. London: Weidenfeld & Nicolson, 1995.

Machiavelli, Niccolo. *The Prince and the Discourses*. With an Introduction by Max Lerner. New York, Modern Library, 1950.

Maheu, Robert, and Richard Hack. *Next to Hughes: Behind the Power and Tragic Downfall of Howard Hughes by His Closest Advisor*. New York: HarperCollins, 1992.

Mahoney, Richard D. *Sons & Brothers: The Days of Jack and Bobby Kennedy*. New York: Arcade Pub., 1999.

Maier, Thomas. *Mafia Spies: The Inside Story of the CIA, Gangsters, JFK, and Castro*. New York: Skyhorse, 2019.

Manchester, William. *The Death of a President: November 20–November 25, 1963*. New York: Harper & Row, 1967.

Mankiewicz, Frank, and Kirby Jones. *With Fidel: A Portrait of Castro and Cuba*. New York: Ballantine Books, 1976.

Marks, John. *The Search for the "Manchurian Candidate": The CIA and Mind Control*. New York: Times Books, 1979.

Marrs, Jim. *Crossfire: The Plot that Killed Kennedy*. New York: Carroll & Graf, 2002.

Martin, David C. *Wilderness of Mirrors*. New York: Harper & Row, 1980.

Martin, Ralph G. *Seeds of Destruction: Joe Kennedy and His Sons*. New York: G.P. Putnam's Sons, 1995.

Martin, Raymond V. *Revolt in the Mafia: How the Gallo Gang Split the New York Underworld*. New York: Duell, Sloan and Pearce, 1963.

McClellan, Barr. *Blood, Money & Power: How L.B.J. Killed J.F.K.* New York: Hannover House, 2003.

McNicoll, Susan. *Sam Giancana: The Rise and Fall of a Chicago Mobster*. London: Arcturus, 2016.

Meskil, Paul. *Don Carlo: Boss of Bosses*. New York: Popular Library, 1973.

———. *The Luparelli Tapes*. Chicago, IL: Playboy Press, 1977.

Meyer, Karl E., and Tad Szulc. *The Cuban Invasion: The Chronicle of a Disaster*. New York: Frederick A. Praeger, 1962.

Miller, Merle. *Lyndon: An Oral Biography*. New York: G.P. Putnam's Sons, 1980.

Moldea, Dan E. *The Hoffa Wars: Teamsters, Rebels, Politicians, and the Mob*. New York: Paddington Press Ltd, 1978.

Molière, Jean Baptiste Poquelin de. *Molière: The Complete Richard Wilbur Translations*, Volume 2. New York: Library of America, 2021.

Mollenhoff, Clark R. *Despoilers of Democracy: The Real Story of What Washington Propagandists, Arrogant Bureaucrats, Mismanagers, Influence Peddlers, and Outright Corrupters are Doing to Our Federal Government*. Garden City, NY: Doubleday & Co., 1965.

———. *Strike Force: Organized Crime and the Government*. Englewood Cliffs, NJ: Prentice-Hall, 1972.

———. *Tentacles of Power: The Story of Jimmy Hoffa*. Cleveland & New York: The World Pub. Co., 1965.

Morin, Relman. *Assassination: The Death of President John F. Kennedy*. New York: Signet Books, 1968.

Morrow, Robert D. *First Hand Knowledge: How I Participated in the CIA-Mafia Murder of President Kennedy*. New York: S.P.I. Books/Shapolsky Publishers, 1992.

Mosley, Leonard. *Dulles: A Biography of Eleanor, Allen, and John Foster Dulles and Their Family Network*. New York: Dial Press/James Wade, 1978.

Moyar, Mark. *Oppose Any Foe: The Rise of America's Special Operations Forces*. New York: Basic Books, 2017.

Munoz, Heraldo. *The Dictator's Shadow: Life Under Augusto Pinochet*. New York: Basic Books, 2008.

Nasaw, David. *The Patriarch: The Remarkable Life and Turbulent Times of Joseph P. Kennedy*. New York: Penguin Press, 2012.

Navasky, Victor S. *Kennedy Justice*. New York: Atheneum, 1971.

Neff, James. *Mobbed Up: Jackie Presser's High-Wire Life in the Teamsters, the Mafia, and the FBI*. New York: The Atlantic Monthly Press, 1989.

———. *Vendetta: Bobby Kennedy Versus Jimmy Hoffa*. New York: Little, Brown & Co., 2015.

Newman, John. *Oswald and the CIA*. New York: Carroll & Graf Publishers, 1995.

Nixon, Richard. *The Memoirs of Richard Nixon*. New York: Grosset & Dunlap, 1978.

North, Mark. *Betrayal in Dallas: LBJ, the Pearl Street Mafia, and the Murder of President Kennedy*. New York: A Herman Graf Book, 2011.

Norwich, John Julius. *Absolute Monarchs: A History of the Papacy*. New York: Random House Trade Paperbacks, 2012.

———. *Byzantium: The Decline and Fall*. New York: Alfred A. Knopf, 1996.

Noyes, Peter. *Legacy of Doubt: Did the Mafia Kill JFK?*. Orlando, FL: P & G Publications, 2010.

O'Donnell, Kenneth P., and David F. Powers, with Joe McCarthy. *"Johnny, We Hardly Knew Ye": Memories of John Fitzgerald Kennedy*. Boston, MA: Little, Brown & Co., 1972.

O'Neill, Tip, with William Novak. *Man of the House: The Life and Political Memoirs of Speaker Tip O'Neill*. New York: Random House, 1987.

Opotowsky, Stan. *The Kennedy Government*. London: George G. Harrap & Co., 1961.

O'Sullivan, Shane. *Who Killed Bobby? The Unsolved Murder of Robert F. Kennedy*. New York: Union Square Press, 2008.

Oswald, Robert L., with Myrick and Barbara Land. *Lee: A Portrait of Lee Harvey Oswald by His Brother*. New York: Coward-McCann, 1967.

Piper, David (ed.). *James R. Hoffa: Messages to the Membership*. Commemorative Edition Honoring the Contributions of Teamster Retirees. Peake Delancey Publishing, 2009.

Ragano, Frank, and Selwyn Raab. *Mob Lawyer*. New York: Charles Scribner's Sons, 1994.

Ranke, Leopold. *The Popes of Rome: Their Ecclesiastical and Political History During the Sixteenth and Seventeenth Centuries*. Translated from the German by Sarah Austin. Fourth Edition, Volume 1. London: John Murray, 1866.

Rappleye, Charles, and Ed Becker. *All American Mafioso: The Johnny Rosselli Story*. New York: Doubleday, 1991.

Reeves, Richard. *President Kennedy: Profile of Power*. New York: Touchstone/Simon & Schuster, 1993.

Reeves, Thomas C. *The Life and Times of Joe McCarthy: A Biography*. New York: Stein and Day, 1982.

Reid, Ed. *The Grim Reapers: The Anatomy of Organized Crime in America*. New York: Bantam Books, 1970.

Reid, Ed, and Ovid Demaris. *The Green Felt Jungle*. New York: Pocket Books, 1964.

Roemer, William F. Jr. *Accardo: The Genuine Godfather*. New York: Ivy Books, 1996.

———. *The Enforcer: Spilotro: The Chicago Mob's Man Over Las Vegas*. New York: Donald I. Fine, 1994.

———. *Roemer: Man Against the Mob*. New York: Donald I. Fine, 1989.

Rogers, Warren. *When I Think of Bobby: A Personal Memoir of the Kennedy Years*. New York: HarperCollins, 1993.

Ross, Janet. *Lives of the Early Medici: As Told in Their Correspondence*. London: Chatto & Windus, 1910.

Royko, Mike. *Boss: Richard J. Daley of Chicago.* New York: E.P. Dutton, 1971.

Russo, Gus. *Live by the Sword: The Secret War Against Castro and the Death of JFK.* Baltimore, MD: Bancroft Press, 1998.

———. *The Outfit: The Role of Chicago's Underworld in the Shaping of Modern America.* New York: Bloomsbury, 2001.

———. *Supermob: How Sidney Korshak and His Criminal Associates Became America's Hidden Power Brokers.* New York: Bloomsbury, 2007.

Salerno, Ralph, and John S. Tompkins. *The Crime Confederation: Cosa Nostra and Allied Operations in Organized Crime.* Garden City, NY: Doubleday & Co., 1969.

Salinger, Pierre. *P.S.: A Memoir.* New York: St Martin's Press, 1995.

———. *With Kennedy.* New York: Doubleday & Co., 1966.

Schiem, David E. *Contract on America: The Mafia Murder of President John F. Kennedy.* New York: Shapolsky Publishers, 1988.

Schlesinger, Arthur M. Jr. *Robert Kennedy and His Times.* Volumes I and II. Boston, MA: Houghton Mifflin Company, 1978.

———. *A Thousand Days: John F. Kennedy in the White House.* Boston, MA: Houghton Mifflin Co./Riverside Press, 1965.

Seedman, Albert A., and Peter Hellman. *Chief!* New York: Arthur Fields Books, 1974.

Semple, Robert B. Jr (ed.). *Four Days in November: The Original Coverage of the John F. Kennedy Assassination by the Staff of the New York Times.* New York: St Martin's Press, 2003.

Server, Lee. *Handsome Johnny: The Life and Death of Johnny Roselli: Gentleman Gangster, Hollywood Producer, CIA Assassin.* New York: St Martin's Press, 2018.

Sforza, Count Carlo. *Count Carlo Sforza Presents the Living Thoughts of Machiavelli.* New York: Fawcett World Library, 1958.

Shakespeare, William. *Julius Caesar.* Edited by Richard Grant White. Boston, MA: Houghton Mifflin Co./The Riverside Press, 1894.

Shannon, William V. *The Heir Apparent: Robert Kennedy and the Struggle for Power.* New York: Macmillan, 1967.

Shapiro, Fred R. (ed.). *The New Yale Book of Quotations.* New Haven, CT: Yale University Press, 2021.

Sheridan, Walter. *The Fall and Rise of Jimmy Hoffa.* New York: Saturday Review Press, 1972.

Shesol, Jeff. *Mutual Contempt: Lyndon Johnson, Robert Kennedy, and the Feud That Defined a Decade.* New York: W. W. Norton & Co., 1998.

Sloane, Arthur A. *Hoffa.* Cambridge, MA: The MIT Press, 1991.

Smith, Sally Bedell. *Grace and Power: The Private World of the Kennedy White House.* New York: Random House, 2004.

Srodes, James. *Allen Dulles: Master of Spies*. Washington, DC: Regnery Pub., 1999.

St Augustine. *City of God*. Translated by Henry Bettenson. London: Penguin, 2003.

Stockton, Bayard. *Flawed Patriot: The Rise and Fall of CIA Legend Bill Harvey*. Washington, DC: Potomac Books, 2006.

Stone, Roger, and Mike Colapietro. *The Man Who Killed Kennedy: The Case Against LBJ*. New York: Skyhorse, 2013.

Sullivan, William C., with Bill Brown. *The Bureau: My Thirty Years in Hoover's FBI*. New York: W.W. Norton & Co., 1979.

Summers, Anthony. *Official and Confidential: The Secret Life of J. Edgar Hoover*. New York: G.P. Putnam's Sons, 1993.

Summers, Anthony, and Robbyn Swan. *The Arrogance of Power: The Secret World of Richard Nixon*. New York: Viking, 2000.

——. *Sinatra: The Life*. New York: Vintage Books, 2006.

Szulc, Tad. *Fidel: A Critical Portrait*. New York: William Morrow & Co., 1986.

Talbot, David. *Brothers: The Hidden History of the Kennedy Years*. New York: Free Press, 2008.

——. *The Devil's Chessboard: Allen Dulles, the CIA, and the Rise of America's Secret Government*. London: William Collins, 2015.

Tanzer, Lester (ed.). *The Kennedy Circle*. Washington, DC: Luce, 1961.

Teresa, Vincent, with Thomas C. Renner, *My Life in the Mafia*. Garden City, NY: Doubleday & Co., 1973.

Thimmesch, Nick, and William Johnson. *Robert Kennedy at 40*. New York: W.W. Norton & Co., 1965.

Thomas, Evan. *Robert Kennedy: His Life*. New York: Simon & Schuster, 2000.

——. *The Very Best Men: Four Who Dared: The Early Years of the CIA*. New York: Touchstone/Simon & Schuster, 1995.

Thomas, Gordon. *Secrets & Lies: A History of CIA Mind Control & Germ Warfare*. London: JR Books, 2008.

Thompson, Josiah. *Six Seconds in Dallas: A Micro-Study of the Kennedy Assassination*. New York: Bernard Geis Associates, 1967.

Thompson, Nelson. *The Dark Side of Camelot*. Chicago, IL: Playboy Press, 1976.

Thompson, Robert E., and Hortense Myers. *Robert F. Kennedy: The Brother Within*. New York: The Macmillan Company, 1962.

Toynbee, Arnold J. *A Study of History*. Abridgement of Volumes I–VI by D.C. Somervell. New York: Oxford University Press, 1987.

Trento, Joseph J. *The Secret History of the CIA*. New York: MJF Books, 2001.

Trevelyan, Janey Penrose. *A Short History of the Italian People: From the Barbarian Invasions to the Attainment of Unity.* New York & London: G.P. Putnam's Sons, 1920.

Trollope, T. Adolphus. *A Decade of Italian Women.* Volume I. London: Chapman and Hall, 1859.

Tuchman, Barbara. *The March of Folly: From Troy to Vietnam.* New York: Alfred A. Knopf, 1984.

United States, Federal Bureau of Investigation, *The F.B.I. Transcripts on Exhibit in U.S.A. V De Cavalcante, Vastola, and Annunziata: U.S. District Court, District of New Jersey; Index Number: Criminal 111-68, Volume 2.* New York: Lemma Pub., 1970.

United States Warren Commission. *The Warren Report: The Official Report on the Assassination of President John F. Kennedy.* The Associated Press, 1964.

Velie, Lester. *Desperate Bargain.* New York: Reader's Digest Press, 1977.

Vidal, Gore. *Palimpsest: A Memoir.* New York: Penguin Books, 1996.

Villano, Anthony, with Gerald Astor. *Brick Agent: Inside the Mafia for the FBI.* New York: Ballantine Books, 1977.

Volz, Joseph, and Peter J. Bridge (eds.). *The Mafia Talks.* Greenwich, CT: Fawcett, 1969.

Waller, Douglas. *Wild Bill Donovan: The Spymaster Who Created the OSS and Modern American Espionage.* New York: Free Press, 2012.

Warren, Earl. *The Memoirs of Chief Justice Earl Warren.* New York: Doubleday & Co., 1977.

Watters, Pat, and Stephen Gillers (eds.). *Investigating the FBI.* New York: Ballantine Books, 1973.

Weiner, Tim. *Legacy of Ashes: The History of the CIA.* New York: Anchor Books, 2008.

Weisberg, Harold. *Oswald in New Orleans.* New York: Canyon Books, 1967.

Wills, Garry, and Ovid Demaris. *Jack Ruby.* New York: New American Library, 1968.

Wise, David. *The American Police State: The Government Against the People.* New York: Random House, 1976.

Wise, David, and Thomas B. Ross. *The Invisible Government.* New York: Random House, 1964.

Wofford, Harris. *Of Kennedys and Kings: Making Sense of the Sixties.* Pittsburgh, PA: University of Pittsburgh Press, 1980.

Wyden, Peter. *Bay of Pigs: The Untold Story.* New York: Simon & Schuster, 1979.

Young, G.F. *The Medici.* New York: Modern Library, 1933.

Zeiger, Henry A. *Sam the Plumber: One Year in the Life of a Cosa Nostra Boss.* New York: Signet, 1970.

Zirbel, Craig I. *The Texas Connection: The Assassination of JFK.* Scottsdale, AZ: Wright & Co., 1991.

Additional Sources

Brown, James. S. 'Profaci Builds Central Jersey Land Empire'. *Asbury Park Press*, 13 August 1969.

Conohan, Sherry, and Robin Goldstein. 'Profaci Family Empire Continuing'. *Asbury Park Press*, 27 February 1983.

Dannen, Fredric. 'The G-man and the Hit Man'. *The New Yorker*, 16 December 1996.

Green, Sterling F. 'Oswald Alone Killed Kennedy, FBI Will Say'. *Washington Evening Star*, 3 December 1963.

Keshner, Andrew. 'Ailing Mobster, 90, Wants to Die in Italy as Feds Fight to Keep Him on Supervised Release'. *New York Daily News*, 18 March 2018: https://www.nydailynews.com/new-york/nyc-crime/mobster-die-italy-da-fights-locked-article-1.3882981

McLain, Gene. 'Butcher Knife Used in Brutal Killing'. *Arizona Republic*, 4 December 1958.

'President Dead, Connally Shot'. *Dallas Times Herald*, 22 November 1963.

Schaap, Dick. 'The Ten Most Powerful Men in New York'. *New York* magazine, 4 January 1971.

Stackpole, Everett Birney. 'A Visit to Potsdam'. Bowdoin *Quill*, Vol. III, No. 1, January 1899.

'West Virginia: Payola by the Pint'. *Time* magazine, Vol. 75, No. 23, 6 June 1960.

***

Audio lecture: Elizabeth Vandiver. 'Lecture Twenty: Persons, Personalities, and Peoples'. *Herodotus: Father of History*. The Great Courses, Course No. 2353, 2000.

Congressional Record: Proceedings and Debates of the 86th Congress, Second Session. Vol., 106, Part 14 (31 August 1960).

Executive Order 11154 – Exemption of J. Edgar Hoover from Compulsory Retirement for Age: https://www.presidency.ucsb.edu/documents/executive-order-11154-exemption-j-edgar-hoover-from-compulsory-retirement-for-age

Fair Play for Cuba Committee, Hearings Before the Subcommittee to Investigate the Administration of the Internal Security Act and Other Internal Security Laws of the Committee on the Judiciary, United States Senate, Eighty-Seventh Congress, First Session (29 April, 5 May, 10 October 1960, Together with Hearings Held 10 January 1961) (Washington, DC: USGPO).

'Final Report on Improper Activities in the Labor or Management Field'. U.S. Senate, Pursuant to S. Res. 44 and 249, 86th Congress, Part 1, 26 February 1960. 86th Congress, Second Session, Report Number 1139.

Interim Report of the Select Committee on Improper Activities in the Labor or Management Field United States Senate. Eighty-Fifth Congress, Second Session. Report No. 1417, 24 March (Washington, DC: USGPO, 1958).

Investigation of Improper Activities in the Labor or Management Field. Hearings Before the Select Committee on Improper Activities in the Labor or Management Field. Eighty-Fifth Congress. First and Second Sessions. 26 September, 28 October 1957, 15, 16, 17, 18 and 22 April 1958. Part 27. (Washington, DC: USGPO, 1958).

Investigative Report: 'Louisiana's Unshaken Mobster Boss: The Governor Promised a Cleanup, but Mafia Chieftain Carlos Marcello Still Runs Things His Way in a State Where He has Plenty of Friends in High Places'. By David Chandler and *Life*'s Investigative Reporting Team. *Life* magazine, Vol. 68, No. 13 (10 April 1970), 30.

Italian Organized Crime. Federal Bureau of Investigation website: www. fbi.gov/about-us/investigate/organizedcrime/italian_mafia

Kenneth P. O'Donnell, Warren Commission Testimony, 18 May 1964. Investigation of the Assassination of President John F. Kennedy. Hearings Before the President's Commission on the Assassination of President Kennedy. Volume VII (Washington, DC: USGPO, 1964).

Nicholas deB. Katzenbach Oral History Interview by Paige E. Mulhollan, Discover LBJ/LBJ Presidential Library (12 November 1968).

Organized Crime and Illicit Traffic in Narcotics. Hearings Before the Permanent Subcommittee on Investigations of the Committee on Government Operations. United States Senate Eighty-Eighth Congress, First Session. Part 1. 25, 27 September, 1, 2, 8 and 9 October 1963. (Washington, DC: USGPO, 1963).

Robert F. Kennedy Oral History Interview by Anthony Lewis, John F. Kennedy Library (4 December 1964).

'These miserable hypocrites . . .': *Chicago Herald-Examiner*, 'President Wilson Dispatch', 16 January 1929. *Congressional Record*, page 4794. 28 February 1929. Proceedings and Debates of the Second Session of the Seventieth Congress of the United States of America. Volume LXX, Part 5, 26 February to 4 March 1929 (Washington, DC: USGPO, 1929).

PICTURE CREDITS

Page 13) Joe Kennedy Snr, *Toni Frissell Collection: Library of Congress*

Page 16) John F Kennedy on his Naval patrol boat, *United States Navy*

Page 25) Johnny Dio socks a reporter, *Bettmann Archive: Getty Images*

Page 26) Hoffa testifies before the Rackets Committee, *U.S. News & World Report magazine photograph collection: Library of Congress*

Page 27) Sam Giancana, *New York World-Telegram and the Sun Newspaper Photograph Collection: Library of Congress*

Page 30) 'Crazy Joe' Gallo, *Wikipedia*

Page 38) Johnny Roselli mug shot, *FBI Media Archives*

Page 39) Frank Sinatra, *National Archives and Records Administration*

Page 40) Cal-Neva Lodge, *Author's own postcard*

Page 45) Judith Campbell, *Associated Press: Alamy Stock Photo*

Page 48) President Kennedy with Mayor Daley, *Robert Knudsen. White House Photographs. JFK Presidential Library & Museum, Boston*

Page 54) JFK, Hoover and RFK, *Library of Congress*

Page 55) RFK at the Justice Department, *New York World-Telegram and the Sun Newspaper Photograph Collection: Library of Congress*

Page 64) Carlos Marcello, *Louisiana Bureau of Investigation*

Page 65) Frank Costello, *New York World-Telegram and the Sun Newspaper Photograph Collection: Library of Congress*

Page 69) Town and Country Motel, *Author's own postcard*

Page 79) Allen Dulles with brother John Foster Dulles, *New York World-Telegram and the Sun Newspaper Photograph Collection: Library of Congress*

Page 98) Santo Trafficante, *Wikipedia*

Page 107) Joe Profaci, *New York World-Telegram and the Sun Newspaper Photograph Collection: Library of Congress*

Page 119) Larry Gallo with a rope burn around his neck, *New York Daily News Archive: Getty Images*

Page 120) Joey Gallo and Mondo leave the courthouse together, *New York Daily News Archive: Getty Images*

Page 126) Joe Valachi, *US Government Archive*

Page 127) 'Joe Beck' Di Palermo, *US Government Archive*

Page 145) Soviet nuclear missile reach from Cuba, *The John F. Kennedy Presidential Library and Museum, Boston: National Archives and Records Administration*

Page 149) Lyndon Jonson chats with Richard Nixon, *U.S. News & World Report Magazine Photograph Collection: Library of Congress*

Page 151) Joe Valachi testifies before Congress, *U.S. News & World Report Magazine Photograph Collection: Library of Congress*

Page 154) David Ferrie, *Bettmann Archive: Getty Images*

Page 158) Ferrie and Oswald together at the Civil Air Patrol
Page 160) Oswald hands out leaflets, *House Select Committee on Assassinations*
Page 166) Texas don Joe Civello *Associated Press: Alamy Stock Photo*
Page 167) Egyptian restaurant, *Lorie Shaull: Wikipedia*
Page 169) Jack Ruby with his employees at the Carousel Club, *New York World-Telegram and the Sun Newspaper Photograph Collection: Library of Congress*
Page 174) Thomas Arthur Vallee
Page 178) Rose Cheramie
Page 179) Billie Sol Estes, *U.S. News & World Report Magazine Photograph Collection: Library of Congress*
Page 180) Bobby Baker, *New York World-Telegram and the Sun Newspaper Photograph Collection: Library of Congress*
Page 182) Eugene Hale Brading, *House Select Committee on Assassinations*
Page 183) Jacqueline Marcello, *Associated Press: Alamy Stock Photo*
Page 185) Presidential motorcade, Dallas, *Victor Hugo King*
Page 187) Hickory Hill, *Carol M. Highsmith Archive*
Page 193) Alamotel, *Author's own postcard*
Page 194) Oswald in police custody, *Dallas Police: Wikipedia*
Page 200) Ruby shoots Oswald, *New York World-Telegram and the Sun Newspaper Photograph Collection: Library of Congress*
Page 206) Warren Commission with former CIA director Allen Dulles, Louisiana representative Hale Boggs and representative Gerald Ford, *U.S. News & World Report Magazine Photograph Collection: Library of Congress*
Page 211) Jack Ruby in custody, *House Select Committee on Assassinations*
Page 211) Ruby's revolver, *House Select Committee on Assassinations*
Page 223) Jim Garrison, *Wikipedia*
Page 225) Fontainebleau Hotel in New Orleans, *Author's own postcard*
Page 228) Eladio del Valle, *Miami Dada County Medical Examiner*
Page 238) Simone 'Sam the Plumber' DeCavalcante, *New York Daily News Archive: Getty Images*
Page 241) Joe Bonanno wanted poster, *New York World-Telegram and the Sun Newspaper Photograph Collection: Library of Congress*
Page 248) Joseph 'Joe Yak' Yacovelli
Page 254) Joe Colombo 'Man of the Year'
Page 258) Joe Colombo with Sammy Davis Jr
Page 259) Colombo shot, *Bettmann Archive: Getty Images*
Page 264) Bolex Camera, *Wikipedia*
Page 273) Carmine 'Sonny Pinto' DiBiase, *U.S. Government Archive*
Page 289) Frank Fitzsimmons with Richard Nixon, *White House Photo Office Collection: US National Archives and Records Aministration*
Page 299) Anthony 'Tony Jack' Giacalone, *FBI: Wikipedia*
Page 305) Tony Pro questioned by reporters on his front lawn, *Bettmann Archive: Getty Images*
Page 308) Salvatore 'Sally Bugs' Briguglio, *Bettmann Archive: Getty Images*
Page 310) Peter Vitale and Jimmy Quasarano, *FBI Archive*
Page 317) Johnny Roselli, *Bettmann Archive: Getty Images*

INDEX

Page numbers in *italic* refer to images

ABOUT THE AUTHOR

Louis Ferrante led a professional heist crew within the Gambino crime family and served nearly a decade in America's worst prisons after refusing to inform on his former associates. While in prison, he educated himself and studied law, science and history, ultimately becoming a writer. His book *Mob Rules* was an international bestseller translated into twenty languages, and his Discovery Channel series, *Inside the Gangsters' Code*, earned him a Grierson Award nomination for Presenter of the Year. His last book, *Borgata: Rise of Empire*, was the first volume in a trilogy recounting the history of the American mafia.